Max Bill

max bill

This publication appears in conjunction with the exhibition organized by James N. Wood and Max Bill for the Albright-Knox Art Gallery.
In cooperation with the Los Angeles County Museum of Art and the San Francisco Museum of Art.

Published by The Buffalo Fine Arts Academy and the Albright-Knox Art Gallery, Buffalo, New Y

Exhibition dates: **Buffalo – September 28 to November 17, 1974**
Los Angeles – December 17, 1974 to February 16, 1975
San Francisco – March 4 to April 20, 1975

This exhibition is made possible with the support of the New York State Council on the Arts. It is also supported by a grant from the National Endowment for the Arts in Washington, D.C., a Federal agency created by act of Congress in 1965, and by a grant from the Pro Helvetia Foundation, Zurich, and the Carborundum Company, Niagara Falls, New York. The production of this catalogue was made possible through a donation from the Members' Council of the Albright-Knox Art Gallery and the cooperation of the Marlborough Galleries in making available their existing material and thereby allowing additional colour reproduction to be included in this catalogue.

Foreword

There has been a long and deep association between the artist and the Albright-Knox Art Gallery over the years. It is, therefore, a special pleasure for us to present the first major museum exhibition of Max Bill's work in this country. Since 1959 the Gallery has acquired several of his works including two major sculptures, *Construction From a Ring,* 1942–63, and *Continuous Surface in Form of a Column,* 1953–58; and two important paintings, *Field of Thirty-two Parts in Four Colors,* 1965 and *Nine Fields Divided by Means of Two Colors,* 1968. The latter three of these works were given to the collection by Seymour H. Knox. In 1972, the Members' Council of the Albright-Knox Art Gallery commissioned an edition of a serigraph from the artist, and the Council has also generously supported this exhibition.

I would like to express our thanks for support of the exhibition granted by the National Endowment for the Arts, the New York State Council on the Arts, and the Pro Helvetia Foundation. In addition, we are grateful to Kenneth Donohue, Director, Los Angeles County Museum of Art, and to Henry Hopkins, Director, San Francisco Museum of Art for their institutions' continued support of and participation in the exhibition.

To Jim Wood, my colleague, I would like to express my deepest appreciation for having realized the project with enthusiasm and for having ably organized every detail of this extensive undertaking. The major documentation which the catalogue represents will shed much light on Bill's achievement, especially in this country, and in great part, this accomplishment is Jim Wood's. I would also like to thank Lawrence Alloway for his essay on the artist's importance.

To Max Bill, whose friendship I have much enjoyed these past years, I extend my personal admiration and appreciation for his great talent and for his creations which have enriched, and continue to enrich, our vision.

Robert T. Buck, Jr.
Director
Albright-Knox Art Gallery

Acknowledgments

Since the Spring of 1971, when Bob Buck and I met with Max Bill in Zumikon and had the pleasure of exploring first hand much of his extensive œuvre, this exhibition has gradually taken shape. From the outset, the project has been indebted to Seymour H. Knox for both his encouragement and his gifts of Bill's work which have made the Albright-Knox Art Gallery the American museum where his painting and sculpture can be adequately seen.

This exhibition could not have been realized without the support and enthusiasm of many individuals. In particular, I would like to thank His Excellency Felix Schnyder, Ambassador of Switzerland to the United States for granting his patronage and Dr. Hans Muller, Cultural Counselor of the Embassy of Switzerland, who has given generously of both his time and diplomacy; Luc Boissonnas, Director of the Pro Helvetia Foundation for his personal interest in addition to the Foundation's financial support; the Carborundum Company for their generous cooperation; and Mrs. William P. King, Chairman of the Members' Council of the Albright-Knox Art Gallery, for the Members' Council's broad involvement which has helped make possible the extensive use of color in the catalogue.

I am particularly grateful to Binia Bill for the loan to this exhibition of a great many pieces from her personal collection.

Maurice Tuchman, Senior Curator of Modern Art, and Jeanne Doyle, Coordinator-Exhibitions and Publications, of the Los Angeles County Museum of Art, Henry Hopkins, Director, and Suzanne Foley, Curator, of the San Francisco Museum of Art, have been of particular help in arranging for the exhibition's travel. Janice Gray Ury, of Belvedere, California; Celia Ascher, Curator for the McCrory Corporation; George Staempfli of the Staempfli Gallery, New York; Donald McKinney and Pierre Levai of the Marlborough Gallery, New York; Mira Godard of Marlborough-Godard, Toronto; and Brigitte de Almeida Lopes of Marlborough Galerie, Zurich, have aided with documentation and in the securing of essential loans.

Both Nicole Buck and Katherine Kline have been of great help with the preparation of translations. Annette Masling, Librarian, and Margaret Cantrick, Assistant Librarian, are responsible for the extensive bibliography. Douglas G.

Schultz, Assistant Curator; Jane Nitterauer, Registrar; John
D. O'Hern, Coordinator of Public Relations and Publications;
Serena Rattazzi, Publications Assistant; Elizabeth Burney,
Executive Secretary; and Norma Bardo, Secretary; all of the
Albright-Knox Art Gallery staff, have provided invaluable
assistance throughout the preparation of both the exhibition
and the catalogue.

I would like to express my debt to Margit Staber and
Edward Fry, both of whom have clarified, in conversation
and through their writings, many questions concerning Bill's
work; and to Lawrence Alloway for contributing an essay to
the catalogue.

To Binia and Max Bill my gratitude for their friendship and
hospitality which have made my repeated visits to Zumikon a
great personal pleasure.

Max Bill has taken an active and formative role in this
exhibition from the outset, despite his usual hectic schedule.
Both the exhibition and this catalogue bear the stamp of his
long experience, an experience which I consider a rare
opportunity to have been able to share.

James N. Wood
Associate Director
Albright-Knox Art Gallery

In December of this year, Max Bill will be sixty-six years old. Forty-five years will have passed since his departure from the Bauhaus at Dessau and arrival in Zürich to begin work as an artist and launch his architectural office. However, this exhibition, which spans a half century of one man's work, cannot be considered a retrospective. First, because Bill is currently producing painting, sculpture, and graphics at as intense a tempo as at any previous time in his long career and, second, because only certain aspects of that all-around creative intellect which is fundamental to his conception of the artist can be adequately presented in an exhibition format. Missing is Bill the architect, urban planner, product designer, publicist, typographer, teacher, and theorist.

We are particularly fortunate, therefore, to have had Max Bill design and supervise the production of this catalogue and grant permission for the reprinting of the selection from his writings which it includes. As an introduction to the latter, an excerpt from Bill's own preface to the writings of Vantongerloo is particularly appropriate.

«One might say that the written formulation of the artist's ideas does not necessarily provide the easiest approach to an understanding of a work of art; the writings of artists are inevitably liable to misinterpretation and misunderstanding. Nevertheless, such writings have always been important documents not only in understanding the individual artist, but, above all, in revealing his problems and his trend of thought in a manner free from outside interpretation.»

James N. Wood

Lawrence Alloway

Max Bill's work spans two very different phases of art. He attended the Bauhaus at Dessau in 1927–29 and in 1951 was one of the founders of the Hochschule für Gestaltung at Ulm. The curriculum at Ulm, as at the Bauhaus, assumed the possibility of a unified theory of art, one that would be effective across the board from product design to painting. In addition, Bill's age, he was born in 1908, enabled him to span vigorously pre-World War II and post-war art. The pioneer Abstract artists did not survive the war, or if they did their important contributions were concluded. The war intercepted an internationally-based coalition of Abstract painting and Constructivism: the resumption of Abstract art on an international basis rests largely on the shoulders of a few individuals like Max Bill.

His special position between pre- and post-war Abstract art can be clarified by reference to the situation in the United States. The development of so-called Hard-Edge painting in the 50's produced a style that was in an equivocal relationship to earlier Geometric art. On the one hand, the paintings presented clean, simple shapes, cooly devised and rigorously executed; on the other hand, their scale and the amplitude of color were new factors. These stemmed from the shift of sensibility initiated by the Field painters among the Abstract Expressionists, that is to say, Barnett Newman, Jackson Pollock, Mark Rothko and Clyfford Still. Additionally, Frank Stella, in 1959, declared himself an opponent of «relational» composition. Though his own pictures were geometric, they were symmetrically locked, unlike the more open asymmetrical compositions of earlier Geometric painters which is what he meant by «relational». Thus, the move away from Abstract Expressionism towards a more tightly structured art was not a simple revival of earlier style, but an extension complicated by new experiences and new demands.

One other factor separates early- from mid-twentieth century Abstract art and this is a philosophical point. Earlier painters were confident that the mastery of geometry brought with it exceptional powers. Mondrian, for example, believed in geometry as a code by means of which absolute values could be signified, a view that manifests itself later in Auguste Herbin's plastic alphabet. The platonic optimism of these artists, believing that geometric forms could symbolize a realm of ideas, was deflated, partly by the war and partly by the increasing sophistication of artists. Thus, the geometrics of post-war art acquired a kind of existential base: geometry is no longer regarded as a mysterious symbolizing agent; it is, on the contrary, humanized. Order is taken as an arbitrary proposal of the artist's, a personal project against the void. Hence, the internal consistency of individual works and their succession in time became expressive of a specifically human order. Mondrian, of course, can be viewed fruitfully from this angle, but it is neither the basis on which his painting was originally conceived nor the basis on which it evolved. It is Bill's extraordinary achievement to bridge the platonic and the existential phases of Abstract art and to have retained a high sense of order.

To define Bill's role it is necessary to look at his work against some of the long-term issues of Abstract art. Unless we do this the originality and probity of his œuvre will not be sufficiently clear. Abstract art, according to the theory and practice of its proponents, certainly relied on the idea of the work of art as an object. This shows in two ways: there is the non-referential display of forms and colors; and there is the material character of the work. Thus, there is a display of syntax (the internal relationships of the work) but it is restricted to a literal reading, in which red is red, a triangle is a triangle, paint is paint, and so on. The internal disposition of the forms in the painting, though isolated from direct references to nature as something outside the painting, did not yield all potential allusions. What happened is that the reduction of the specificity of the signs made possible the conversion of architecture-derived motifs into universal pattern (Mondrian) and of airplane squadrons into symbols of Flight (Malevich). This easily-acquired and rather naive claim to higher significance became hard to take seriously after the war. There was, however, an increase in confidence in the material character of Abstract art at the expense of its surreptitious universals.

In the United States, Hard-Edge painters who were reacting against the metaphysics of the Abstract Expressionists even as they were learning from their color, stressed the reduction of elements with a polemical vigor. The appearance of massively simplified works of great visual aplomb which denied signifying activity was salutory in opposing «the myth of depth» (Alain Robbe-Grillet's term). On the other hand, the development of American Abstract art in the absence of content or, at least, with a theoretical hostility to signifying functions, has not been satisfactory. A number of painters who began early with reduced forms ran into trouble sustaining their work, except by introducing decorative complications, perhaps because the dismissal of content removed an essential factor.

Bill represents another possibility. He is not burdened with Mondrian's metaphysics but continues firmly certain of Mondrian's ideas. He is rationalistic in his claims for the function of art, but has avoided the risks of reducing art to an aggressive muteness.[1] In an article of 1956 he scrutinized one of «about twenty paintings by Mondrian that are square and stand on one corner... He called the shape of these paintings ‹lozenge› or ‹rhombic›. But both are misnomers since a square never becomes rhombic by virtue of merely being placed on its tip. It might have been preferrable had Mondrian called them ‹acute› pictures».[2] Bill examines the formal properties closely: «A horizontal-vertical structure accords itself with a horizontal-vertical environment. However, a square placed on a point cannot be assimilated to this order, but develops as another form of activity which extends itself on the wall surrounding it in four horizontal and vertical directions.»[3]

In addition, Bill examines the possibility that some of the forms can be said to extend beyond the canvas. This is a theory of Mondrian's based on the claim that his lines are infinite, but Bill applies the notion more specifically to the tipped squares. Since Mondrian only used horizontal and vertical forms it follows that when he tips his canvas, the lines that cross it hit the edges hard and appear to run off: the physical square of the canvas is thus made to carry forms of which it is implied that they complete themselves outside the picture space. In some recent «pointed» paintings, as he calls them, of his own, Bill has developed this format systematically. Inside the «pointed» square canvas, that is, tipped on one point, he paints a central square whose corners touch the picture's boundaries. Another square can be made of the sum of the four corners of the tipped canvas; however, these areas also point outwards like arrow heads, away from their implicit unification as one square. There is an interplay of logical containment and expansion, the latter effect obtained by the subtle pulse of close-valued colors. In his color Bill has

1. Lucy R. Lippard wrote, to separate Bill from the systematically structured work of Donald Judd and (early) Robert Smithson: «Less theoretically sophisticated than their European counterparts, the Americans seem to stress the object as object in a more direct though perhaps more naive manner.» («Diversity in Unity: Recent Geometricizing Styles in American Art», in *Art Since Mid-Century,* vol. 1 [Greenwich, Conn.: New York Graphic Society, 1971], p. 234). This really amounts to (1) a defense of American simplicity and (2) the mute presence of primary forms against European skills. Something comparable is found in Judd who wrote that Bill's «paintings are able but just involve the various public geometric formats: checkers, bands, Mondrian's diamonds [sic], and the progressive halving of areas.» («In the Galleries,» *Arts Magazine* 37, 9 [1963] :102). It is the continuity of Bill with earlier Abstract art that separates Judd's taste from Bill's work, its intricacy as opposed to a monolithic presence.

2. Max Bill, «Composition 1 with Blue and Yellow», in *Piet Mondrian* (New York: Solomon R. Guggenheim Museum, 1971), p. 74.

3. Ibid., p. 75

4. Margit Staber, *Max Bill* (St. Gallen: Erker-Verlag, 1971), p. 23. I have kept Bill's preference for the term ‹Concrete art› in mind, but don't feel that Abstract art will be misunderstood in this context. I use it to refer to art that is not iconic, that does not match some aspect of visual experience.

moved far beyond the simple primaries of Mondrian but without any slackening of Mondrian's original pictorial clarity. Bill has preserved the definition of art that he gave in 1936, but without becoming repetitive. «We call Concrete Art those works of art which originate on the basis of means and laws of their own, without external reliance on phenomena or any transformation of them, in other words, without undergoing a process of abstraction. Concrete painting and sculpture are the formulation of what is optically perceptible. Their means of formulation are colors, space, light, and movement.»[4]

The problem of the meaning of Abstract art has not been resolved by the formalist tactic of concentration on the physiognomy of the work of art. An interest in the possible meanings of Abstract art would not conceivably neglect the presence, or aura, of the work of art itself. If we take Bill's definition of Concrete art we can discuss meaning without insisting on locating an external point of reference in nature. What we cannot do, however, is suppose that nobody made the work: it has its origin in a series of human decisions and the work must be considered as, in some way, signifying those decisions and hence, the artist. This is not a form of expression-theory because decisions concerning the internal development of a work of art are very different from emotional cues.

The meaning of Bill's work must be sought, therefore, in his geometrics and in the concepts that they embody. The ideas of the artist as to how his work is to be structured constitute surely an exhilarating area of meaning. It is not only visual nicety or advances in the state of the art that can be adduced from the identification of semantic content with the optical plane. We can interpret the visual display, the syntax, as signifying regularities put into the picture by the artist in accordance with his ideas of order.

Bill has retained a belief in non-arbitrary order, but he has expanded its definition in accordance with later experience. This can be indicated by the changes from Mondrian's work to his own. Mondrian used simple elements (line and plane) inscribed on the canvas in full visibility: they were reduced but they were not predictable; one part of the picture did not follow logically from another, though there is a final effect of balance of course. A part of Mondrian's point, in fact, is to make equivalences of unlikes. Bill, however, uses systematic

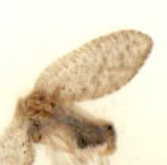

5. Polygon: «a figure, esp. a closed plane figure, having 3 or more us. straight sides.» (Random Unabridged Dictionary).

6. Max Bense, «Max Bill 1963,» *Art International 7* (1963): 35.

7. Ibid., p. 35. Noise: the term is taken from telecommunications and refers to disturbances on a channel that are not part of a transmitted message. Hence its use here as a combination of order (message) and disorder (accidental factors).

8. Ibid., p. 35.

forms and sequences of forms so that each part of a picture is continuous with other parts. It is not that he is using simple forms but that he takes known polygonal forms and divulges their sequence logically.[5] The evident order of the polygon is inserted into a less evident pictorial order of the artist's invention. To quote from Max Bense: «Creations by Max Bill give the impression of being higher degrees of order gained from given lower degrees of order plus disorder.»[6] Bense observes that the notion of «the scheme of ‹order-from-disorder› more strongly represents individual graduations within order, while the scheme of ‹order from noise›, in other words, ‹order from order-plus-disorder›, represents the scheme of subjugating lower degrees of order under higher degrees.»[7] Art is usually said to give or to bring order, and of course it does, but Bense's point is that the use of existing ordered forms, such as polygons and mathematical sequences, is a special case. «It is not the square as such which is presented in its aesthetic reality, but the aesthetic inclusion of this structure into a higher order and complexity scheme [that] is demonstrated.»[8] This is a great departure from Mondrian: it is a move from visual improvisation to systematic structure, one of the fundamental differences between pre- and post-war Abstract art.

Bill structures his art mathematically, which is still, even today, sometimes taken to constitute an impersonal basis. However, there are two points to bear in mind about the use of mathematical forms in painting and sculpture. First, the act of choice by the artist, *this* formula as opposed to another one, is irreducibly personal. It amounts to an objective found element, because the formula exists before the painting and can be deduced by ourselves, as spectators. Secondly, the recognition of visual nuance is only possible within a learnable system, that is to say, a system with sufficient regularities for the artist's purpose to be clear. To Bill, a work of art that is loosely structured must dissolve into a mass of probabilities. Thus, one can only say, that his use of mathematics is no less personal than his choice of color or his decisions about size and medium. Characteristic of his method of work is the permutation of his selected themes, so that particular formats recur with color differences, for instance. In this respect he is like Ingres whose art is not an endless pursuit of new inventions but taking possession of the multiple possibilities of a few subjects. The rules by which the paintings and sculpture develop, rules formulated by the artist, are themselves a part of the meaning of his art. It is notable, for instance, that Bill is at pains to preserve a sense of whole forms in his art, whether by division or extension. In some of his work clearly legible large forms, such as circles or squares, are opened up, entered, sectionalized; in others, clearly legible small forms are presented sequentially, in additive rows. In both cases a known unit of form is subsumed into complex relationships.

To compare the surface of a painting by Mondrian with that of a Bill is to see another change between earlier and later abstract art. A Mondrian, though composed of «pure» discrete elements, is always characterized by a terrain of directional brushstrokes and of irregular densities of paint. The surface of a Bill, however, is very different: the physical deposit of the paint is clarified, its paste-like facture is reduced to continous color planes with smooth junctions between areas. This has the effect of releasing his exquisite color from its material embodiment so that the color vibrates without surface intereference (or «noise»). It must be admitted that a good deal of early Abstract art, though arrived at heroically, as by the efforts of Mondrian and Malevich, is disappointing technically; the manual customs of figurative oil painting are laboriously adapted to the depiction of spare geometric forms. Later Abstract artists, however, have found ways to apply paint so that there is no intervention of the medium into configurations that depend on conceptual rigor and color as vibration. This holds true of Bill's sculpture, also, in which the continuous flow of his surfaces, whether manifested in granite or brass, is not predominantly characterized by the material. In the metal pieces, high polish is a constituent of the conception of the work; the sleek mirror-like surfaces condense a maximum of reflections from their surroundings. Their partial dematerialization by light corresponds to the immaculate skin of optically active color in the paintings. The factual basis of Bill's art has never inhibited his extraordinary sensitivity to zones of ambiguous visibility and complex color.

In addition to the idea of art as an object, there is another constant in the aesthetics of Abstract art and this is the belief in art's connection to the other arts and to the environment. Obviously these links are not to be thought of as references to objects and events in the world; rather, the painting is regarded as a model to which the world can be made to conform. Both Mondrian and Malevich regarded their paintings as, among other things, models of a better world. The personal geometry of their paintings was supposed to be isomorphic to industrial design, architecture, city planning. In assuming that the arts were thus exchangeable in principle, the Abstract artist's withdrawal from the world was turned around and made into an advantage. Abstract art offered the basis of an aesthetic system unadulterated by physical contingencies (architecture), exigencies of mass production (industrial design), or historical complexity (city planning). Thus, the painting of pictures could be defined as one aspect of building a great totality of the arts. In the 19th century, the theory of the *Gesamtkunstwerk,* or Totalwork, is embodied by opera and architecture. The synthesis of the arts was attempted on the basis of incorporating the other arts into a capacious form: Wagner subsumed literature, visual art, and national myth into one «musicodramatic unity»; Camillo Sitte in his city planning proposed the incorporation of sculpture, painting, gardening and architecture. Abstract painting picked up the architectonic line and has continued to provide the model for the unification of urban arts and design. This prolongation of Abstract art into society was most nearly achieved, though briefly, by the Russian Constructivists, but the link to revolutionary politics turned out to be illusory. However, the desire to confer political relevance on Abstraction was preserved in the effort to make Abstract art the nucleus of a new *Gesamtkunstwerk.*

Bill has worked in architecture, industrial design (including exhibition display), stage design, typography, education, and politics. It cannot be stressed enough that none of these activities is occasional and none of them are confined to project form, Utopian schemes with no serious chance of realization. On the contrary, his range of work all has to do with interventions in the real world. To take examples from one field, that of industrial design: Bill was responsible in the 50's for a sunlamp, a wall clock, an electric kitchen clock with timer, a stackable chair, all of which were mass-produced and distributed. To quote Margit Staber, originally a student at Ulm: «his whole activity is methodically concerted with a view to the coherent shaping of the human environment and forms

9. Staber, Op. cit., p. 24.

an aggregate of creative inventions which serve the interests of man.»[9] The weakness of earlier approaches to the *Gesamtkunstwerk* via rational planning is that the artists held too simple and too elitist a view of the inter-relations of art, the arts, and society. It was assumed to be sufficient to apply art-derived principles to the rest of the environment. However, looking at, say, Bauhaus products we can see that although individual pieces were admirable, no unified aesthetic emerged on the basis of extrapolated art principles. It is important not to confuse Bill's numerous activities with this aestheticizing mode. He considers the different tasks as different kinds of operation. The kinds of decision that are appropriate in painting a picture are not of a kind that can be transferred to, say, the layout of a catalogue. There is no assumption of one universal design principle, elastic and omnivorous, that can engulf all artifacts. On the contrary, Bill works so well in his wide field, because of his exceptional grasp of specific objectives and of the costs or resources to be used in achieving them. There are functional differences between the various tasks.

The complex social adaptation that is required of the designer is not effective in art. For example, Bill considers painting and sculpture to be absolutely unlike other activities, because of the artist's freedom. In making a work of art one is in a situation of complete control, from concept, through work procedures, to final state. This unique control, including feedback from the work process that can change the original destination, is surely one of the main satisfactions in producing art, and a source of its special value in society. It is on the basis of such a view of the artist's responsibility towards his art that Bill's forms must be viewed, as beautifully completed expressions of debated order.

James N. Wood

To deal with Max Bill solely as a painter, sculptor, and graphic artist is to make a distinction which he has never made in his work: the distinction between Fine Art and the other areas of his activity.

From the outset, his position, encouraged by his study at the Bauhaus and elaborated later in his own teaching and writing, has been to see the creative intellect as having a central moral purpose regardless of what area of the arts it might be involved with. This purpose is to bridge the division between art and daily life. Bill has summarized it in the phrase, «shaping the environment». Any and every man-made object represents the solution to a problem. Bill believes that the purely technical solutions which our culture equates with progress are not adequate to our spiritual needs. He insists that at a time when «moral and ethical measurements are no longer stable, or are no longer used as they were in older societies... somebody must take the responsibility for interpretation».[1] Bill strives to make his solutions, be they for buildings, utilitarian objects, or works of Fine Art, as comprehensible as possible and to this end he brings a finely-honed analytical intellect and a life-long commitment to basing formal solutions on the study of human needs.

But human needs are infinitely complex and Bill insists that the attempt to meet them not be deflected by an appeal to universals. The design of a commercial product or a piece of architecture must take into account a priori functional and economic requirements of varying degree, while it is in the Fine Arts that creativity enjoys maximum freedom. This very freedom, however, in no way lessens the social significance of the work produced. In his words: «Many people are shocked when they see something that is clear;...furthermore it is wrong to assume that this clarity merely represents ‹art for art's sake›; it is really a programme in itself. Works of art enable certain problems to be solved without compromise, in a world which is full of compromises and failed speculations.»[2] The result is works of art with two primary intentions; first, as concretions of symbolic information for the pleasure and spiritual use of individuals and, second, as prototypes for a broader social use – for as Bill has repeatedly stressed, he is convinced that the Fine Arts are the primary formative influence on all design.

These characteristics have separated Bill's work from the

1.
Max Bill, «Responsibility in Design and Information», *American Scholar* 35 (Spring 1966), p. 312

2.
«Max Bill Answers Questions by Margit Staber», in *Max Bill: Recent Works* (Zurich: Marlborough Galerie AG, 1972).

mainstream of post-war American art. His conscious effort to undertake all his activities within a social context, while having deep roots in the history of twentieth century European art, is fundamentally foreign to the more individualistic tradition in the United States. Similarly, Bill's pluralistic approach, where aesthetic problems and their solutions are pursued simultaneously in several mediums and disciplines, goes against that ingrained reverence for specialization so consistent with the economic priorities which have determined the form of so much of American life. This attitude has only been compounded by a native criticism which claims that self-definition is the overriding goal of each of the arts. While Bill's adherence to his work and his concept of the artist was often solitary in the forties and fifties, the past decade has witnessed a growing interest, at first among younger artists and gradually, a larger public. Today, as has recently been the case with his longtime friend and colleague, Albers, many in this country are making the «discovery» of Bill's painting and sculpture after years of familiarity with his reputation as architect, designer and educator.

Max Bill was born in Winterthur on December 22, 1908. Among his family an uncle on his mother's side, who had first studied science and later become a serious painter in the circle of Cuno Amiet, stimulated his early interest in art. Winterthur provided an active cultural life, the museum mounting frequent exhibitions of contemporary European art, and at an early age, after first considering a career in geology, Bill decided to become a painter. The family agreed to this with the stipulation that he learn a trade to support himself and in 1924 he entered the School of Applied Arts in Zurich where he remained four years, apprenticing as a silversmith.

In 1925 Bill visited Paris and the Exposition Internationale d'Art Decoratif which proved a formative experience. «I can still visualize», he later recalled, «what made such a strong impact on me at the age of sixteen: the Pavilion de l'Esprit Nouveau, with pictures and plans by Le Corbusier, and the Austrian Pavilion by Josef Hoffman, with Frederick Kiesler's section.»[3] Kiesler's contribution included *The City in Space,* a room-sized, suspended framework constructed on a tension system. With neither static axis nor walls, it produced a dynamic equilibrium of closed and open spaces.

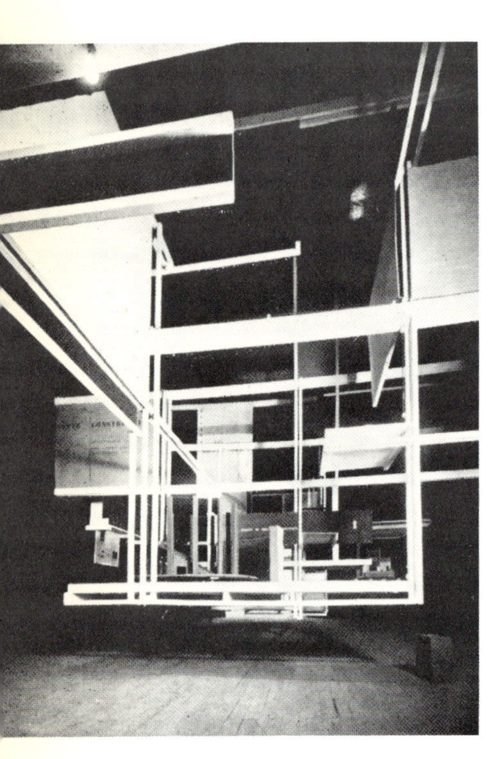

Frederick Kiesler
The City in Space
model in Austrian section,
International Exposition, Paris, 1925

3.
Margit Staber, *Max Bill* (London: Methuen, 1964).

4.
Ibid.

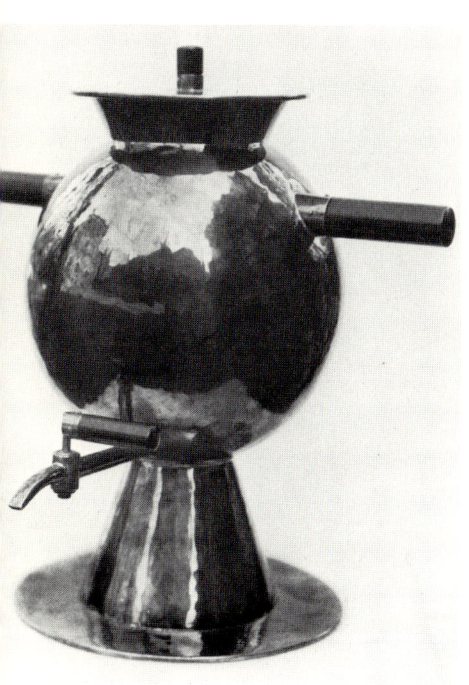

Max Bill
Electric Samovar, copper, 1925

5.
Max Bill, «The Bauhaus Idea from Weimar to Ulm», *Architect's Yearbook* No. 5
(1953), p. 31

The following year Bill travelled the length of Italy in search of clues for his own development. On his return the Bauhaus handbook was brought to his attention and shortly thereafter Le Corbusier lectured in Zurich, impressing Bill with his concepts of the responsibility and breadth of involvement of the modern architect. Bill recalled later that: «My field of interests had widened. A friend of mine pointed out that my fondness of spheres, cylinders, and other stereo-metric forms had been anticipated in Germany, where a new style employing these forms had come into being. He brought me a book called, *Staatliches Bauhaus Weimar: 1919–1924.* ...Hammering away in a workshop now seemed to me terribly outmoded. I began to take an interest in architecture, and this led me to apply for admission to the Bauhaus, which I entered in 1927.»[4]

The first Swiss citizen to enroll in the Dessau Bauhaus with its newly completed quarters by Gropius, Bill arrived well equipped to make the most of its extraordinary faculty. The Euclidian clarity of his 1925 design for a samovar shows a thoroughly digested trade skill applied with a highly developed sense of three-dimensional form. He followed the normal curicullum and in addition continued his interest in painting. Art as such was never stressed at the Bauhaus, but Bill attended the informal classes of Klee and Kandinsky. His 1928 oil, *Spatial Composition No. 9,* takes the volumetric vocabulary of the samovar and explores it on a flat surface. While this picture shows the influence of Bill's other instructors – Moholy-Nagy, Schlemmer, and more specifically, the contemporary «thermometer» style work of Albers – its mastery of the use of restricted formal means to achieve a subtle spatial ambiguity is a clear indication of things to come. Writing on «The Bauhaus Idea» twenty-five years later, Bill observed: «In Dessau Gropius realized what were at and for that time, almost ideal conditions because he was able to gather round him a body of highly qualified teachers who, though leading artists in their own right, were ready to give pride of place to working on the practical problems of design for utility and knew how to do so without the slightest derogation of their high aesthetic standards. That conscientious fusion of the most vital elements in modern art with the essential principles of modern technical design was the Bauhaus's most decisive achievement.»[5]

6.
Stephen Bann, *The Tradition of Constructivism* (New York: The Viking Press, 1974), pp. 136-7.

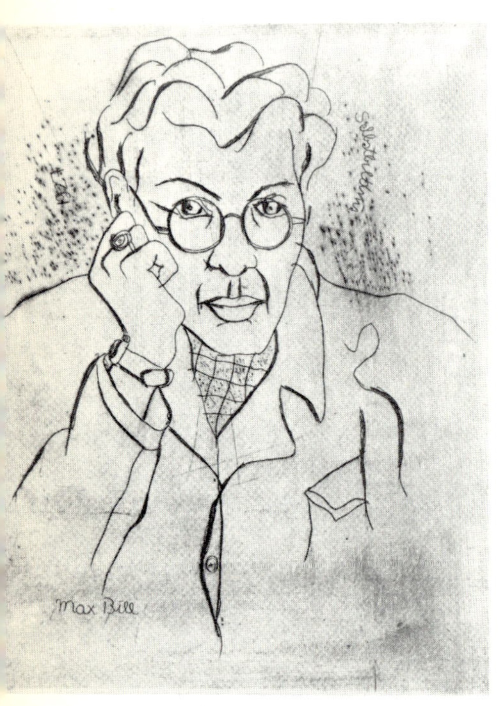

Max Bill
Self-portrait, etching, 1927

In April of 1928 when the Swiss architect Hannes Meyer was appointed director following Gropius's resignation, Bill was one of thirty-seven foreigners in a student body of one hundred sixty-six. Beginning five years earlier, with the arrival of Moholy-Nagy and the departure of Johannes Itten, the Bauhaus's initial atmosphere of romantic expressionism with its focus on the artist as «an exalted craftsman» was redirected toward the goal of «art and technology, a new unity». Now Moholy-Nagy was himself departing and in his letter of resignation he argued for a position of «equilibrium», opposed to an extreme and exclusive adherence to either the expressive (formalist), or the utilitarian (functionalist) position. He wrote: «There must be room for teaching the basic ideas which keep human content alert and vital. For this we fought and for this we exhausted ourselves. I can no longer keep up with the stronger and stronger tendency toward trade specialization in the workshops... It remains to be seen how efficient will be the decision to work only for efficient results. Perhaps there will be a new fruitful period. Perhaps it is the beginning of the end.»[6]

Bill's etched self-portrait of 1927, executed before his arrival at the Bauhaus and conspicously labeled «selbstbildnis» in the plate, is a confident self-image of the artist as thinker. As a student, sensitive to the growing need for functional solutions, but by nature skeptical of ideological arguments, this atmosphere of debate surely encouraged his growing stress on personal conception as opposed to personal execution; for only through the former could one hope to create prototypes which might positively affect the broad level of design quality. He was evolving his own theory of equilibrium to prevent the isolation of the creative talent (himself) from an increasingly technical system of mass production. A means of achieving a clearly defined sense of order was now seen to be essential. He studied closely the geometrically inspired figurative art of Schlemmer, but the influence of Klee's inquiries into the control of movement on a painted surface – particularly through his schematic lecture diagrams – and his articulation of the laws of a systematic theory of form where logic and mystery miraculously managed to coexist, were the primary Bauhaus elements in Bill's later development as an artist.

In the Fall of 1929, Bill left the Bauhaus and returned to

7.
Peter Gay, *Weimar Culture* (New York: Harper and Row, 1968), p. 1.

8.
Quoted in: Ibid., p. 55.

Zurich. For a young architect and artist who came convinced that the answers needed to solve the problems confronting his generation would only be found through more and not less rationalism, it was not an auspicious date to embark upon a career. With the death of Stresemann that year, the Weimar Republic began to disintegrate and with it the brief interlude from 1924 to 1929 of monetary stabilization, relaxation of political tension and general prosperity.

The Weimar Republic has been called «an idea seeking to become reality,»[7] a characterization which could be applied equally well to the Bauhaus. Both struggled with the same basic enemy, as prevalent within the arts as without: irrationality. Heidegger had given philosophical respectability to the growing belief that thinking was antagonistic to true understanding. The threat this attitude posed to European culture and the wedge it drove between the artistic activity of the time and society itself was fully understood by few. An exception was the poet Rilke who saw tragedy in the fact that the youth of this age «had so often understood the call of art as a call to art»[8] and therefore away from life.

The Bauhaus was no exception to the fact that the culture of the Weimar republic rested primarily on the accomplishments of outsiders to the accepted social structure who for a brief historical moment achieved a central position. However, unlike many of the faculty and students who were soon to leave as exiles, Bill was returning home to Switzerland with its tradition of democracy and neutrality. While this hardly assured support for the innovations he now undertook, it reinforced his identity as, if not an insider, at least a citizen working for change within society. This unalienated stance is reaffirmed throughout Bill's career as an artist and in his activity as teacher, propagandist and politician.

Switzerland provided a haven from the gathering storm, but one which Bill was to be constantly leaving in search of people and ideas. While living in Zurich from this time on, he remained in close touch with the shifting centers of European art. The following year, 1930, he was in Paris, where he returned regularly, meeting Mondrian for the first time in 1932 and Vantongerloo in 1933. Both Ernst and Giacometti he was to meet in Zurich in 1935. From 1932 until it dissolved in 1936 he was active in the group «Abstraction-Création», participating in its yearbooks and Paris exhibitions. In addi-

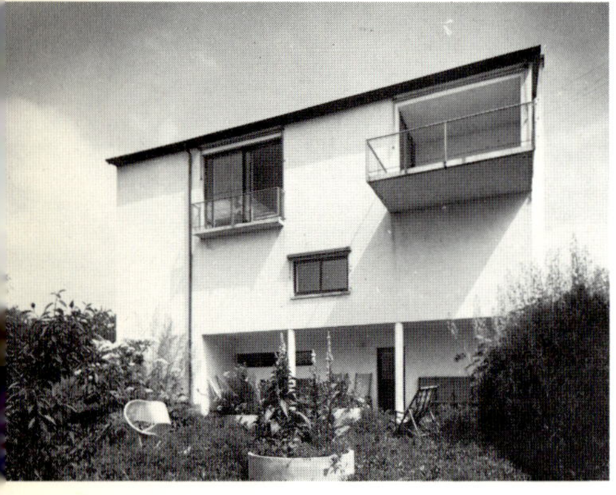

Max Bill
Home and Studio of Max Bill at Zurich-Höngg,
1932–1933

9.
Abstraction, Création, Art Non-Figuratif
No. 1 (1932), title page.

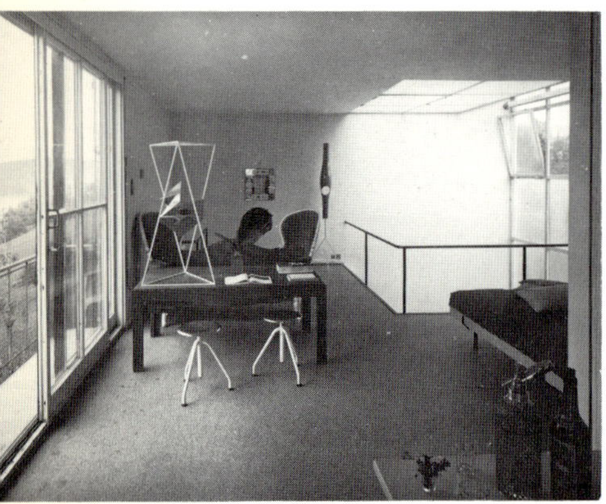

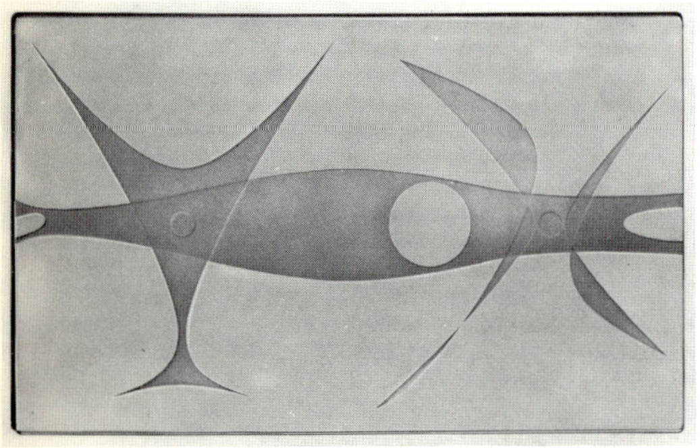

Max Bill
Glass Painting, flashed glass, 1933

tion to Mondrian and Vantongerloo, Hans Arp, and Sophie Taeuber, Moholy-Nagy, Albers, Kandinsky, Pevsner, Herbin, and Kupka were among the diverse membership.

While the program of the group was expressed more in negative than in positive terms: «Cultivation of pure plastic art, to the exclusion of all explanatory, anecdotal, literary, and naturalistic elements,»[9] it provided a rallying point for the growing number of «constructive» artists fleeing Germany (the Bauhaus was closed by the Nazi's in 1933), Eastern Europe and Soviet Russia (Stalinism had clearly expressed its taste by 1931 with the rejection of Le Corbusier's project for Moscow's Palace of the Soviets and the substitution of a neo-classical fantasy of immense proportions). The additional presence of the leading De Stijl artists as well as many of the Russian avant-guard made Paris the world center of abstract art for most of the thirties.

Bill thrived on the intellectual contact with these, primarily older, colleagues which Paris afforded, becoming particularly close to Vantongerloo who remained a life-long friend. The illustrations of his work which appeared in the group's annual publication *Abstract, Création, Art Non-Figuratif* stand out with those of Mondrian, Vantongerloo, Van Doesburg, Albers, and Vordemberge-Gildewart for their clarity and geometric structure against the dominant tendency toward more amorphous styles of abstraction. Among these, the *Relief, Undulating Surface* of 1931–32 and *Long Sculpture* of 1933 initiated his concern with sculpture, and specifically with sculpture that would stimulate a new awareness of space and volume. In 1932–33, Bill designed a home and studio for himself at Zurich-Höngg on a plan of crisply defined, interlocking open and closed spaces. Both this house and the *Relief Undulating Surface* utilized pre-fabricated materials, and all these works, as well as his contemporaneous experiments with flashed glass pictures, made brilliant use of the spatial effects of controlled light and shadow. This development of solutions to a given concern simultaneously in sculpture, painting, and architecture was to become a standard Bill procedure.

The original pioneers of abstract art shared El Lissitzky's view that: «Our generation was born in the last decade of the 19th Century and called to the colours of an era which

10.
Sophie Lissitzky-Kuppers, *El Lissitzky* (London: Thames and Huston Ltd., 1968), p. 326.

11.
John Elderfield, «The Paris–New York Axis: Geometric Abstract Painting in the Thirties» in *Geometric Abstraction: 1926–1942* (Dallas: Dallas Museum of Fine Arts, 1972). Another version of this essay appeared as «Geometric Abstract Painting and Paris in the Thirties; Part One», *Artforum* 8 (May 1970), p. 54 and «... Part Two», *Artforum* 8 (June 1970), p. 70. See also Robert Welsh, «Abstraction and the Bauhaus», *Artforum* 8 (March 1970), p. 46, for an additional viewpoint.

marked a new beginning to the history of mankind.»[10] To the artists reaching maturity in the thirties a less utopian and more pragmatic view of history was essential. Not only had the great political and cultural experiment in Russia, which provided the context for El Lissitzky's statement, gone sour, but they had been born into «the non-objective world» which Malevich, Kandinsky and Mondrian's generation had discovered. It is Bill's response to this particular historical moment of the modern movement, a moment demanding consolidation of the radical innovations of the pioneer generation and a sober rethinking of much of its theory, that distinguishes his art and thought from that of his contemporaries.

In an essay on «Geometric Abstract Painting in the Thirties», John Elderfield has pointed out that in Paris at this time non-objective art, particularly in the hands of younger artists, began to be employed increasingly as style before philosophy and that the resulting preoccupation with this new range of formal issues served to undermine the bond which had linked geometric abstraction to its philosophical and environmental foundations. He concludes that: «Advanced art, once more alienated from its social context, was forced back onto itself – to delve anew into issues unique to each individual medium.»[11]

This attitude and the floating, nature-derived forms which the fusion of eastern non-objective art and the Synthetic Cubist heritage of the French tradition encouraged, were diametrically opposed to Bill's developing style and concept of the artist. While Mondrian's growing willingness to experiment, as Van Doesburg and Vantongerloo had, with the strict limitations of his De Stijl principles certainly encouraged younger artists to explore more personal styles, he remained adamant abouth the dangers of eclecticism and decorativeness when abstract forms were taken over with no concern for understanding their motivating spirit. The result, he and Van Doesburg had warned earlier, was all too often a «quadratic Baroque» where the illusion of personal freedom only masked a derivative style. Their concerns reinforced Bill's own insistence on an art for his time which would be abstract without being arbitrary. Rather than reject the philosophical component of earlier art, he updated it to conform with the requirements of a new world şituation and the more pragmatic values of his own beliefs and his Bauhaus training.

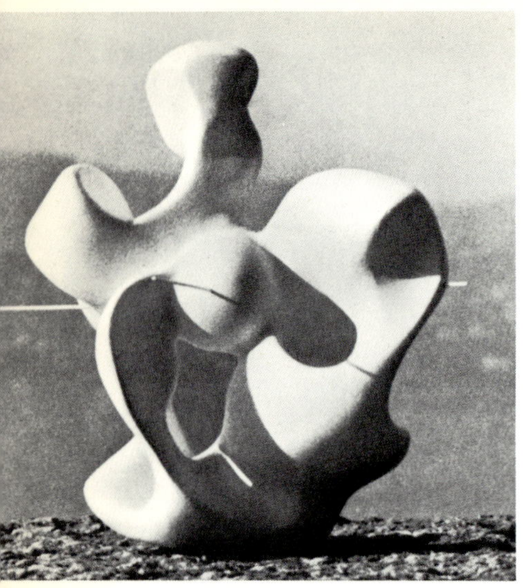

Georges Vantongerloo
Construction in a Sphere
plaster, 1917

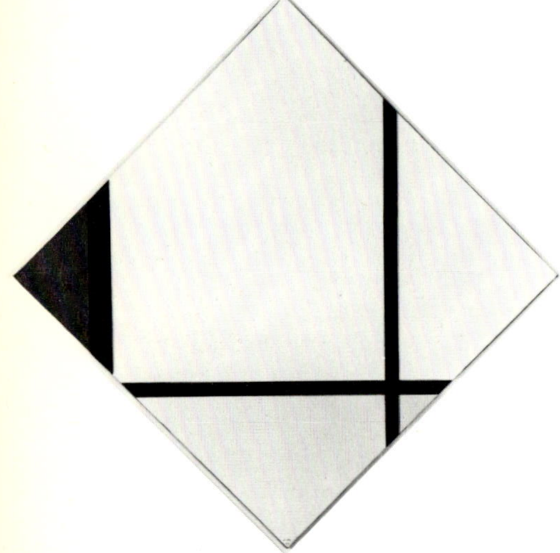

Piet Mondrian
Composition I with Blue and Yellow
oil on canvas, 1925,
Kunsthaus, Zurich

12.
The artist, in conversation with the author.

13.
Max Bill, «Composition I with Blue and Yellow, 1925», in *Piet Mondrian* (New York: The Solomon R. Guggenheim Museum, 1971), pp. 74–75.

14.
Ibid., p. 75.

15.
Ibid., p. 76.

He rejected as being just as naive as the utopian panaceas of much first generation abstraction, the widespread association among his contemporaries of totalitarian control with self-discipline, rationalism and a scientific approach to defining social and aesthetic problems. Eventually, these convictions led Bill to formulate the concept of «Concrete Art» and develop his «mathematical approach» to the control of each stage in the creation of a given work.

Of this period Bill recalls, «My generation could look at things another way», – after the expressionistic innovations of the first decades of the century – «we needed a new organization and could learn from other fields of experience».[12] In sculpture and painting it was Vantongerloo and Mondrian who provided the most influential lessons of the regulation of surface and space. The former, from 1917, the date of his *Construction in a Sphere,* had brilliantly explored the relationship of intuitive form to geometric, and often mathematically derived, structure. In painting, as well as sculpture, he provided the examples of actual art that did not look arbitrary, that had an air of freedom, while leaving nothing to chance. The latter, in those pictures which are «square and stand on one corner», as Bill describes them in an essay written in 1956 on *Composition I with Blue and Yellow* of 1925, developed a format where a «fixed center» – the material rectangle of the canvas – became a «nucleus surrounded by possibilities of unlimited extension».[13] Since 1946 Bill has put this specific form and concept to a wide variety of uses, by determining the compositions systematically. In his essay, Bill stresses that: «It is exactly in this principle of a nucleus as the starting point of an order capable of unlimited extension that the true greatness of Mondrian's achievement and his œuvre's compelling artistic quality is found.»[14] Here was a new principle of organization, visually and symbolically expansive, as opposed to the hermetic grid of cubist-derived composition contained by the surface edge. Bill concluded his essay with the statement: «The principal merit of this picture seems to be that Mondrian has achieved a combination of actual appearance – with its absolute restrictions – and a freedom of imaginative possibilities, for which, like the well-defined rules of a game, only the nucleus was defined.»[15] This treatment of a flat surface, just as Vantongerloo's constructions in space, allowed a strict formal control and a drive to

16.
«Max Bill Answers Questions by Margit Staber», op cit.

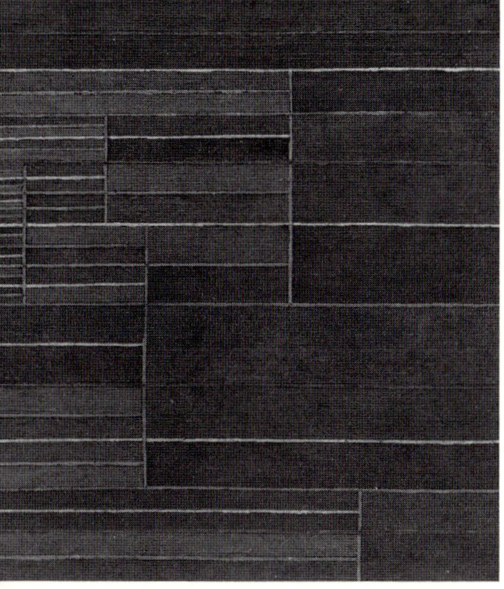

Paul Klee
In the Current Six Thresholds
tempera and oil on canvas, 1929,
The Solomon R. Guggenheim Museum,
New York

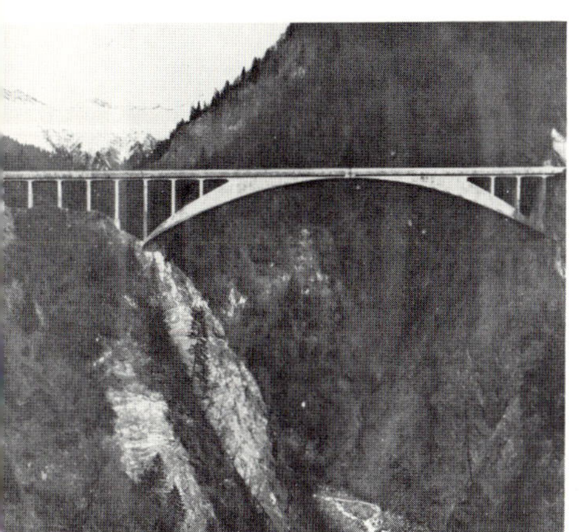

Robert Maillart
Salgina-Tobel Bridge
1929–1930, Switzerland

shape the environment beyond the framing edge to be mutually enhancing. In Bill's hands this concept of the nuclear character of works of art in relation to their environment has been developed into one of the most potent and versatile artistic concepts of the last quarter century.

The other fields of experience in which Bill sought clues to a new organization have been varied, for as he explains, «art is just as pluralistic a thing as our society itself… I can do my paintings and sculptures only if I constantly follow the course of political and economic events, and of scientific research and discovery, and only in close relation to practical experience… I don't believe that I would be capable of developing as an artist, with any confidence or optimism, if I were not constantly dealing with reality.»[16]

Specific examples offering solutions which deal with problems relevant to Bill's own are music, engineering, and mathematics. Music had always held a central place in Klee's teaching, particularly in his more systematic works, such as *In the Current Six Thresholds* of 1929, where the integration of two linear systems and four colors within a restricted compositional and tonal scale is virtually a pictorial equivalent to a Bach fugue. Bill also shared this interest, particularly in music's ability through variations and developments on a theme to produce great variety with strictly limited means and soon after its publication in 1937, he read James Jean's *Science and Music* which explored and illustrated the shape of sound through harmonic motion and the sound-curve of various tones.

In engineering, the relationship between functional and aesthetic form is often a particularly close one, and nowhere is the expressive tension which this can produce more apparent than in the bridges of the Swiss engineer, Robert Maillart. This pioneer of ferro-concrete construction, by reducing the traditional supporting mass to a minimal structural system, freed the basic building unit (the reinforced flat or curved concrete slab) to be used as an element of nearly pure plastic expression. Just as a Bill sculpture, a Maillart bridge imprints the presence of rational man on the landscape without the slightest note of intrusion. In fact this respect for the environment, with its own imposing sense of scale, and concern for the work's integration rather than competition with it, appears to be a typically Swiss trait.

17.
Siegfried Giedion, «Construction and Aesthetics», in *Circle* (London: Faber & Faber, 1937. Reprint New York: Praeger, 1971), p. 223.

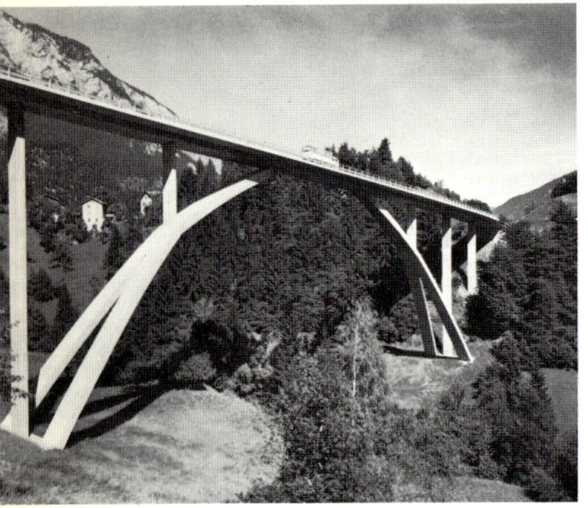

Lavina-Tobel Bridge
Tamins, Switzerland 1966–67
Concept by Max Bill, Engineers Roš &
Coll. Aschwanden & Speck

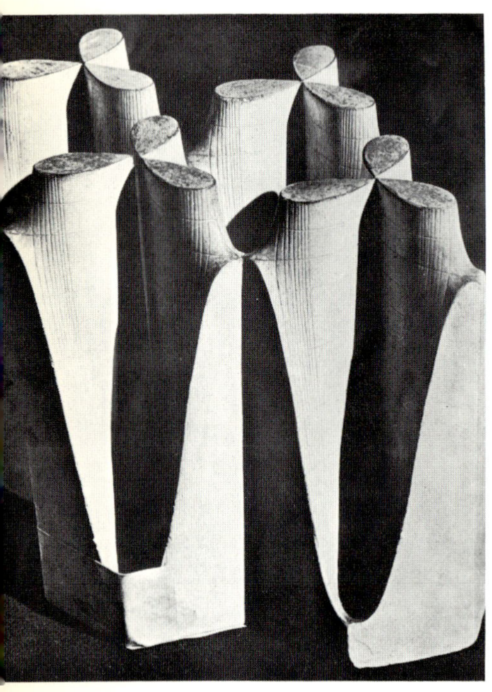

The Elliptical Function P'(U) for G2 = 0 and G3 = 4
model, photo by Man Ray

18.
Georges Vantongerloo, *Paintings, Sculptures, Reflections* (New York: Wittenborn, 1948).

In 1949 Bill published the first monograph on Maillart's work, stressing its aesthetic importance. In addition, Bill's own work bears a strong spiritual relationship to Maillart's conception of engineering where, because «it is very difficult to determine the forces present in slabs... by calculation alone, ...the final forms were based partly on calculation and partly on experiment».[17] These structures are prototypes of a humanized application of technology, and as totally functional works of sculpture, it is more than a pun to point out that Maillart's work bridges the gap between art and everyday life with almost unique success. In the nineteen-sixties Bill proposed the structural system for the Lavina-Tobel bridge, which through the use of the new technique of pri-stressed concrete, further developed Maillart's philosophy.

While Bill's formal study of mathematics has never gone beyond ordinary architectural calculations, his interest in exploring its relation and application to the arts has been continous. In his 1949 essay on «The Mathematical Approach in Contemporary Art» (reprinted in this catalogue) he summarizes his working philosophy and the lessons of his own development and locates the importance of measurement and the determination of accurate relationships at the very threshold of cognition and rationality. By stressing this very fundamental level of mathematical organization, a shared characteristic of music and engineering, as well as the Fine Arts, Bill has been able to derive inspiration from modern science and technology without the fear of mimicking or competing with their physical forms.

Just as Vantongerloo, who was the first to claim mathematics as a tool which could be «used as one uses a hammer and chisel to cut marble»[18] to express abstract concepts in art, Bill had confidence, in the face of widespread criticism, that mathematical means could be frankly employed without undermining the uniqueness of the artist. In fact he reversed the argument by stressing that the generative power of his ideas was the contemporary artist's primary source of originality rather than expressionistic or personal execution. It cannot be overstressed that it is the very strength of Bill's conviction that art and science, while capable of a rich cross-fertilization, are clearly distinct, which allows him to explore their points of similarity so clearly.

A result of this is that Bill has always been open about his

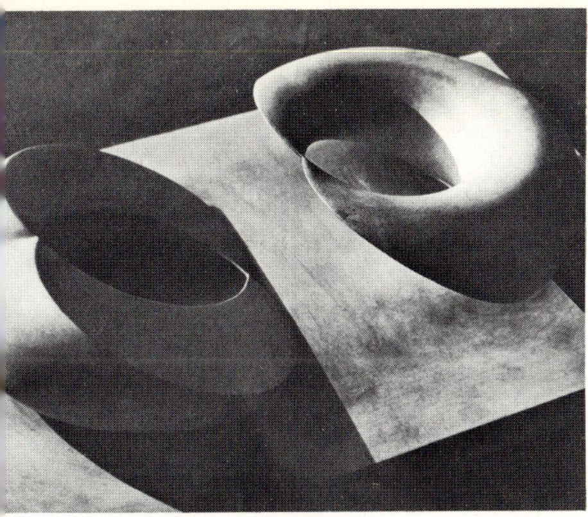

A Plane Bitangent to a Torus Cut by Two Circles
model, photo by Man Ray

19.
It is of interest to note that Man Ray translated his photograph of the model of the elliptical function $P'(U)$ for $G2 = 0$ and $G3 = 4$ directly and unchanged into *The Merry Wives of Windsor,* an oil of 1948 belonging to a series titled «Shakesperean Equations».

20.
Jack Burnham, *Beyond Modern Sculpture* (New York: Braziller, 1968), p. 129.

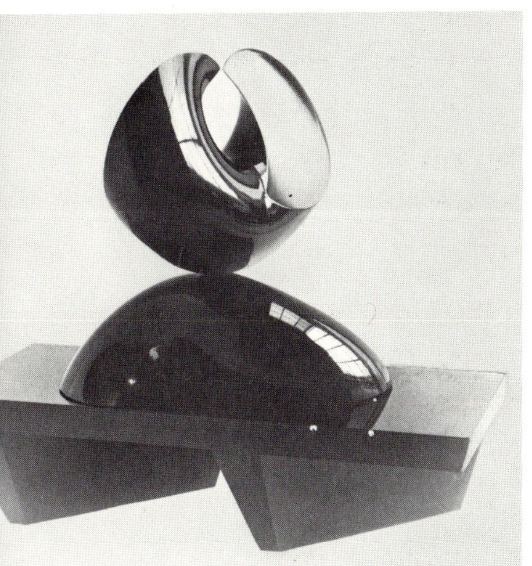

Max Bill
Construction from a Ring
1940–41, black polished wood,
Collection Georges Baines, Antwerpen

debt to mathematics and interest in such things as scientific models which he first saw in Paris at the Palais de la Découverte. In the essay mentioned above, he compares their fascination to that which African sculpture held for the Cubists, while pointing out that they were equally inappropriate for direct assimilation into modern European art. The Surrealists «discovered» examples of these models in the Musée Poincaré and published Man Ray's photographs of a number of them with a lead article by Christian Zervos on «Mathematics and Abstract Art» in the 1936 *Cahiers D'Art.*[19] This issue is of particular interest as it conveys the dominant aesthetic climate in Paris the year both Abstraction-Création folded and Bill first formulated the principles of Concrete Art. Zervos's article is a diatribe condemning the use of mathematics as anti-humanist and Man Ray's photographs, with their dramatic lighting, underscore the Surrealists interests in these models as bizarre and provocative «found objects.»

For Bill their actual forms, which when looked at as sculpture tend to be overly complicated, were not of primary interest, but their content was; for here were objects which bore no abstracted relationship to the visible world, but were solely the concrete realizations of ideas. While certain models produce impressive examples of formal harmony, the mathematical equations they embody are completely impersonal. In contrast, a sculpture by Bill provides an affirmation of individual expression.

There is irony in the fact that Zervos leveled the charge that mathematics was devoid of «ambiguity», «introspection», and «irrationality» at just the moment, as Bill points out in the essay mentioned, when it had reached a stage of evolution where much had become unclear and the proof of many apparently logical deductions ceased to be demonstrable. Jack Burnham has observed that at the very time when artists became interested in scientific models they were losing their validity for mathematicians and physicists. «Yet many scientists concede that the decline of the physical model has been a loss for purposes of conceptualization – making it now more difficult to grasp problems through common sense perception.»[20] It is Bill's belief that art, through its ability to create new symbols, can provide a new means of conceptualization, without which we run the growing danger of drifting out of touch with a rapidly changing reality.

From 1936 on, Paris steadily declined as a center of contemporary art. Bill's formulation of the principles of Concrete Art that year was not so much intended as a new «ism» to rally the dispersed proponents of abstract art as an elaboration of his own developing position and a recognition of the need to provide it with a firm and positive theoretical foundation in the face of growing hostility. While Bill took the term and general principles from Van Doesburg's 1930 manifesto, *Art Concret,* which culminated the latter's attempt to systematize the means of artistic expression, he drew on and clarified a central strain of the modern movement. This strain reaches back at least to Wilhelm Worringer's pivotal treatise of 1907, *Abstraction and Empathy,* which asserted that the existence of formal laws was central to the very concept of aesthetics. In Worringer's words, «The aesthetic effect can only issue forth from that higher condition which we call form, and whose essence is to conform to certain rules, no matter whether this conformity is simple and easily discernible, or whether it is differentiated in such a way that it can only be sensed as the conformity of the organic».[21]

In 1944 Bill organized the first international exhibition of *Concrete Art* in Basel and in 1960 a retrospective, *Concrete Art, Fifty Years of Development,* in Zurich. Between 1944 and 1945, twelve issues of the revue, *Abstrakt-Konkret,* founded by Bill, and to which he contributed regularly, appeared in the bulletin of the gallery, Des Eaux-Vives, Zurich. Despite the hyphenated title, Concrete Art was defined in deliberate contrast to Abstract Art. During this period, Bill taught the introductory course on the theory of form at the School of Applied Arts in Zurich, at the request of its Director, Johannes Itten, and this may have been one reason he now concentrated in his writings on clarifying the meaning of these terms. One has the impression that, aware of the vacuum the war had created in European culture, Bill was preparing the pedagogical tools that would soon be needed for the massive challenge of rebuilding which lay ahead – a task he was to be centrally involved in at the Hochschule für Gestaltung at Ulm, Germany from 1951 to 1956, and elsewhere.

«I am obliged over and over again», he wrote, «to explain why I call one direction in art ‹abstract› and another ‹concrete› …The difference between abstract art and concrete art

21.
Wilhelm Worringer, *Abstraction and Empathy* (New York: International Universities Press, Inc., 1967).

22.
Max Bill, «Of the Meaning of Terms in the New Art», in *Max Bill* (Geneva: Musée Rath, 1972), pp. 72–74, first published in *abstrakt/konkret* Zürich 1944.

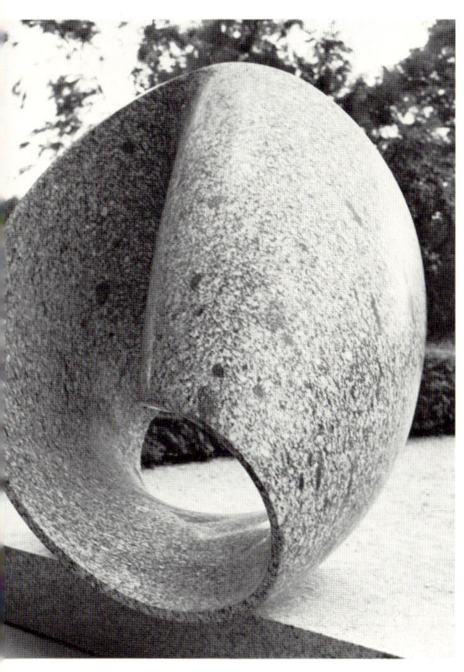

Max Bill
Endless Ribbon, 1935–53
Musée Nationale d'Art Moderne, Paris

lies in this, that in abstract art the pictorial content is still tied to images from nature, whereas the pictorial content of concrete art emerges without the intermediary intervention of the later ...Concrete Art renders visible abstract thought as such, by purely artistic means, and in so doing creates new objects. It is the goal of concrete art to create objects for spiritual use by analogy to the manner in which man creates objects for his material use.»[22] Concrete Art's significance for post-war painting and sculpture has not been felt as an exclusive movement, but as an inclusive, creative program cutting across a wide variety of personal styles. The common characteristic of its most able adherents is the attempt to re-introduce the intellectual rigour of the pioneer generation into a new cultural context. In this attempt, the originality of Bill's art stands out as a true prototype.

Turning to Bill's work, it is clear that theory followed invention. His instinctive search for forms which were neither arbitrary nor abstracted from nature had led by 1935 to the creation of the *Endless Ribbon,* his first single-sided sculpture, and the start of his suite of lithographs, *Fifteen Variations on a Single Theme* (published in 1938). Together with the *Construction with Suspended Cube* of 1935–36 they stand within his development as a clear breakthrough to a fully realized, personal style. The *Variations* went much further than merely establishing the validity of serial development. They stressed integrity and applicability of concept rather than the dogma of one «correct» structural system, producing straight and curved, open and closed, colored and monochrome solutions. Furthermore, the geometric surface configuration of *Variation I* unleashed Bill's bold, personal sense of color, in a premonition of his later paintings. And both the *Variations* and the *Endless Ribbon,* which as a theme was eventually to undergo a fascinating variety of transformations, led to an interest in topology.

A relatively young branch of geometry, topology is the study of those properties of an object which are the most permanent, the most capable of undergoing distortion without destroying their topological constants in terms of edges, faces, vertices, and connectedness. Topology had little to offer as far as actual forms. It should be remembered that Bill invented his original endless loop in response to problems posed by a specific commission and only later learned that he

23.
See: Max Bill, «How I started making Single-Sided Surfaces», in *Max Bill: Surfaces* (Toronto: Marlborough-Godard, Ltd., 1972).

24.
Jack Burnham, op cit., p. 143.

had reinterpreted the «moebius strip», one of the few aesthetically effective topological models.[23] What it did offer, as a versatile mathematical concept of formal relativity and complexity within an underlying order, was content.

Just as the *Endless Ribbon* confronts us with the fact of finite infinity, all Bill's central themes challenge both perceptual assumptions and accepted notions of the forces regulating our environment. This is not, however, accomplished at the expense of the aesthetic quality of the object. To the contrary, the total interdependence of form and content, of object and idea, is one of the distinguishing characteristics of his work and central goals of Concrete Art in general.

Frequently, as in the theme of the half sphere, Bill has produced a number of distinct variations each with such compelling individuality that we find it hard to accept their common topological identity. Jack Burnham has pointed out that by doing this, «Bill demonstrates both a topological truth and an artistic principle; there are no ‹perfect forms›, only the ability of the artist to reveal meaningful aspects of the same reality»,[24] However, where so much recent art which concerned itself with the new realities of science ended by rejecting painting and sculpture as viable means, in Bill's hands, such traditional qualities as the sensuality of logical form, pure color, and the innate beauty of fine materials have been accentuated.

Because of the central role afforded mathematically deduced order in his work, some have attacked it as impersonal and lacking in originality – «cold, kitchen art» was one of the more memorable epithets. To the contrary, a Bill painting or sculpture stresses with exceptional clarity the personal decisions leading to its final state. His titles are factual descriptions of a theme, while each individual work is one distinct and conscious choice from an infinity of possible variations. The original theme, the specific choice, the materials, color and scale of execution all are decisions made no less personal by the final geometric configuration. In a group installation, Bill's works instantly proclaim his conceptual authorship, their very lack of expressionistic handwriting an unmistakable signature.

The almost total absence of public monuments of quality in the twentieth century is a clear indication of the disappearance of widely shared symbolic concepts and imagery. This

See: page 102–108

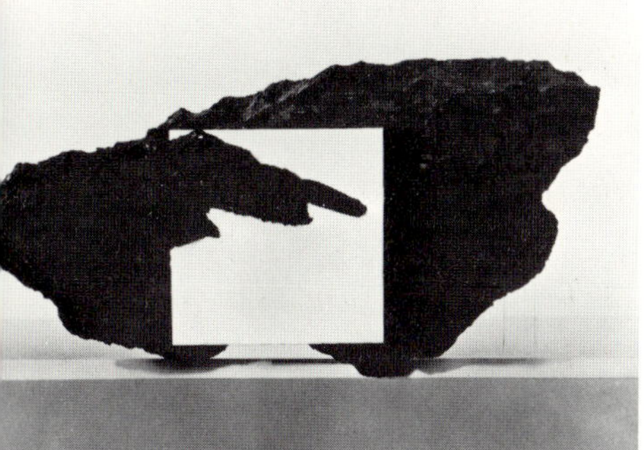

Max Bill
Monument for *George Büchner* at
Darmstadt, 1955

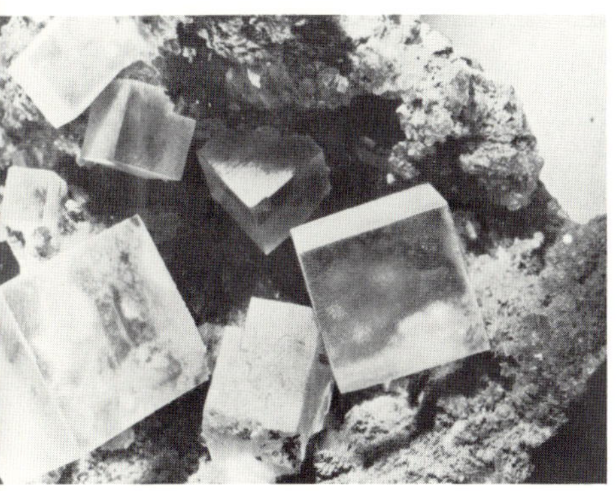

Transparent Crystals of Fossil Salt found
at Wiediczka in Calicia

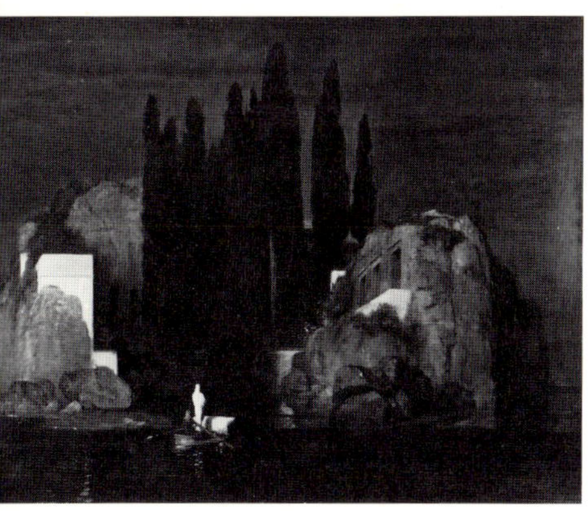

Arnold Böcklin
The Isle of the Dead: First Version
tempera on canvas, 1880,
Kunstmuseum, Basel

problem of investing a given theme with a viable contemporary form has been seen by Bill as a challenge modern art cannot afford to ignore. On two occasions he has entered proposals for specific competitions. In 1953 his *Monument to the Unknown Political Prisoner* dealt with a quintessentially twentieth century subject – the anonymous, mass hero – where the very idea of a rhetorical statement would have been unfitting.

A trip to Ravenna the previous year, where he saw the fifth century Mausoleum of Galla Placidia, had impressed on him the fact that monuments need not be large to trigger profound emotions. The very humility of scale and intense focus on the momentarily «imprisoned» visitor, which his solution achieves, creates a microcosm with truly monumental implications. Bill's description of this project and its goal of achieving symbolic meaning through purely sculptural means (reprinted in this catalogue), provides an insight into a central motivation for all his work.

Two years later, in 1955, Bill designed a monument for the nineteenth century German writer and scientist Georg Büchner, who died a political exile in Zurich at the early age of twenty-two. Here Bill created a bold image of absolute contrasts. The white cube standing for the rationality and ultimate durability of Büchner's ideas, the enclosing, organic mass for the repressive and transitional times with which he struggled. The image expresses a primal, recurring contrast and its forms recall a natural crystal in nature, similar to those Bill had illustrated in his publication *Form* of 1952.

With this proposal Bill produced a concrete solution to the iconography of the subject, which nevertheless was in keeping with the Romantic character of Büchner and his times. The symbolic contrasts of black and white and organic and geometric, which a true Romantic such as the Swiss Arnold Böcklin used in his *Isle of the Dead,* are here drastically simplified without sacrificing their emotional appeal. The failure of both these proposals to be realized has been a major loss to contemporary sculpture in an area where few definitive solutions exist.

From the late thirties on, Bill's development has been continuous but not linear. Just as his work as a whole benefits from the feedback of problems and solutions in his other areas of activity, his painting and sculpture are constantly

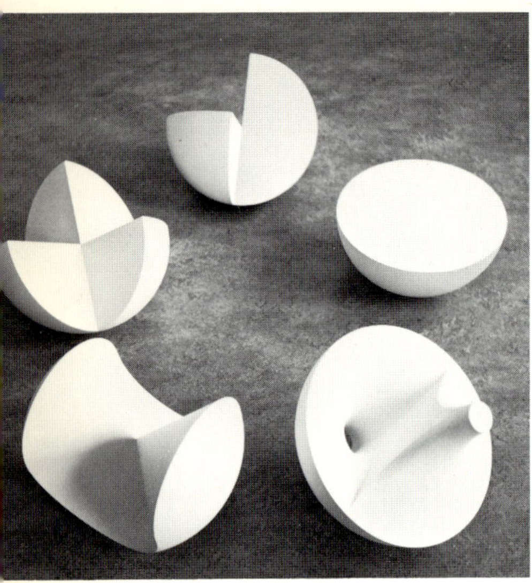

Max Bill
Family of Five Half Spheres
1965–1966

See: page 171

See: page 49

See: page 134

redefining earlier themes and adding new interpretations to a number of central problems which run like leitmotifs through his art. While Bill rejects formalist reductivism as a legitimate source of invention (see his article «Structure as Art? Art as Structure?» reprinted in this catalogue), he is extremely sensitive to the formal concerns of the separate media in which he works.

In sculpture he sees the central problem to be that of spatial expression. Beginning with the *Long Sculpture* of 1933, his first, freestanding piece, Bill has cut into solids to link interior and exterior space. The *Construction with Suspended Cube* of 1935–36 began a lifelong study of the balance between solid and void which can be achieved by cutting into geometric masses. The result, as in the case of this cube, one half of which has been cut out, is a form that is visually clear, but conceptually complex.

Similarly, one of Bill's most recent works, *The Solid Half of a Sphere* of 1972, repeats the same procedure, only now the resulting mass balances evenly in apparent contradiction to the visual illusion of an off-axis center of gravity. Here, as in his other pieces on the theme of the half-sphere, the solid form molds space with such authority that its conceptual twin, which would restore the original sphere, is sensed as an almost palpable presence. Invariably, however, Bill's formal solutions merge into symbols. In this particular case the profile of the division of the sphere is the same as that of the *yin-yang* unity of active and passive cosmic principles in Chinese, dualistic philosophy.

The *Construction* of 1937 alternates from closed to open form as we move around it, while its tremendous physical mass rests weightlessly on that invisible point where a sphere meets a flat plane. Questions central to the development of modern sculpture – the elimination of the base, the relation of fragment to whole, and three-hundred sixty degree frontality – are all clearly resolved in this piece.

The economy of means with which Bill can produce a work of great physical beauty and thought-provoking complexity is nowhere more apparent than in his *Pyramid in the Form of One-Eighth of a Sphere* of 1965. Somewhere near its center the characteristics of a sphere – curved, free rolling and unstable – are replaced by those of a pyramid – angular, stationary and stable. As if to accentuate its mixed parentage,

the resulting object can be easily rocked, but moved only
with difficulty.

In painting, Bill sees the primary problem as that of expressing color and rhythm on a flat surface. His development led
quickly to a rejection of relational composition and the
demonstration that mathematical organization could be an
effective means for freeing color. His compositional systems
produce the initial impression of an overall, balanced gestalt;
only later, with further observation, do we notice the specific
organizing principle.

While the particular composition developed in a given
work produces its individual rhythm, it also provides a
vehicle for presenting color with little or no connotation of
anything other than itself. What analogy there is in Bill's
work tends toward music. Increasingly since the late forties,
he has tightened and simplified the rules governing his compositions and simultaneously intensified his use of color. His
choice of tone is wide and extremely personal; and while he
frequently uses the primaries and secondaries in structural
relationships, the hues are never those of the first generation's «absolutes». In fact Bill's color sense shares little with
recent painting, and one must go back to the work of Hodler,
Böcklin and, before them, Niklaus Manuel Deutsch to locate
the tradition in which it falls.

George Kubler has pointed out that: «A signal trait of our
time is an ambivalence in everything touching upon change.
Our whole cultural tradition favors the values of permanence, yet the conditions of present existence require an
acceptance of continual change.»[25] This pervasive sense of
relativity is central to any contemporary definition of reality.
Similarly, a central concern of Bill's art is to express in comprehensible terms this ambiguous, modern relationship
between permanence and change. The solution which he has
evolved is to produce concrete, often tactile, formulations of
ambiguous concepts. Tangible ambiguity may at first appear
to be a contradiction of terms, but in its resolution resides a
precise mathematical poetry of which Bill is an undisputed
master.

While the variations on the theme of the endless ribbon are
probably the best known examples, all his work touches on
this question at least indirectly. The various constructions
from a ring are among his most definitive solutions. A ring is

25.
George Kubler, *The Shape of Time* (New
Haven: Yale University Press, 1962), p. 62.

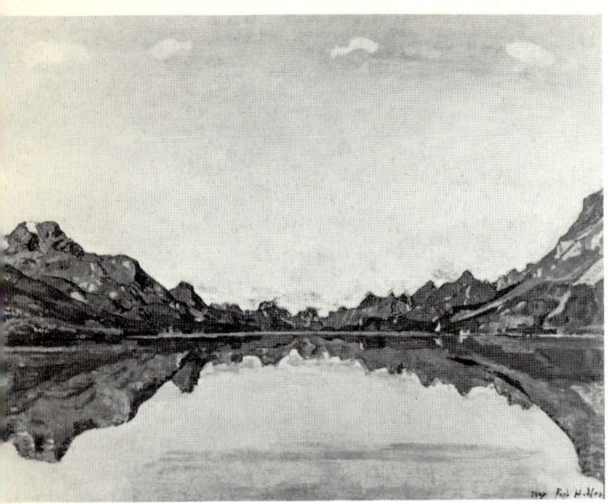

Ferdinand Hodler
Silvaplanersee, oil on canvas, 1907,
Kunsthaus Zürich

26.
Margit Staber, *Max Bill* (St. Gallen:
Erker-Verlag, 1971), p. 27.

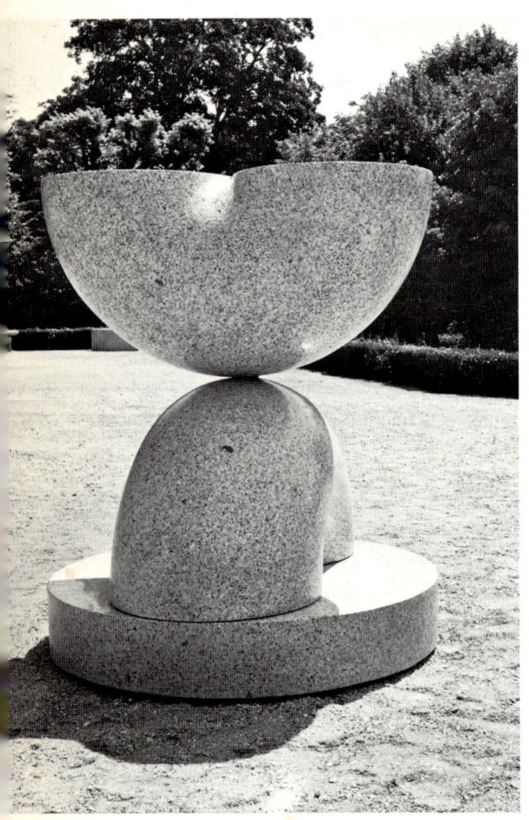

Max Bill
Construction from a Ring
1942–44, gray granit,
Albright-Knox Art Gallery

sliced through the center producing two identical halves which are then reassembled to make their characteristics totally contradictory. The bottom half achieves absolute, immobile permanence, the top half – precarious balance, suggesting imminent change. Yet the concept and its formal resolution are so strong and conveyed with such clarity that the ambiguity of the parts is submerged in the integrity of the whole.

Bill's use of the reflection image recalls the work of another Swiss, Ferdinand Hodler, who was equally determined to capture the spiritual intensity of nature's contradictions. His *Silvaplanersee* exploits the only straight line in the Swiss landscape – the surface of a body of water – to contrast the identical curves of massive peaks and their immaterial reflection. As in Bill's observation on his own work, «The greatest reality engenders the greatest unreality».[26]

By accepting the «responsibility for interpretation» which be believes is the artist's, Max Bill has attempted to produce objects which both help define the world we live in and clarify our perceptions of it. His painting, sculpture and graphic work, all to varying degrees, represent a struggle to produce prototypes of clearly solved problems. His pictorial and sculptural style has a higher goal in his mind than style itself. The aesthetic quality of his work is there to see. The question of to what degree this quality is the result of the philosophical and social convictions underlying it is one which, regardless of the answer, will be of central importance for the future.

List of Works Exhibited

All dimensions are given with width proceeding height.

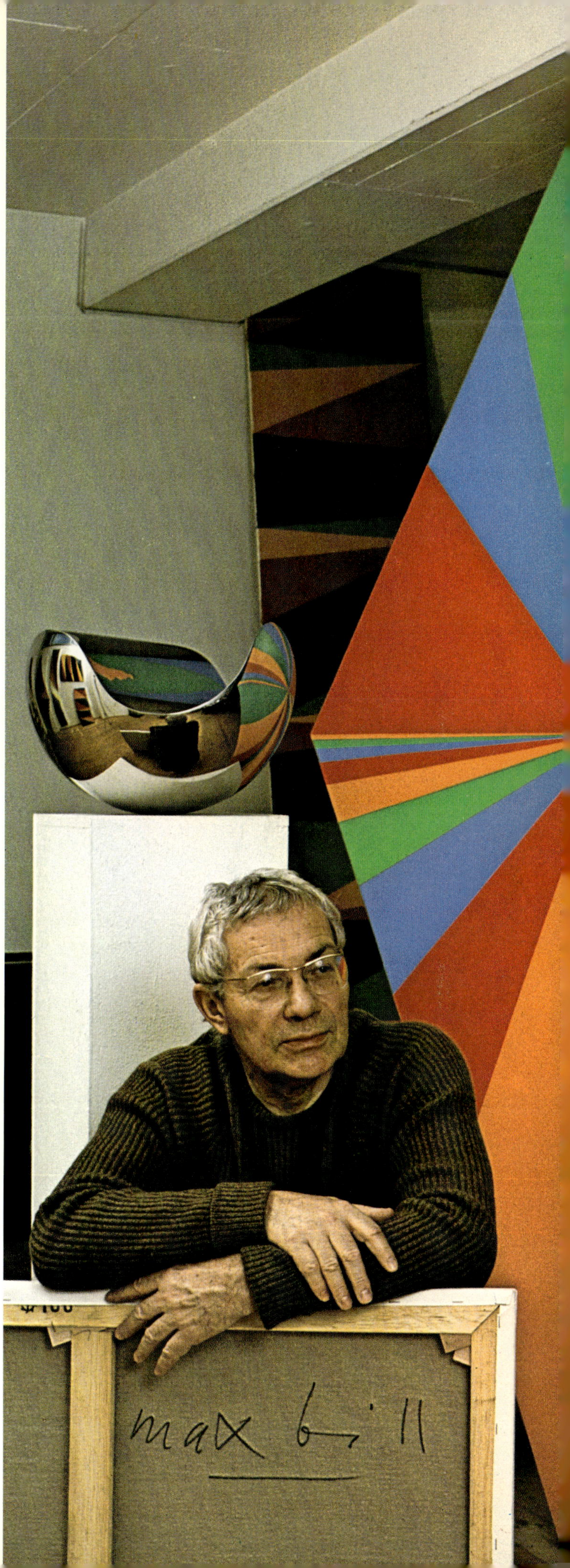

Max Bill in his studio at Zumikon-Zürich,
on his 65th birthday
december 22nd 1973

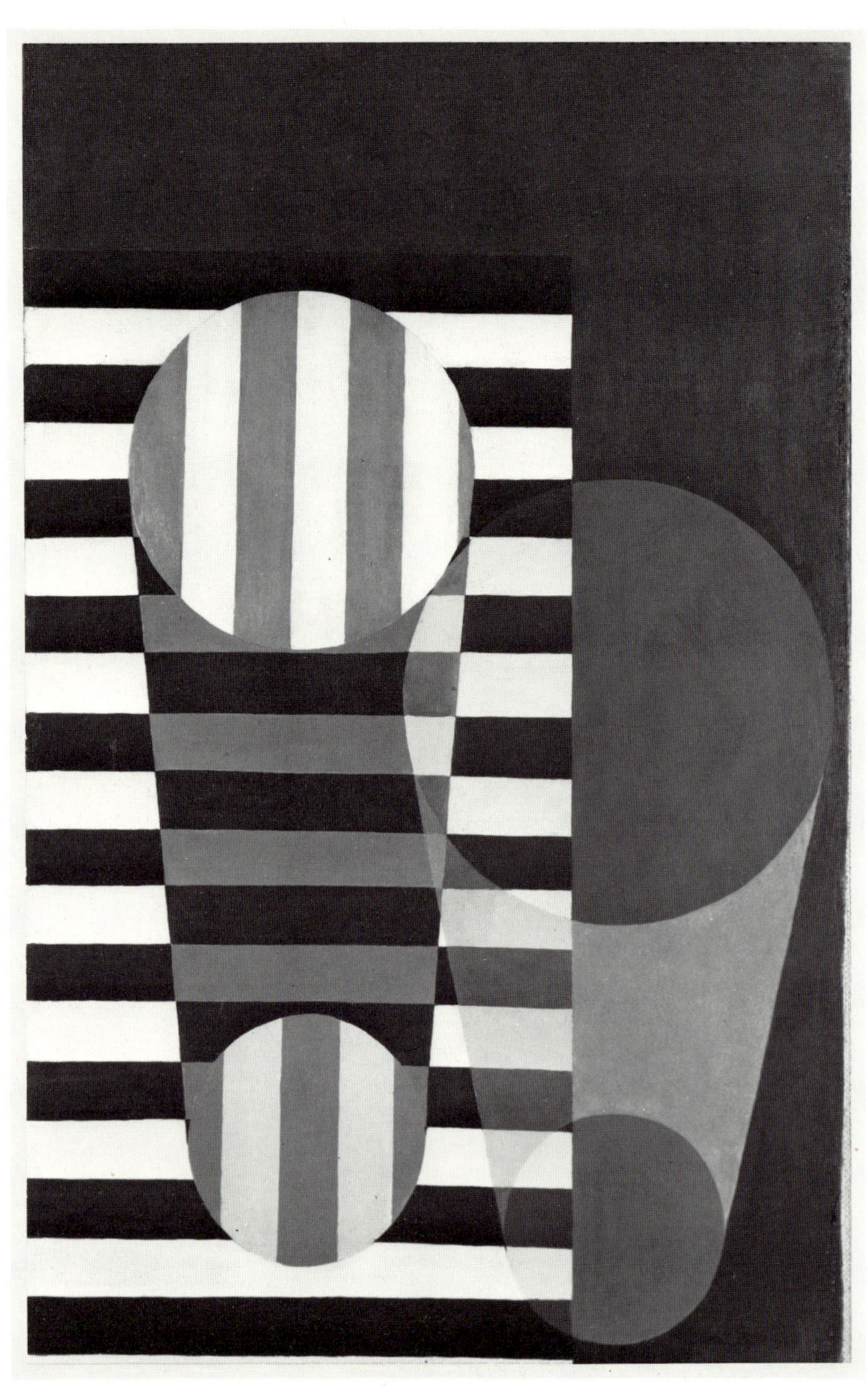

1928
Spatial Composition no. 9
oil on canvas, 17¼″ × 29¼″,
(44 × 69 cm)

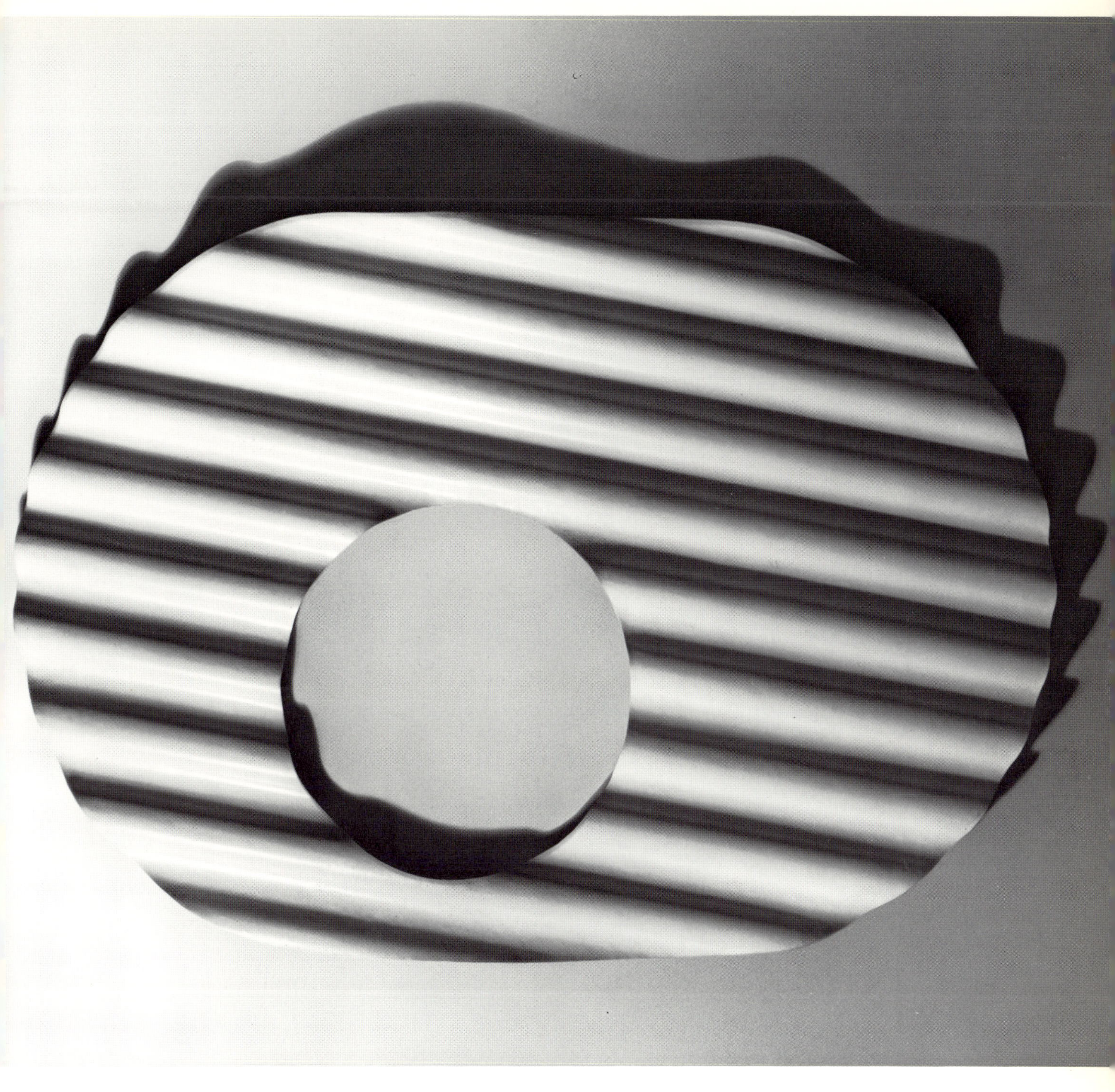

1931–32
Relief/Undulated Surface
corrugated iron, 47¼″ × 31½″,
(120 × 80 cm)

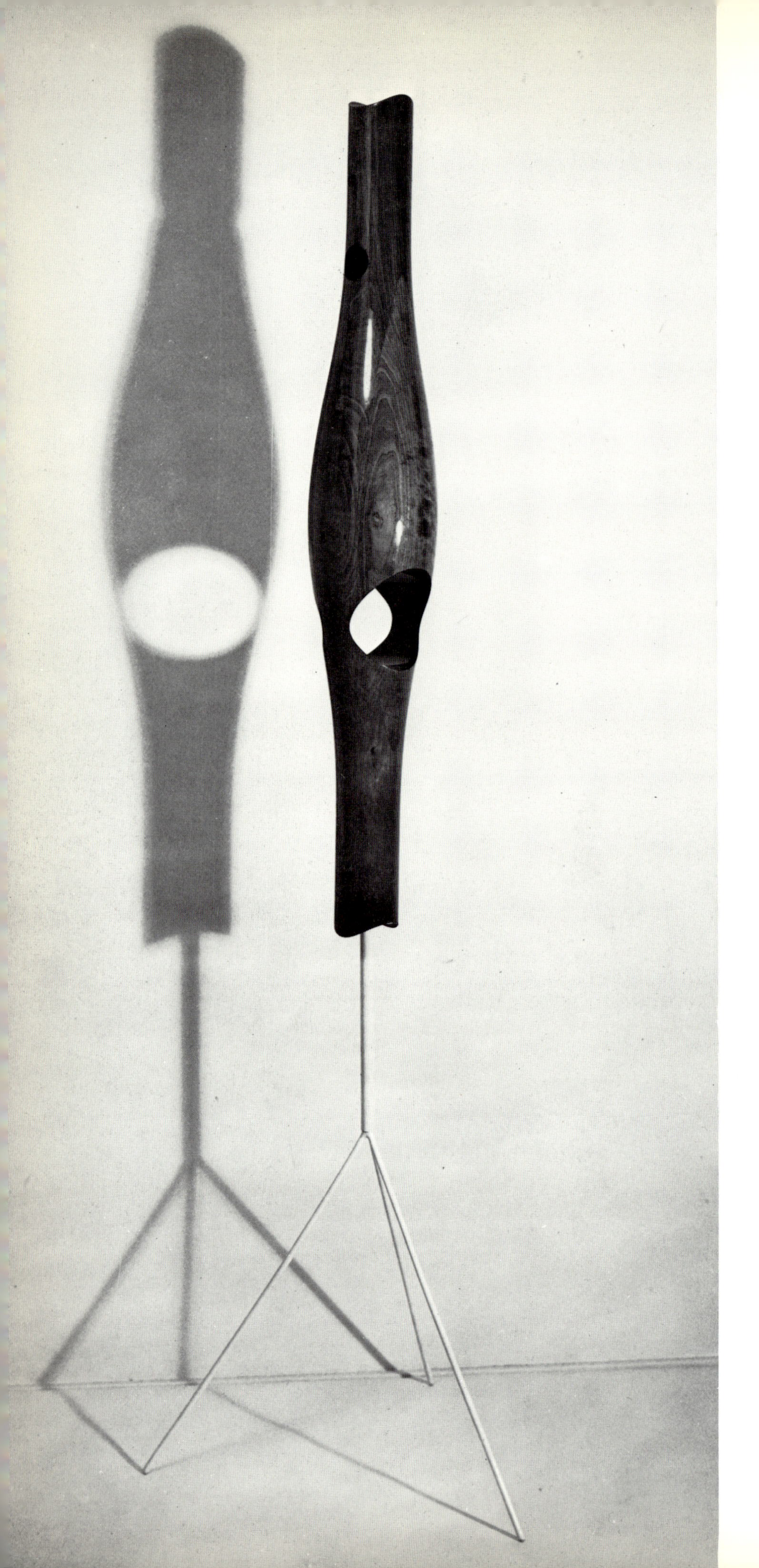

1933
Long Sculpture
wood and iron, height, 78¾″,
(200 cm)

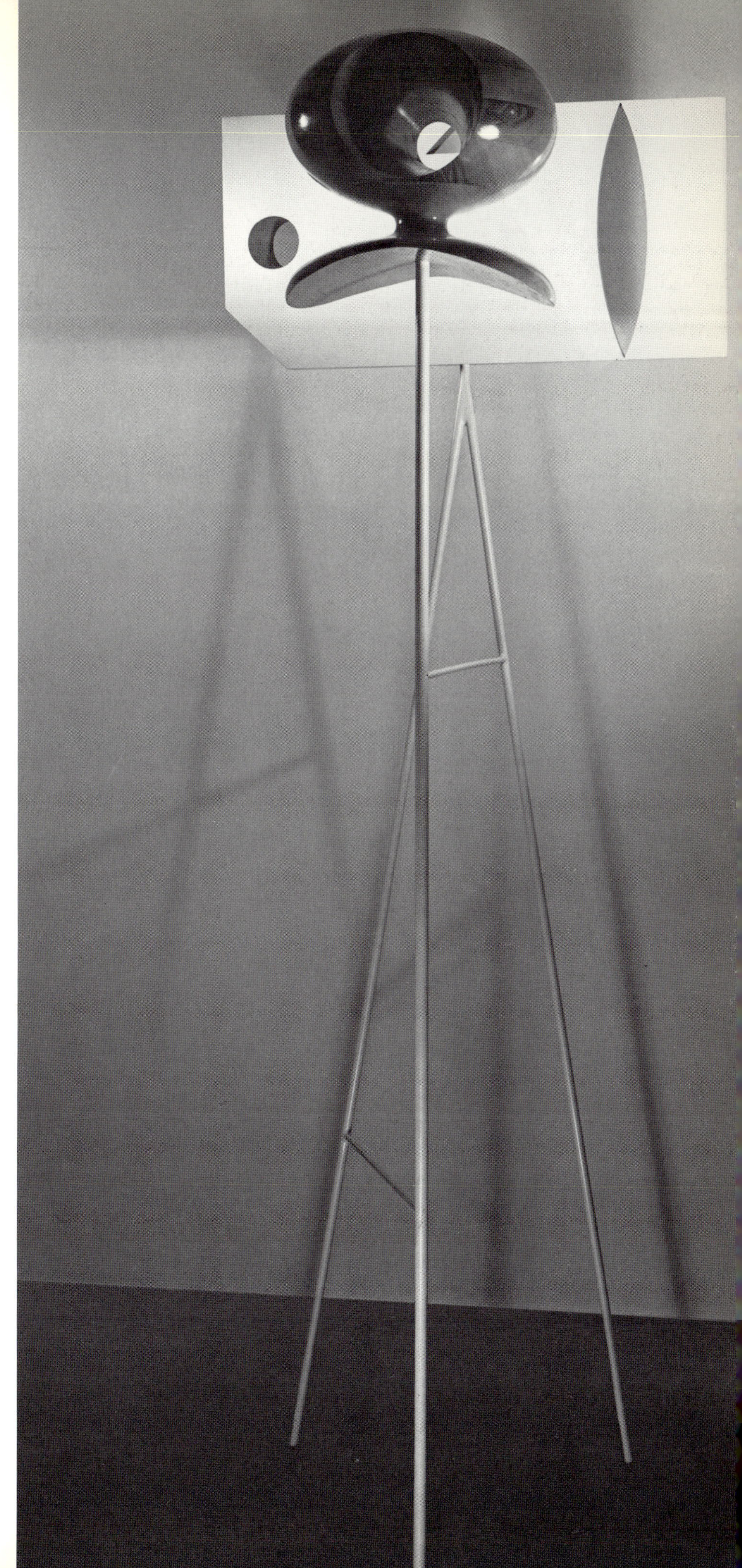

1934
Sculpture in Two Parts
wood and iron, height, 90½″,
(230 cm)

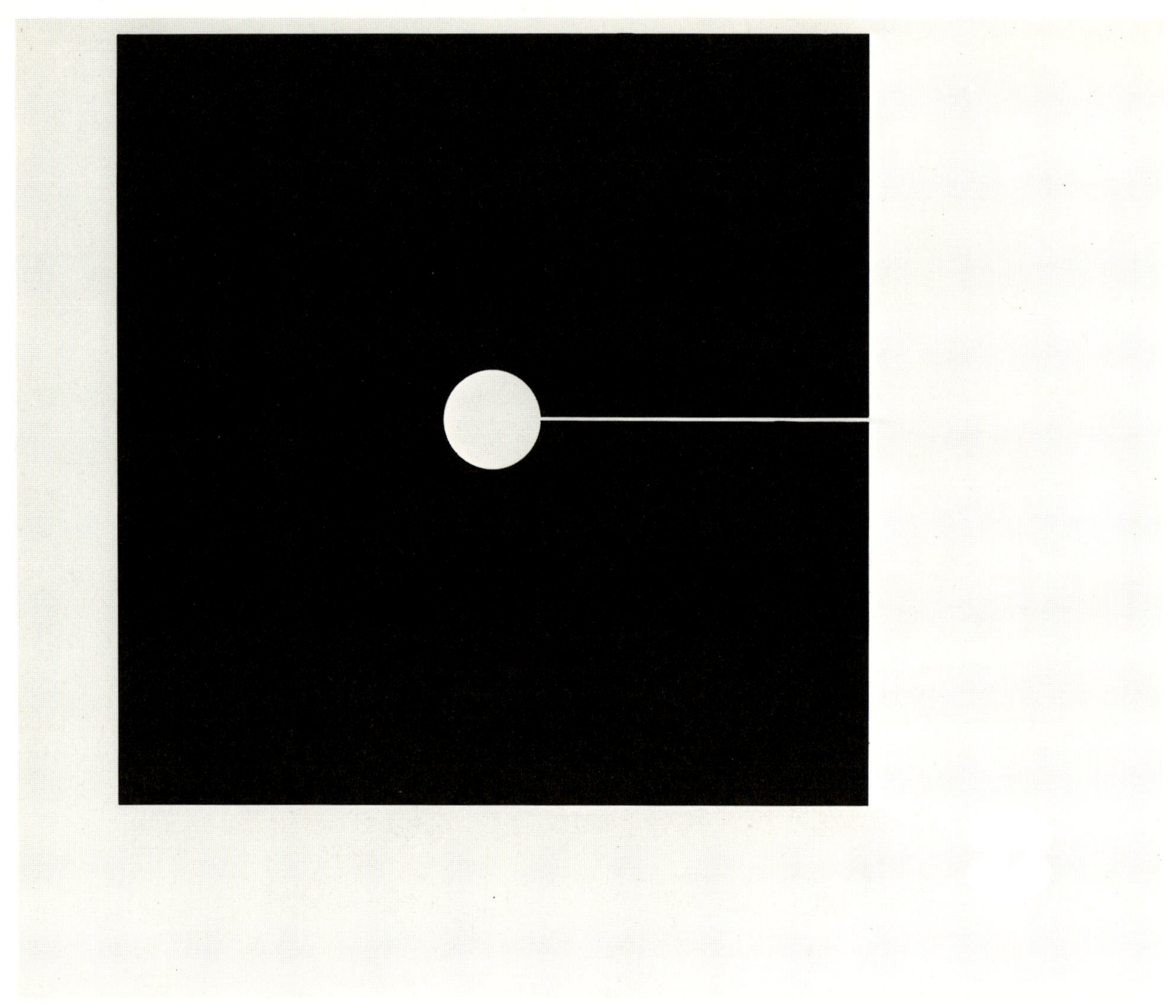

1934
Construction
oil on masonite, 23⅝″ × 19¾″,
(60 × 50 cm)

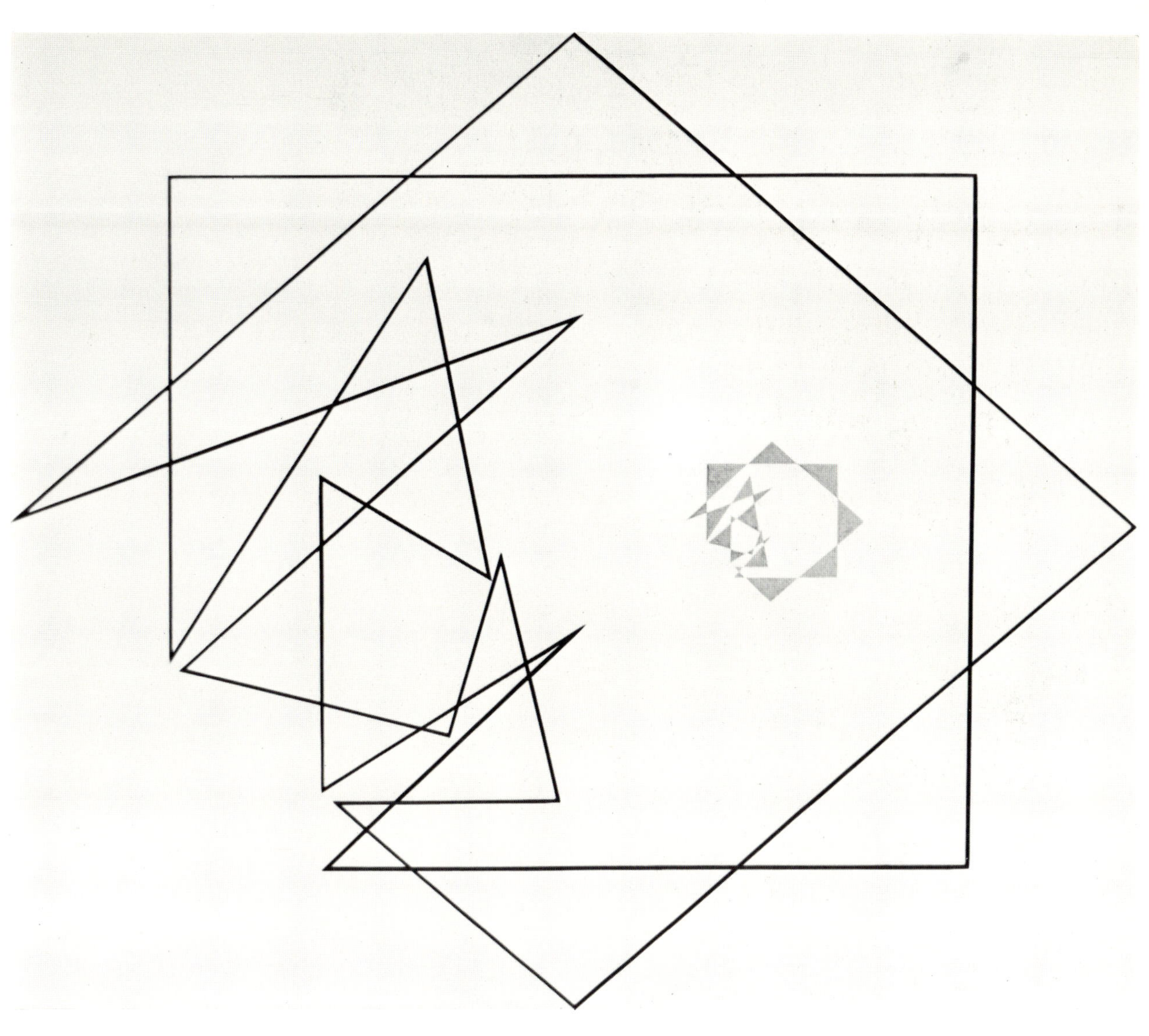

1934
Construction in Two Parts
oil on masonite, 23⅝″ × 19¾″,
(60 × 50 cm)

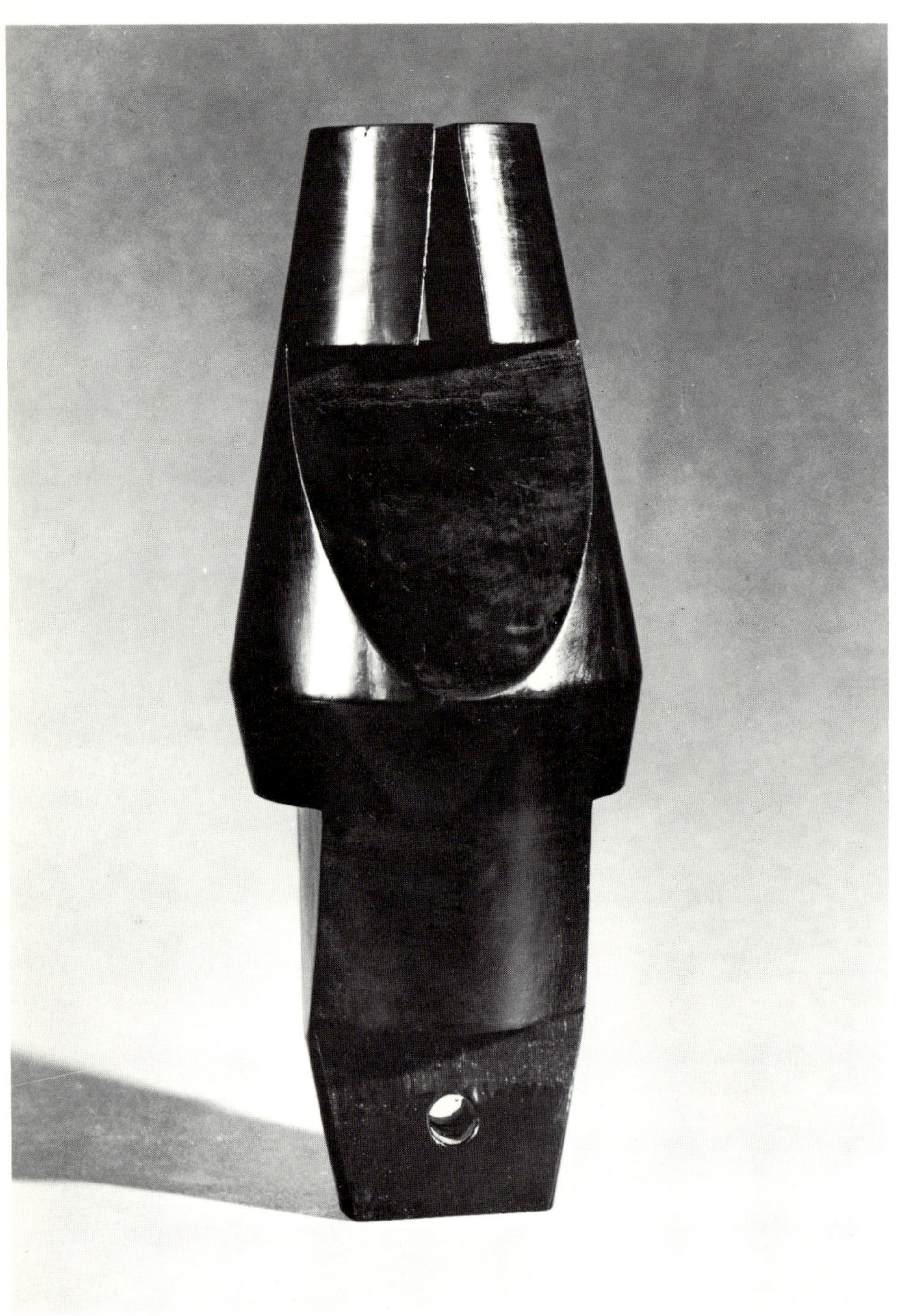

1934–35
Black Sculpture
wood, 3⁷⁄₈″ × 9⁷⁄₈″, (10 × 25 cm)

1935–36
Construction With a Suspended Cube
brass and iron, 19¾″ × 23⁵⁄₈″ × 47¼″,
(50 × 60 × 120 cm)

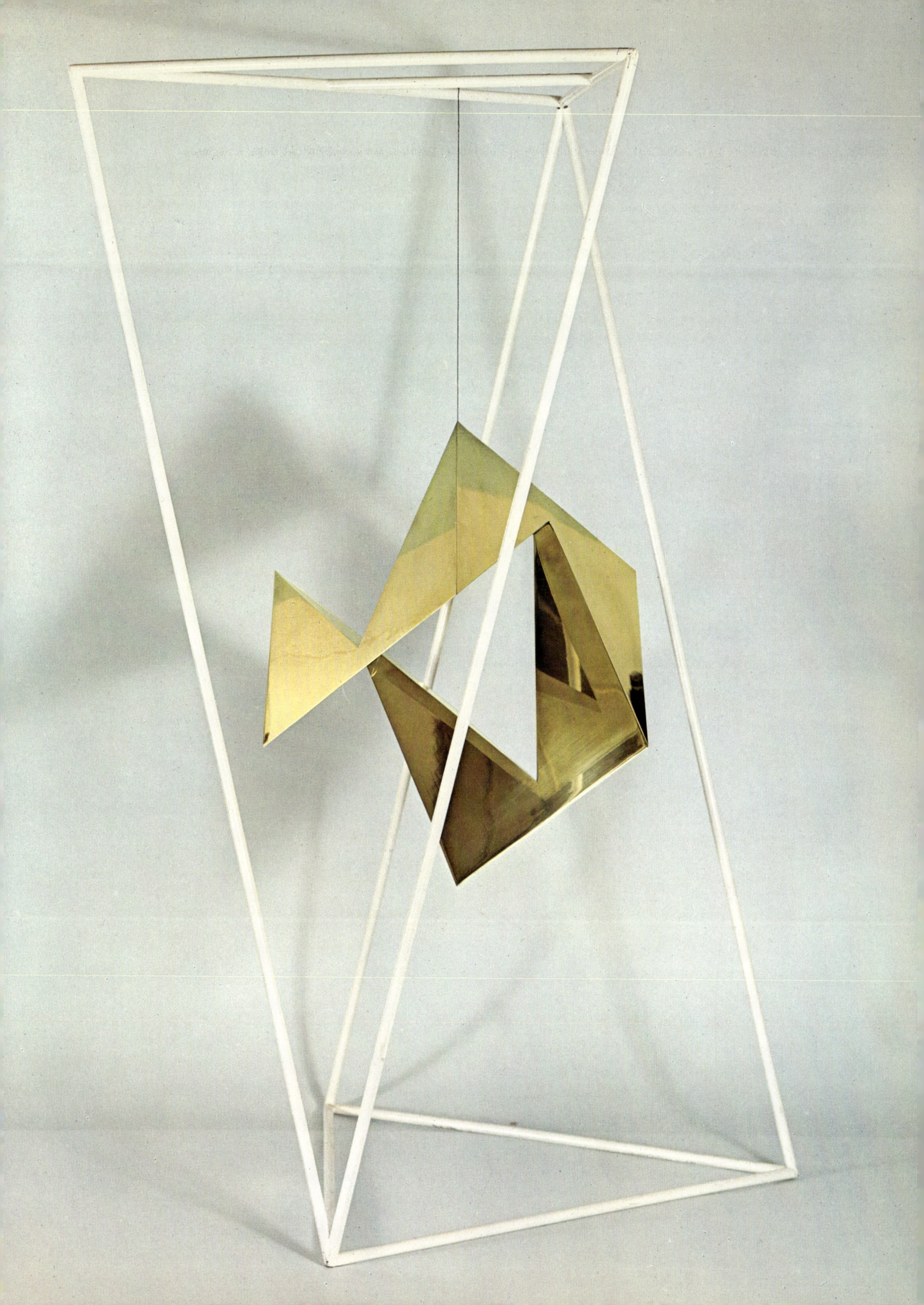

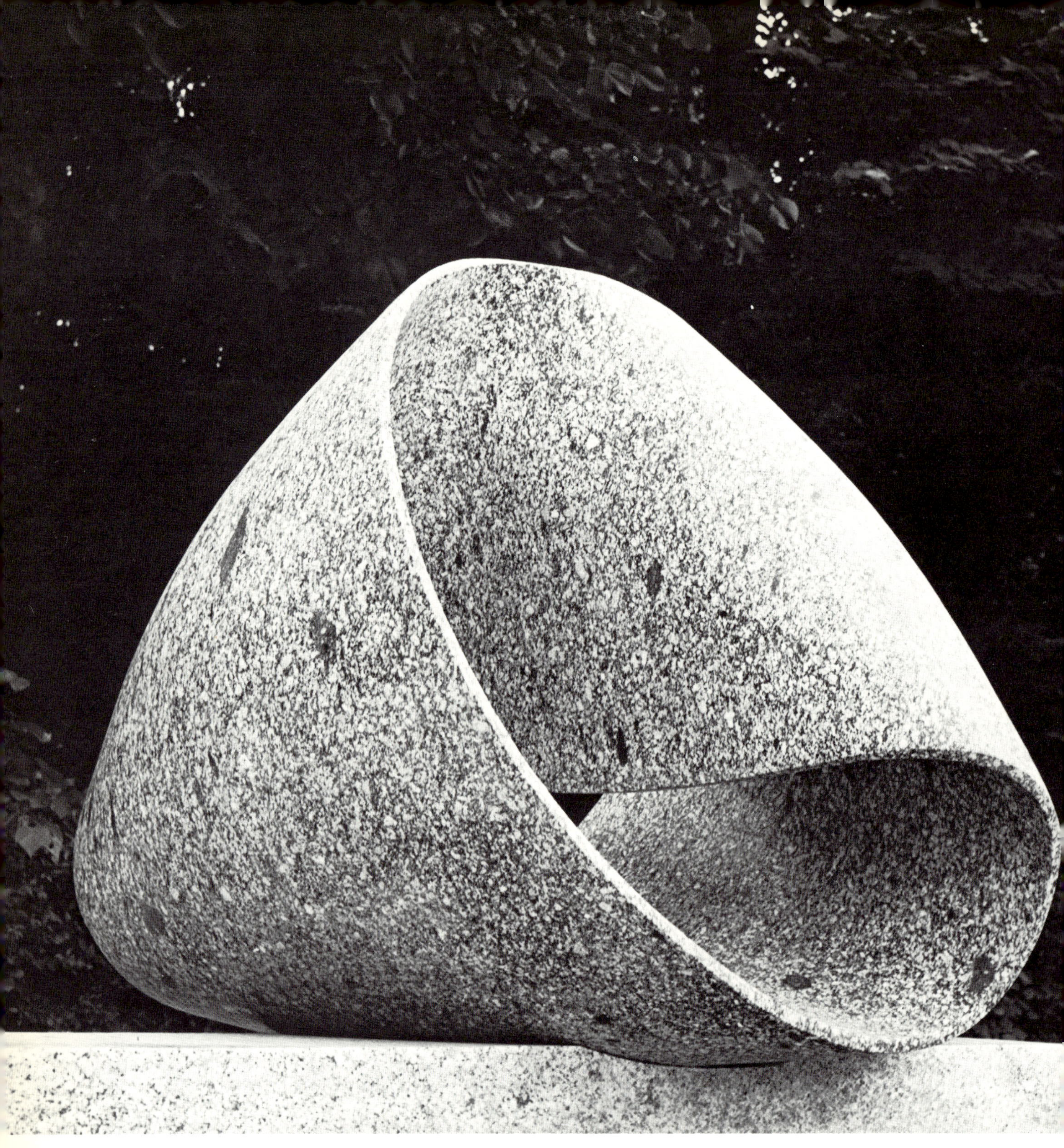

1935–53
Endless Ribbon
granite, 59″ × 39½″ × 47¼″,
(150 × 100 × 120 cm),
Musée National d'Art Moderne, Paris

Concrete Art

In the catalogue of the exhibition *Zeit-probleme in der Schweizer Malerei und Plastik (Current Problems in Swiss Painting and Sculpture),* Max Bill formulated in 1936 the principles of Concrete Art, conceived as an elaboration of the ideas that Theo Van Doesburg expressed in 1930 in the publication, *Art Concret.* He revised his text in 1949 for the introduction to the catalogue of the exhibition *Zürcher Konkrete Kunst (Zurich Concrete Art)* which travelled in Germany. This text is included in the publication *Konkrete Kunst* edited by Margit Staber (in *Gesammelte Manifeste* by Margit Staber, 1966, Edition Galerie Press, Saint Gallen).

We call «Concrete Art» works of art which are created according to a technique and laws which are entirely appropriate to them, without taking external support from experiential nature or from its transformation, that is to say, without the intervention of a process of abstraction.

Concrete Art is autonomous in its specificity. It is the expression of the human spirit, destined for the human spirit, and should possess that clarity and that perfection which one expects from works of the human spirit.

It is by means of concrete painting and sculpture that those achievements which permit visual perception materialize.

The instruments of this realization are color, space, light, movement. In giving form to these elements, one creates new realities. Abstract ideas which previously existed only in the mind are made visible in a concrete form.

Concrete Art, when it is true to itself, is the pure expression of harmonious measure and law. It organizes systems and gives life to these arrangements, through the means of art. It is real and intellectual, anaturalist while being close to nature. It tends toward the universal and yet cultivates the unique, it rejects individuality, but for the benefit of the individual.

[1936–1949]

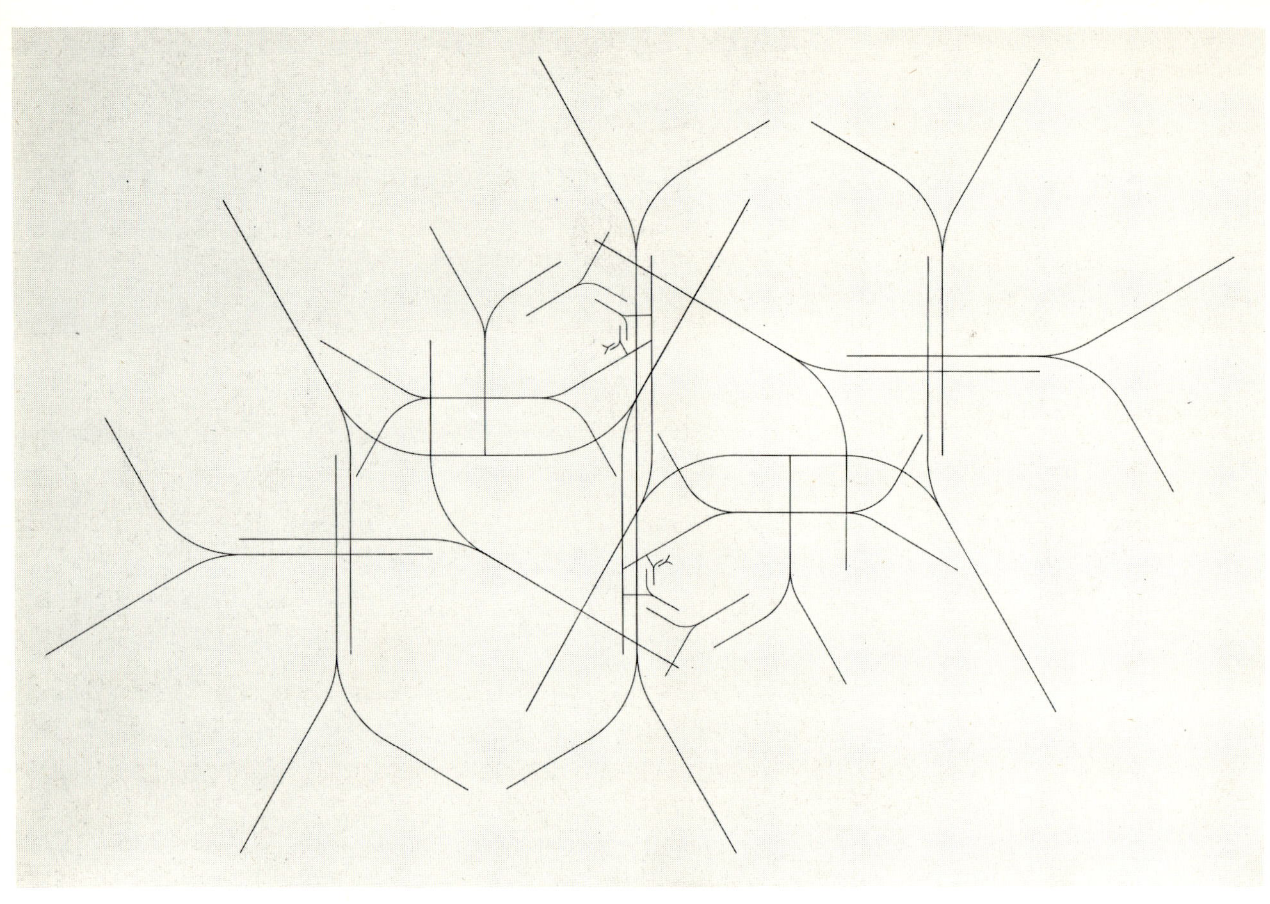

1937
Construction on the Formula $a^2 + b^2 = c^2$,
ink on cardboard, 20½″ × 13¾″,
(52 × 35 cm)

1937
Construction
grey granite, diameter, 47¼″,
(120 cm)

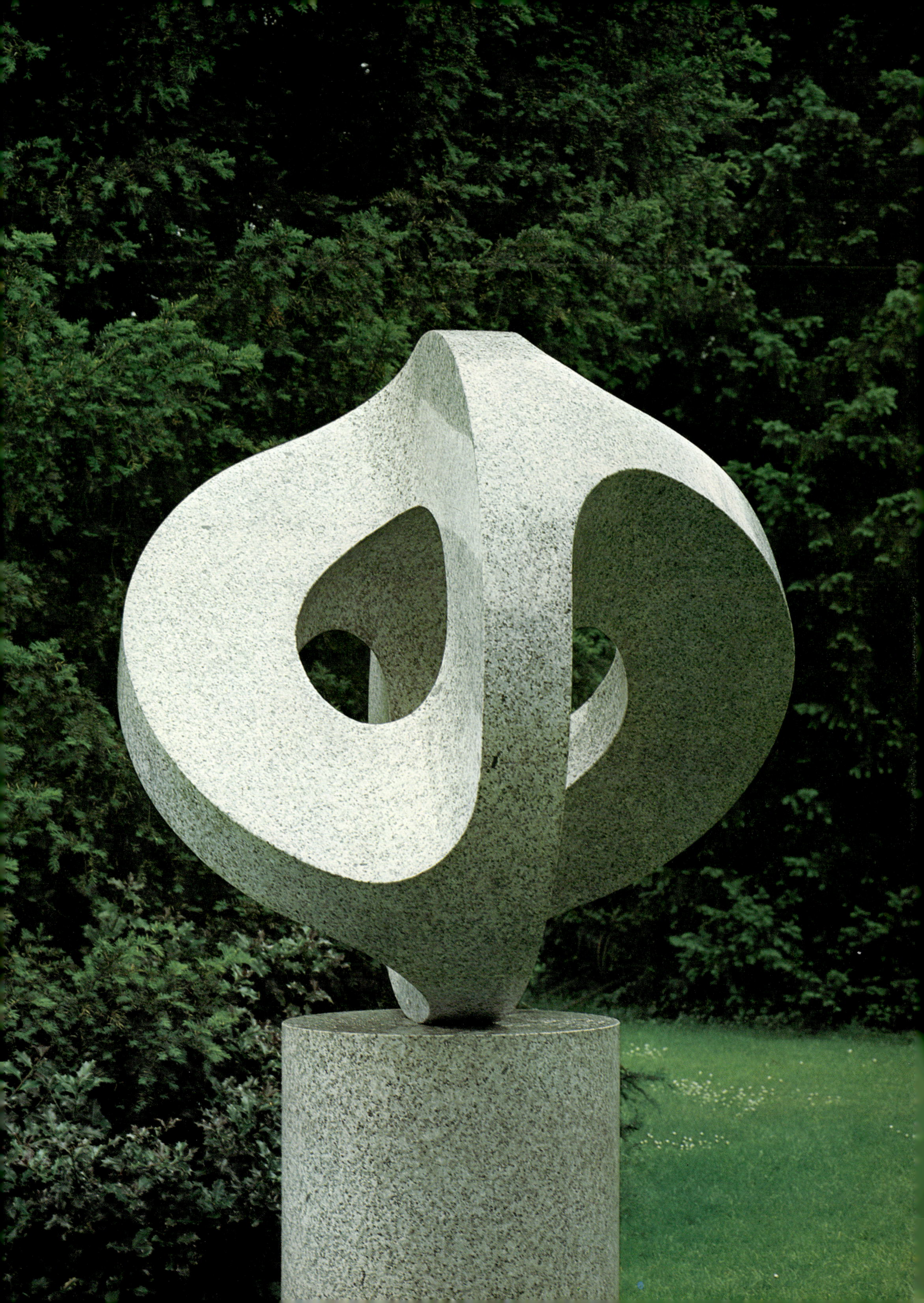

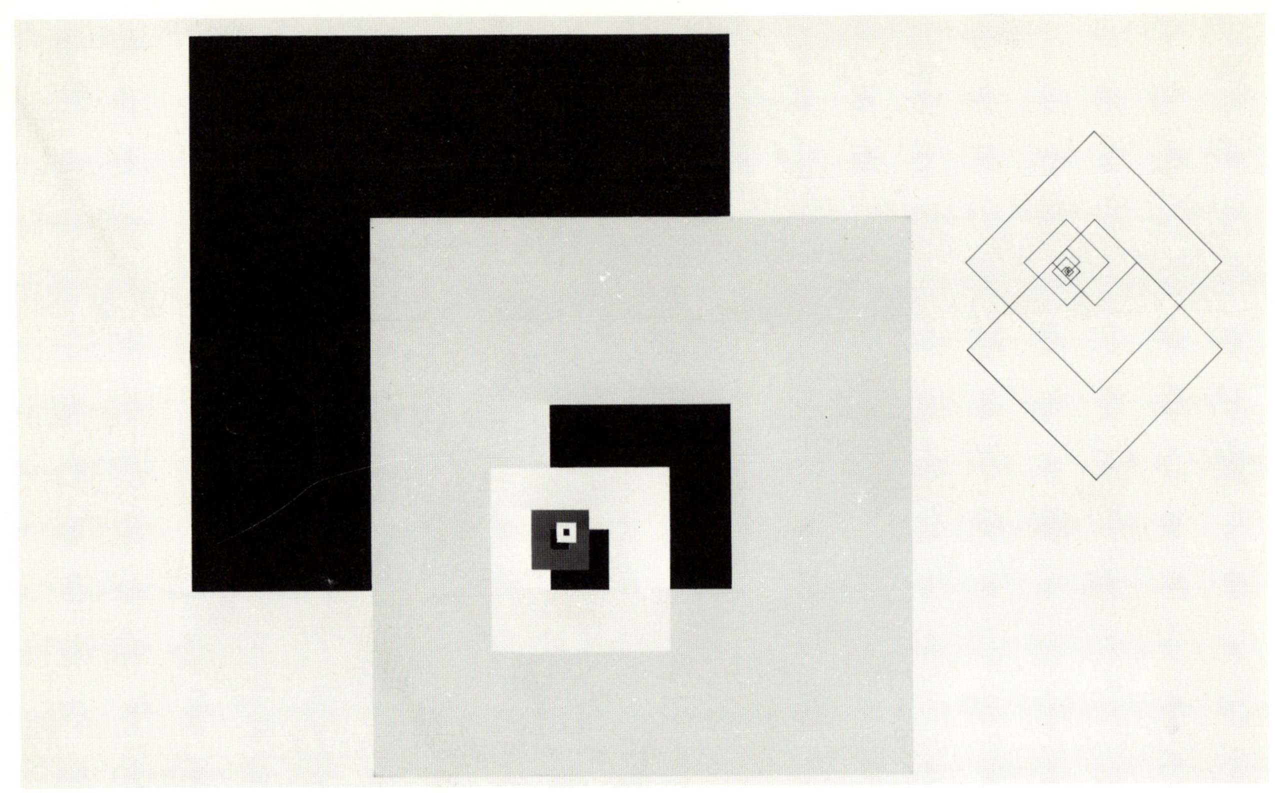

1937
Tectonic Construction
gouache on cardboard, 19¾″ × 11¾″,
(50 × 30 cm)

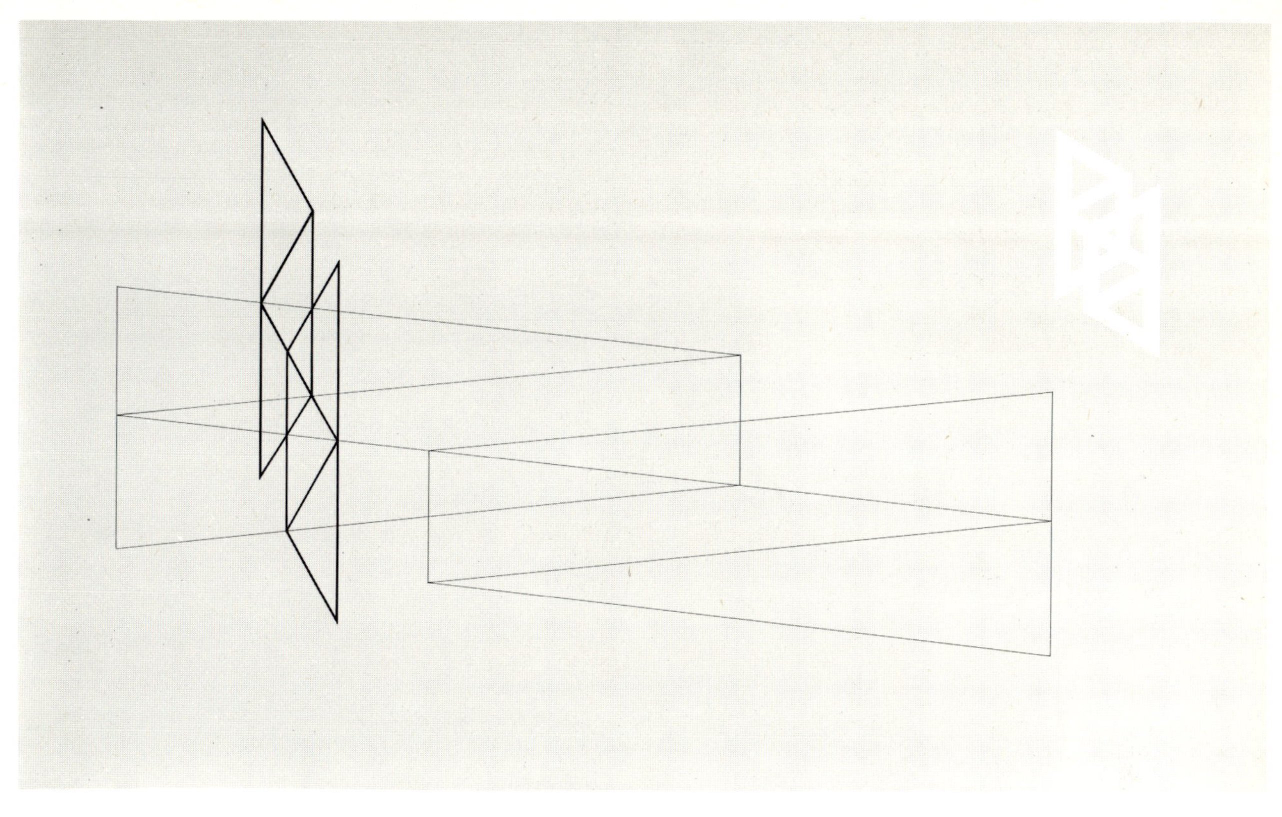

1938
Construction black-white
ink and gouache on cardboard, 19¾″ × 11¾″,
(50 × 30 cm)

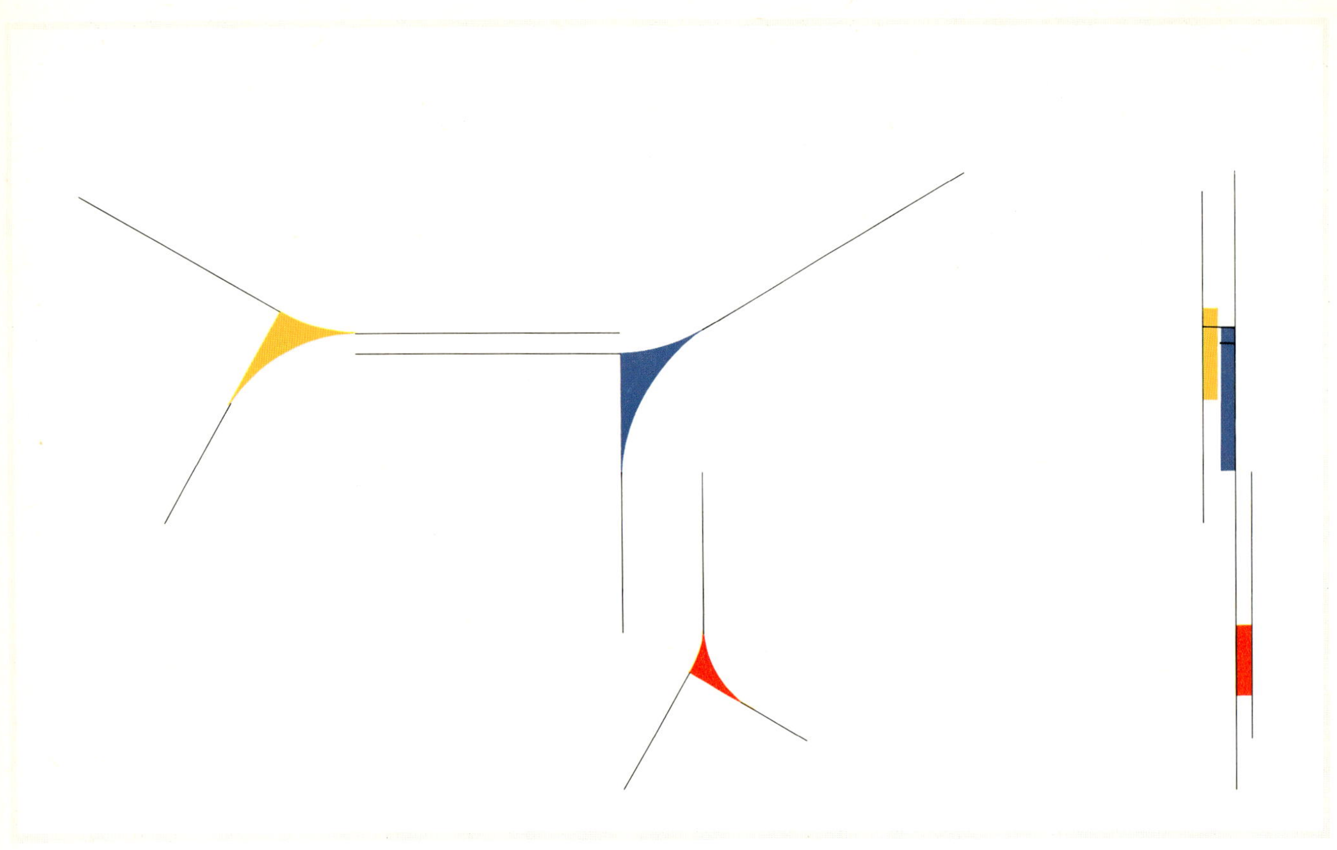

1938
Construction with Two Groups
gouache on cardboard, 19¾″ × 11¾″
(50 × 30 cm)

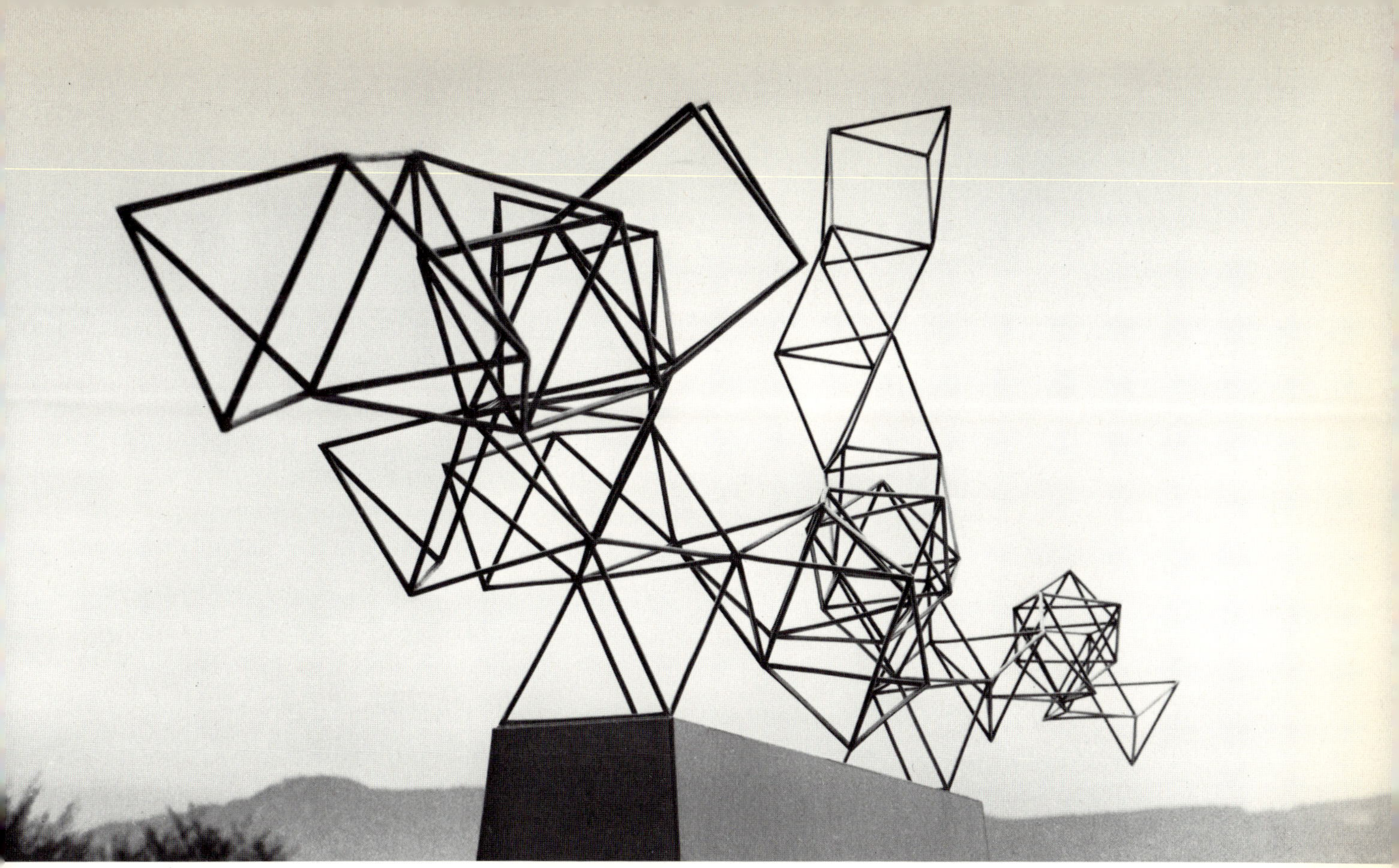

1938-39
Construction of 30 Equal Elements
stainless steel, 180¾″ × 29⅞″ × 60¼″,
(459 × 76 × 153 cm)

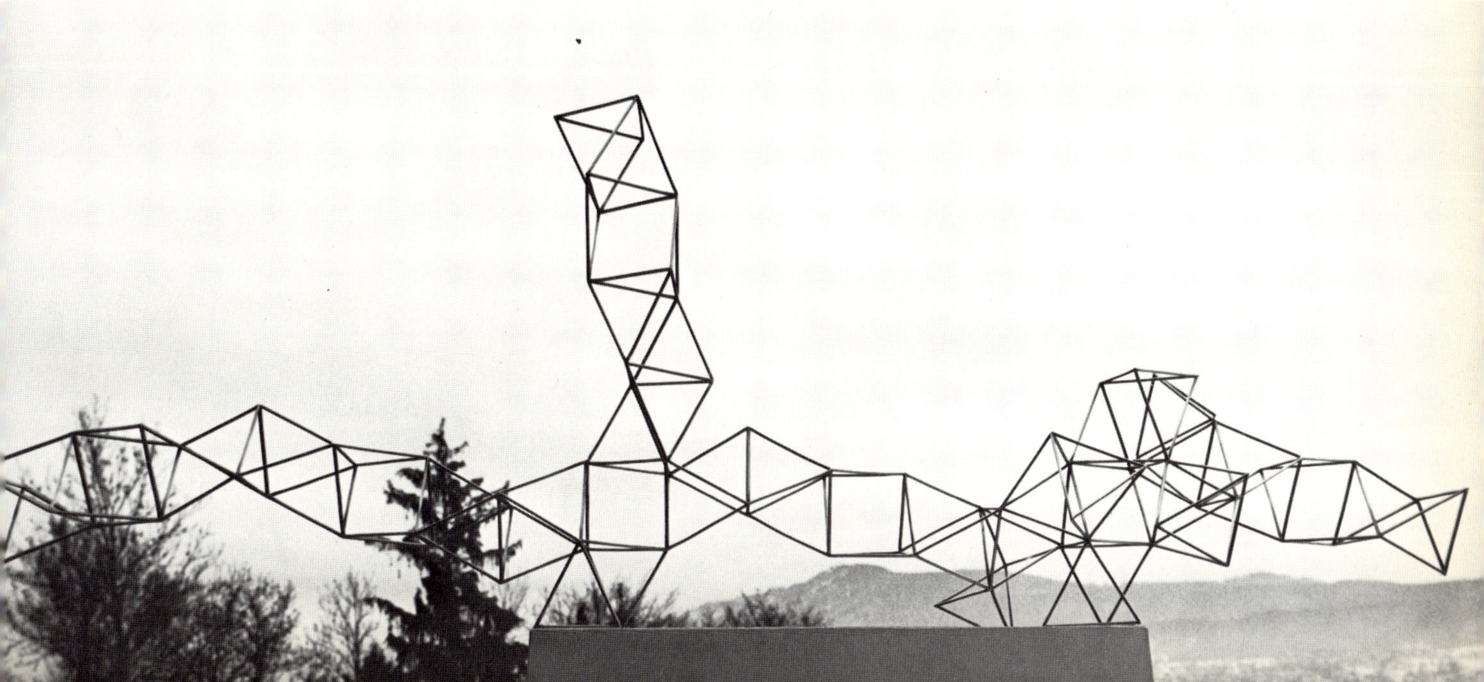

**fifteen variations
on a single theme**

1935–38
Fifteen Variations on a single Theme
16 lithographs, 12″ × 12⅝″,
(30.5 × 32 cm)
Paris: Editions des
Chroniques du Jour, 1938

my «fifteen variations on a single theme» were produced between 1934 and 1938 and i have decided to publish them in their present form only because i feel that a great many of those who are interested in art have no clear idea of how works of art are created and are without any clear understanding of the internal and external construction of such works.

although it is possible to like our creations without fully understanding them, one is scarcely able to extract from them all the pleasure they can give without at least a little insight into the methods by which they have been evolved. the purpose of this brief introduction is to give a glimpse of what a group of these methods consist of and to give anyone who takes the trouble to look at the plates the opportunity of following certain operations by means of the examples shown on them. this introduction, therefore, draws attention to a certain number of relationships which show themselves both in the theme and in the fifteen variations and which, indeed, bind all the variations together.

as there exist within these narrow and clearly defined limits such a large number of possible variations, the fact that a single theme – that is to say a single fundamental idea – leads to fifteen very different developments can be considered the proof that concrete art holds an infinite number of possibilities. such constructions are developed only on the basis of their given conditions and without any arbitrary attempt to modify them for reasons of proportion. with this method once the basic theme has been chosen – whether it be simple or complex – an infinite number of very different developments can be evolved according to individual inclination and temperament. this method of thus developing and transforming a fundamental idea – a theme – into a variety of expressive forms derived from the theme itself is used by various artists in the realm of concrete art. knowledge of these methods ought to enable the observer to discern the methods by which other works of art have been created. a number of these last are essentially more complex than «the fifteen variations on a single theme» although superficially they may appear simpler. even for the person who has some knowledge of the subject the underlying constructive thought is often difficult to distinguish because the bias of the personal element in the composition comes more to the surface not only in the general presentation of the work but also in its opposition to the system of variations in its individuality, and also because personal interpretations are more possible and permissible than in the case of a group of variations on a construction worked out without compromise.

everything which is not strictly a part of the «construction» theory outlined above is omitted in the following analysis. all the personal considerations which were responsible for the choice of the figures have also been omitted – that is with the exception of the methods by which the figures have been evolved from each other. it must also be pointed out that it would be possible to develop other variations on the same theme and that no attempt has been made to reverse or develop the theme itself or to combine the variations with each other or to try other colour combinations. these possibilities have been omitted here in order to keep the drawings as clear as possible and to eliminate all those developments which would lead to constructions of a too personal nature and which would only tend to make the explanations more confused.

it is possible that some, on reading these notes, may find nothing in the «fifteen variations on a single theme» other than a mere amusement of a pseudo-mathematical or geometrical nature. although the exact placing of the spaces and surfaces of these figures was obviously done by geometrical methods, the controlling idea which produced the figures was neither mathematical nor geometrical. what is brought out in the «fifteen variations on a single theme» is the pure play of form and colour freed from the compulsion of being something other than it really is, of which the sole aim is to give pleasure by the fact of its own independent existence.

max bill
zurich november 1938

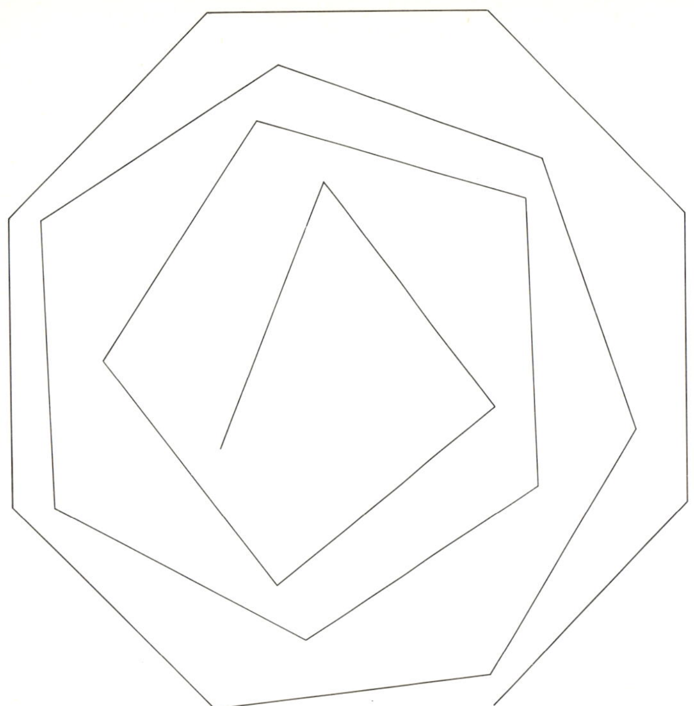

the theme

the theme consists of the continuous development of an equilateral triangle to a regular octagon. in other words the third side of the triangle which would close it is moved outwards so as to form one of the sides of the quadrilateral (square). in this way the area of the triangle remains open and is merely suggested. the transitions from one polygon to the next are all made in the same fashion. the resultant figure is a spiral composed of straight lines of equal length. the angles and the areas between these lines show a great variety of form and tension.

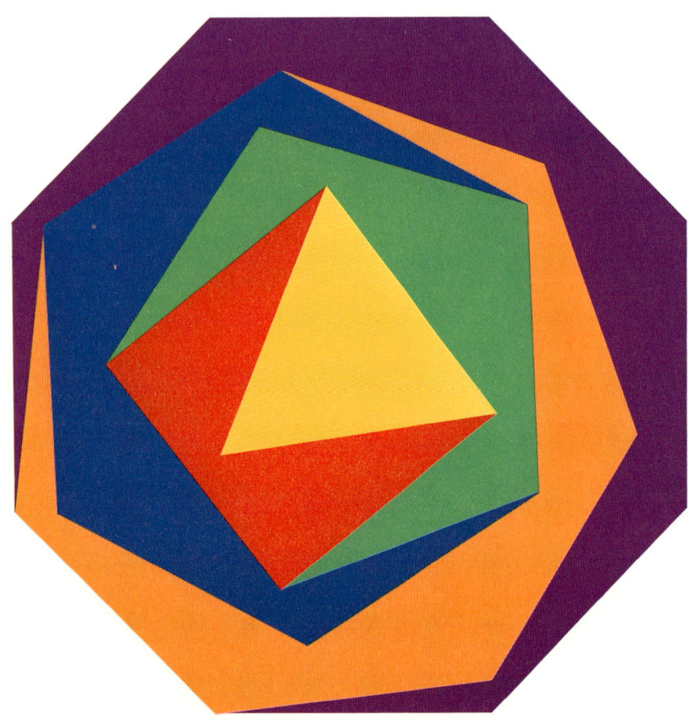

variation 1

all the regular polygons of the theme are here entirely closed. that is to say all the lines limiting the areas are put in. one side of each polygon coincides with a side of the polygon coming after it. the areas themselves are clearly visible. they are picked out with colours chosen to correspond with the fundamental forms of the polygons. these colours are constant and appear in the same order in all the following variations. although they are clearly recognisable the polygons do not in reality exist. their places are taken by surfaces of different form and colour which result from the fact that the area of each polygon has superimposed on it the polygon which immediately precedes it.

the theme is shown in heavy line. it is elaborated by circles drawn in a fine line. the
original lines of the theme form the diameters of these circles. the interplay of these
equal circles is interrupted by six semi-
circles which are drawn heavier. the semi-
circles break the development from
triangle to octagon and mark the lines that
would have closed the polygons in the
theme by taking these as their diameters.

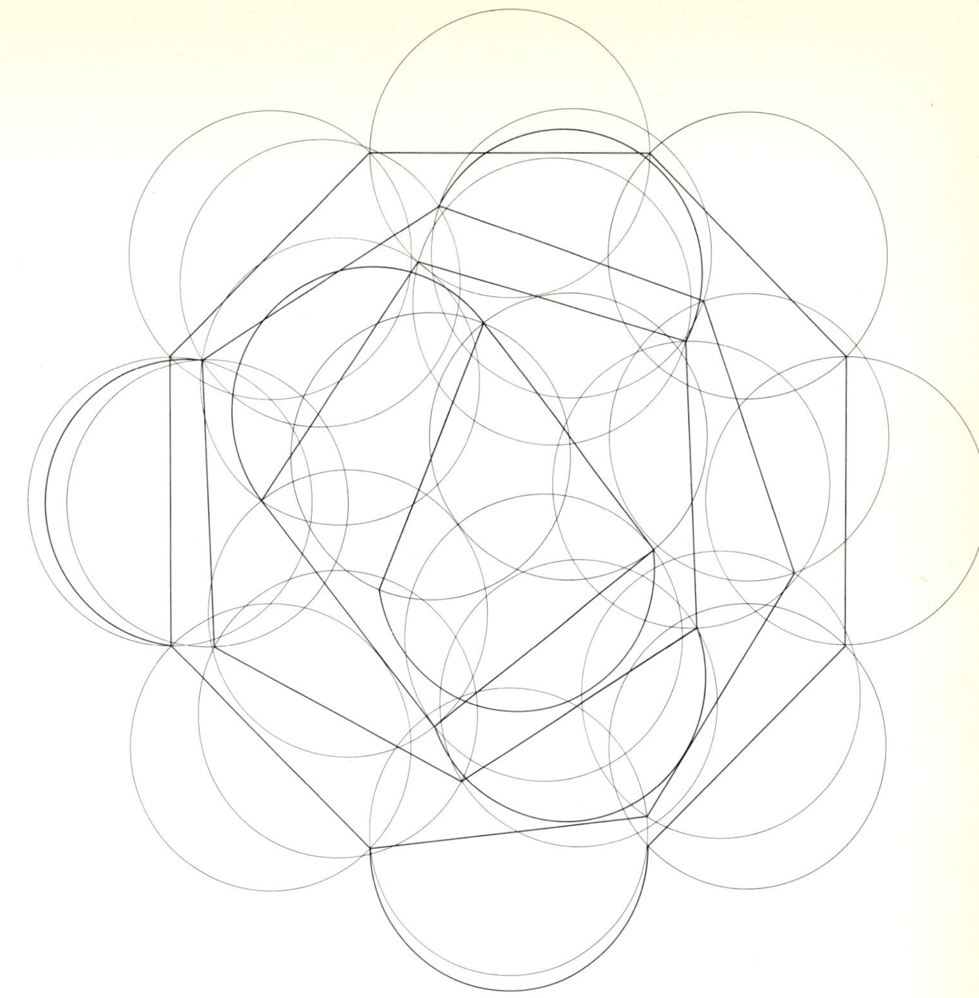

the points in colour mark the angles of the
theme. the points in two colours mark the
lines which are common to two polygons
and therefore indicate a change of direction. the colours are developed in the
same order as in variation 1.

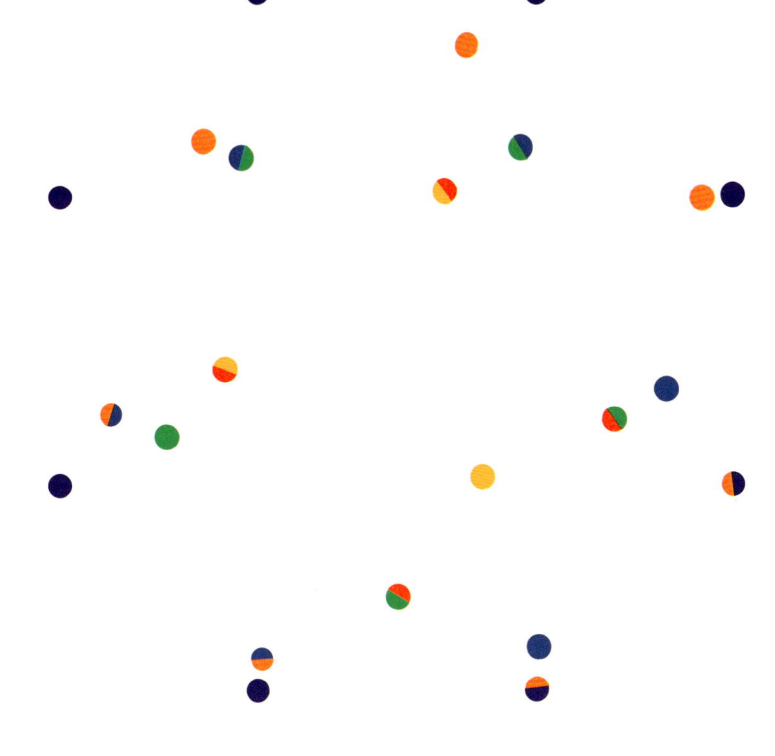

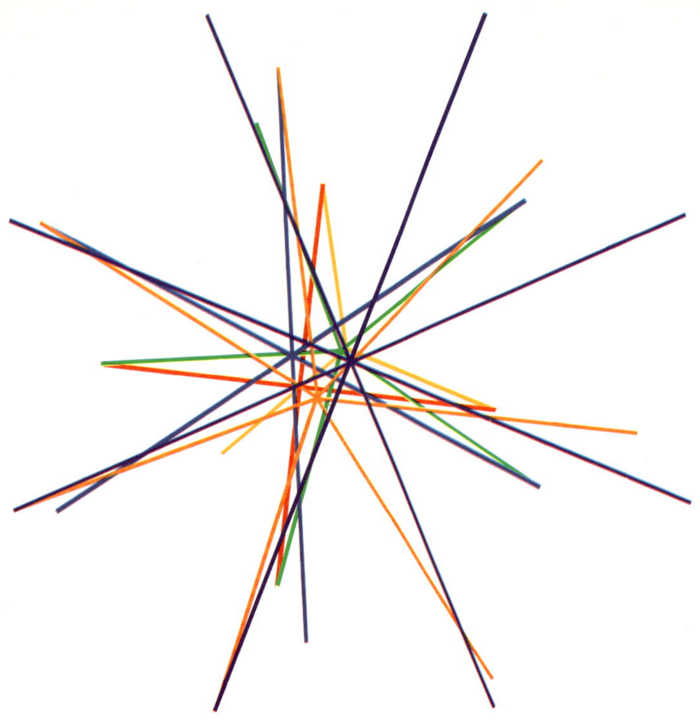

variation 4
the angles of each polygon are connected
to its centre. two of the tips of each of the
resulting coloured stars touch the tips of
the preceding star. for example the yellow
connects with the red and the red with the
green.

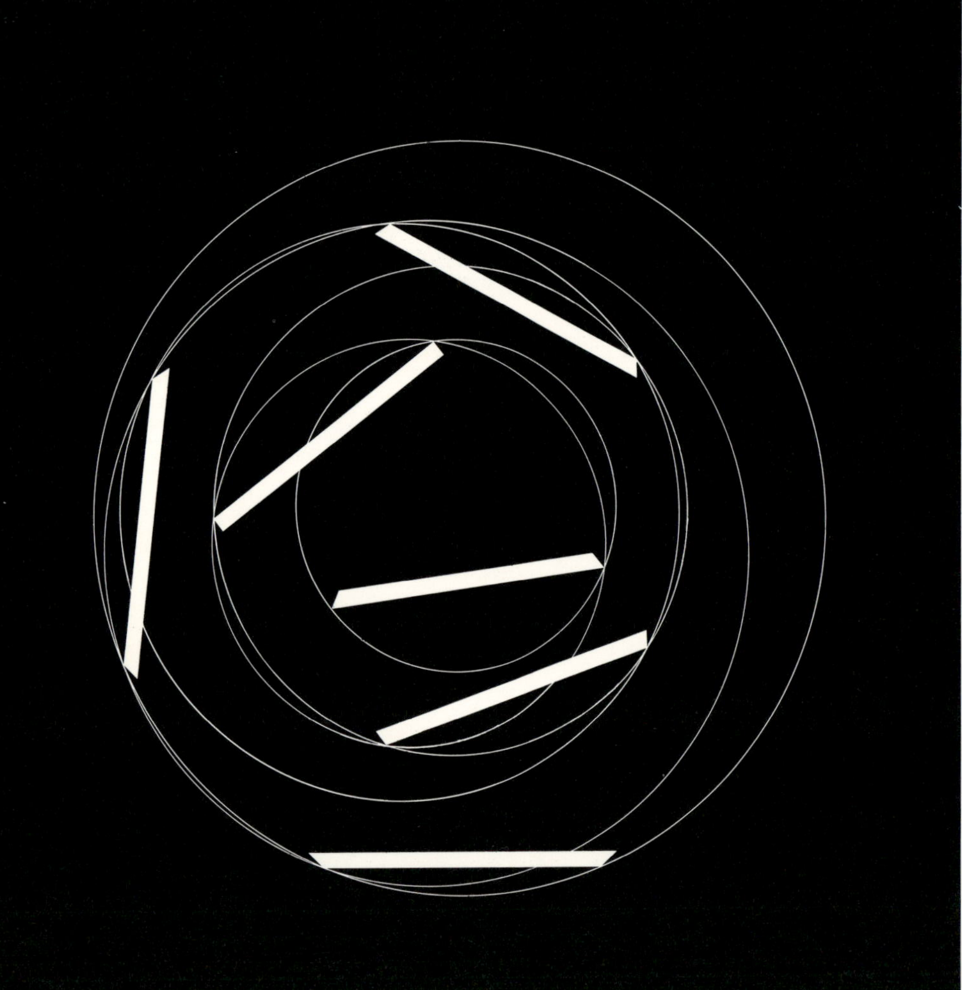

variation 5
the circumscribed circles of the polygons
are connected to those lines of the polygons omitted in the theme. the polygons
form surfaces whose smaller sides
develop in the same rhythm as the theme.

the theme is taken up again by the semi-
circles which have as their bases the
straight lines of the theme. these semi-
circles are described in alternating
opposition to each other. the result is a
continuous movement of changing
colours progressing from yellow to violet.

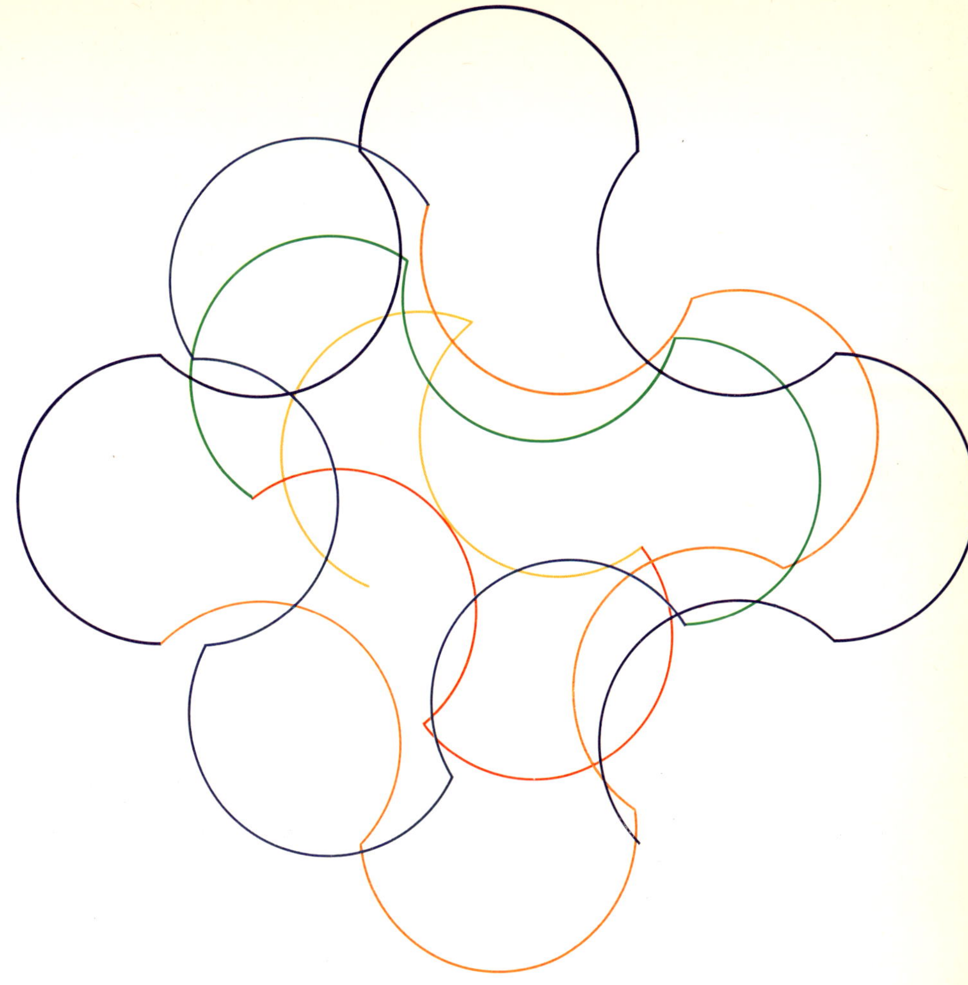

the inscribed circles of the polygons are
drawn so as to form two semi-spirals turning in opposition to one another. the grey
spiral, which is moving in the opposite
direction to the black, is strengthened and
reinforced by the angles of the polygons
themselves. this combination gives all the
inscribed circles of the complete series of
polygons from the triangle to the octagon.

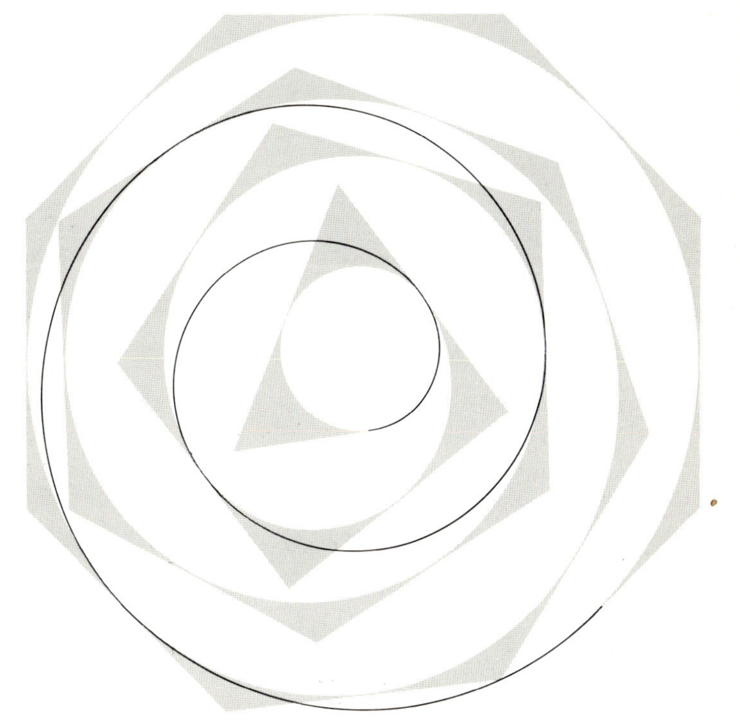

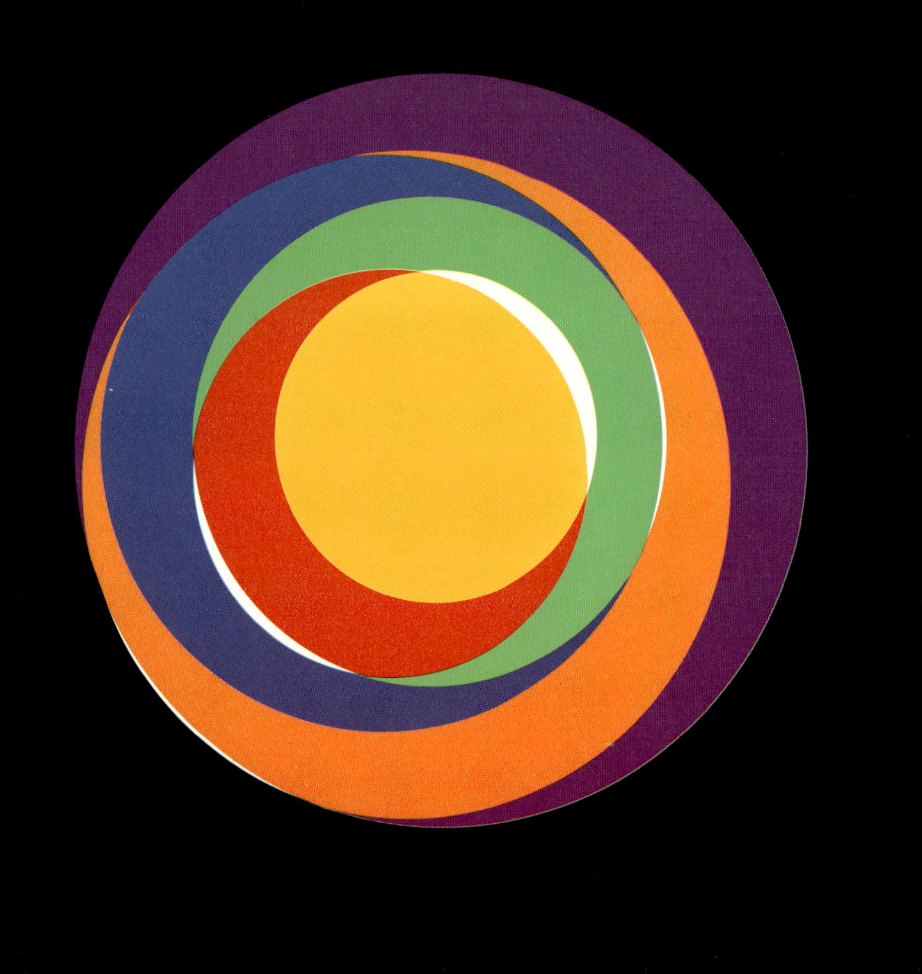

variation 8
the circumscribed circles of the polygons
form segments of circles. these are shown
according to their corresponding colours.
those parts of the circles which are the
same length and in which the colours
would be superimposed on each other are
left white. the order of the colours is as in
variation 1.

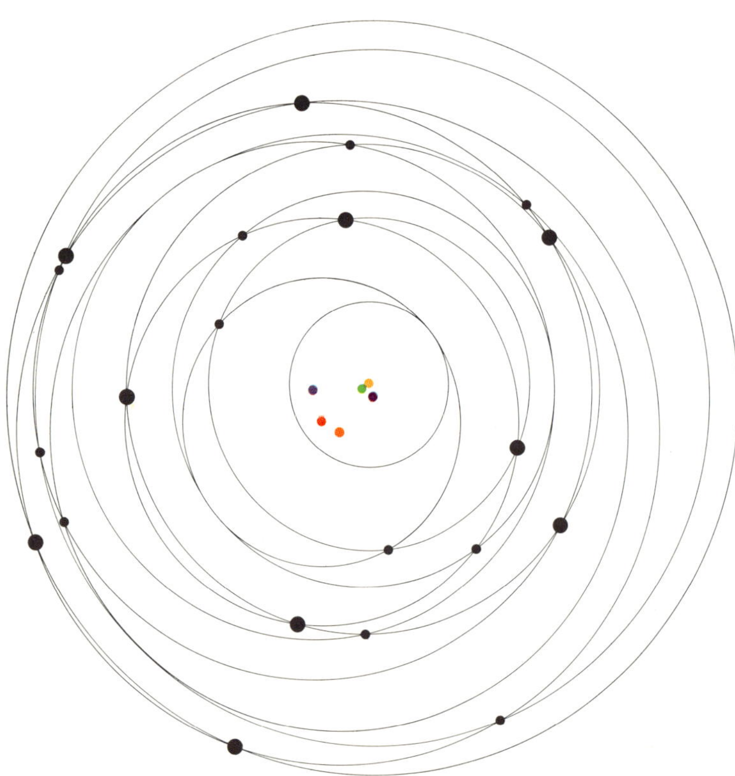

variation 9
a framework is formed by the inscribed
and circumscribed circles. those points
where the cutting of the circles coincides
with the angles of the theme are shown by
large spots. the other points where the
circles intersect are marked with smaller
spots. the colours are concentrated at the
centres of the circles.

variation 10
the inscribed and circumscribed circles
produce thick circular rings. the parts of
these rings where no overlapping takes
place are shown grey.

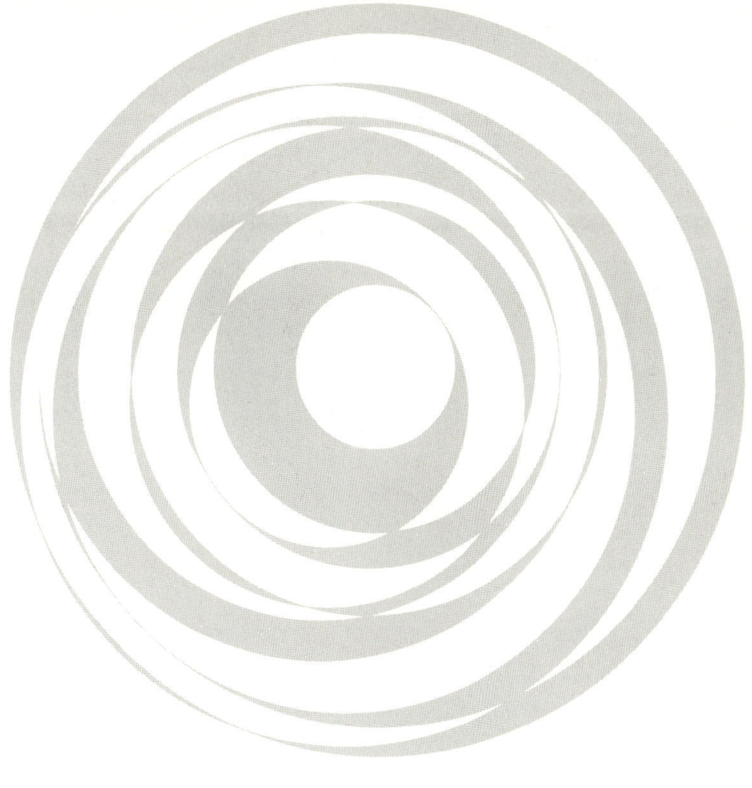

variation 11
the angles of the polygons are joined to
their centres (as in variation 4). the spear-
head shapes thus formed lead from the
middle of the figure to the angles of the
polygons and all are shown in a contrast
of black and white. the corresponding
colours of the polygons appear on areas in
which the centres of the respective polygons occur.

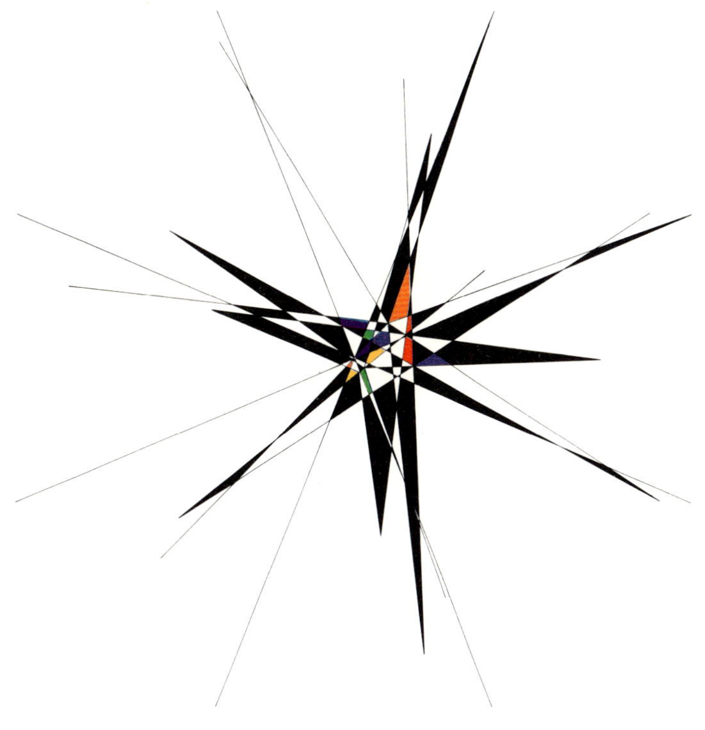

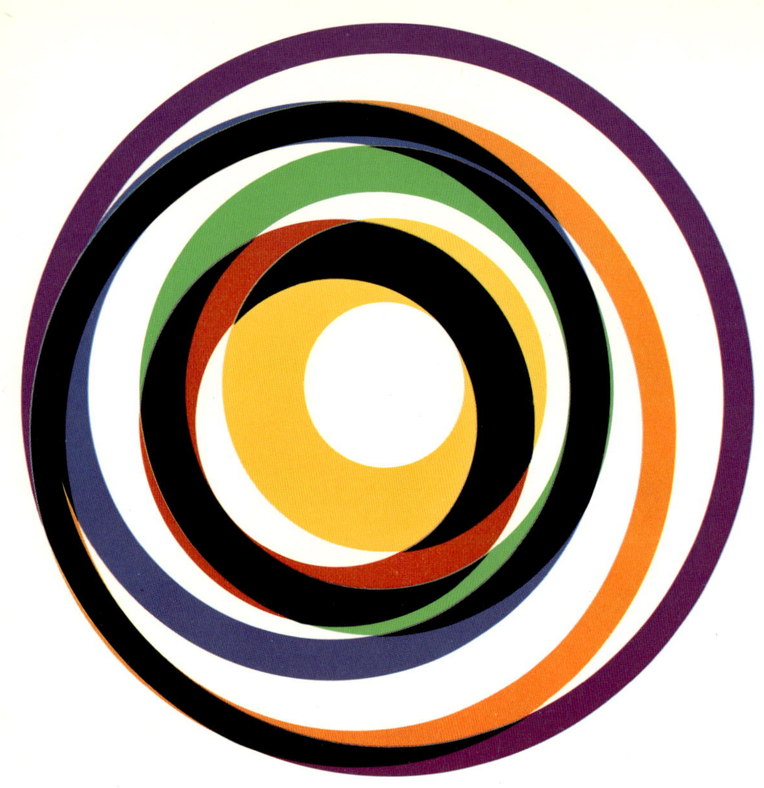

variation 12
the inscribed and circumscribed circles
form thick circular rings. these are shown
in their appropriate colours, while those
parts where overlapping occurs are black.

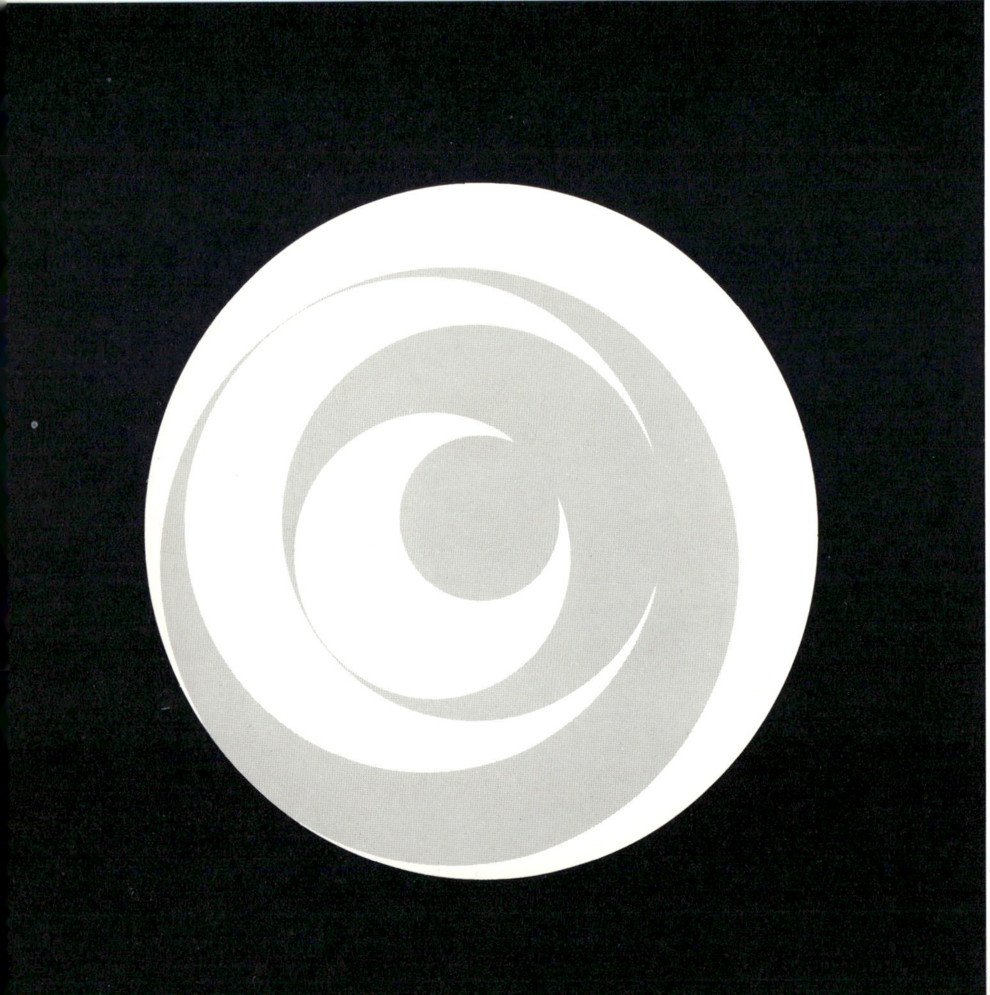

variation 13
the inscribed circles of the polygons touch
each other at one point. the resultant surfaces are shown alternately grey and
white.

variation 14
here only the edges of the surfaces formed
in variation 1 are coloured. the result is a
great variety of colour arising from the
relative positions of the colours. the star
shapes of variation 4 are added in black.

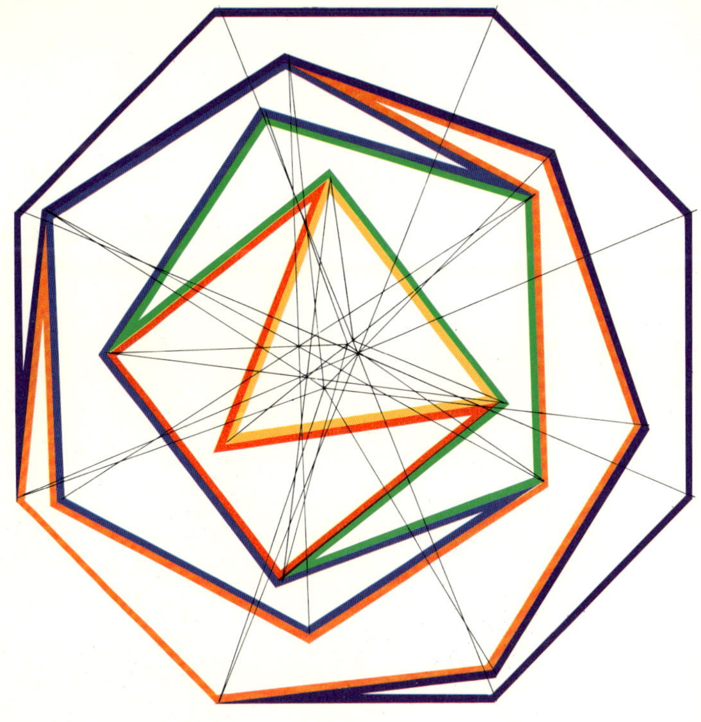

variation 15
the inscribed circles produce a semi-spiral
movement formed by the connecting up
of the thick circular rings. the thickness of
this movement is determined by the distance between the inscribed and the circumscribed circles of the octagon. the
various segments of this semi-spiral form
are connected to their centres by lines.

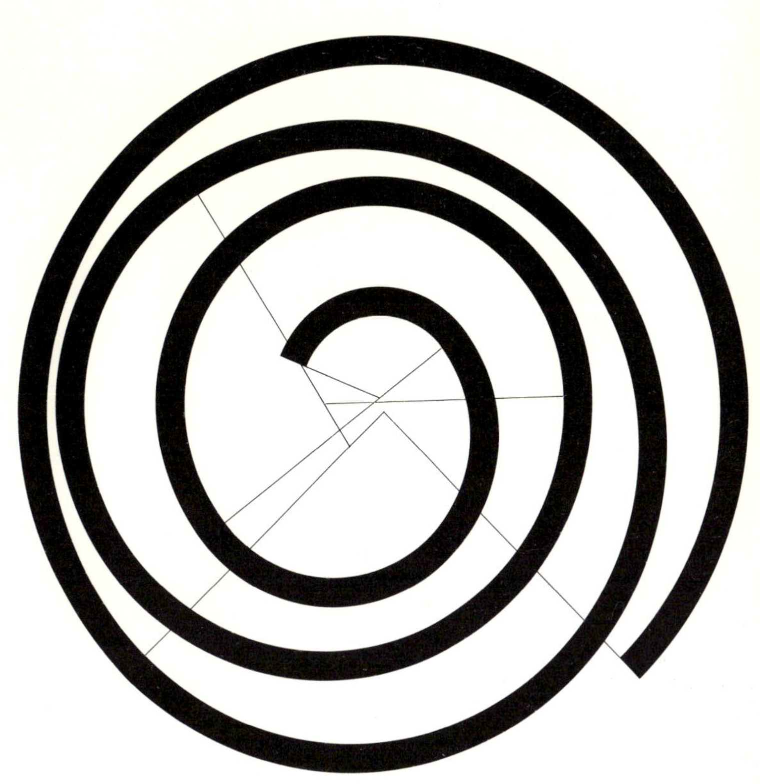

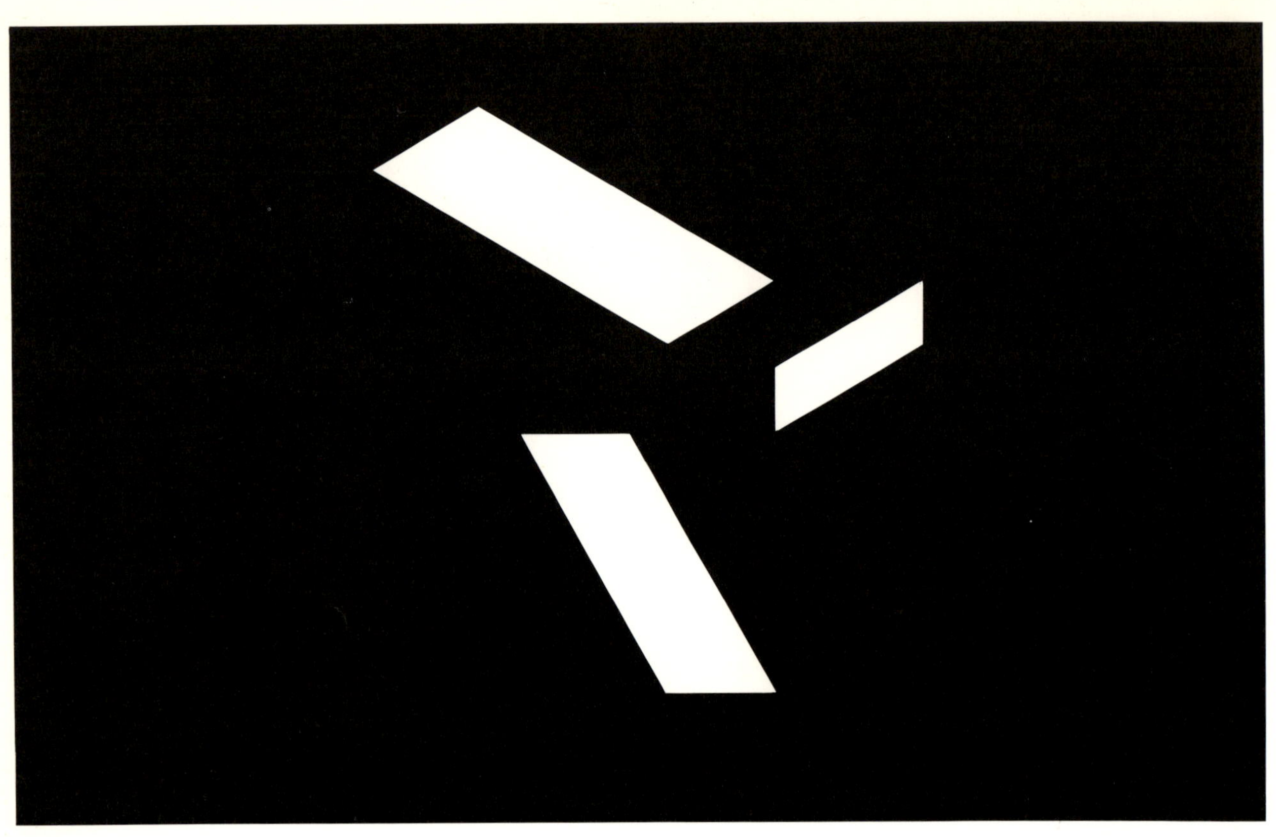

1939
Construction in black
cut in cardboard, 19¾″ × 11¾″,
(50 × 30 cm)

1940–41
Construction From a Ring
gilt bronze, 29½″ × 27½″ × 32¼″,
(75 × 70 × 82 cm)

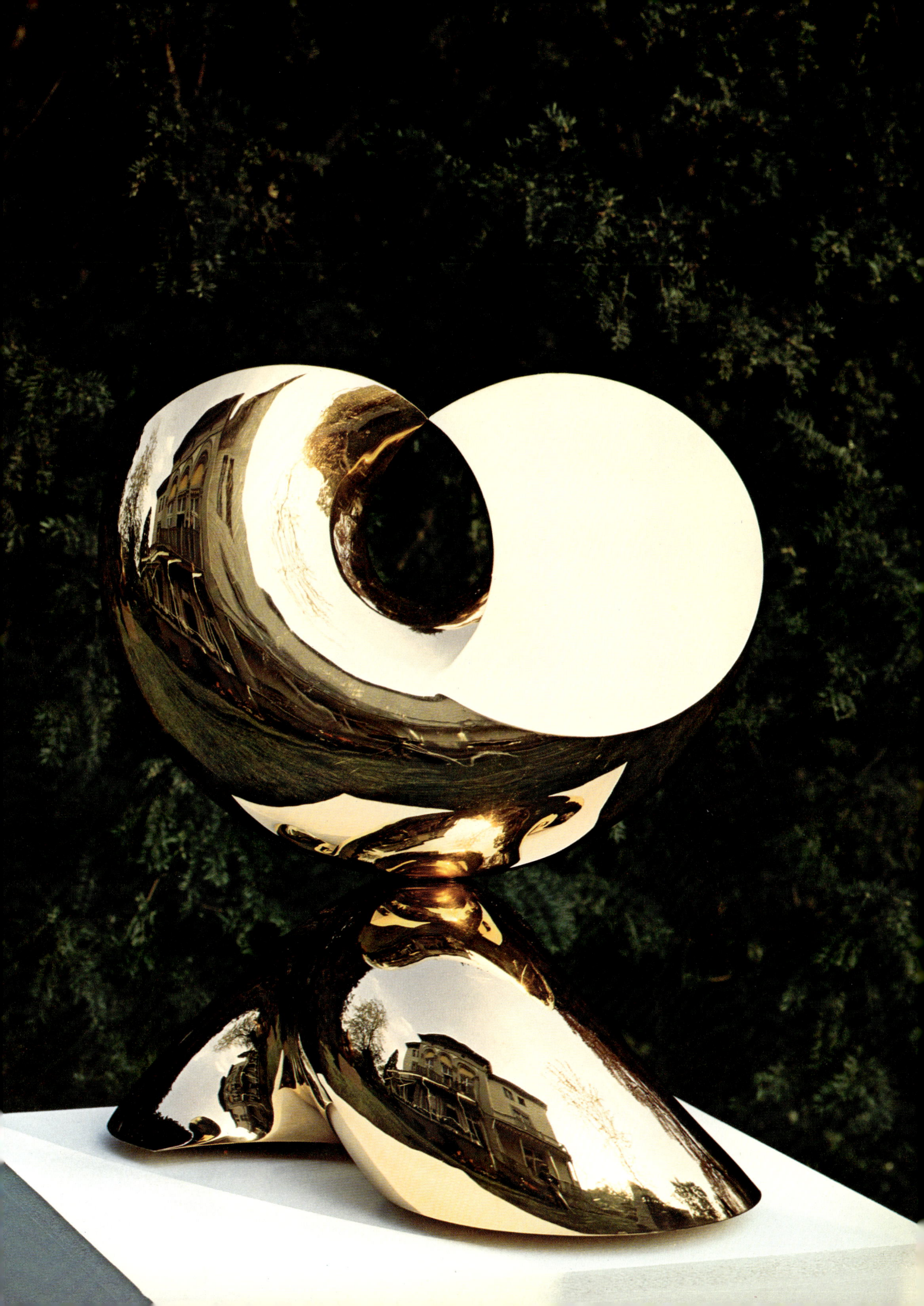

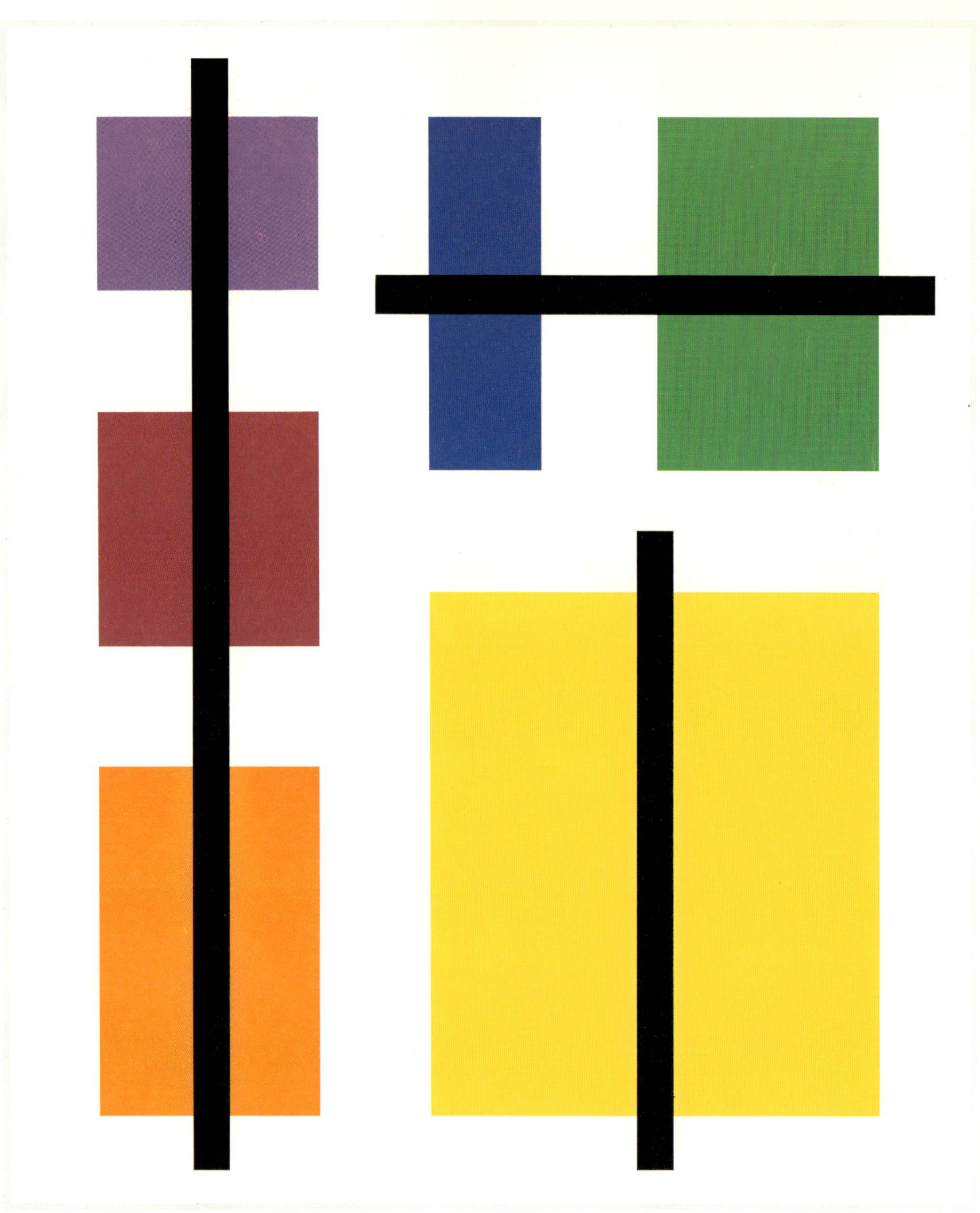

1940–43
Construction with Ten Rectangles
oil on canvas, 29½″ × 35½″,
(75 × 90 cm), Kunstmuseum, Berne

1942
Black Vertical
oil on canvas, 11¾″ × 35½″,
(30 × 90 cm)

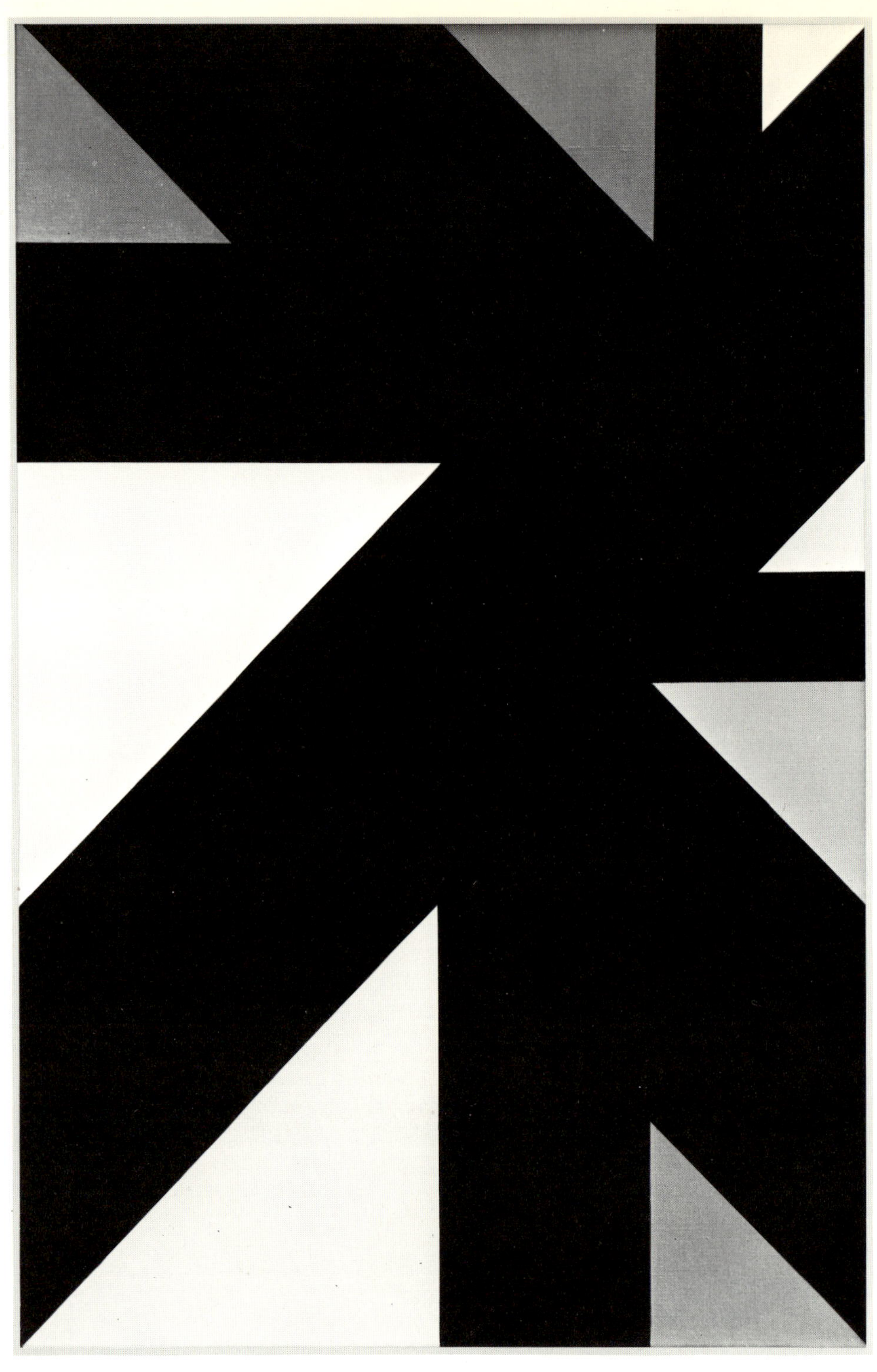

1942
Rythm in Eight Parts
oil on canvas, 31½″ × 47¼″,
(80 × 120 cm)

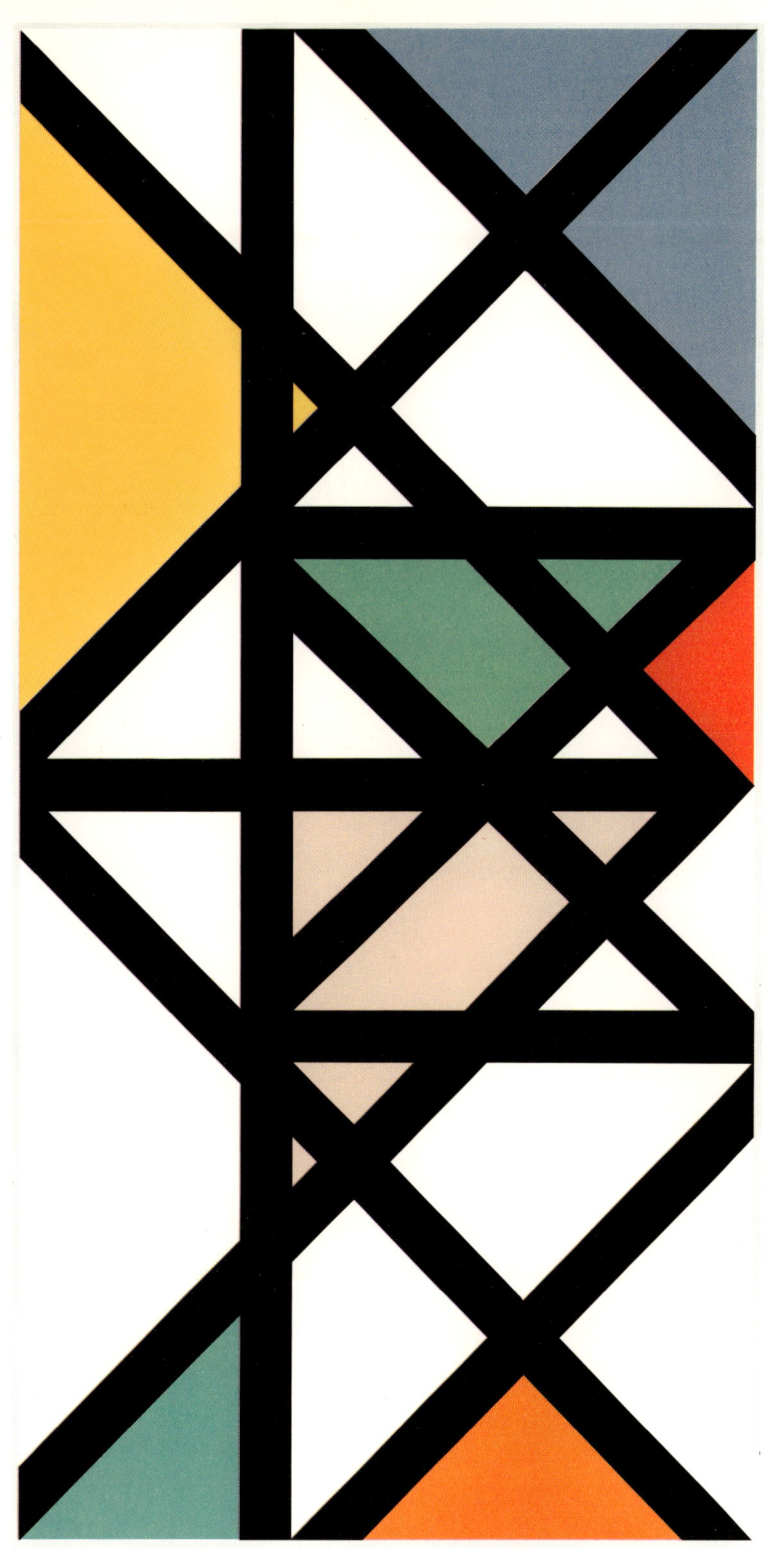

1942
Rythm: horizontal-vertical-diagonal
oil on canvas, 31½″ × 63″,
(80 × 160 cm)

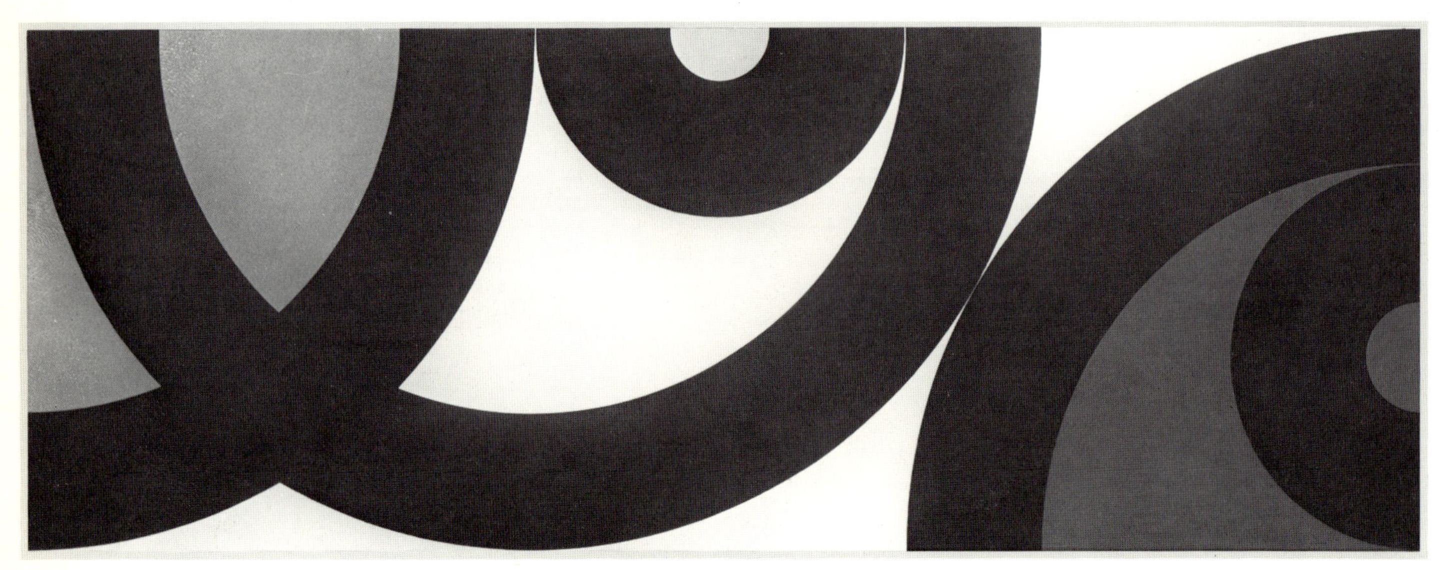

1942
Construction From Two Rings
oil on canvas, $41\frac{3}{8}''$ × $15\frac{3}{8}''$,
(105 × 39 cm)

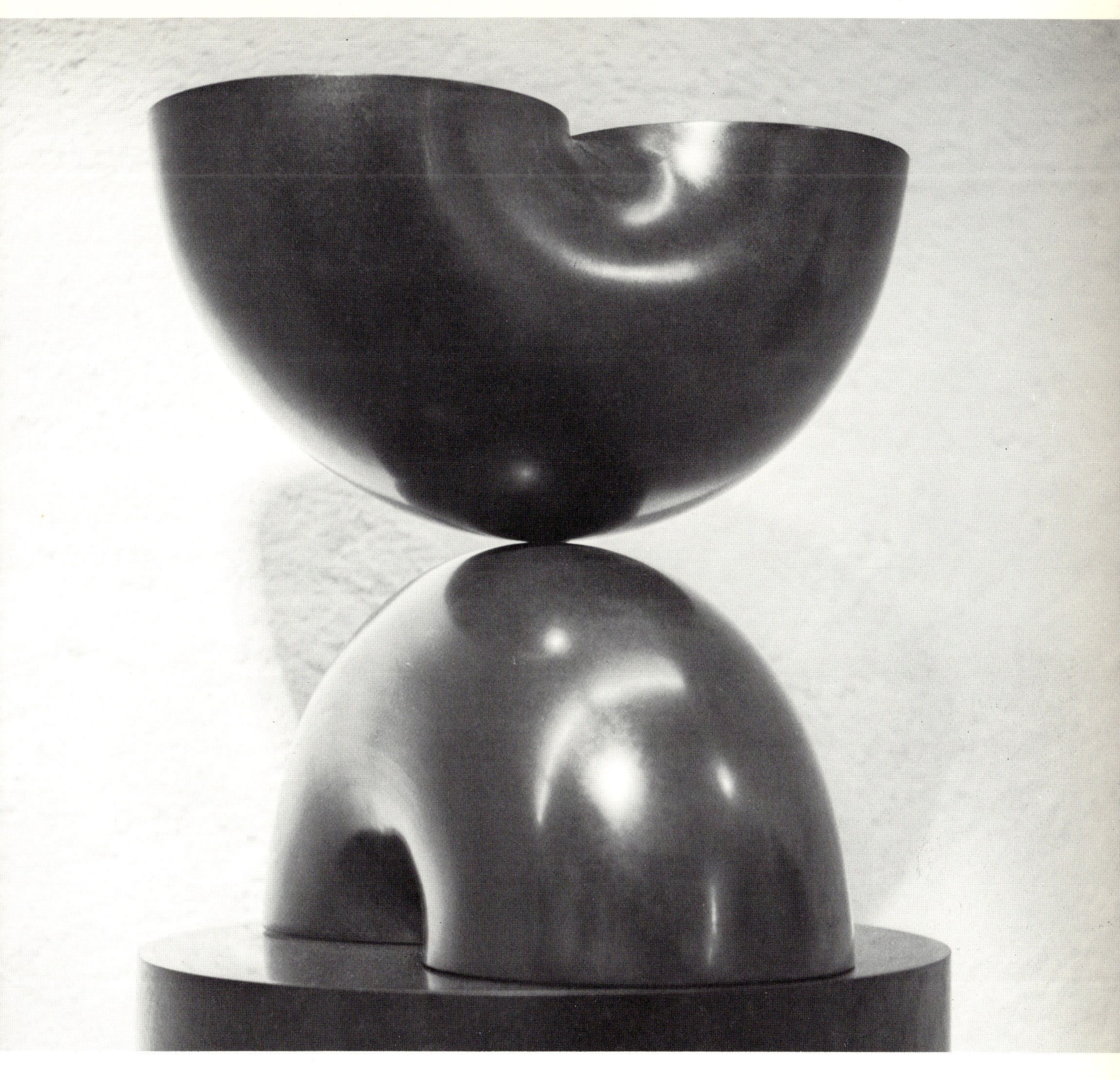

1942–44
Construction From a Ring
black diorite, 15¾″ × 15¾″ × 19¾″,
(40 × 40 × 50 cm),
The Art Institute of Chicago, William
E. Hartmann Fund

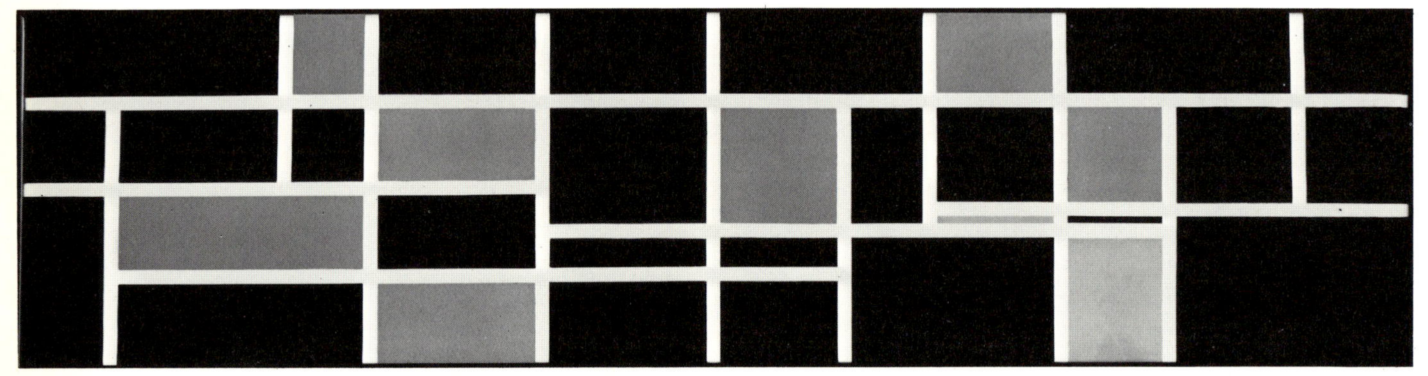

1942
Rythm in Four Parts
oil on canvas, 63″ × 15¾″,
(160 × 40 cm)

1942–70
Progression with Five Squares
oil on canvas, 15¾″ × 78¾″,
(40 × 200 cm),
Marlborough-Godard Ltd., Toronto

73

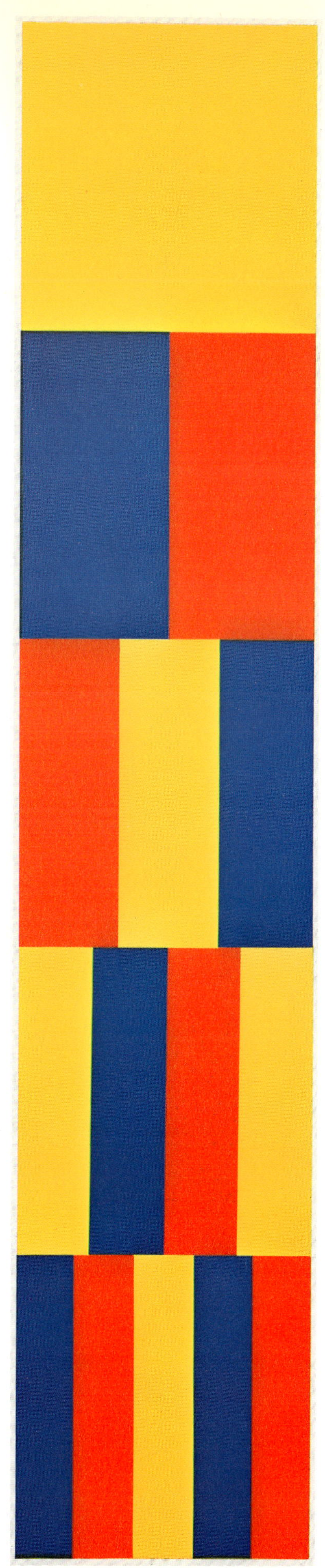

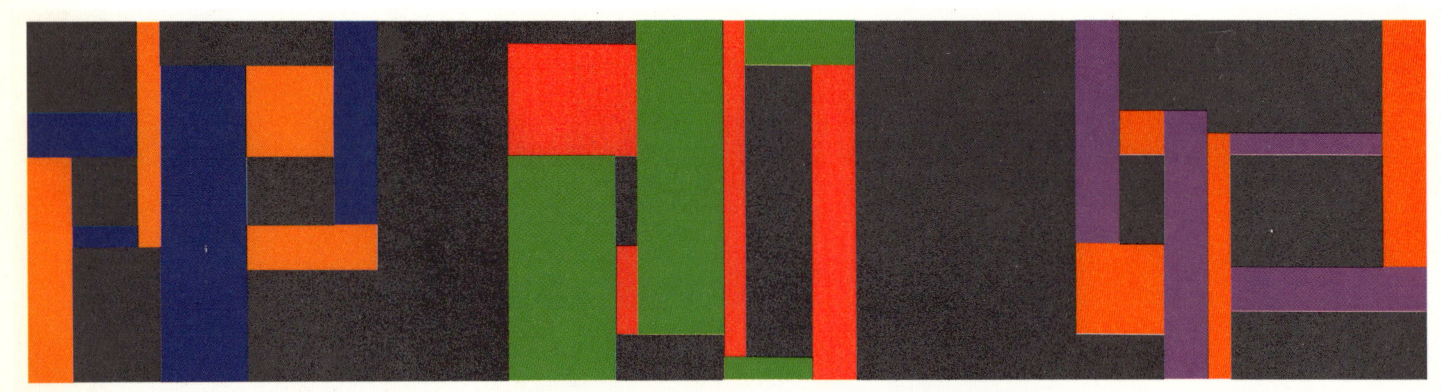

1943
Rythm in Four Squares
oil on canvas, 47¼″ × 11¾″,
(120 × 30 cm),
Kunsthaus, Zurich

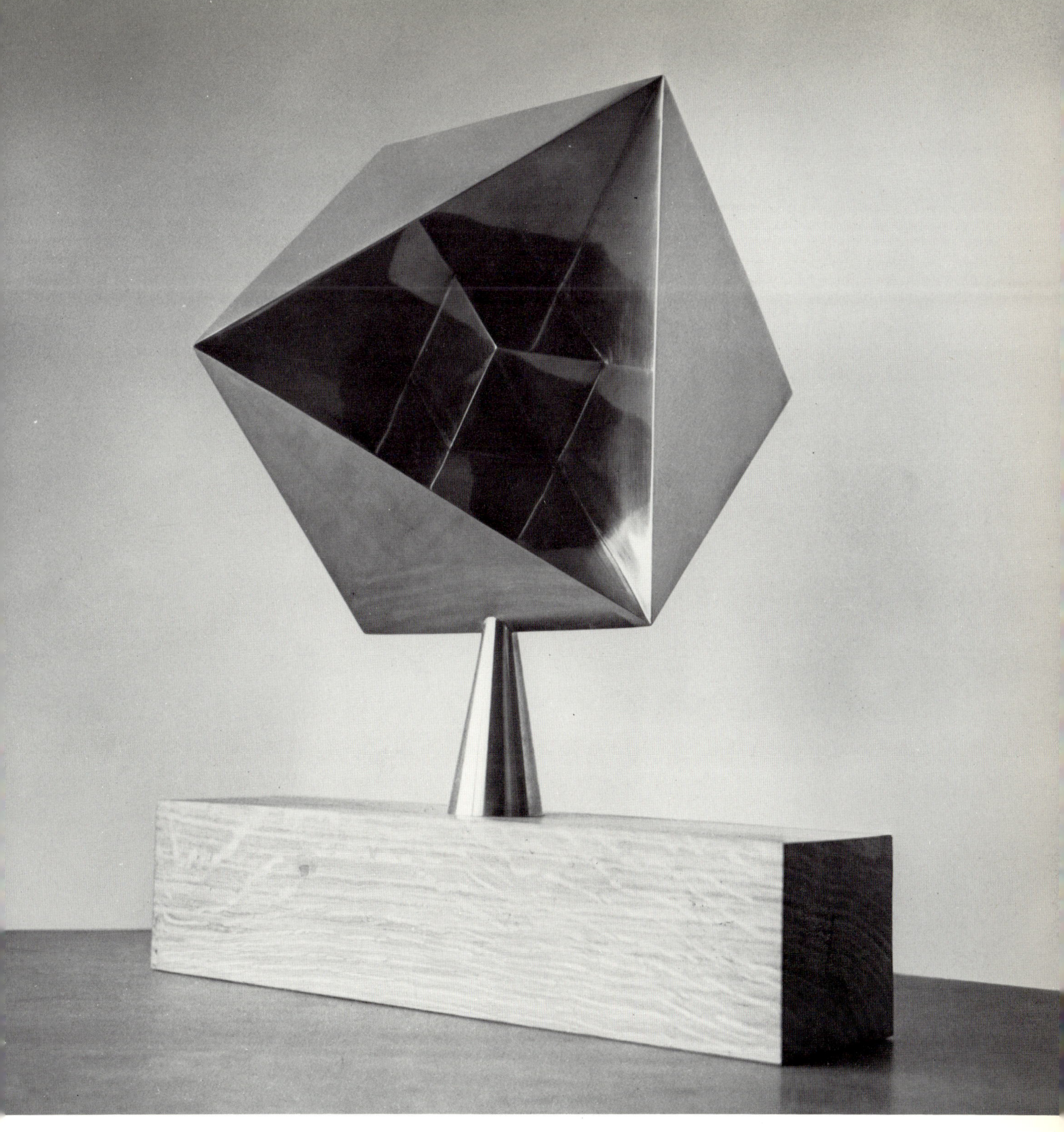

1944–45
Construction With and Within a Cube
brass, 15½″ × 11½″ × 8″,
(39.5 × 29 × 20.5 cm),
Kunstmuseum, Basel, Hans Arp Donation

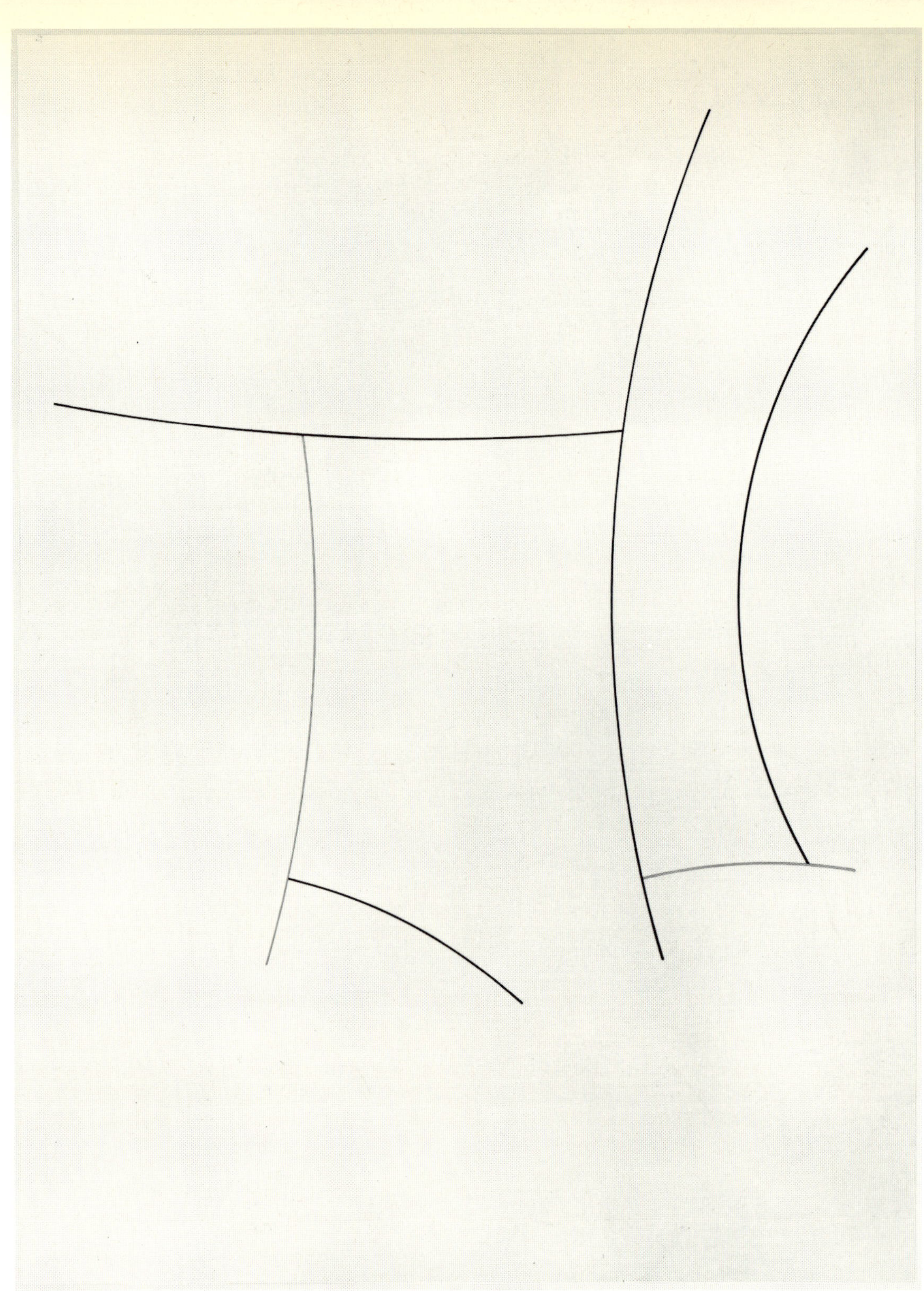

1944–46
Far Away
oil on canvas, 27³/₄″ × 39³/₄″,
(71 × 101 cm)

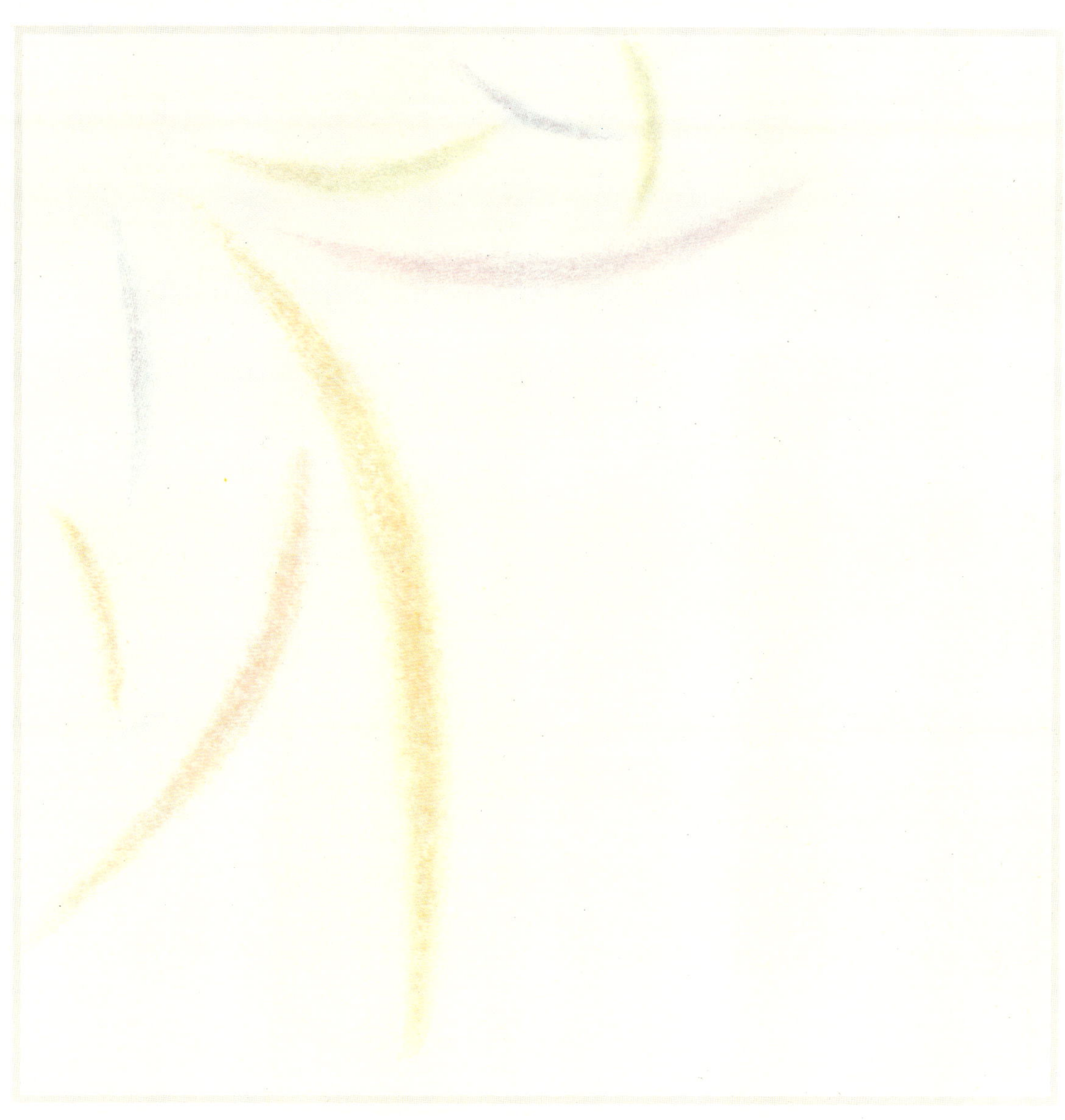

1944–49
Nine Accentuations
oil on canvas, 32¹/₄″ × 32¹/₄″,
(82 × 82 cm)

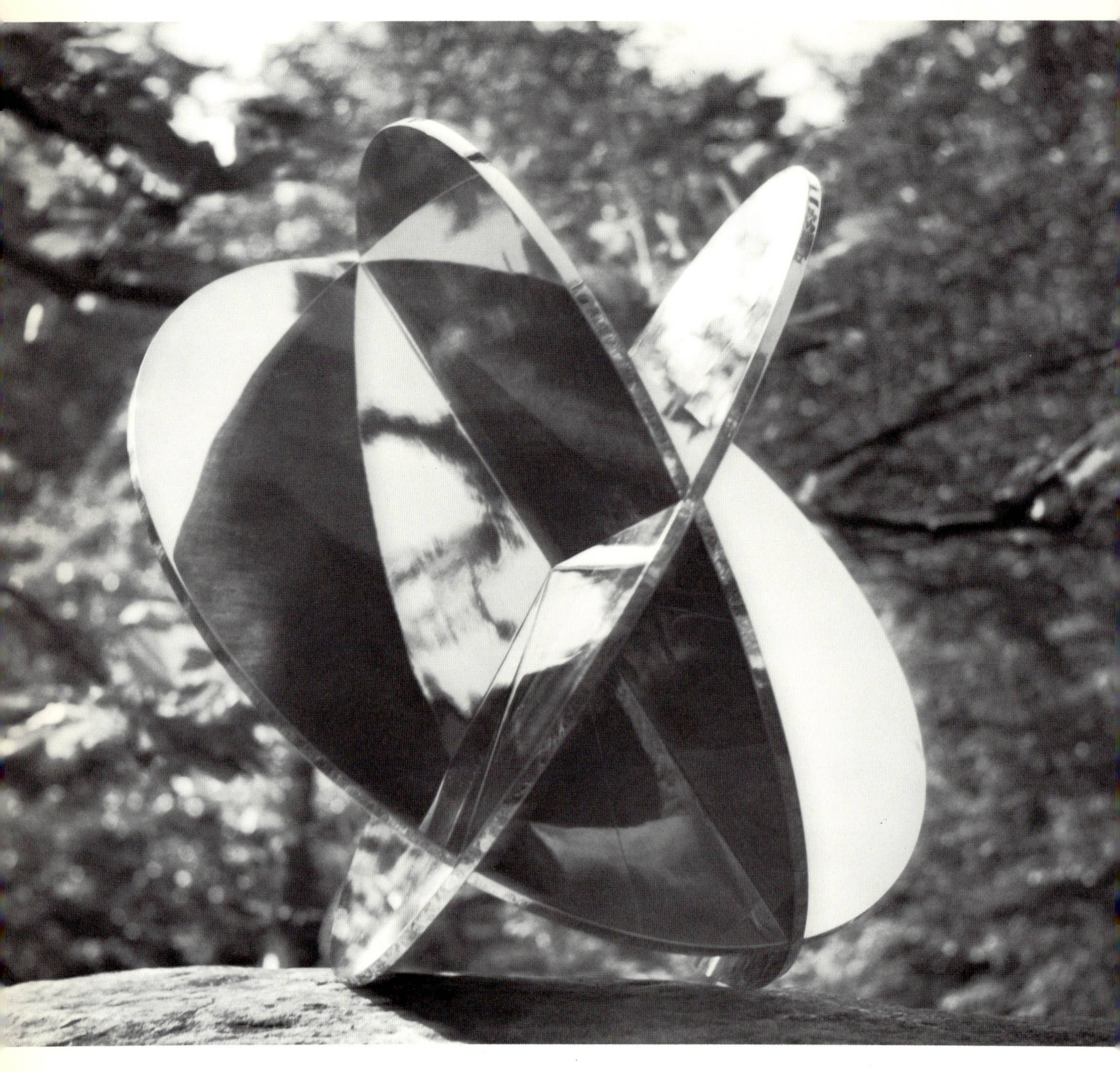

1945–46
Construction From Three Disks
chromed brass, diameter, 19¾″,
(50 cm)

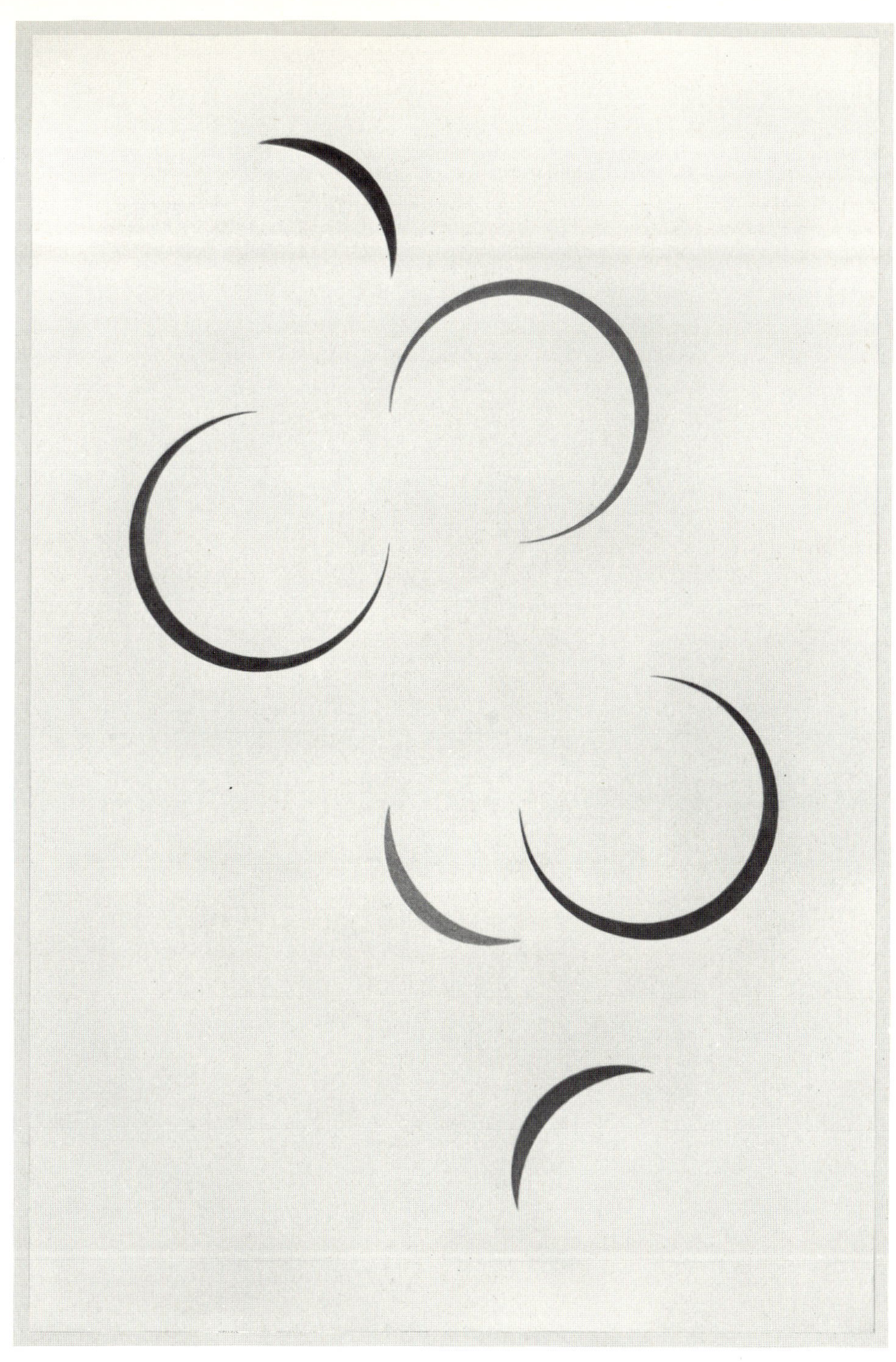

1946
Accents from the Yellow
oil on canvas, 16″ × 23³/₄″,
(40.5 × 60.5 cm),
Kunstmuseum, Basel, Emanuel Hoffmann
Foundation

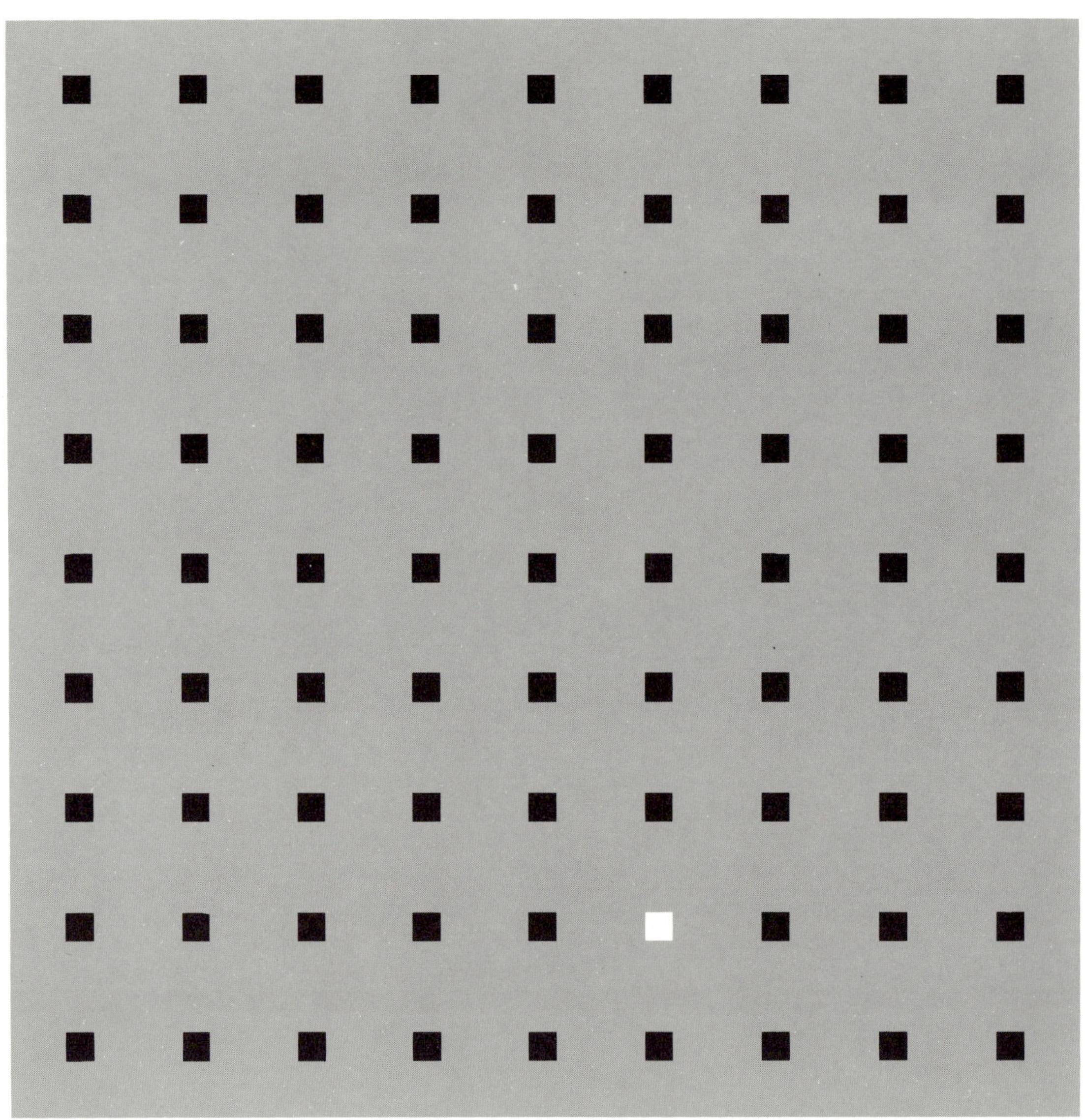

1946
The White Square
oil on canvas, 27½″ × 27½″,
(70 × 70 cm)

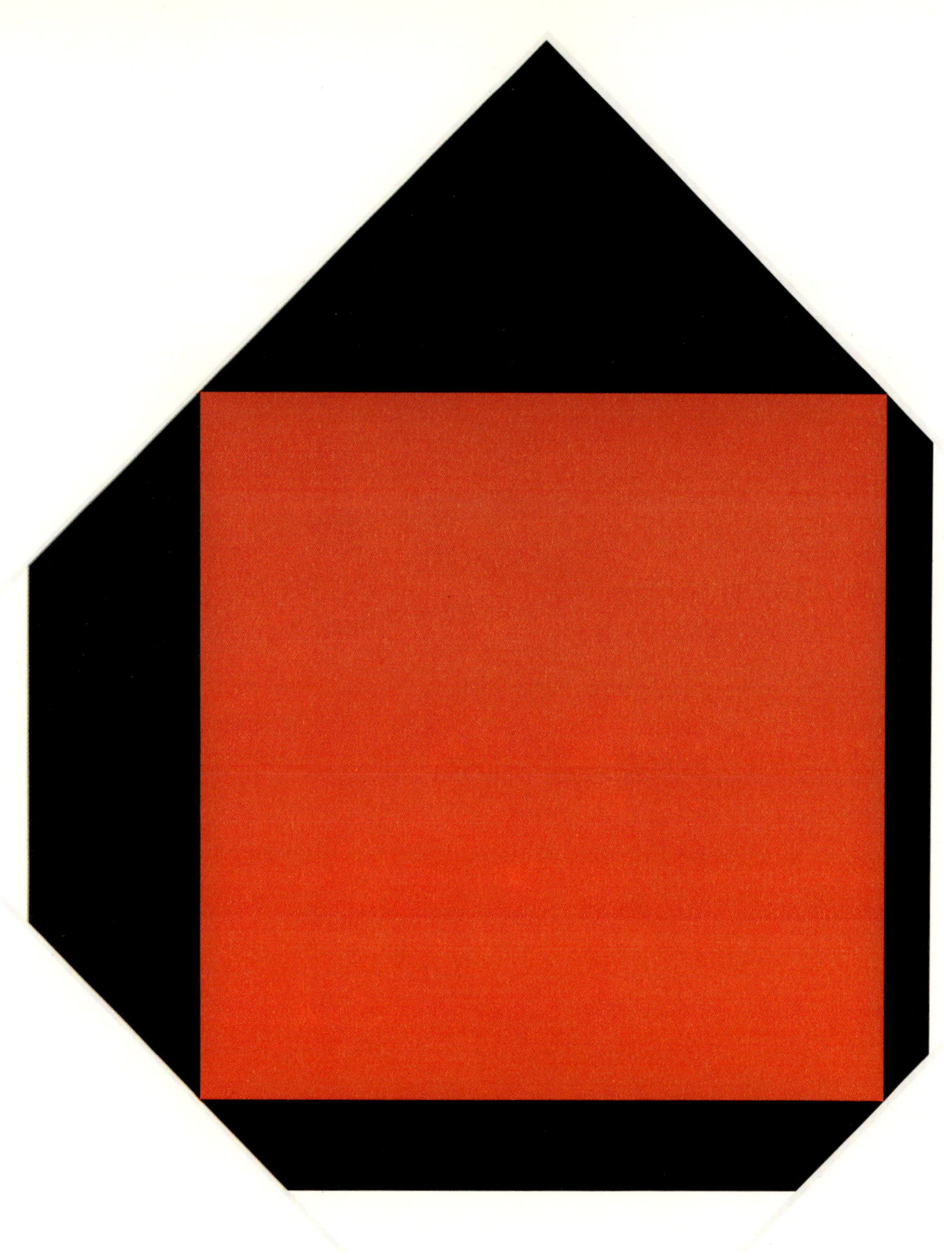

1946
The Red Square
oil on canvas, diagonal, 27½″,
(70 cm)

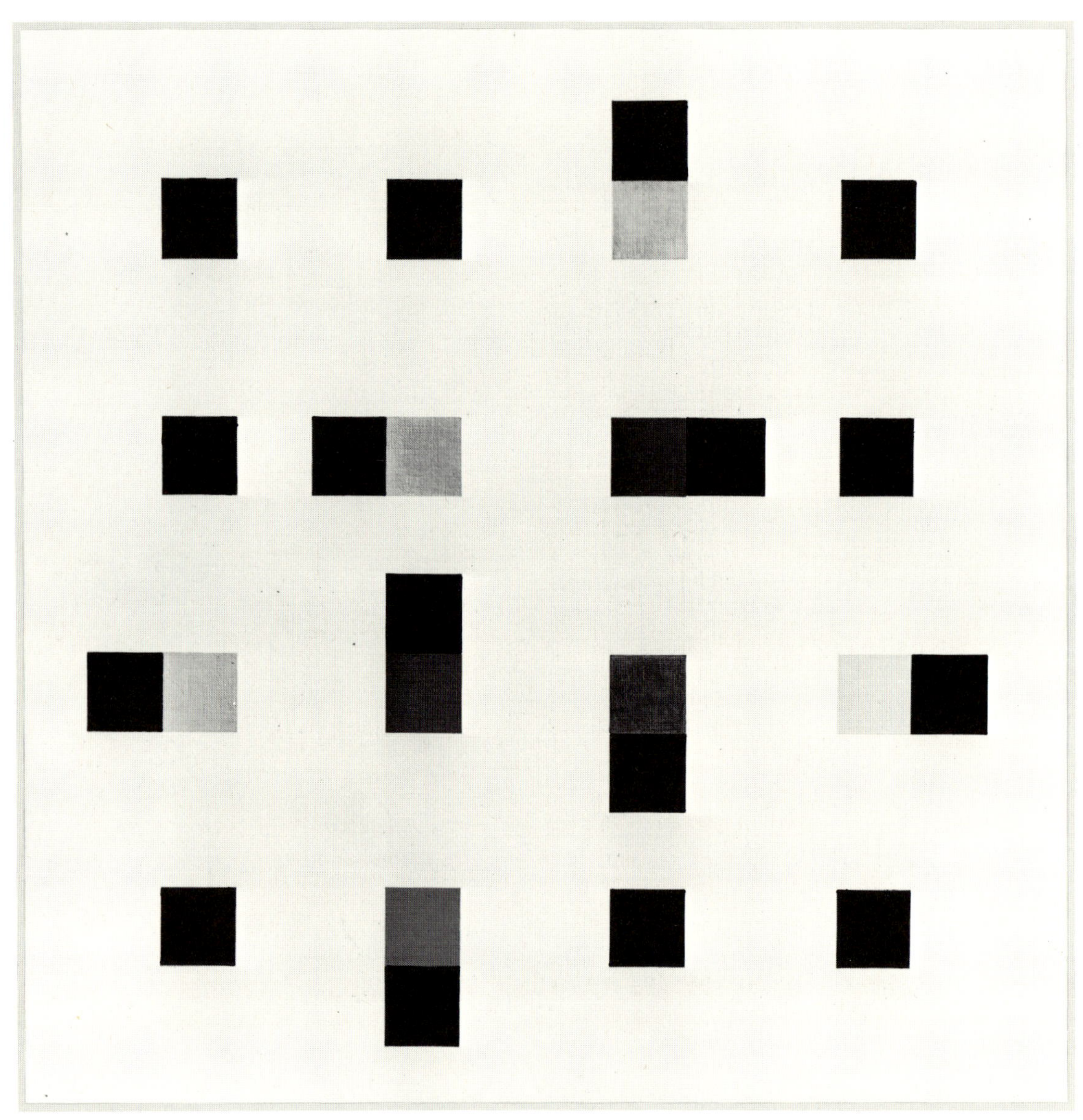

1946
Brightly Colored Accent
oil on canvas, 19¾″ × 19¾″,
(50 × 50 cm)

1947–48
Endless Ribbon from a Ring II
gilt brass, 21⅝″ × 5⅛″ × 15¾″,

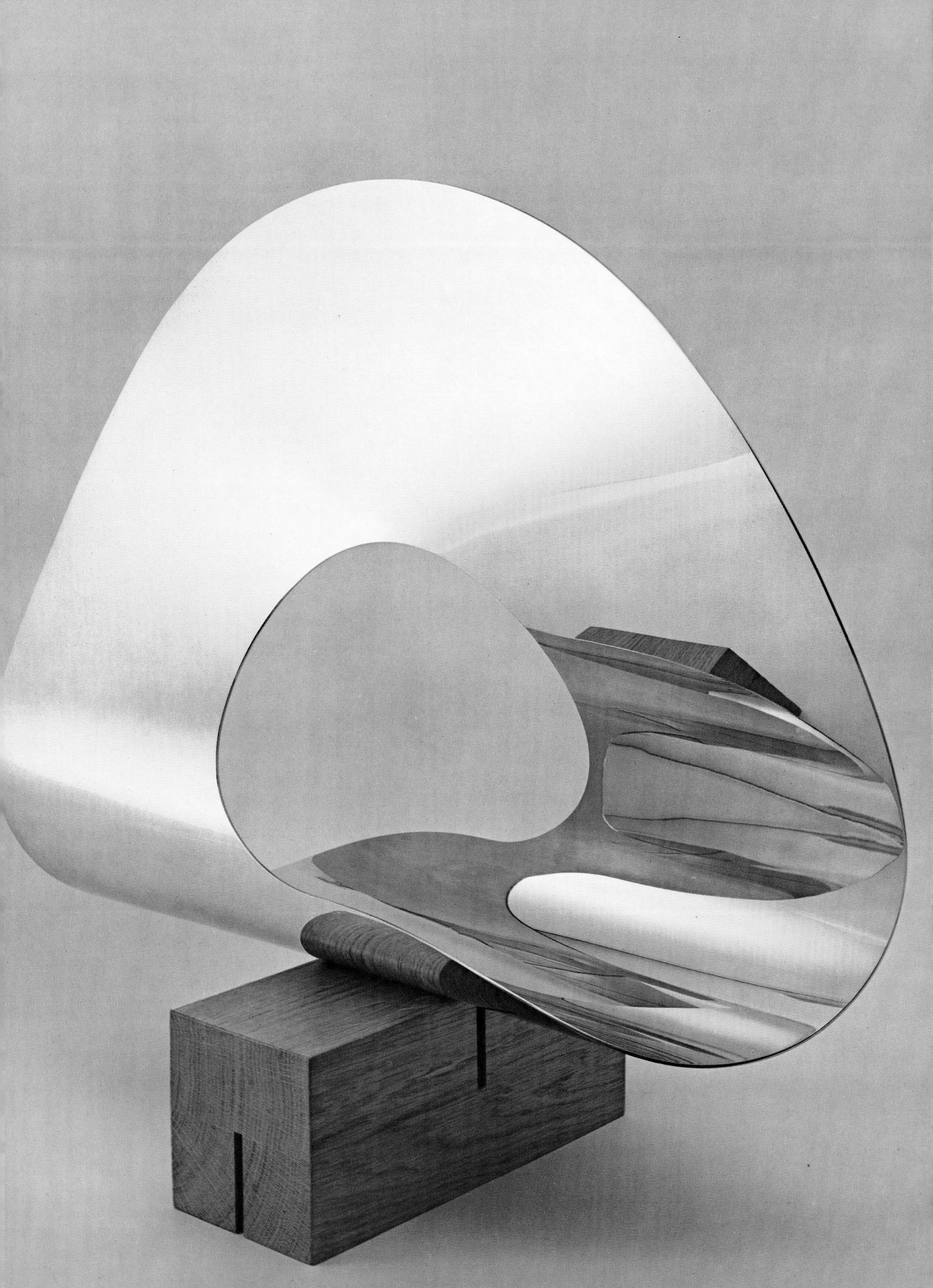

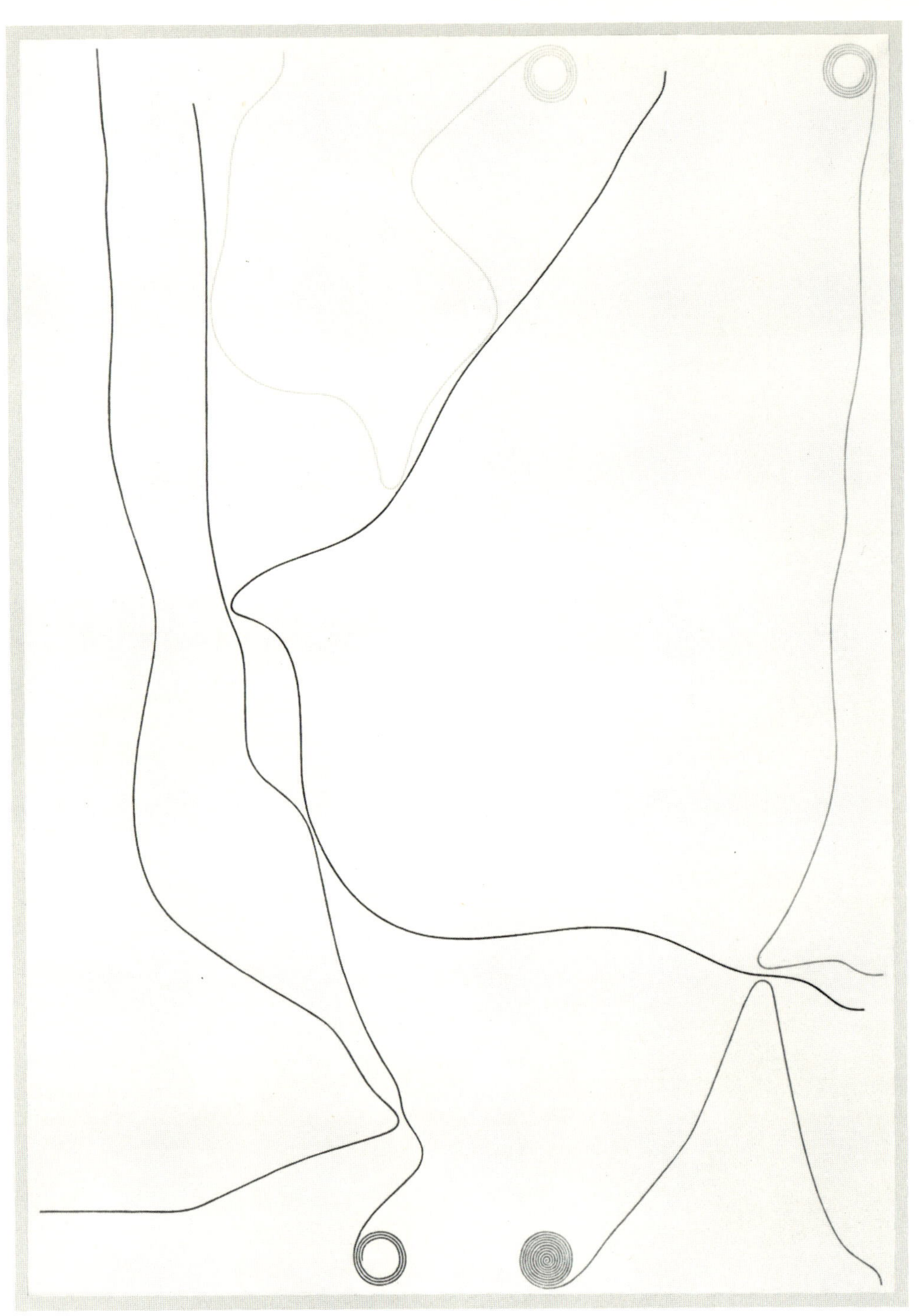

1947
Six Lines of Equal Length
oil on canvas, 27$\frac{1}{2}$″ × 38$\frac{1}{2}$″,
(70 × 98 cm)

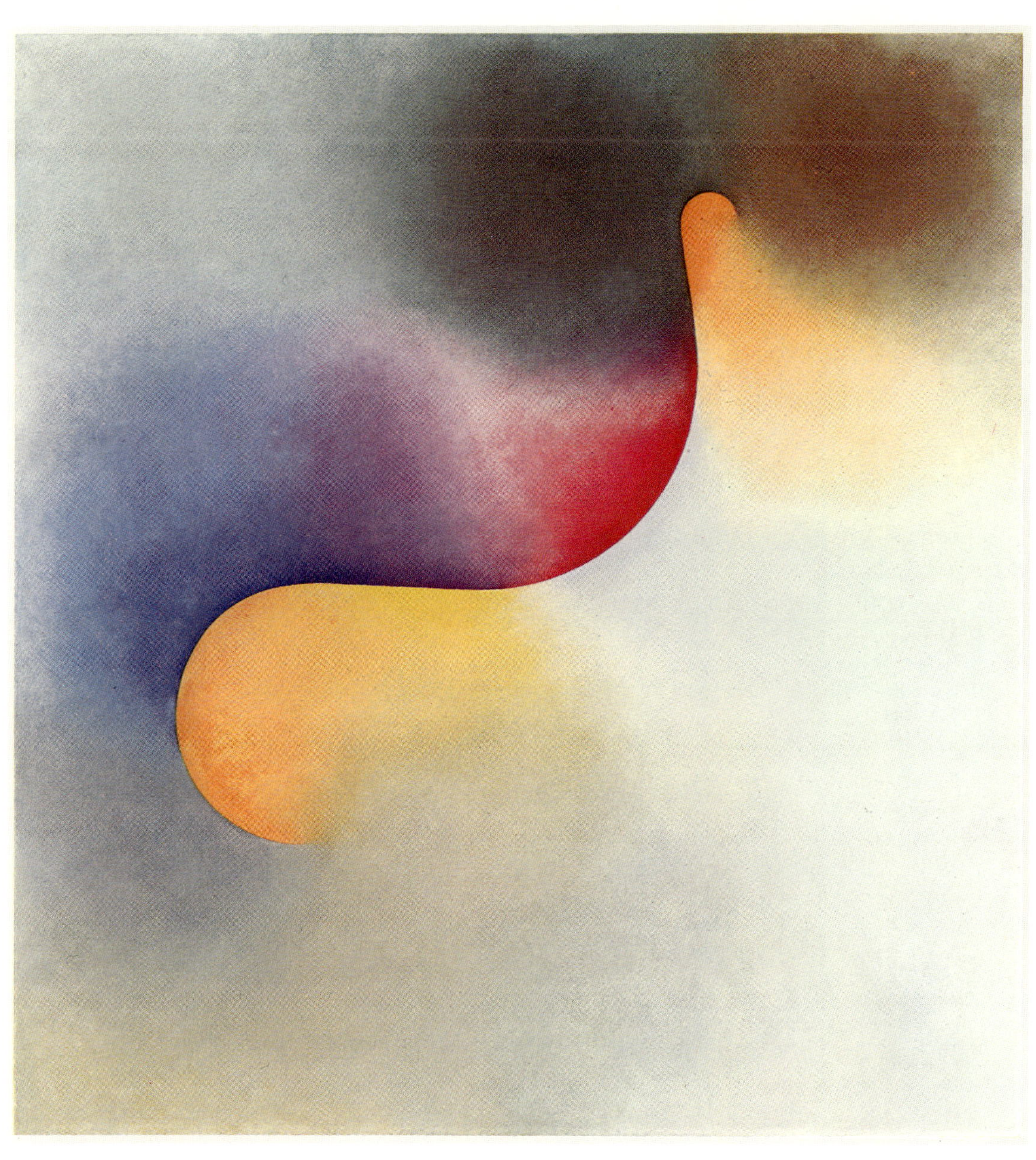

1947
Unlimited and Limited
oil on canvas, 40$\frac{1}{2}$″ × 43$\frac{1}{4}$″,
(103 × 110 cm)

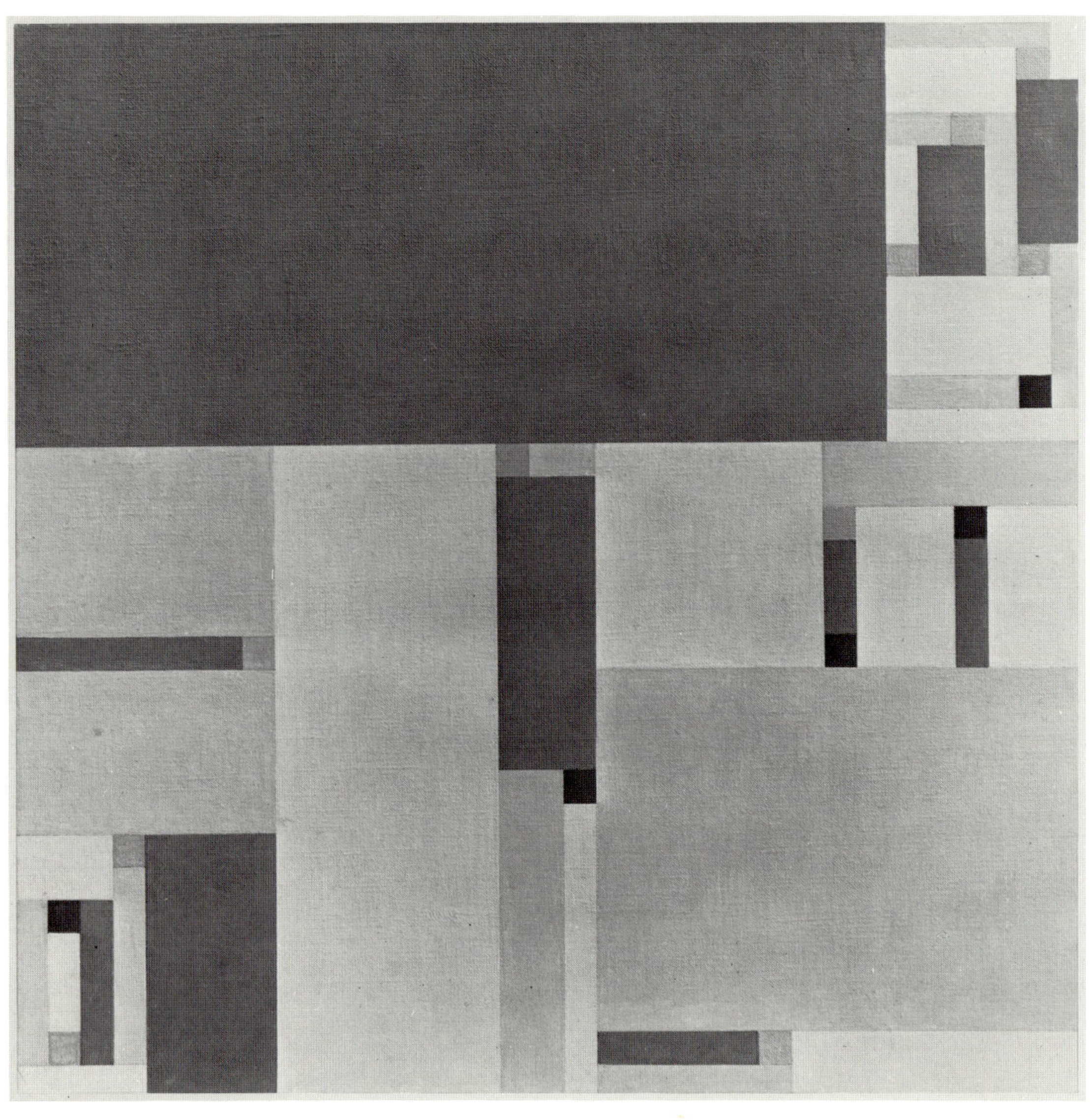

1947
Three Accentuated Groups
oil on canvas, 19¾″ × 19¾″,
(50 × 50 cm)

1947–48
Painting in Form of a Column II
oil on wood, height 78¾″, (200 cm)
(55 × 13 × 40 cm)

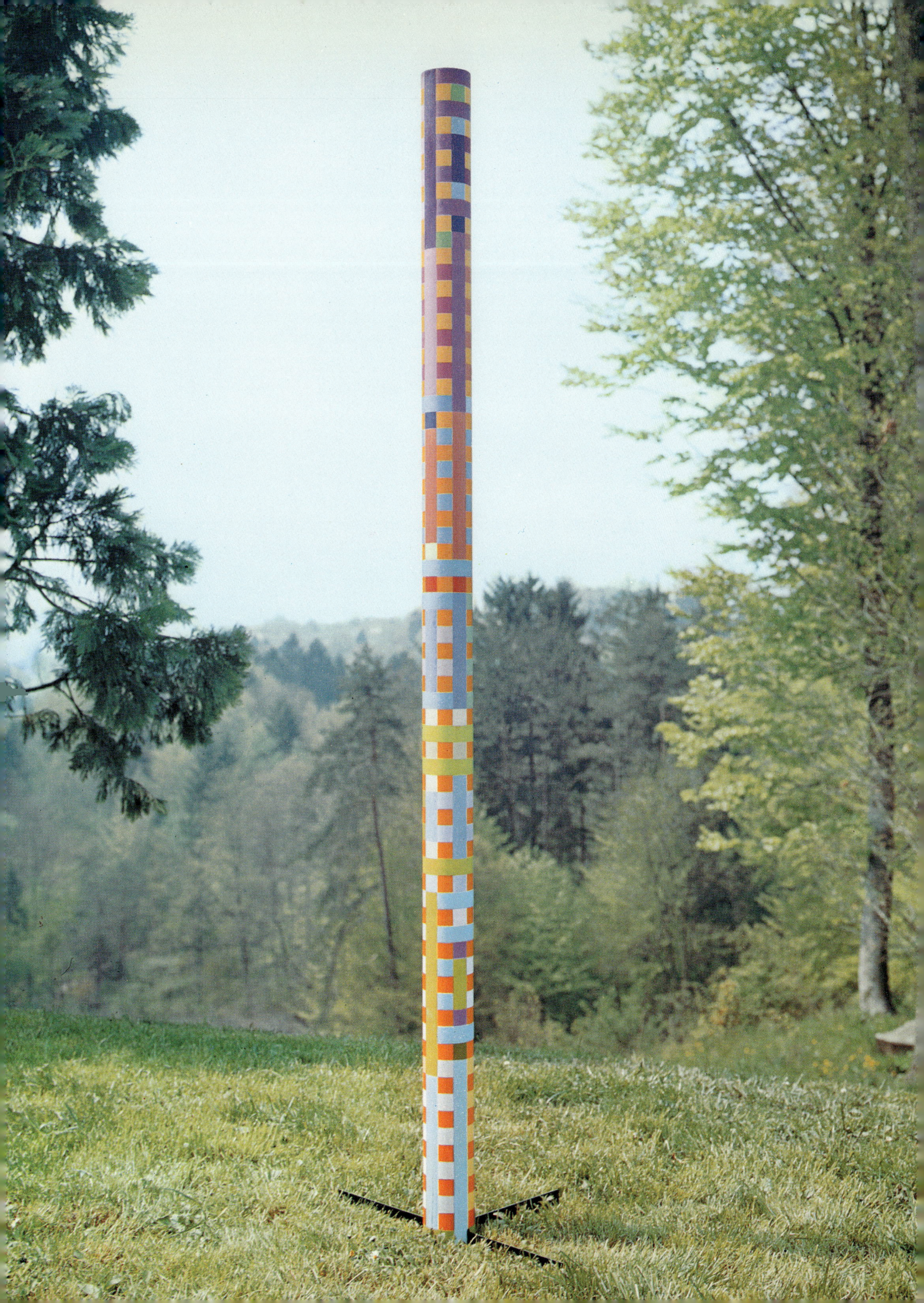

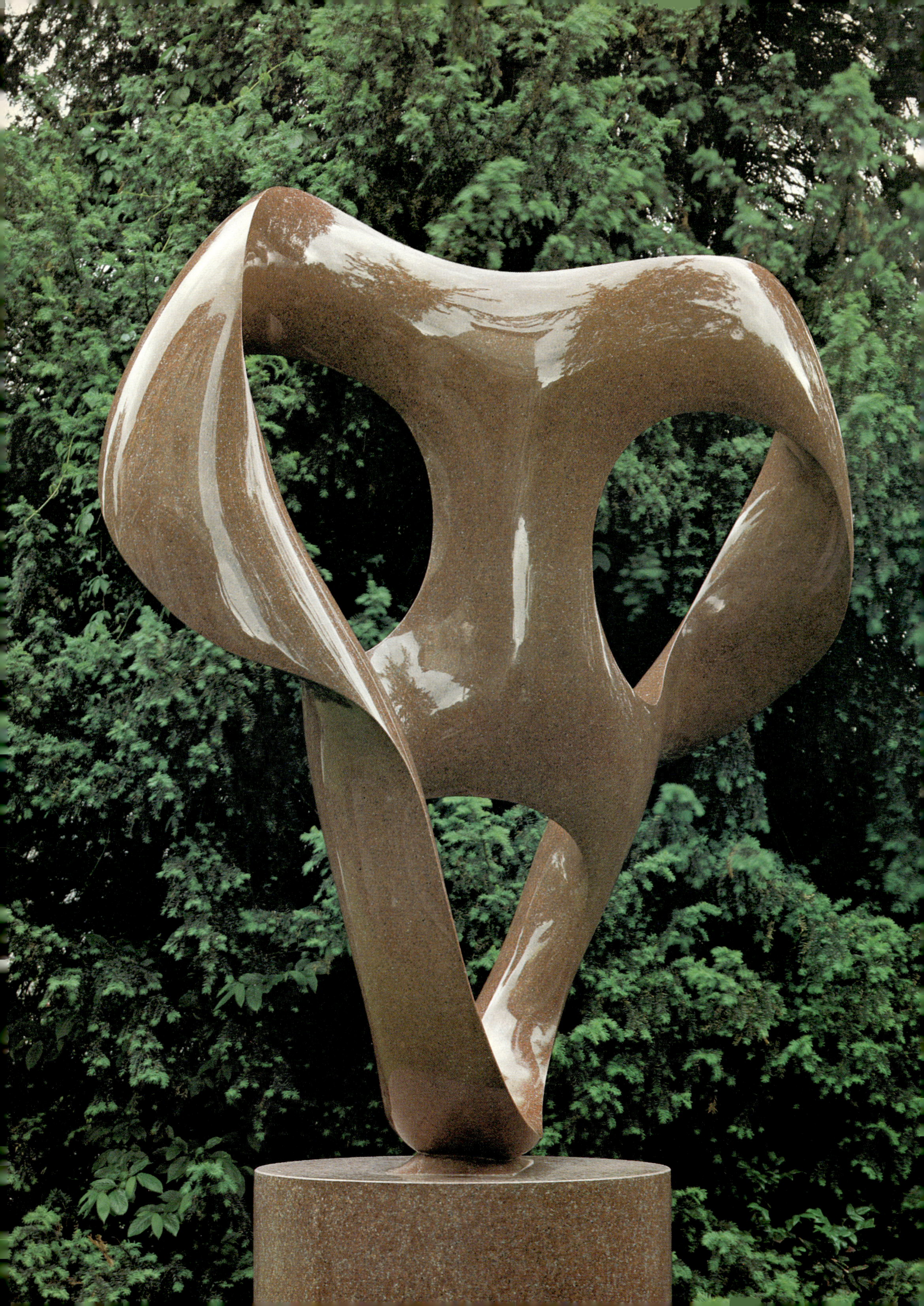

This essay was first printed in the review *Werk* (Nr. 3, 1949, Winterthur). It appeared afterward in another version in the catalogue of the exhibition, *Pevsner, Vantongerloo, Bill* in the Zurich Kunsthaus in 1949 and finally in a monograph, *Max Bill,* published in Spanish, French, English and German, edited by Tomas Maldonado (Buenos Aires, 1955). This essay has been reprinted in several countries and languages. This translation by Morton Shand first appeard in *Arts and Architecture* (Los Angeles), No. 8, 1954.

1947–48
Rhythm in Space
red granite, 88½″ × 29½″ × 98″,
(225 × 75 × 250 cm)

The Mathematical Approach in Contemporary Art

By a mathematical approach to art it is hardly necessary to say I do not mean any fanciful ideas for turning out art by some ingenious system of ready reckoning with the aid of mathematical formulas. So far as composition is concerned every former school of art can be said to have had a more or less mathematical basis. There are also many trends in modern art which rely on the same sort of empirical calculations. These, together with the artist's own individual scales of value, are just part of the ordinary elementary principles of design for establishing the proper relationship between component volumes; that is to say for imparting harmony to the whole. Yet it cannot be denied that these same methods have suffered considerable deterioration since the time when mathematics was the foundation of all forms of artistic expression and the covert link between cult and cosmos. Nor have they seen any progressive development from the days of the ancient Egyptians until quite recently, if we except the discovery of perspective during the Renaissance. This is a system which, by means of pure calculation and artificial reconstruction, enables objects to be reproduced in what is called «true-to-life» facsimile by setting them in an illusory field of space. Perspective certainly presented an entirely new aspect of reality to human consciousness, but one of its consequences was that the artist's primal image was debased into mere naturalistic replica of his subject. Therewith the decadence of painting, both as a symbolic art and an art of free construction, may be said to have begun.

Impressionism, and still more Cubism, brought painting and sculpture much closer to what were the original elements of each: painting as surface design in colors; sculpture as the shaping of bodies to be informed by space. It was probably Kandinsky who gave the immediate impulse towards an entirely fresh conception of art. As early as 1912, in his book on *The Spiritual Harmony in Art,* Kandinsky had indicated the possibility of a new direction which, if followed to its logical conclusion, would lead to the substitution of a mathematical approach for improvisations of the artist's imagination. But as he found other ways of liberating painting from romantic and literary associations he did not adopt this particular line in his own work.

If we examine a picture by Klee or one of Brancusi's sculptures we shall soon discover that, though the «subject» may be an indeterminable echo of something or other in the actual world about us, it is an echo which has been transmuted into a form that is original in the sense of being elemental. Kandinsky confronted us with objects and phenomena which have no existence in ordinary life, but which might well have meaning or be portents on some unknown planet; a planet where we should be quite unable to gauge their purpose or relevance. Yet it was undoubtedly Mondrian who went furthest in breaking away from everything that had hitherto been regarded as art. If the technique of structural design may seem to have inspired his rhythms the resemblance is fortuitous and one which was not present in his own intention or consciousness. Although the specific content of his work is constricted with the utmost discipline, the horizontal-vertical emphasis represents a purely emotional factor in his composition. It is not for any whimsical reason that he called his latest pictures «Broadway Boogie-Woogie» and «Victory Boogie-Woogie», but simply to stress their affinity with jazz rhythms.

If we can agree that Mondrian realized the ultimate possibilities of painting in one direction – that is by his success in eliminating most of the remaining elements which are alien to it – two others still lie open to us: either we can return to traditionalism (in its wider sense), or else we can continue the quest for subjects with a content of a new and altogether different nature.

Let me take this opportunity to explain why it is impossible for many artists to go back to the old type of subjects. In the vast field of pictorial and plastic expression there are a large number of trends and tendencies which have all more or less originated in our own age. Different people look at modern painting and sculpture with different eyes because what they severally recognize as significant of our age is necessarily various. Clergymen have a different idea of art from scientists. Peasants and factory-hands live under radically different conditions. There are inevitable variations in standards of living and levels of culture. Similar differences can be found among artists. They, too, come from different walks of life, and their work reflects different emotional and intellectual undercurrents. There is another attitude to modern art which must not be overlooked as its now numerous followers can always be relied upon to take their stand against every disinterestedly progressive movement. I mean the much-boosted school which demands that, since art itself cannot perhaps solve social and political problems, these shall at least be made dramatically «actual» and suitably glorified through its medium. We have good reason to be skeptical about any «Political Art» – regardless of whether it emanates from right or left; especially when, under the cloak of antagonism to the prevailing social order, its aim is to bring about a new, but in all essentials, almost identical structure of society – because this is not art at all but simply propaganda.

After this digression into the potential alternatives which may be said to have existed prior to somewhere about 1910, let me try to make clear why some of us were unable to rest content with what had then been achieved. That would have meant going on marking time over the same ground during the last forty years and painting in one or the other of those manners which may be called «à la Klee», «à la Kandinsky», «à la Mondrian», or, what was more usual «à la Picasso», «à la Braque», and «à la Matisse». A great many gifted and intelligent artists are still wearing out their talents in ringing the changes on these modern masters. In fact this sort of painting has now become something in the nature of a substitute for the masters themselves, and «à la» pictures begin to rank as interesting variants of their originals. To acquiesce in this state of stagnation was impossible because we have no right to allow a halt to be called in any genuinely creative field of human activity.

We can safely assume that all the various forms of expression open to painting and sculpture at the present day are now sufficiently known, and that the techniques they postulate have been sufficiently demonstrated and clarified in the work of their respective pioneers (except perhaps for a very few which can be already anticipated, but which have not so far been realized). What, then, it may be asked, are the possibilities of further development? But there are two other important points which must be dealt with before that question can be answered: namely, whether the several idioms just referred to can claim general validity in the plastic arts; and whether there is reason to enlarge the existing limits of their content. Careful study of those forms of expression has led me to the conclusion that all of them were the discoveries of individual artists, either born of their will to overcome particular problems or else expedients called forth by exceptional circumstances; and that therefore they cannot be considered universally applicable or appropriate. As regards content, most of the modern work which is often held to have been largely inspired by mathematical principles cannot, in point of fact, be identified with that entirely new orientation I have called the Mathematical Approach to Art. And as this needs to be more nearly defined, I will now endeavor to elucidate it, and at the same time answer the question I have left in suspense.

I am convinced it is possible to evolve a new form of art in which the artist's work could be founded to quite a substantial degree on a mathematical line of approach to its content. This proposal has, of course, aroused the most vehement opposition. It is objected that art has nothing to do with mathematics; that mathematics, besides being by its very nature as dry as dust and as unemotional, is a branch of speculative thought and as such in direct antithesis to those emotive values inherent in aesthetics; and finally that anything approaching ratiocination is repugnant, indeed positively injurious to art, which is purely a matter of feeling. Yet art plainly calls for both feeling and reasoning. In support of this assertion the familiar example of Johann Sebastian Bach may be credited; for Bach employed mathematical formulas to fashion the raw material known to us as sound into the exquisite harmonies of his sublime fugues. And it is worth mentioning that, although mathematics had by then fallen into disuse for composition in both his own and the other arts, mathematical and theological books stood side by side on the shelves of his library.

It is mankind's ability to reason which makes it possible to coordinate emotional values in such a way that what we call art ensues. Now in every picture the basis of its composition is geometry or in other words the means of determining the mutual relationship of its component parts either on plane or in space. Thus, just as mathematics provides us with a primary method of cognition, and can therefore enable us to apprehend our physical surroundings, so, too, some of its basic elements will furnish us with laws to appraise the interactions of separate objects, or groups of objects, one to another. And again, since it is mathematics which lends significance to these relationships, it is only a natural step from

1948
Yellow Field
oil on canvas, 32″ × 32″, (81 × 81 cm),
Kunstmuseum Winterthur

having perceived them to desiring to portray them. This, in brief, is the genesis of a picture. Pictorial representations of that kind have been known since antiquity, and, like those models at the Musée Poincaré in Paris where conceptions of space have been embodied in plastic shapes or made manifest by colored diagrams, they undoubtedly provoke an aesthetic reaction in the beholder. In the search for new formal idioms expressive of the technical sensibilities of our age these borderline exemplars had much the same order of importance as the «discovery» of native West African sculpture by the Cubists; though they were equally inapt for direct assimilation into modern European art. The first result of their influence was the phase known as Constructivism. This, together with the stimulus derived from the use of new materials such as engineering blueprints, aerial photographs, and the like, furnished the necessary incentive for further developments along mathematical lines. At about the same time mathematics itself had arrived at a stage of evolution in which the proof of many apparently logical deductions ceased to be demonstrable and theorems were presented that the imagination proved incapable of grasping. Though mankind's power of reasoning had not reached the end of its tether, it was clearly beginning to require the assistance of some visualizing agency. Aids of this kind can often be provided by the intervention of art.

As the artist has to forge his concept into unity his vision vouchsafes him a synthesis of what he sees which, though essential to his art, may not be necessarily mathematically accurate. This leads to the shifting or blurring of boundaries where clear lines of division would be supposed. Hence abstract conceptions assume concrete and visible shape, and so become perceptible to our emotions. Unknown fields of space, almost unimaginable hypotheses, are boldly bodied forth. We seem to be wandering through a firmament that has had no prior existence; and in the process of attuning ourselves to its strangeness our sensibility is being actively prepared to anticipate still further and, as it were, as yet inconceivable expanses of the infinite.

It must not be supposed that an art based on the principles of mathematics, such as I have just adumbrated, is in any sense the same thing as a plastic or pictorial interpretation of the latter. Indeed, it employs virtually none of the resources

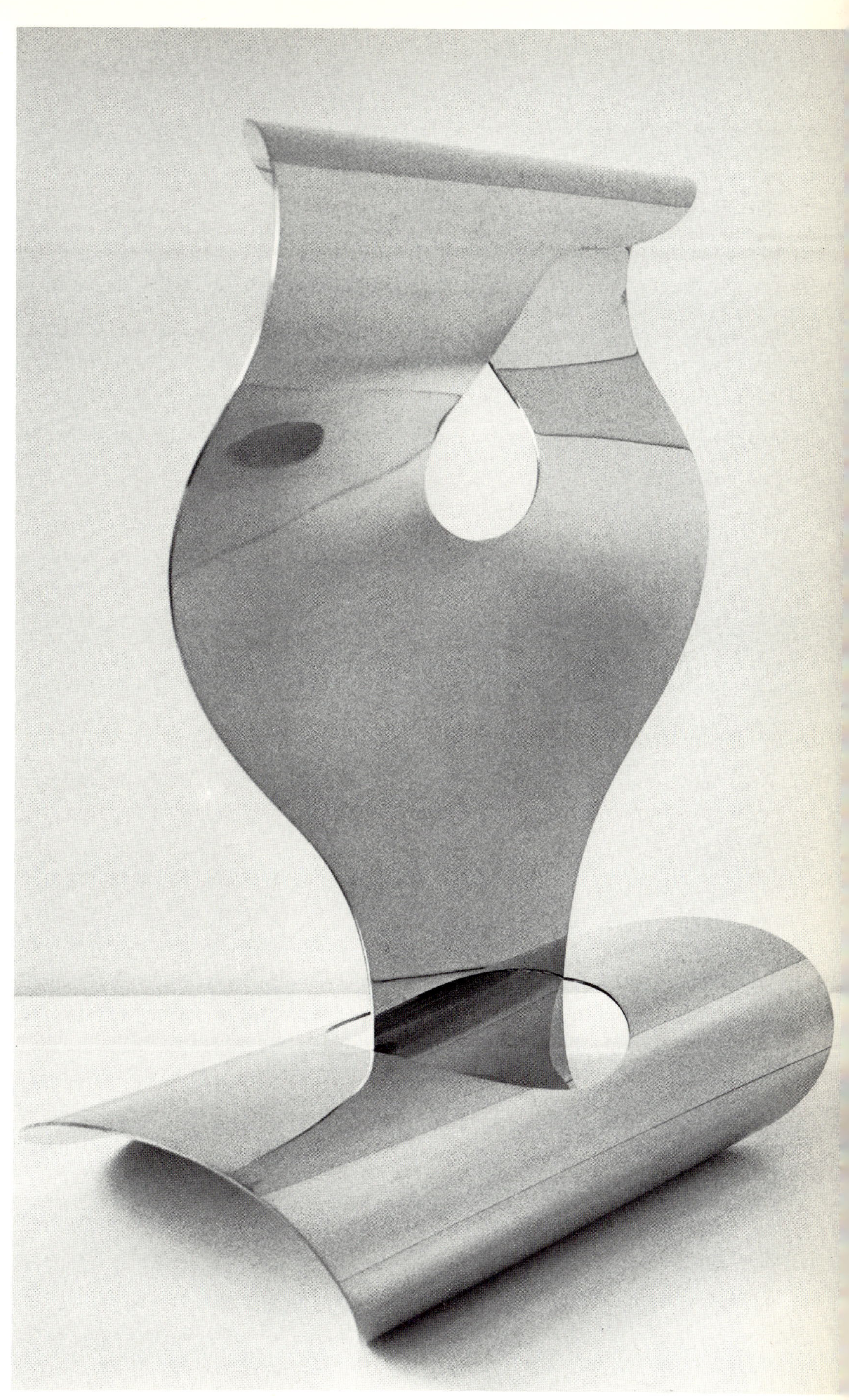

1948–71
Surface in Space
gilt brass, 23½″ × 15″ × 26″,
(60 × 38 × 66 cm)
Marlborough Gallery Inc.,
New York

implicit in the term «Pure Mathematics». The art in question
can, perhaps, best be defined as the building up of significant
patterns from the everchanging relations, rhythms and proportions of abstract forms, each one of which, having its own
causality, is tantamount to a law unto itself. As such, it pre-
sents some analogy to mathematics itself where every fresh
advance had its immaculate conception in the brain of one or
other of the great pioneers. Thus Euclidian geometry no longer possesses more than a limited validity in modern science,
and it has an equally restricted utility in modern art. The concept of a Finite Infinity offers yet another parallel. For this
essential guide to the speculations of contemporary physicists has likewise become an essential factor in the consciousness of contemporary artists. These, then, are the
general lines on which art is daily creating new symbols:
symbols that may have their sources in antiquity but which
meet the aesthetic-emotional needs of our time in a way
hardly any other form of expression can hope to realize.

Things having no apparent connection with mankind's
daily needs – the mystery enveloping all mathematical problems; the inexplicability of space – space that can stagger us
by beginning on one side and ending in a completely changed
aspect on the other, which somehow manages to remain that
selfsame side; the remoteness or nearness of infinity – infinity
which may be found doubling back from the far horizon to
present itself to us as immediately at hand; limitations without boundaries; disjunctive and disparate multiplicities constituting coherent and unified entities; identical shapes
rendered wholly diverse by the merest inflection; fields of
attraction that fluctuate in strength; or, again, the square in
all its robust solidity; parallels that intersect; straight lines
untroubled by any relativity and ellipses which form straight
lines at every point of their curves – can yet be fraught with
the greatest moment. For though these evocations might
seem only the phantasmagorial figments of the artist's inward
vision they are, notwithstanding, the projections of latent
forces; forces that may be active or inert, in part revealed,
inchoate or still unfathomed, which we are unconsciously at
grips with every day of our lives; in fact that music of the
spheres which underlies each man-made system and every
law of nature it is within our power to discern.

Hence all such visionary elements help to furnish art with a

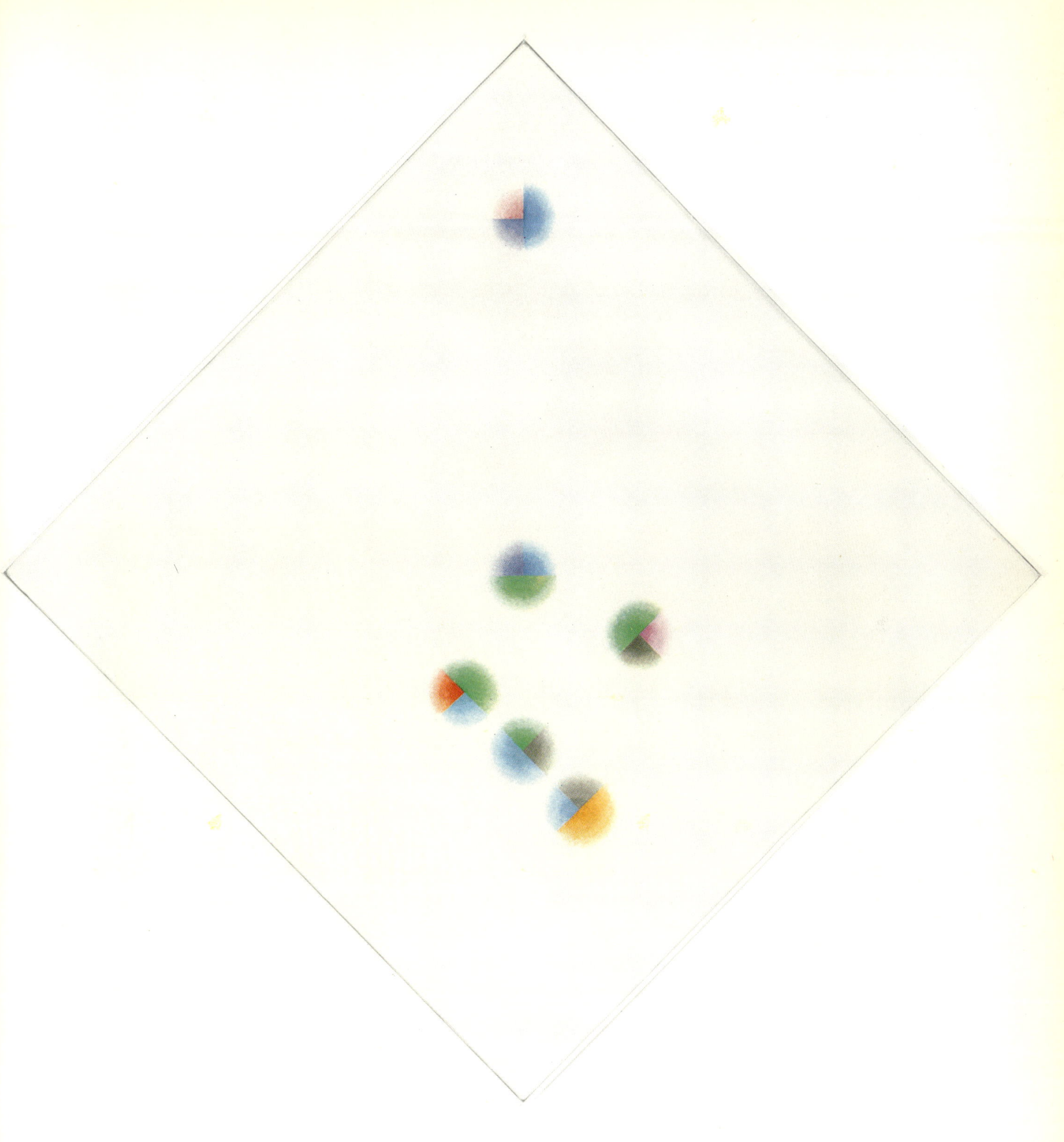

1949–51
Six Centers of Energy
oil on canvas, diagonal, 46⅞″,
(119 cm)

fresh content. Far from creating a new formalism, as is often erroneously asserted, what these can yield us is something far transcending surface values since they not only embody form as beatuy, but also form in which intuitions or ideas or conjectures have taken visible substance. The primordial forces contained in those elements call forth intimations of the occult controls which govern the cosmic structure; and these can be made to reflect a semblance of the universe as we have learned to picture it today: an image that is no mere transcript of this invisible world but a systematization of it ideographically conveyed to our senses.

It may, perhaps, be contended that the result of this would be to reduce art to a branch of metaphysical philosophy. But I see no likelihood of that for philosophy is speculative thought of a special kind which can only be made intelligible through the use of words. Mental concepts are not as yet directly communicable to our apprehension without the medium of language; though they might ultimately become so by the medium of art. Hence I assume that art could be made a unique vehicle for the direct transmission of ideas, because if these were expressed by pictures or plastically there would be no danger of their original meaning being perverted (as happens in literature, for instance, through printer's errors, or thanks to the whim of some prominent executant in music) by whatever fallacious interpretations particular individuals chance to put on them. Thus the more succinctly a train of thought was expounded and the more comprehensive the unity of its basic idea, the closer it would approximate to the prerequisites of the Mathematical Approach to Art. So the nearer we can attain to the first cause or primal core of things by these means, the more universal will the scope of art become – more universal, that is, by being free to express itself directly and without ambivalence; and likewise forthright and immediate in its impact on our sensibility.

To which, no doubt, a further objection will be raised that this is no longer art; though it could equally well be maintained that this alone was art. Such a structure would be like saying that Euclid's was the only geometry, and that the new conception of geometry associated with the names of Lobaschevsky and Riemann was not geometry at all. One claim would stand against the other and that would be that!

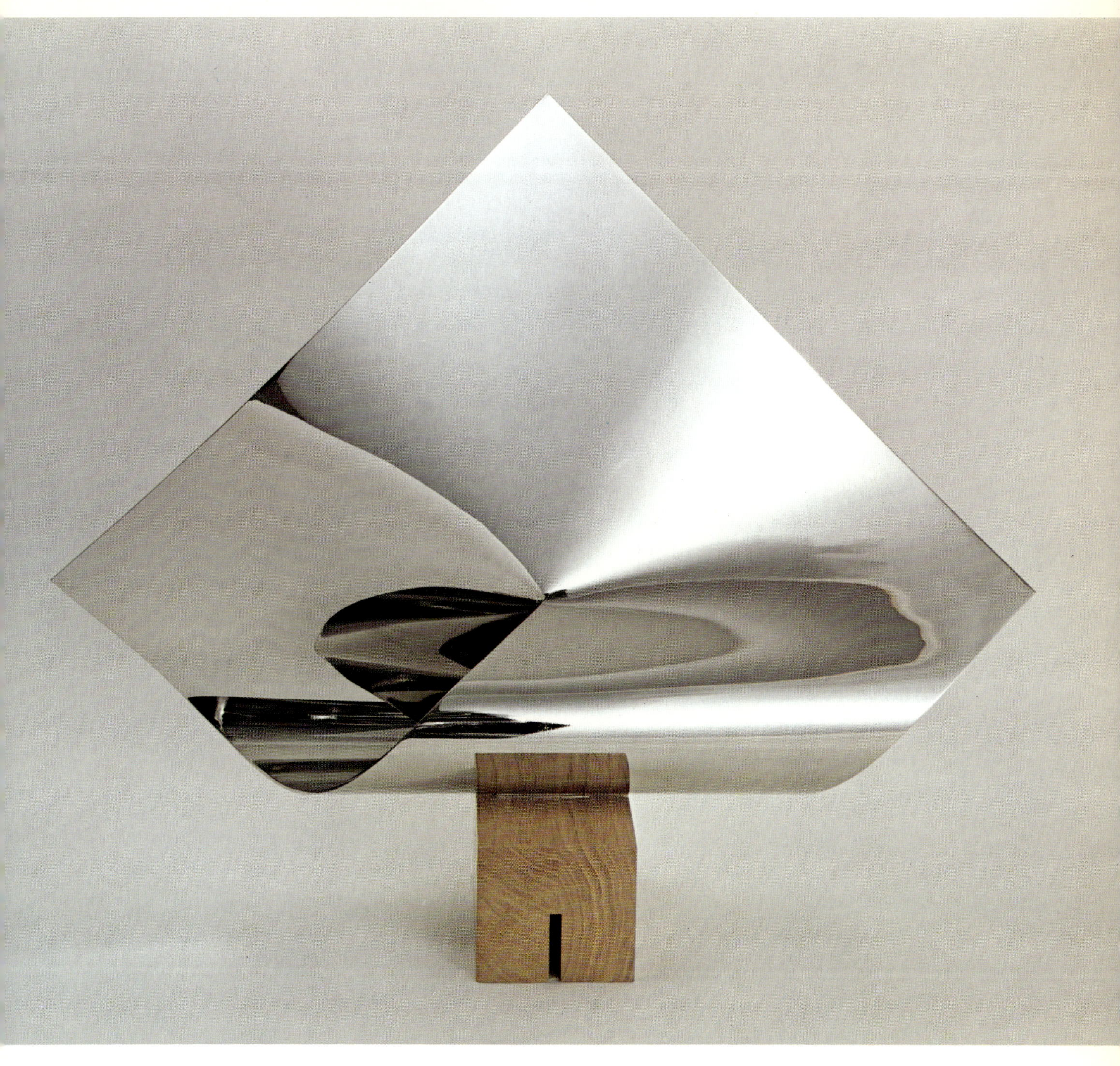

1952
*Quadrilateral Surface in Space with Equal
Delimiting Edges*
chromium plated brass,
$31^{1}/_{2}''\times 4^{3}/_{4}''\times 21^{3}/_{4}''$,
(86 × 12 × 55 cm),
Galerie Beyeler, Basel

Although this new ideology of art is focused on a spectral
field of vision this is one where the mind can still find access.
It is a field in which some degree of stability may be found,
but in which, too, unknown quantities, indefinable factors will
inevitably be encountered. In the ever-shifting frontier zones
of this nebular realm new perspectives are continually open-
ing up to invite the artist's creative analysis. The difference
between the traditional conception of art and that just
defined is much the same as exists between the laws of
Archimedes and those we owe Einstein and other outstand-
ing modern physicists. Archimedes remains our authority in
a good many contingencies though no longer in all of them.
Phidias, Raphael, and Seurat produced works of art that charac-
terize their several epochs for us because each made full
use of such means of expression as his own age afforded him.
But since their days the orbit of human vision has widened
and art has annexed fresh territories which were formerly
denied to it. In one of these recently conquered domains the
artist is now free to exploit the untapped resources of that
vast new field of inspiration I have described with the means
our age vouchsafes him and in a spirit proper to its genius.
And despite the fact the basis of this Mathematical Approach
to Art is in reason, its dynamic content is able to launch us on
astral flights which soar into unknown and still uncharted
regions of the imagination.

[1949]

1952
Surface in Space Delimited by One Line
gilt brass, 26¾" × 7" × 13⅜",
(68 × 18 × 34 cm),
Marlborough Gallery Inc., New York

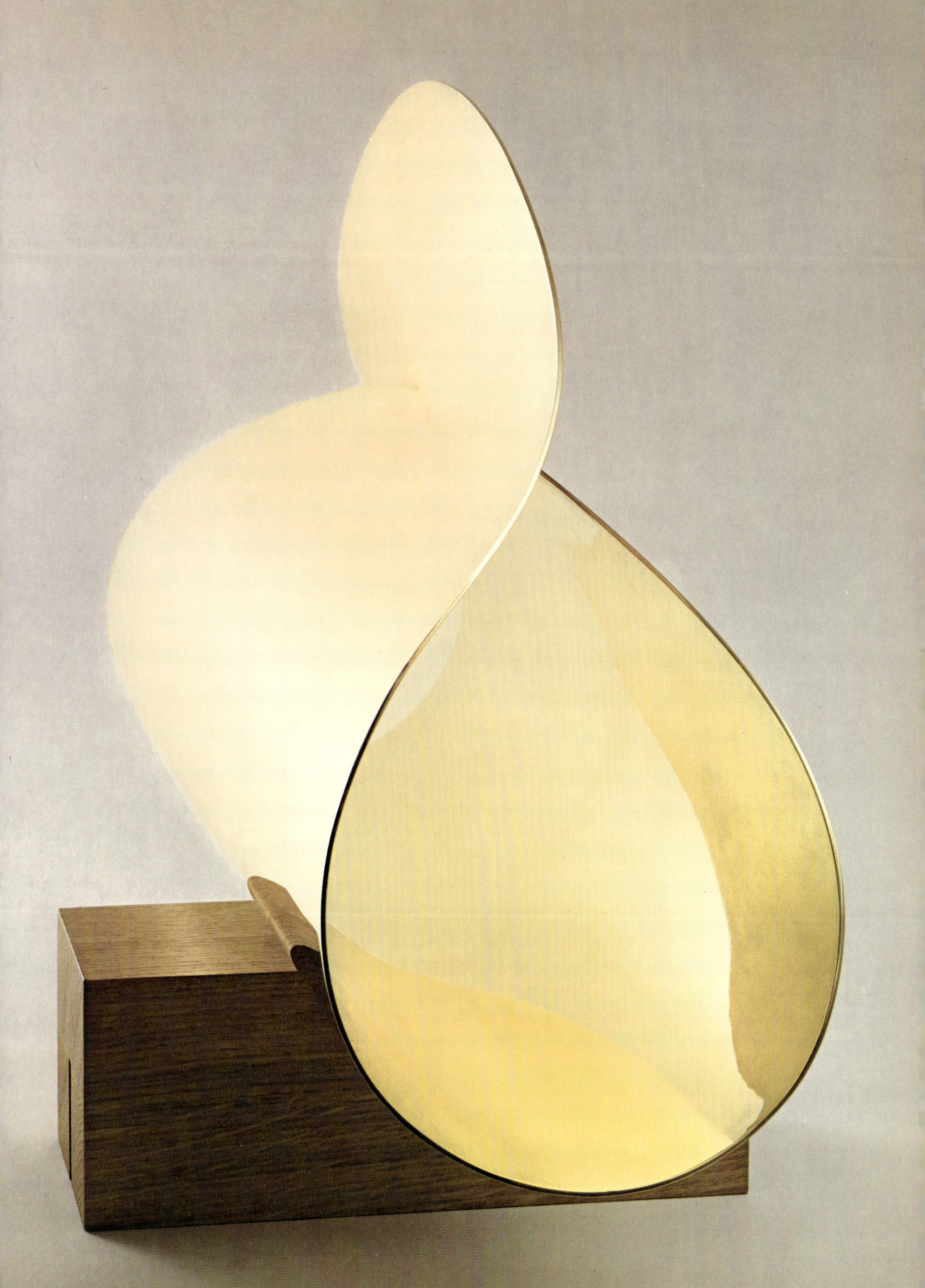

A Monument

Comments by Max Bill about his project on «A monument to the Unknown Political Prisoner» submitted to the Institute of Contemporary Art, London, 1952.

The subject having been given, my first consideration was, has the theme really been correctly expressed? What was the sponsors' objective in assigning this theme? What was meant by the unknown political prisoner? My answer was: the unknown political prisoner is different under each form of government. He is never the recognized leader of an opposing group but always an unknown human being who follows a course of political action which he has not himself created. When the state authority uses its power to suppress the opposition, he is taken prisoner. The state authority can be any of several: fascist, communist, royalist, democratic. In certain cases, and particularly in exceptional circumstances, it resorts to imprisonment to defend itself against its enemies.

Should a memorial really be erected to this anonymous political fellow traveller of some oppugnant tendency?

Was it really the tragedy of this anonymous individual destiny, of this – in all cases – inhuman attitude toward a political opponent, which was to have its monument? In other words, was this to be a monument to the passive endurance of a sentence frequently imposed as a result of a questionable political attitude?

My answer was negative. I came to the conclusion that the sponsors' intention had not been to erect a monument to this anonymous suffering, particularly since it was obvious that an opponent of a dictatorial regime had been meant.

Therefore, it seemed to me that a different theme had been implied if not clearly expressed. This theme I defined as «an honestness of attitude and faithfulness to the awareness of having a free choice on one's own responsibility regarding the way to be taken». Such an attitude can bring the individual into conflict with the social order, according to the degree to which this social order restricts the individual's right to form his opinions freely and his political activity.

It was to this unknown, upright human being, intrinsically free and aware of his responsibility that a monument was to be erected; and for this attitude it was to be the symbol.

This deliberation gave rise to a solution wherein idea and form were identical, and of which I can personally show each detail to be indispensable and deliberate.

The monument consists of a group of three cubes which appear from without as constituting a closed entity. At their center stands a triangular steel column.

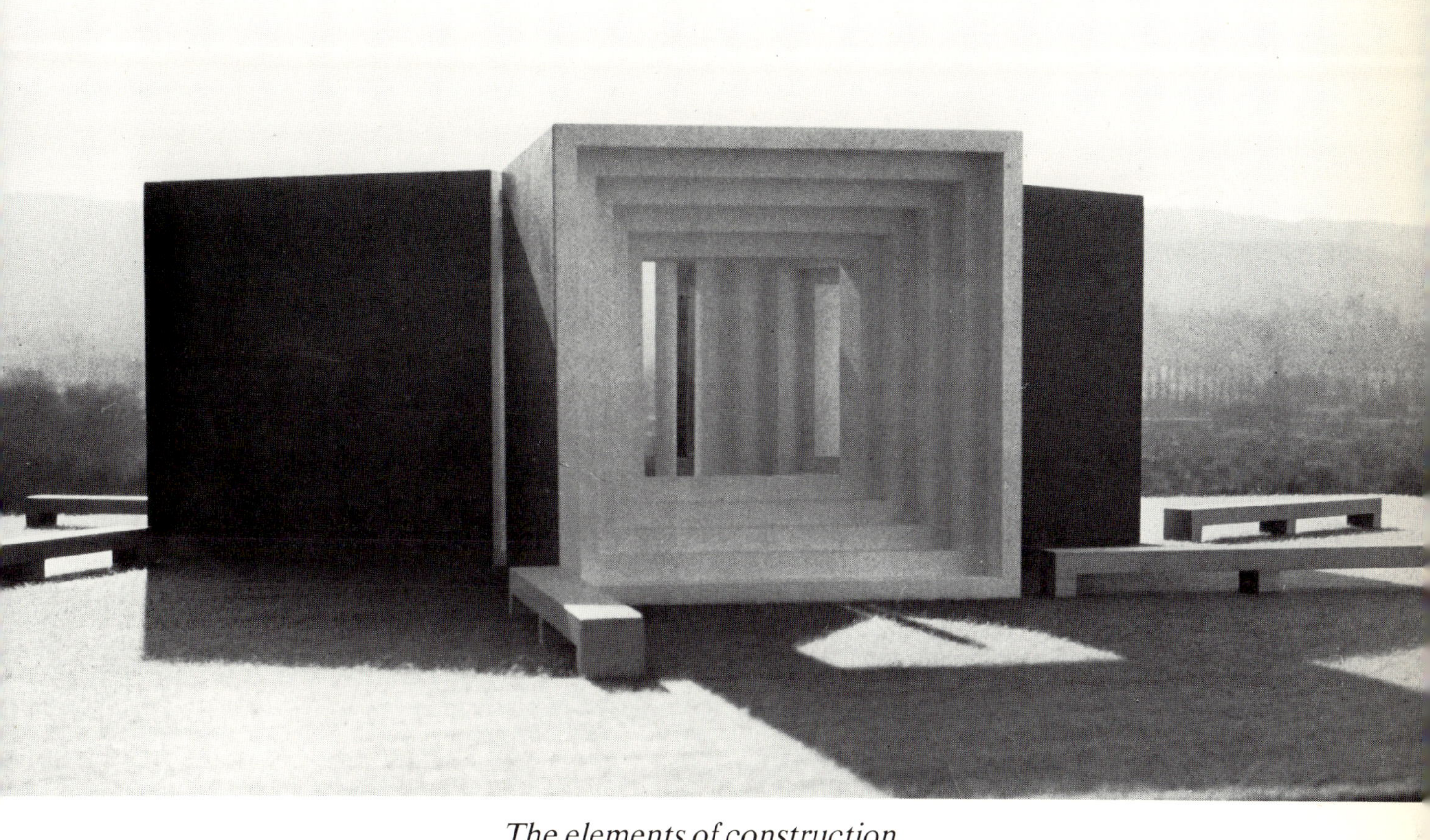

The elements of construction
The cubes are of dark granite on the outer surface, conveying
an outwardly sombre impression. On the inner surface the
cubes are of white marble, which means that the interior of
the space formed by the cubes is lighter than the impression
given by the outside. The space, the actual sculpture, is not
outside but within. This space comes from the internal stepp-
ing of the cubes. The cubes are formed in such a way that no
matter which of the four closed sides they rest on, they are
the same. Instead of forming a stairway within the cube in the
usual sense, a hollow plastic space is created which at the
same time can be used as a stairway.

Distribution in space
The repetition of cube-enclosed hollow spaces results in a
spatial development in which first the free exterior space is

narrowed down and then widened again into the internal «triangular space». This triangular space is not only open in three directions, but also between the cubes and above. A triangular column stands in the center of the triangular space.

The column
The triangular column is the same height as the cubes. It is placed with one corner against each entrance. The width of the column is similar to that which lies between two cubes. The column is in stainless steel and polished to an exact mirror.

The site
No specific site was indicated for the erection of the monument. My opinion is that it should stand in a public park on a lawn among trees, with smaller paths joining it to wider ones.

The symbols
The column stands as the symbol of the precise, unconditional and independent attitude of a responsible human being, who is loyal to his convictions and fights unyieldingly for his personal persuasions. The column is therefore not only sharply edged but also mirror-clear.

The cubes are a symbol of the fact that a situation which is outwardly sombre can be clear and bright on the inside.

The distribution symbolizes the freedom to decide. On entering the space, one is free to go to the left, to the right, or back. However, one is not merely given the freedom to decide which way to take: this decision must be made.

The cubes are approached from without. Granite benches link the monument to the surroundings. To enter the monument, the visitor must ascend the steps. At the center of the cubus, he finds himself in a confine corresponding more or less to a double-width door. He then descends the steps into the inner space, open on all sides, and stands before a sharp edge, facing the column. In passing the column, he sees his own image in the mirror. This should cause him to reflect: «Why do I see myself here in this column, what does this mean?» The column asks the question: «What is your attitude?» Later, the visitor asks himself: «Which way shall I take to leave this enclosure?» Thus, the visitor's action is to ascend – descend – encounter his mirrored image – deliber-

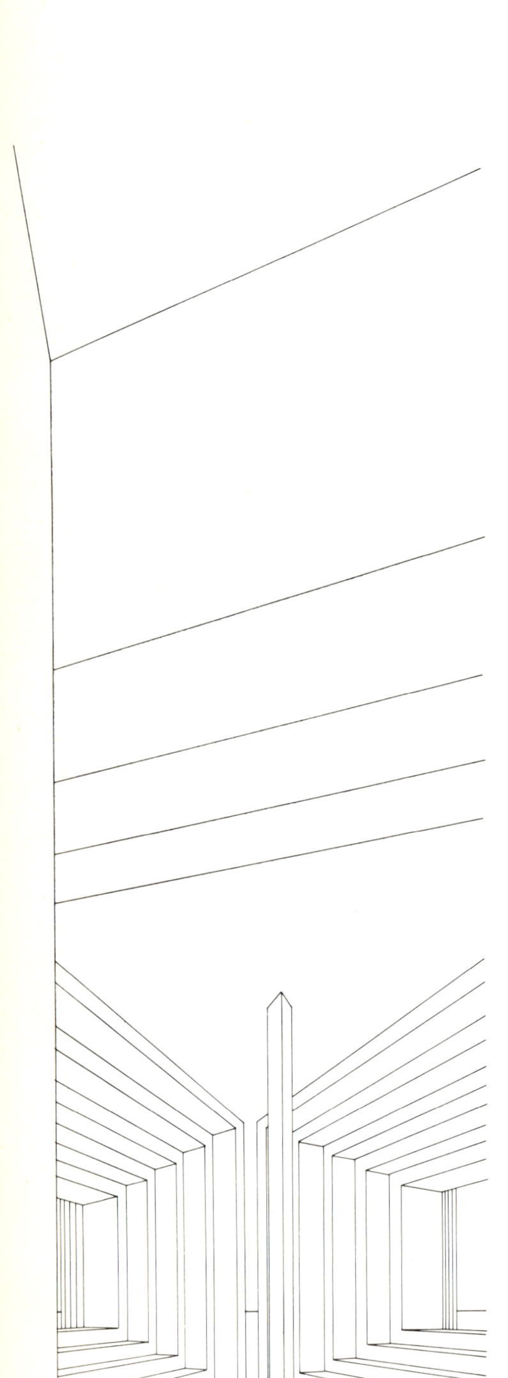

ate – choose a way – ascend and go out into the free surroundings.

Many different objections were raised in connection with my scheme for the monument, all of them based, as I see it, on a misunderstanding of the function of art. The objections may be grouped under the following headings and I shall try to answer all of them.

Sculpture – Architecture

The objection was raised that my project was not sculpture, but architecture. Sculpture and architecture have a common characteristic, namely the composition of space. The case we are discussing is actually a border-line case, in which spatial development, in the plastic sense, is achieved by the use of architectonic means. In contrast to traditional sculpture, which generally represents an image placed into an outlying space (and this is also true of «modern sculpture»), it has been the primary intention here to compose an inner space as plastic, whereby the inner space leads to the outer. In this sense, this monument is an example of the «de-composition» of the concepts of sculpture and architecture, as also of the concept of «painting», which is evident here in the variously colored materials. The result is a composite work, a synthesis of sculpture – architecture – painting.

Material – Modernness

Certain objections have it that the materials I propose are «not modern», that the media I suggest are archaic in contrast with those of the constructivist projects. I gave this problem my careful consideration and this is my conclusion: If an idea is considered worthy of a monument, the monument should be durable. Construction and materials must be able to withstand the deteriorating effects of the elements. A construction such as that of the Eiffel Tower, or a similar one employing so-called modern materials is therefore out of the question. For this reason the outer surfaces of my monument are of granite and the inner surfaces of white marble, both of which are materials capable of withstanding the influence of time. The stainless steel column remains unchanged over a long period of time.

The Monumental – Scale
There were some who objected that my monument was too
small and not sufficiently monumental. What is the true scale
for a monument? And what is true monumentality? The
measure of a monument is its relationship to man. This monument in particular speaks to each human being as an individual. Its proportions should therefore be in proper relationship to the human proportions. This size is achieved by
having the scaling down inside the cubes correspond to
human measurements and also by making the passage in the
cubus 78–3/4"x 78–3/4", as wide as a double-width door. The
visitor thus finds himself in a well-defined and familiar spatial
relationship, which provides the scale for the entire monument.

Monumentality does not, therefore, depend on extension, but
is independent of it. We must be careful not to confuse monumentality with the gigantic. Our era has a tendency towards
the gigantic and the measure of real greatness is lost. It is
precisely in contrast with the fantastic heights, which were
proposed, for instance, in some complicated lattice-work and
other constructions measuring 98'6" × 393'9", that I planned
the size of my project very carefully, as I am convinced that
real monumentality is closely related to true greatness, i.e.,
the gigantic is not grand but rather bombastic, whereas
nowadays the small in size once again gains in strength.

Art of ideas – Concrete art
Certain critics maintain that we have now finally freed art
from the encumbering ideas and that the new art is an «art of

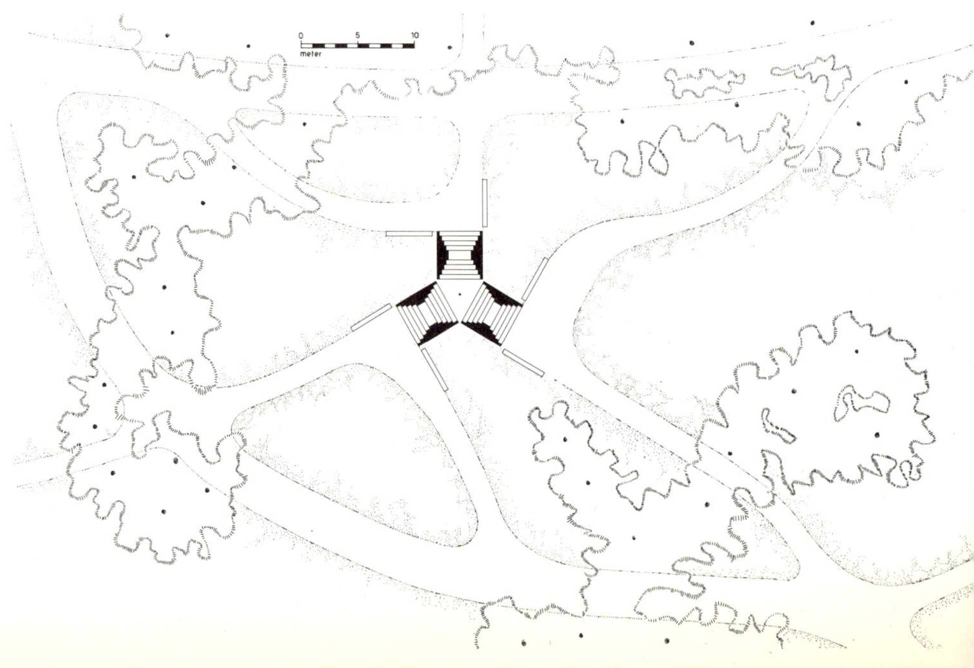

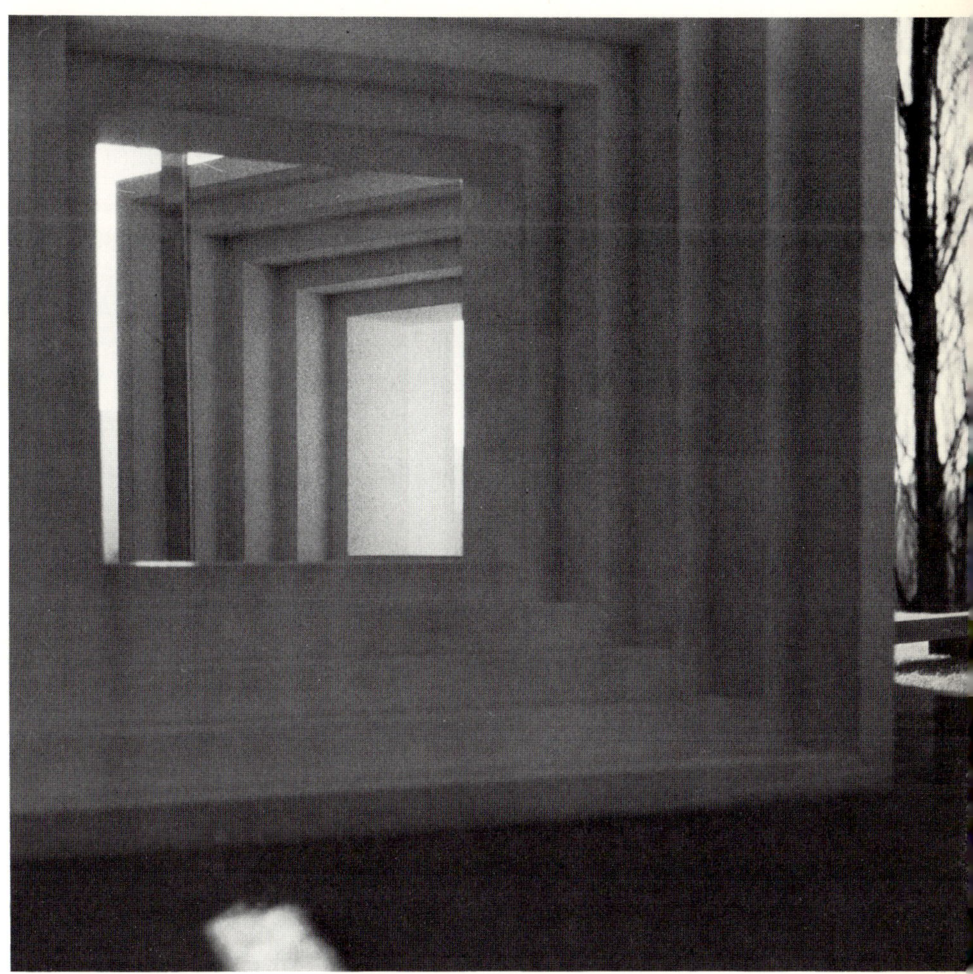

pure relationships», as Mondrian would have it. However, concrete art is the visible form of an idea, it provides an abstract concept with a concrete form. We believe that concrete art can help to express precisely those values which are not encumbered by literary or sentimental connotations. Thus, we attempt to create works with a direct, unequivocal symbolic force, such as symbols for unity, eternity, liberty, human dignity. My project attempted to contribute to this development, at the same time demonstrating that art of ideas and concrete art are not inherently contradictory.

Whether or not I have successfully created in this monument a synthesis between painting-sculpture-architecture, material and modernness, the size and the monumental, art based on ideas and concrete art, I am unfortunately unable to determine, since a proper evaluation of the effect is not possible without actual execution.

The following is a summary of what I have stated above, taken from the explanatory report handed in to the jury:

Idea

As a symbol of unyielding resistance and the power of free determination, a triple-sided column stands at the center, one edge facing each entrance.

As a symbol of freedom, the space opens outwards on all sides.

Due to the differences in level, the passage must be"worked for".

Towards the outside, the entire construction forms a unity composed of large, protective surfaces.

Form

The triple-sided column serves as a mirror, reflecting the image of its surroundings. In contrast to the spatial experience of the three inwardly stepped cubes, the relationship of the column to the human being is not equivalent to that of the latter to the surroundings.

The column reflects a mirrored image which moves in a different way from the space through which the visitor is walking.

The space is developed from the inside outwards, i.e., contrary to the traditional concepts of sculpture, this plastic space has two fundamental aspects:

(1) Outwards: sharply-edged; elemental, closed.

(2) From the inside outwards, its many-faceted articulation is open on all sides.

Benches link the monument to its surroundings, extending the monument into space. They serve simultaneously as seats, as spatial links with the surroundings and to limit the ground plan.

Execution

The stainless steel column at the center is exactly ground and polished, precise as a mirror. The cubes are composed of gray granite slabs on the outside. The interior is entirely of white marble.

The benches are of the same gray granite as the outer surfaces of the cubes.

The perimeter of the cubes is 157-1/2" which is also the height of the steel column.

[1952]

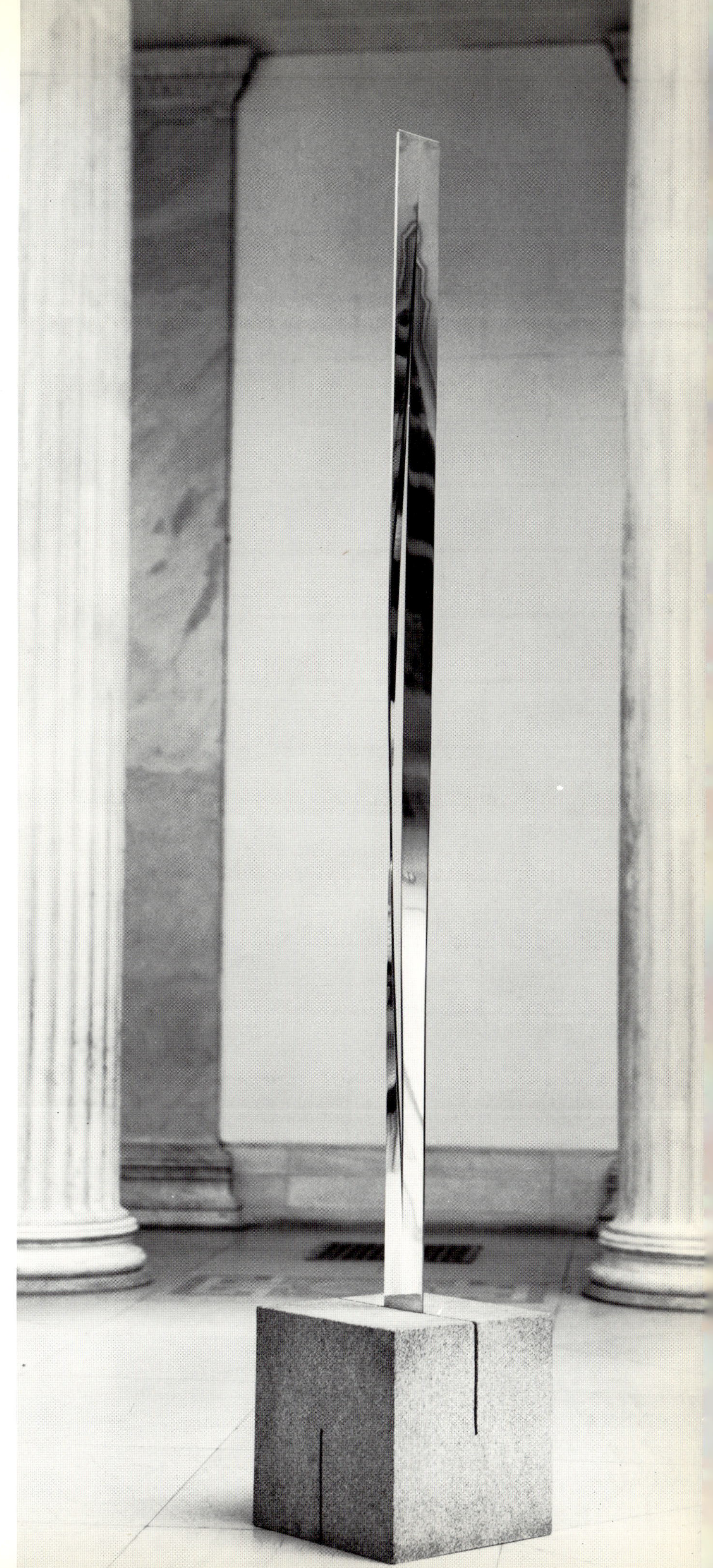

1953
Continuous Surface in Form of a Column
brass, height, 121″, (307 cm),
Albright-Knox Art Gallery, Buffalo,
Gift of Seymour H. Knox

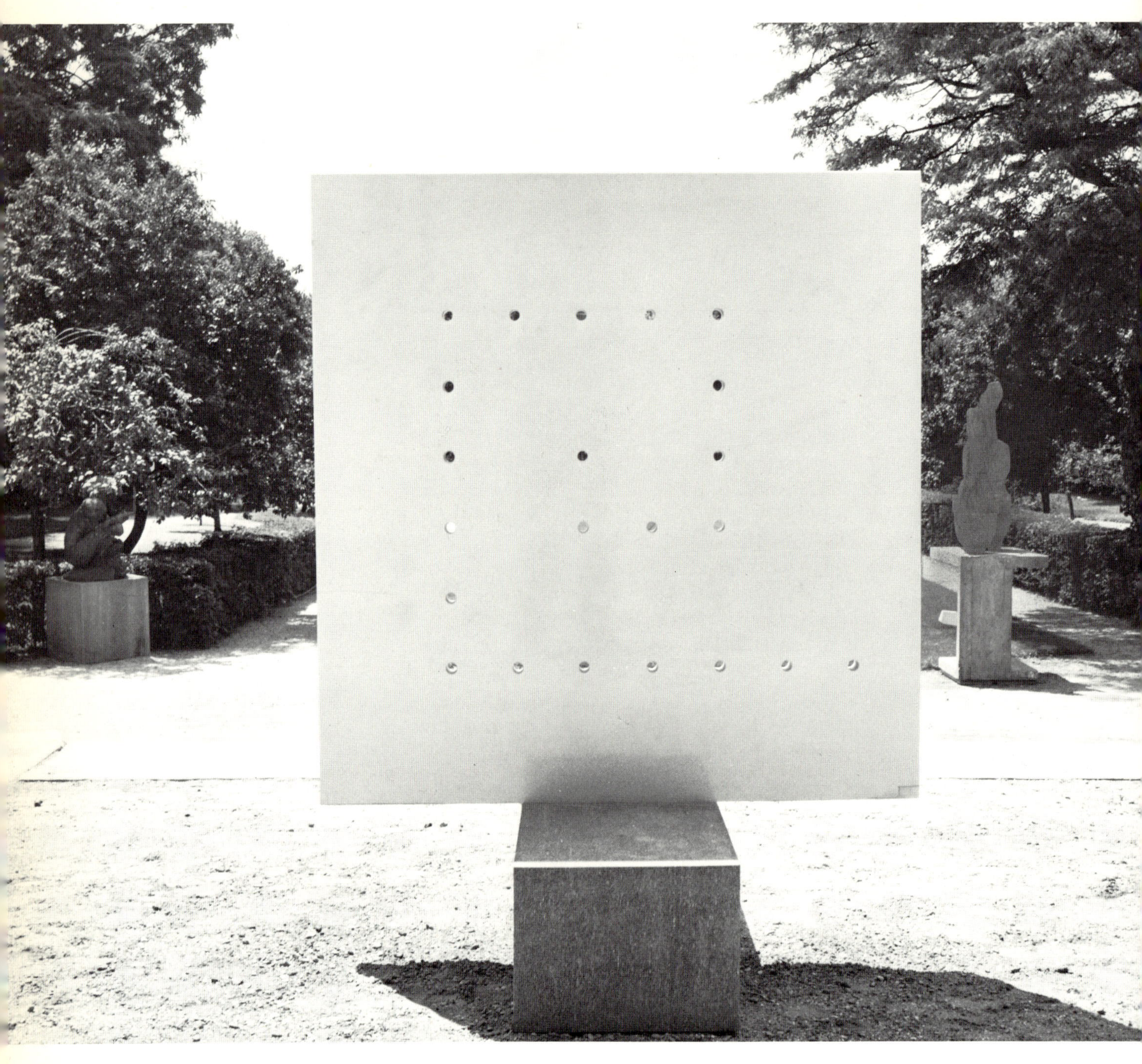

1953
«22»
marble, 55¹/₈″ × 3¹/₈″ × 55¹/₈″,
(140 × 8 × 140 cm)

1955
Accents out of Six Zones
oil on canvas, 41³⁄₈″ × 27¹⁄₂″,
(105 × 70 cm)

1955–69
Red Ninth
oil on canvas, 31½″ × 31½″,
(80 × 80 cm)

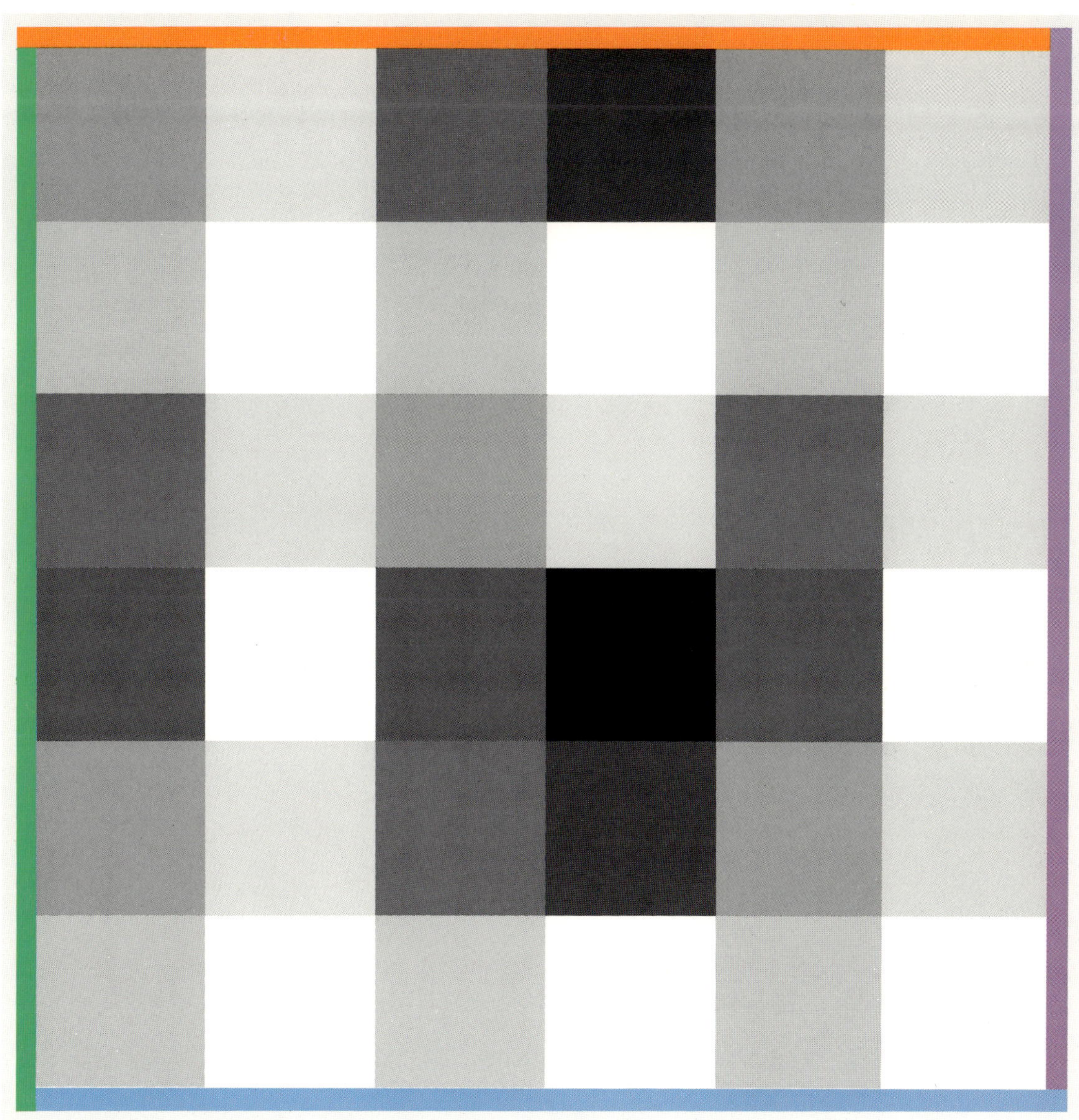

1956
One Black to Eight Whites
oil on canvas, 39⅜″ × 39⅜″,
(100 × 100 cm)

1958–60
Integration of Four Systems
oil on canvas, 26″ × 26″, (66 × 66 cm)

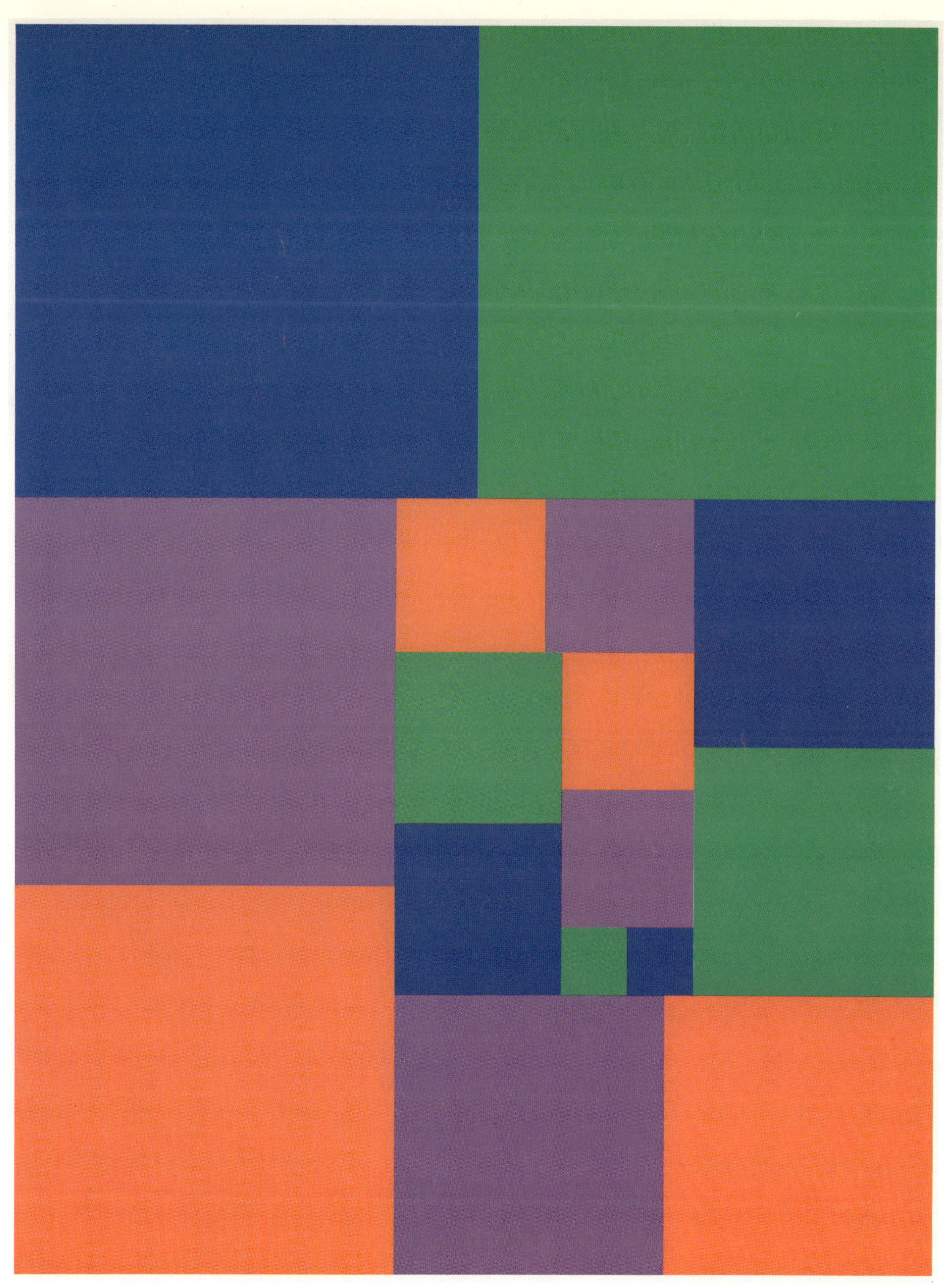

1958–62
Two Groups of Double Colors
oil on canvas, 36⅝″ × 28″,
(93 × 71 cm)

115

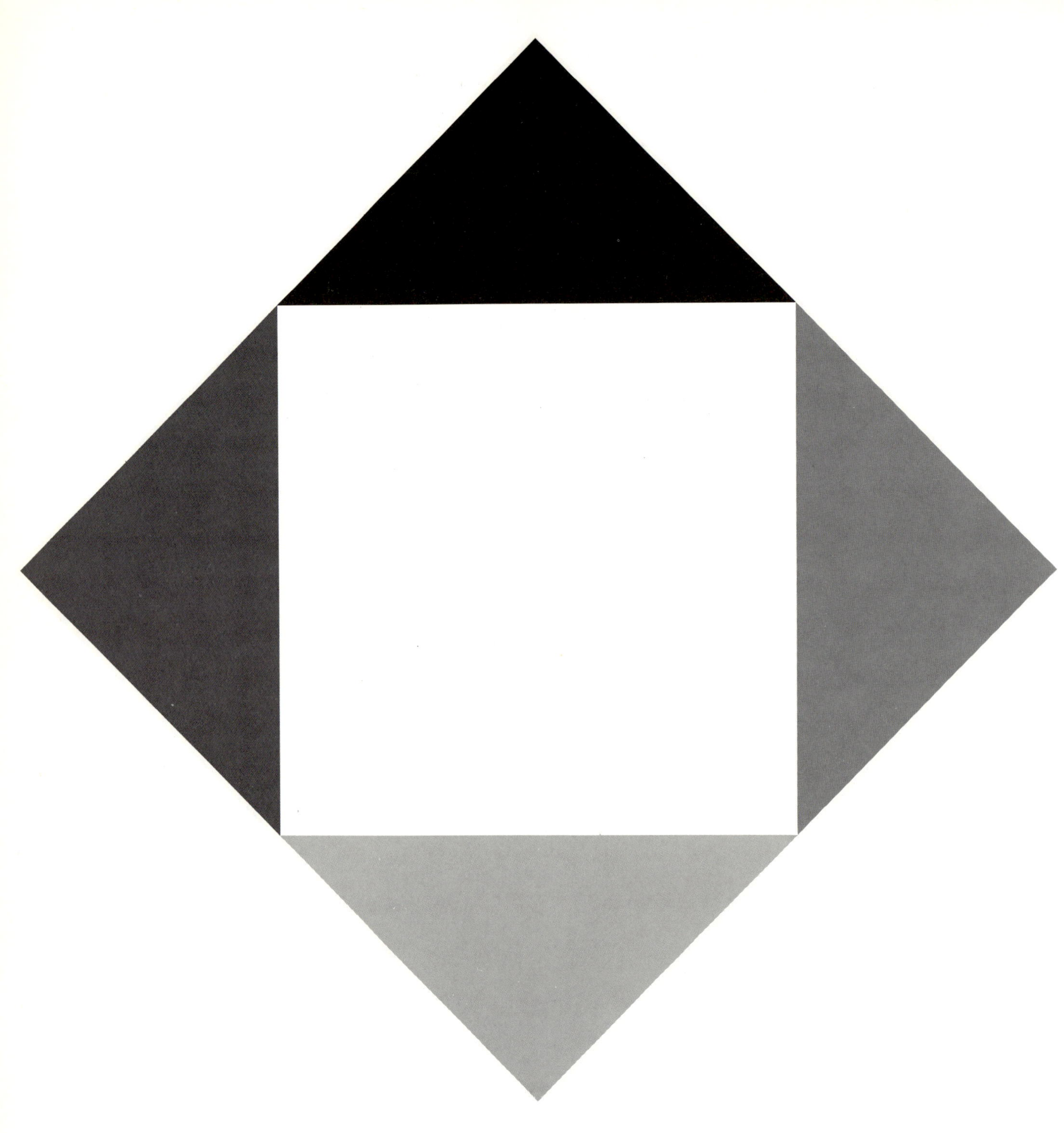

1959
White Element
oil on canvas, diagonal, 26¾",
(68 cm)

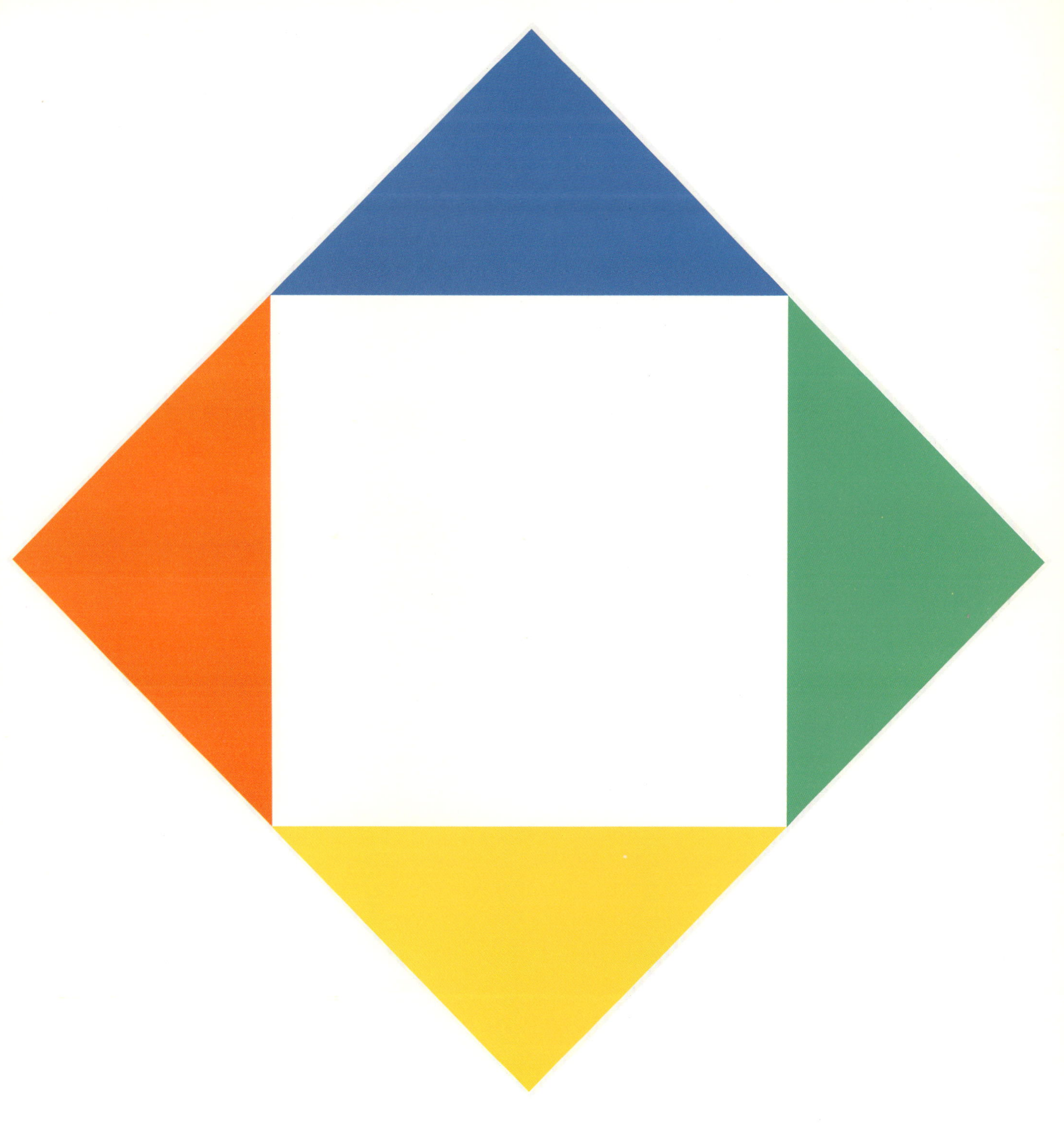

1959
White Resulting from Complementary
Colors
oil on canvas, diagonal, 26¾″,
(68 cm)

117

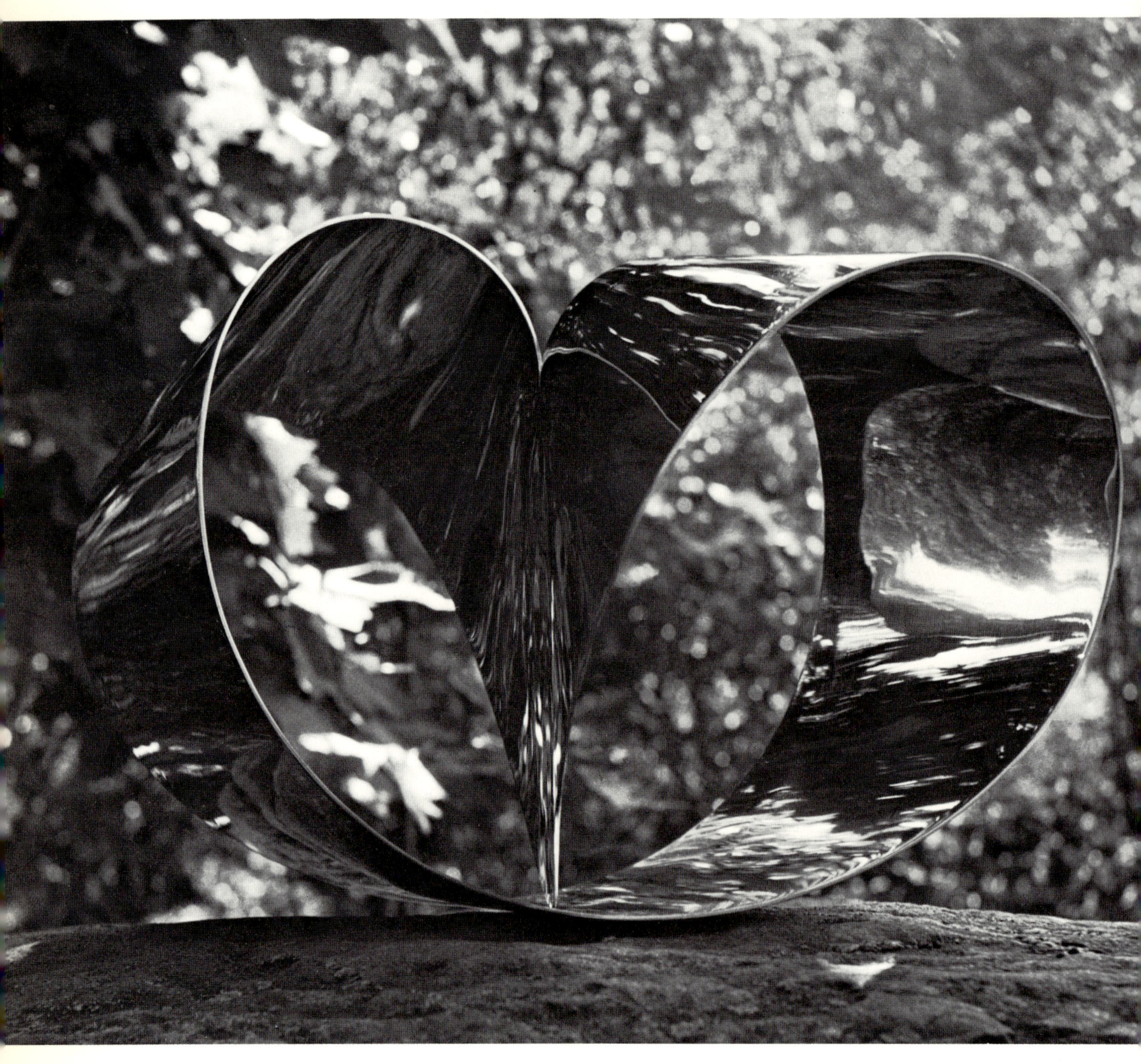

1959
Mono-angulated Surface in Space
gilt brass, 24¾″ × 16½″ × 14¼″,
(63 × 42 × 36 cm),
Detroit Institute of Arts, Detroit,
Gift of W. Hawkins Ferry

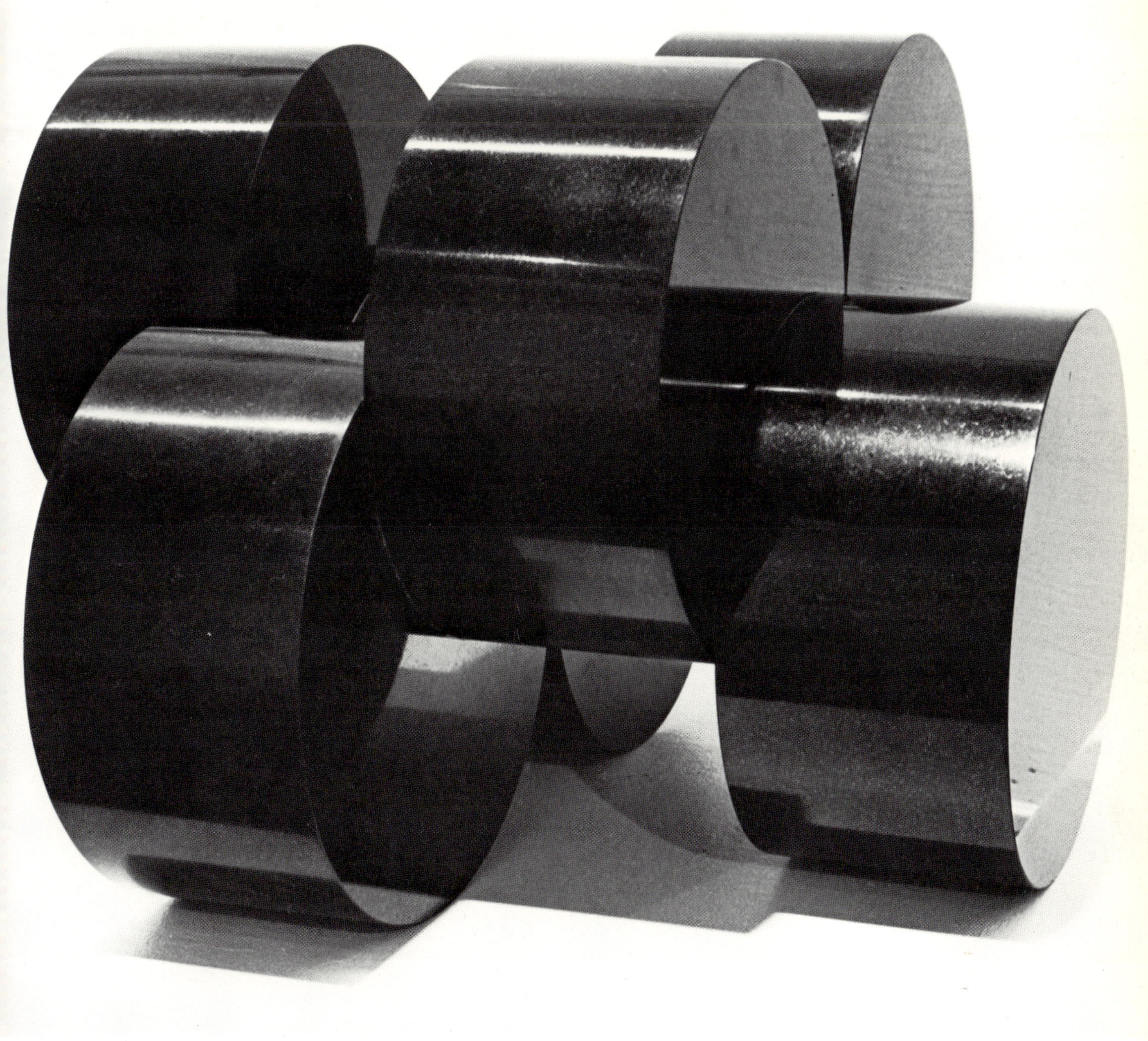

1959
Group of Six Cells
black granite, 14½″ × 22½″ × 20½″,
(37 × 57 × 52 cm),
Coll. Janice Ury, Belvedere, California

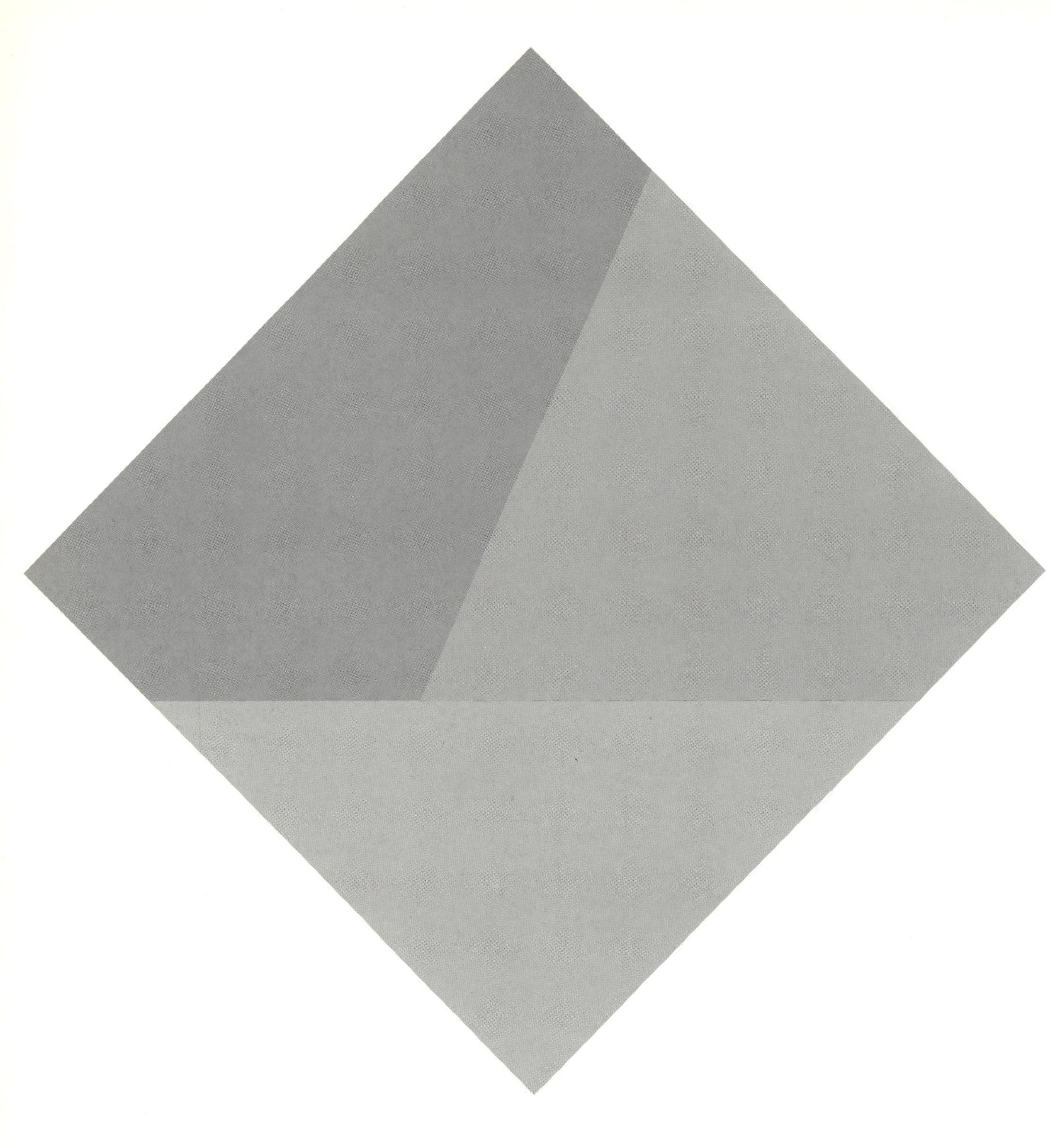

1959
Three Colored Parts of Equal Area
oil on canvas, diagonal, 67″, (170 cm)

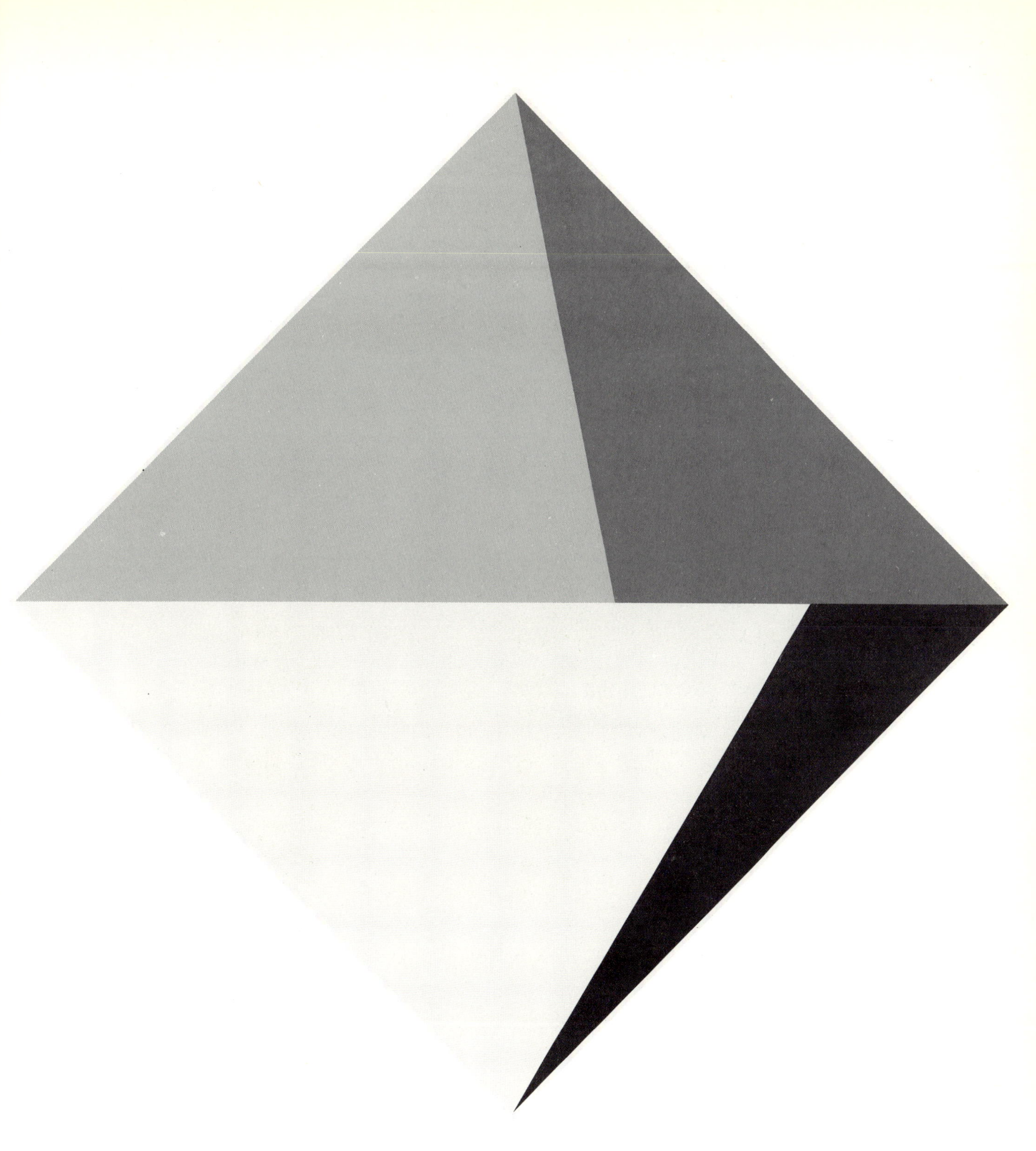

1960
Compression 4 : 3 : 2 : 1
oil on canvas, diagonal, 44½″,
(113 cm)

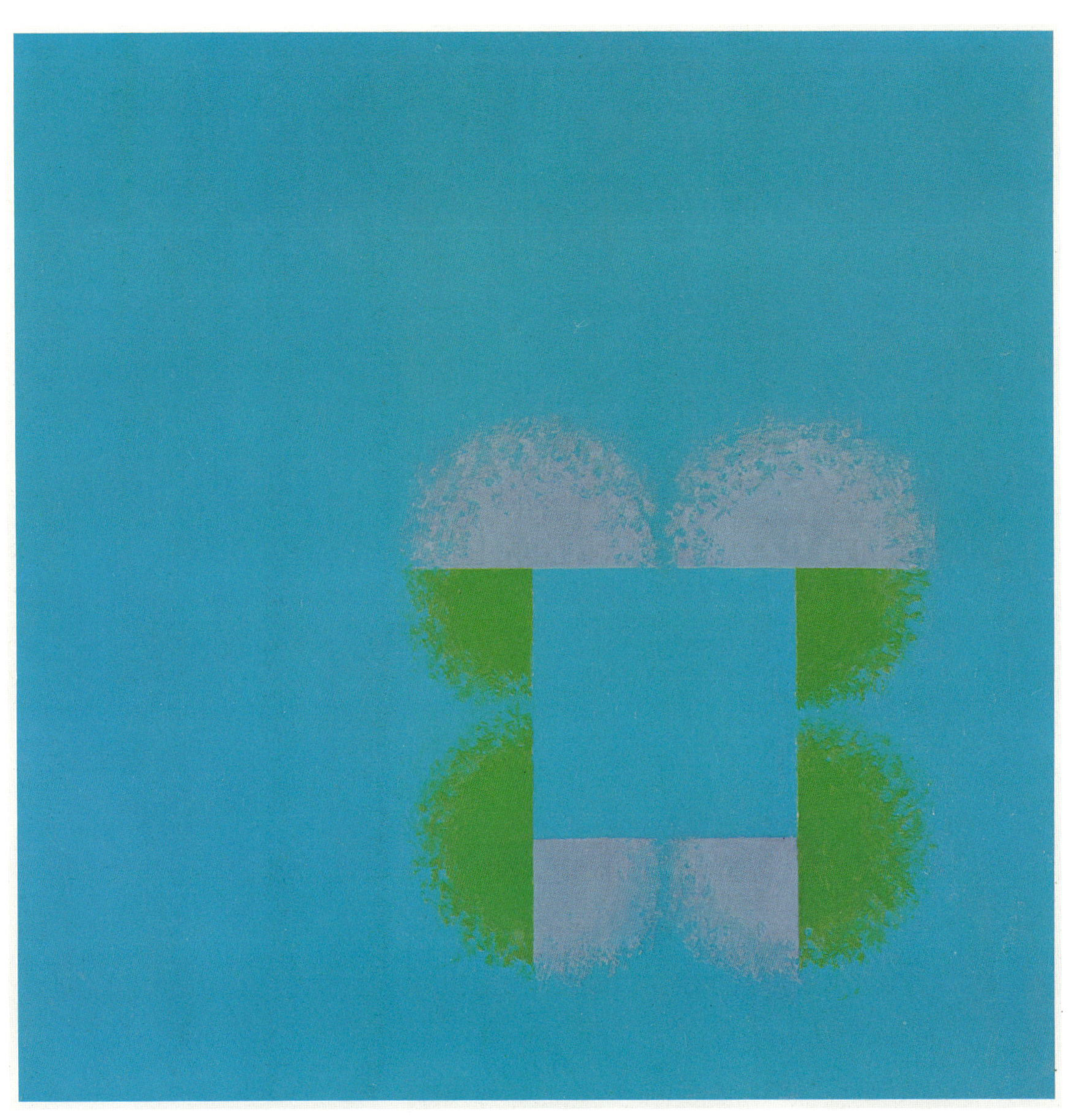

1960
Square Within the Square
oil on canvas, 31½″ × 31½″,
(80 × 80 cm)

1960–61
Horizontal-Vertical Simalton Square
oil on canvas, diagonal, 44½″,
(113 cm)

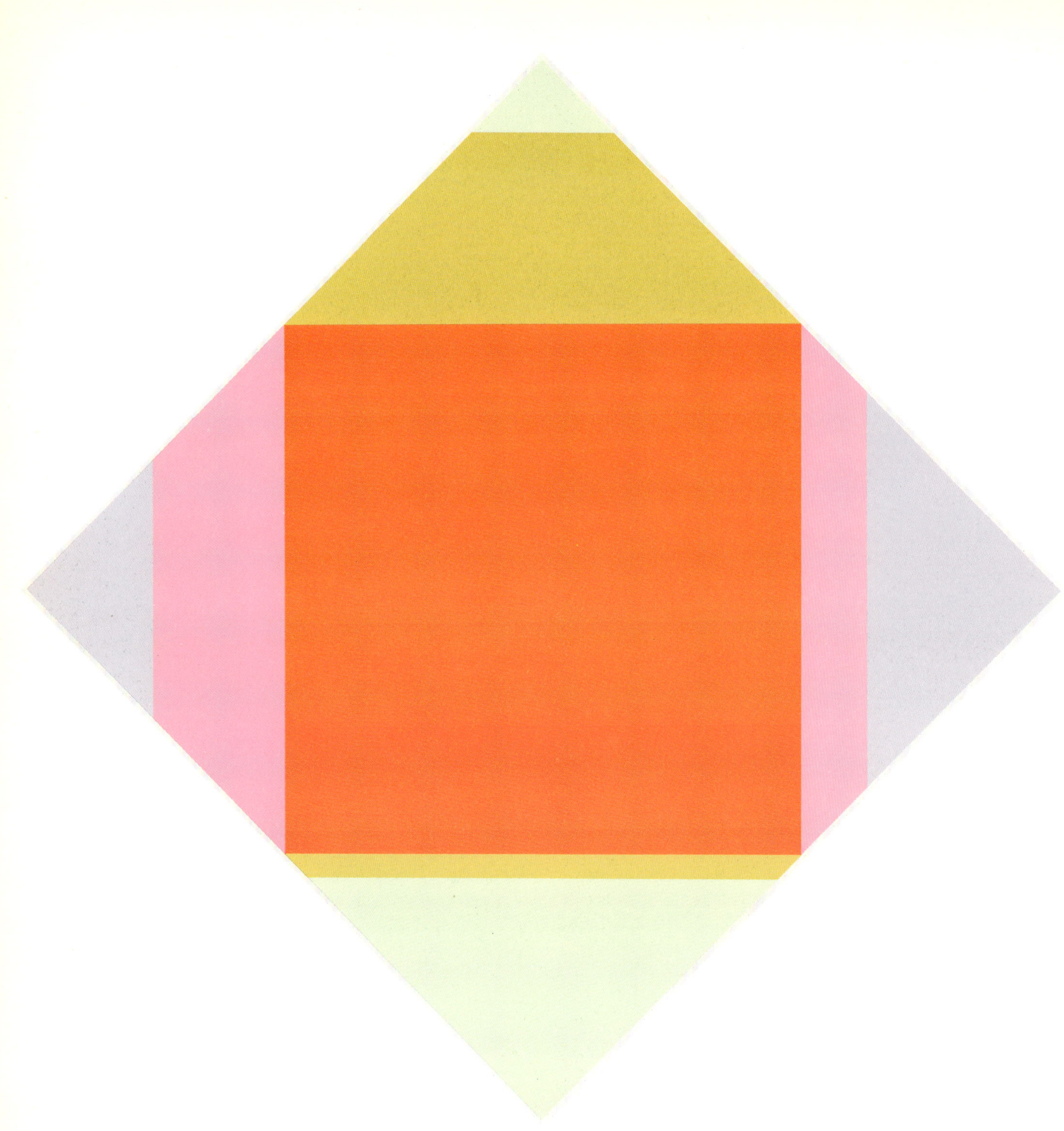

1961–62
Partitions Out of Orange
oil on canvas, diagonal, 67″, (170 cm)

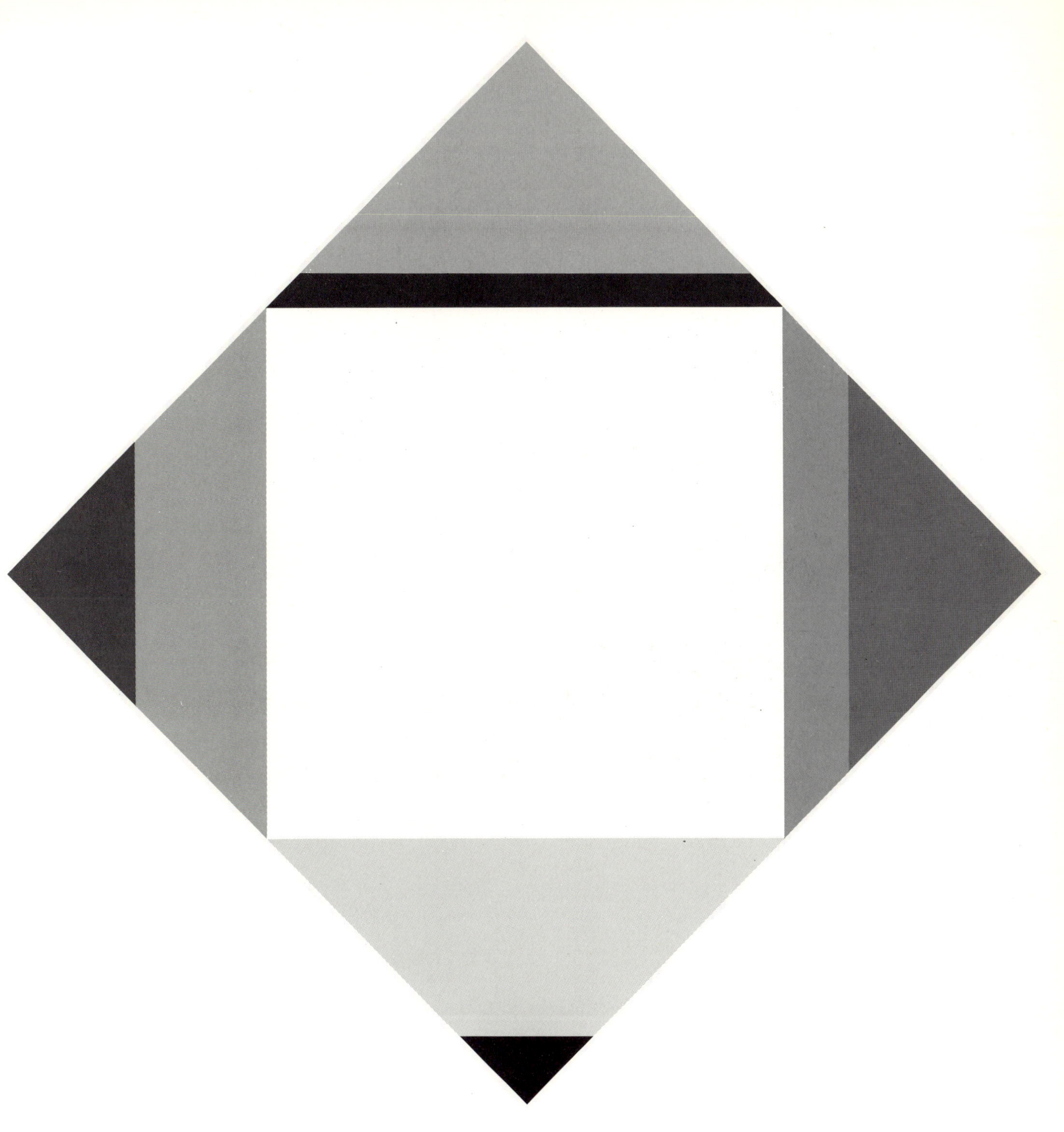

1961–65
Extension From Black to the White Square
oil on canvas, diagonal, 55½″,
(141 cm)
Coll. Richard Zeisler, New York

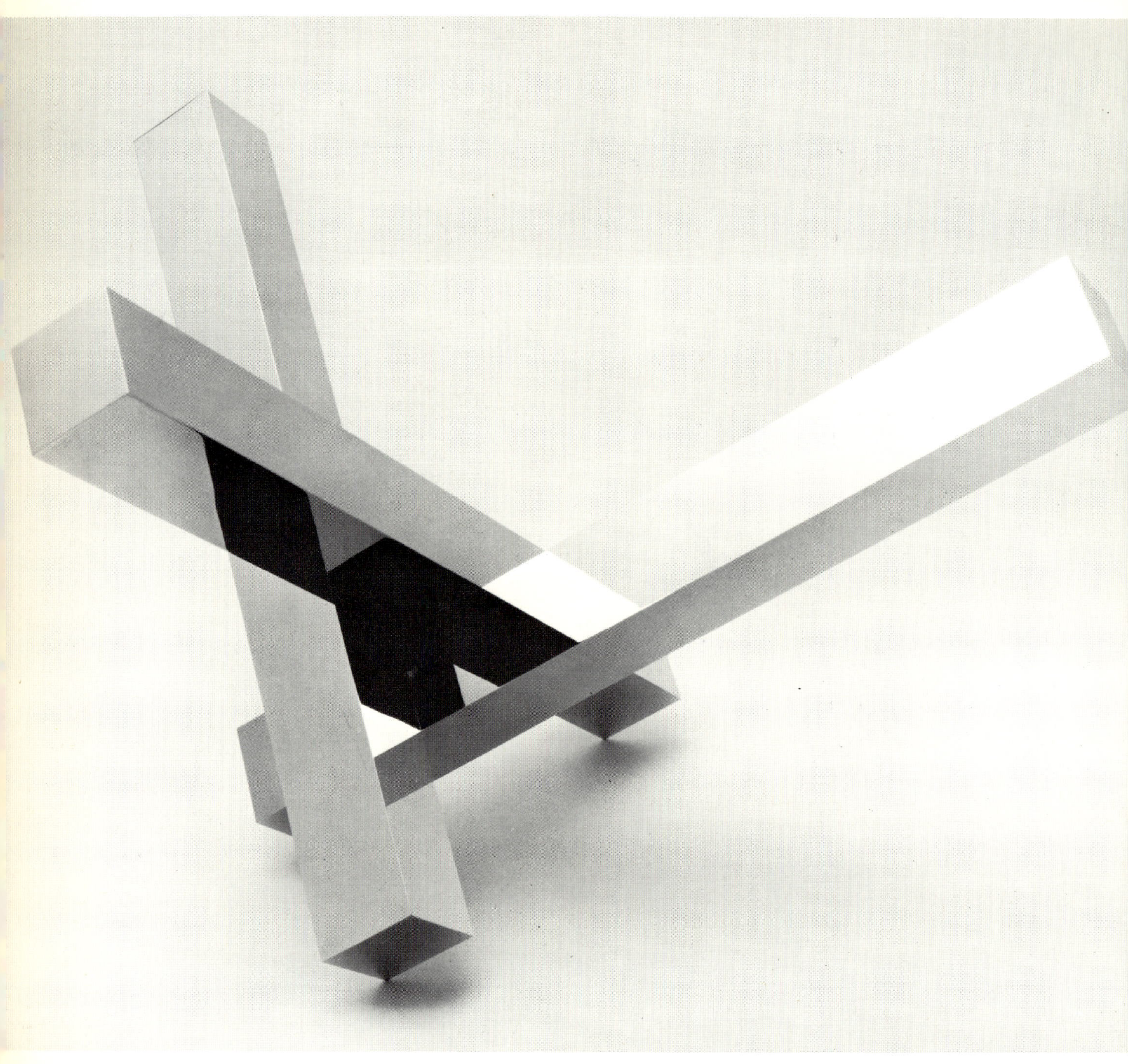

1961
Unity of Three Equal Volumes
black granite, 55⅛″ × 41⅜″ × 32¼″,
(140 × 105 × 82 cm)
Illustrated version in gilt brass

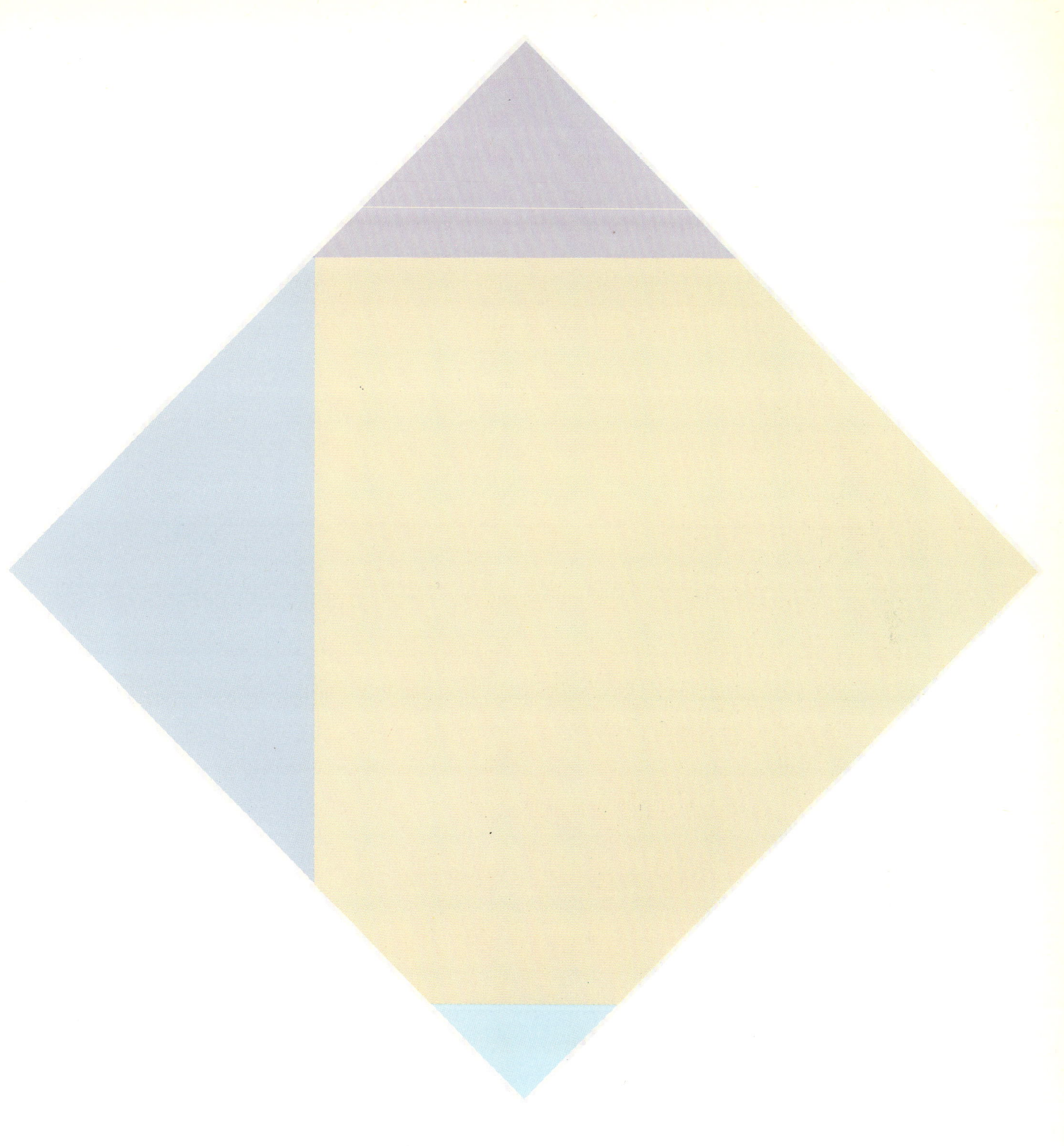

1962
Square from Parts
oil on canvas, diagonal, 55⁷/₈″,
(142 cm)

127

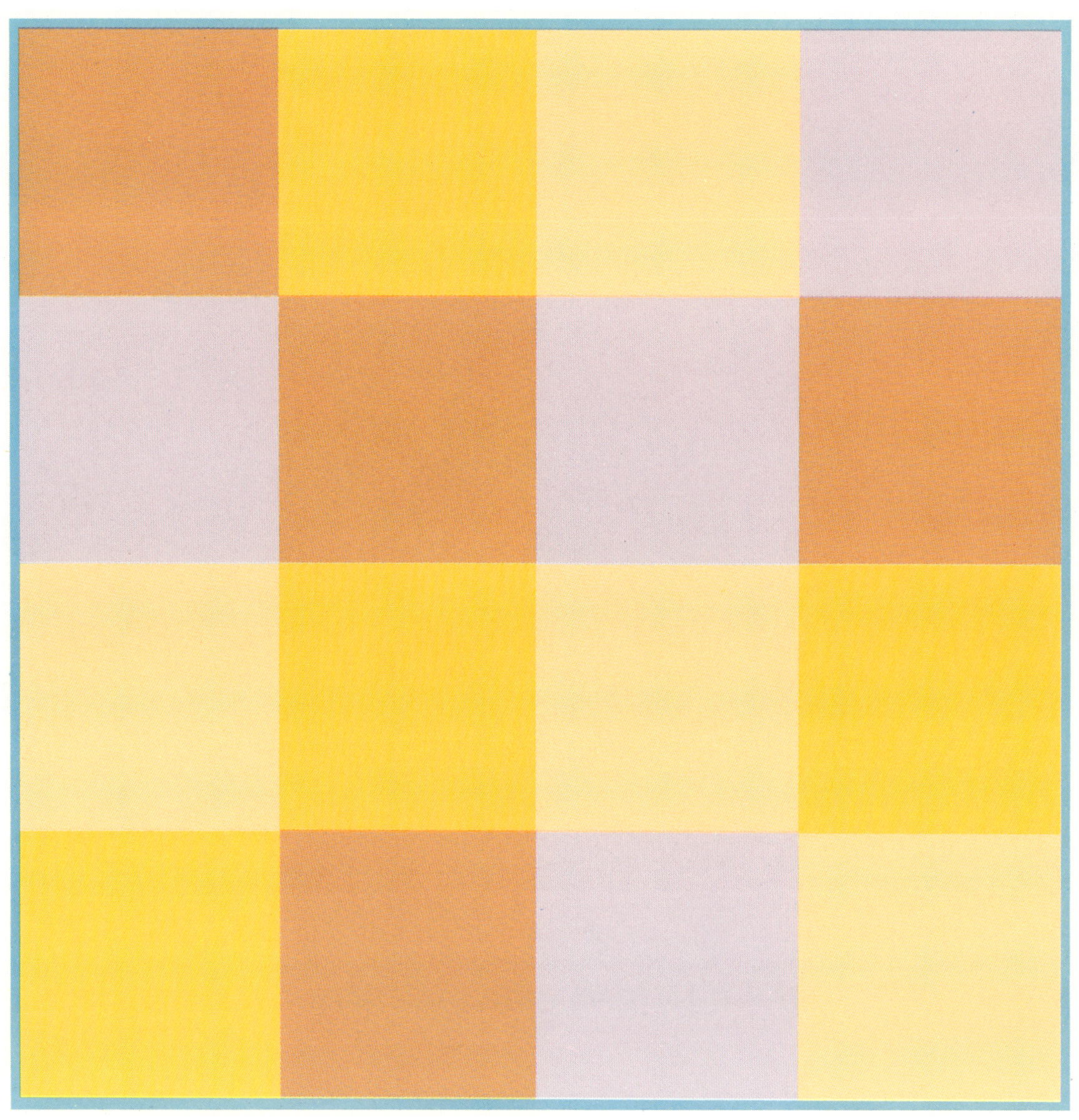

1963
Four Colors in Equal Groups
oil on canvas, 39⅜″ × 39⅜″,
(100 × 100 cm)

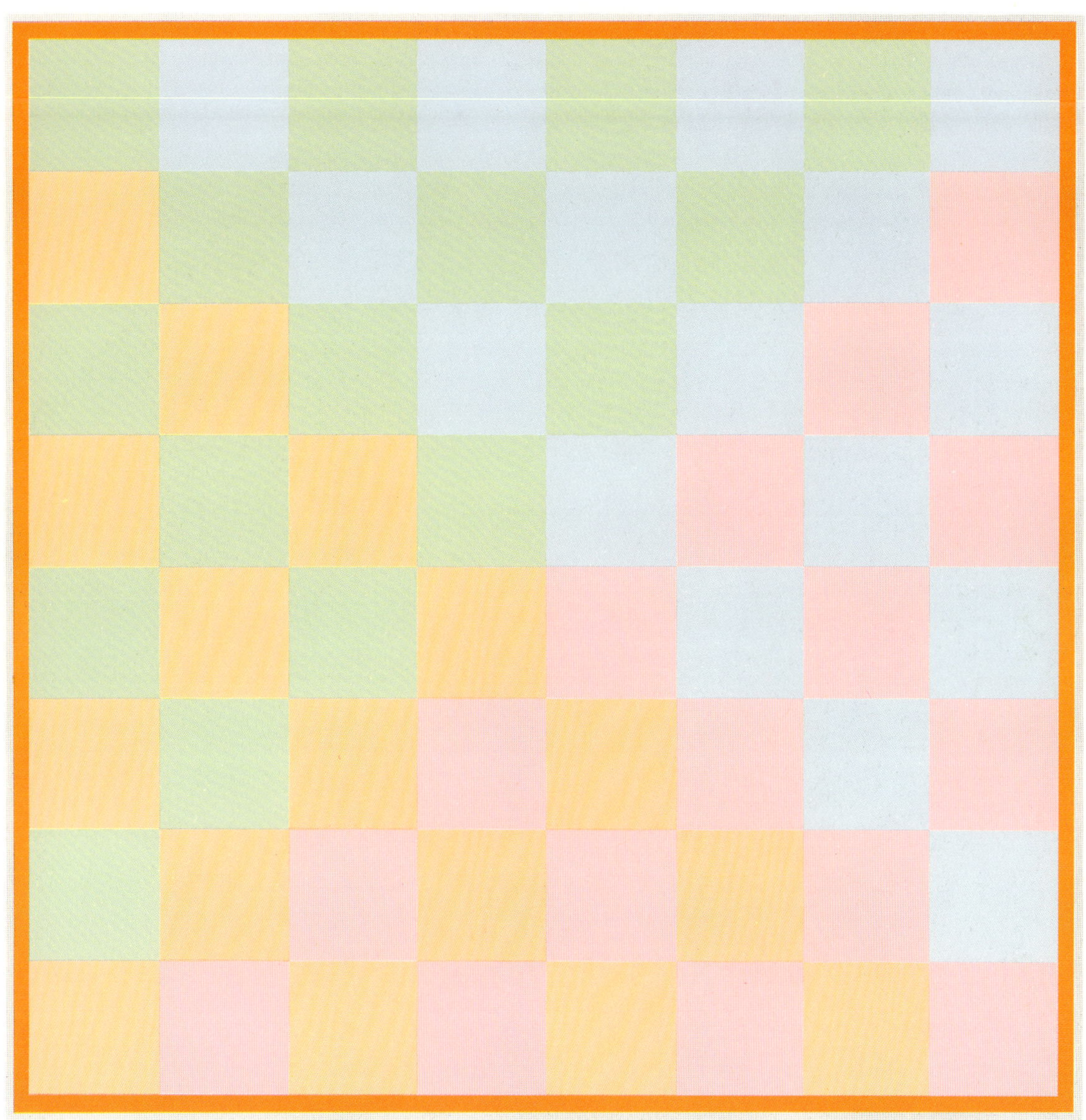

1963
Four Colors in Equal Groups
oil on canvas, 31½″ × 31½″,
(80 × 80 cm)

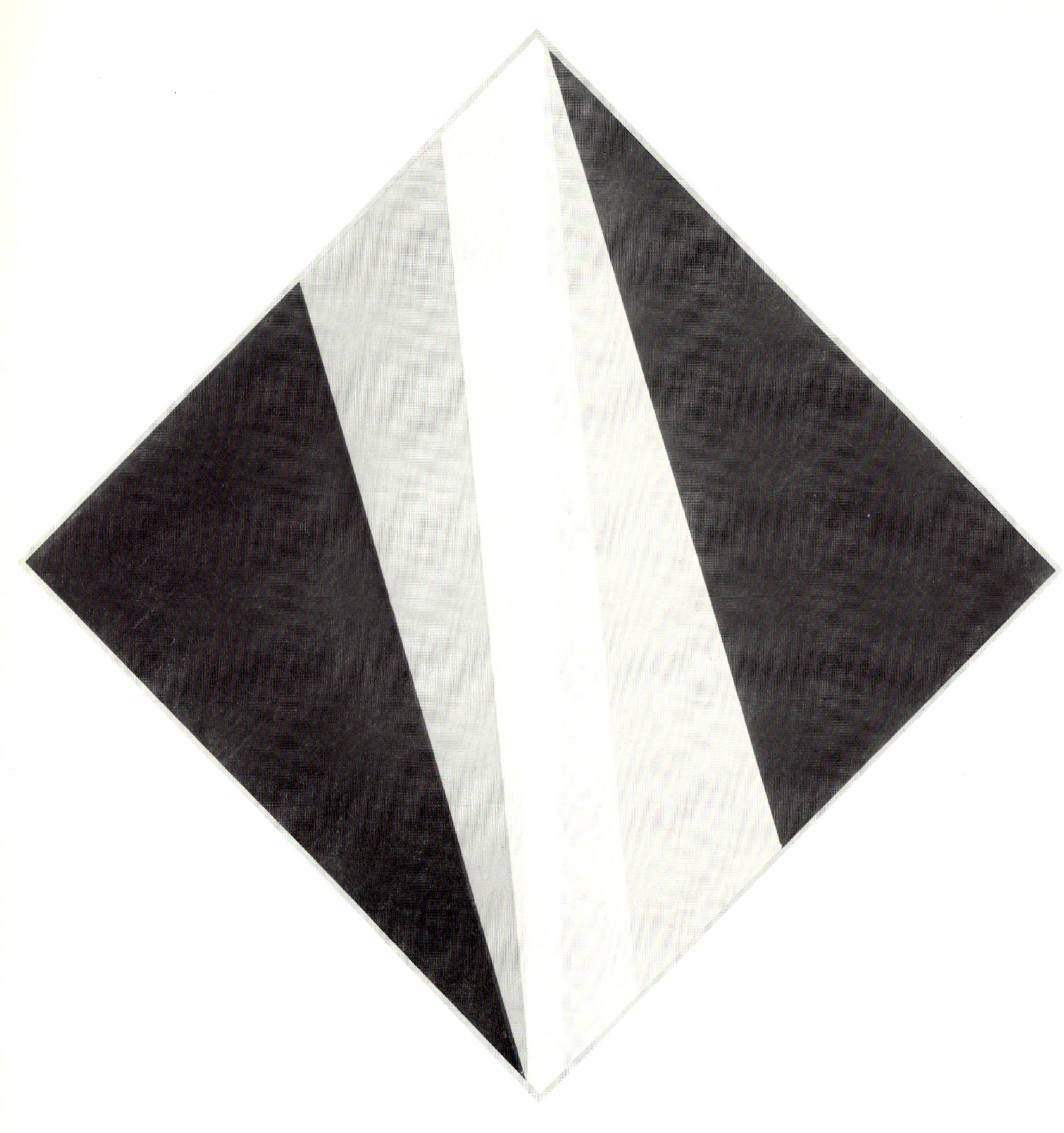

1964
Condensation Towards Brightness
oil on canvas, diagonal, 44½",
(113 cm)

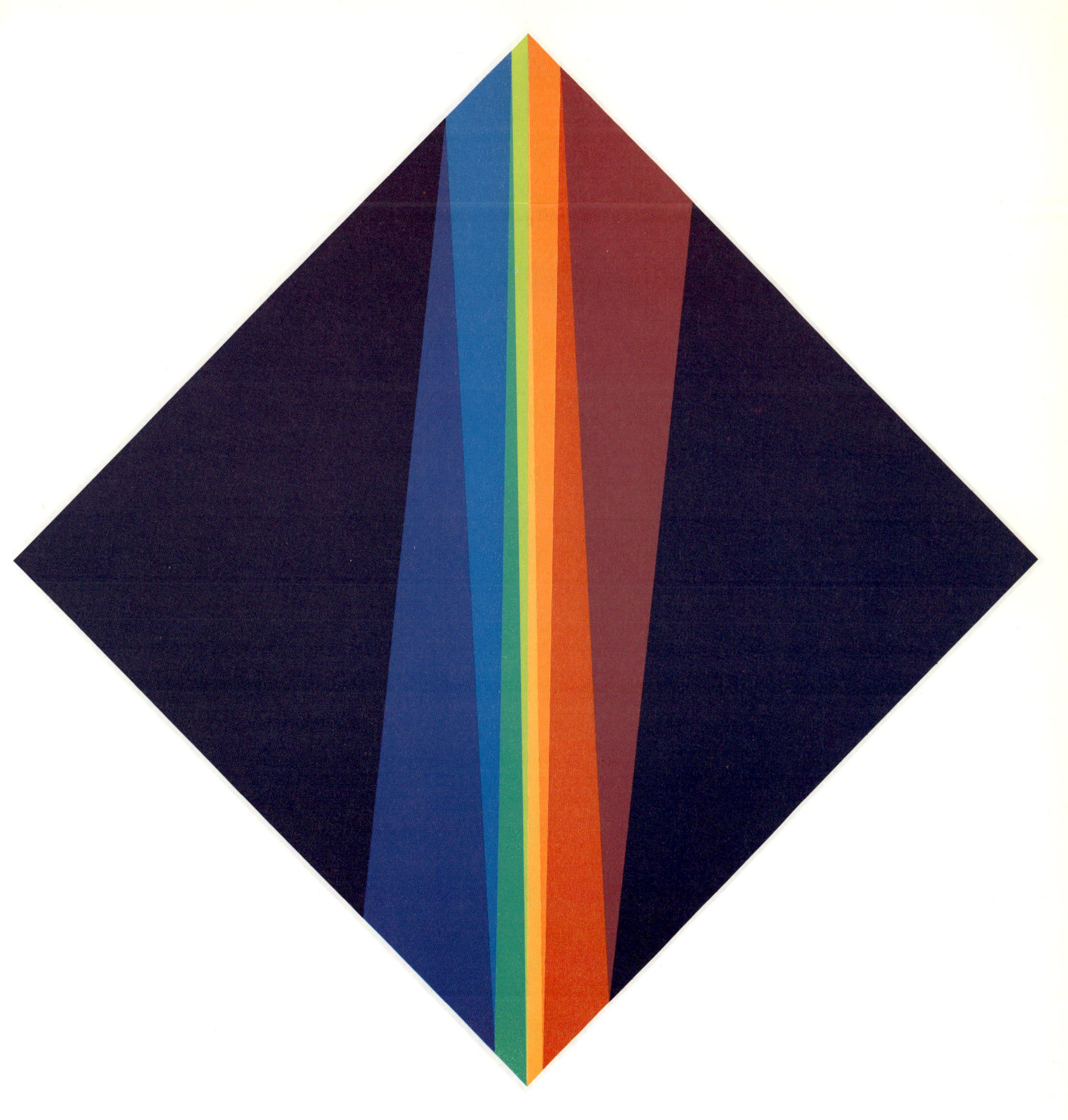

1964
Condensation Towards Yellow
oil on canvas, diagonal, 83½″,
(212 cm)

131

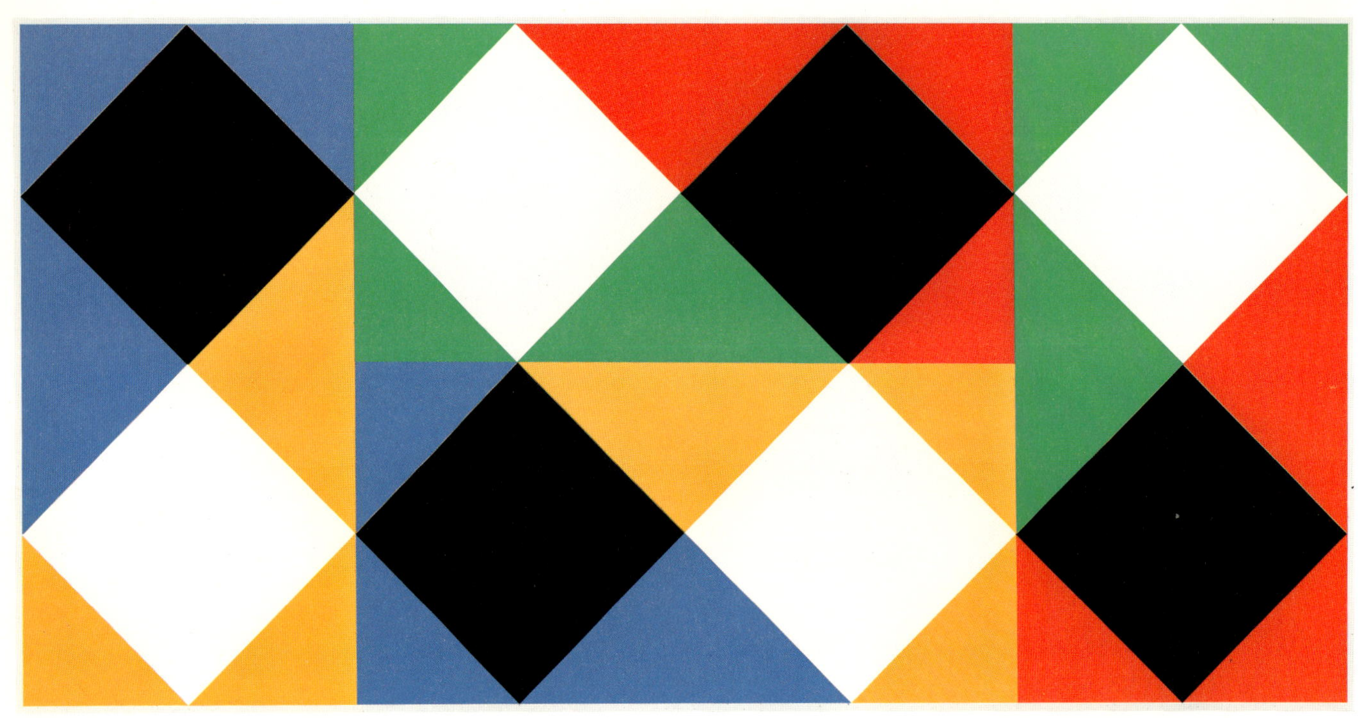

1964-66
Color Field With White & Black Accents
oil on canvas, 78¾″ × 39⅜″,
(200 × 100 cm)

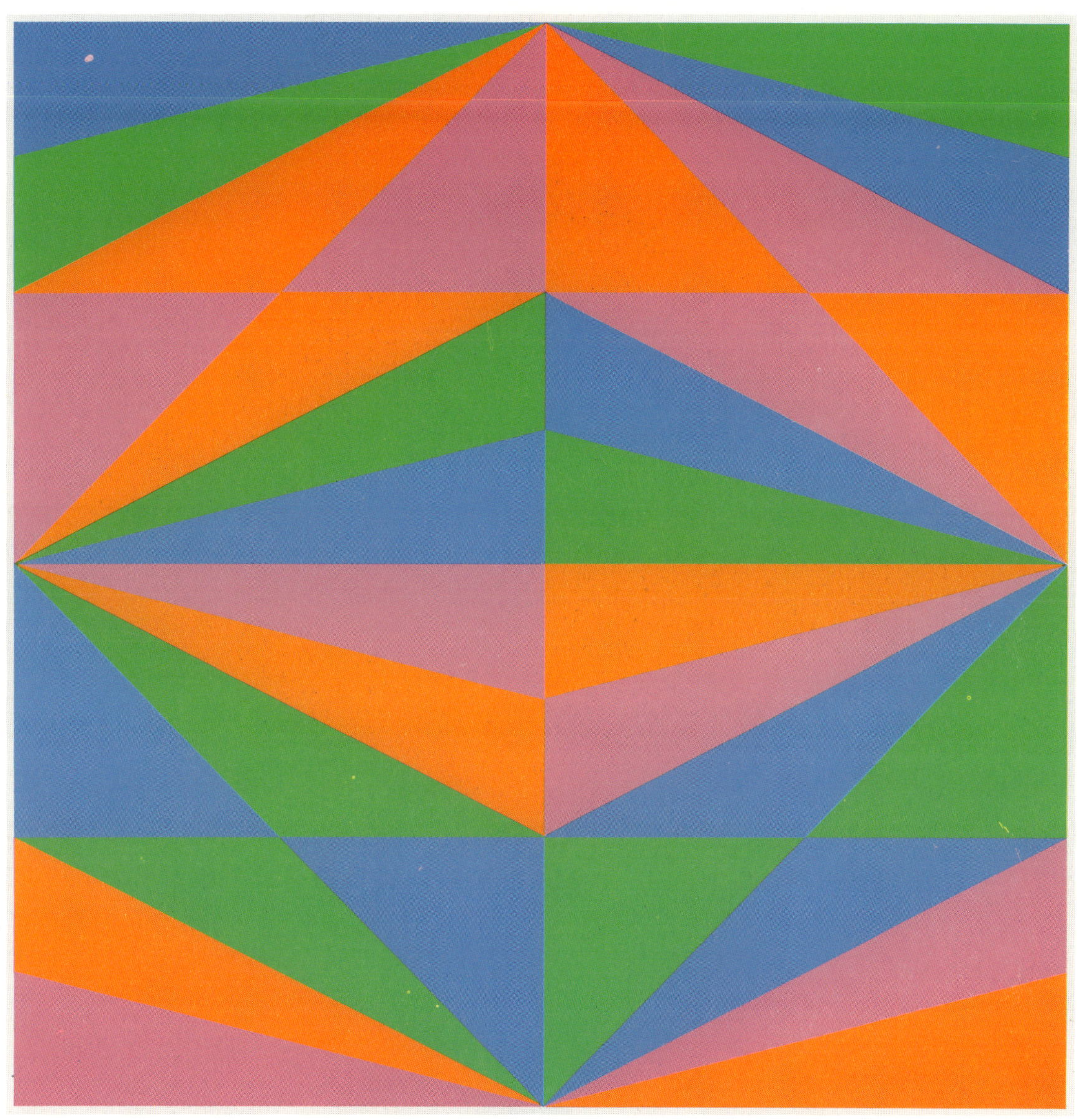

1965
Field of Thirty-two Parts in Four Colors
oil on canvas, 52″ × 52″,
(132 × 132 cm),
Albright-Knox Art Gallery, Buffalo,
Gift of Seymour H. Knox

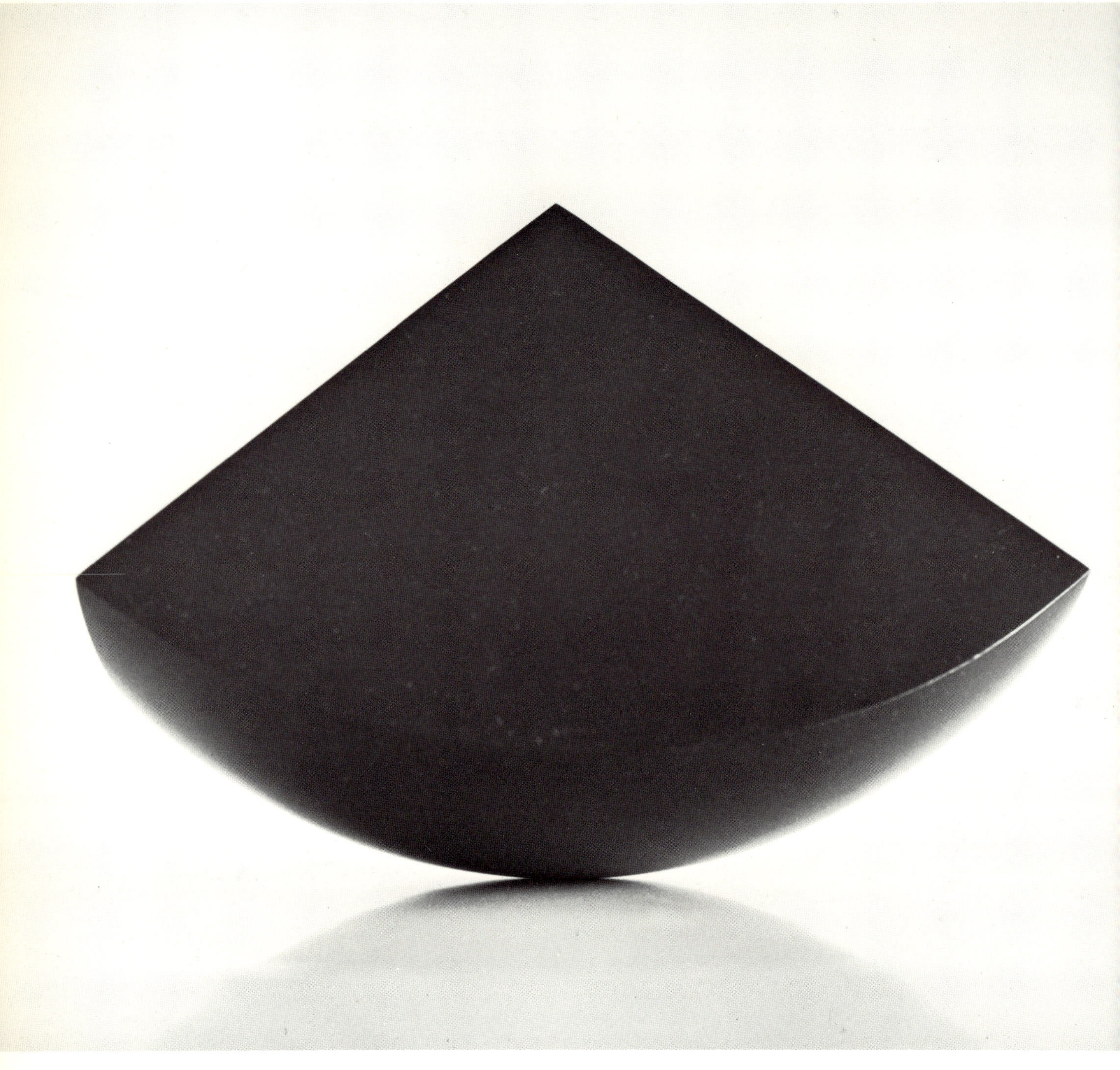

1965
*Pyramid in Form of One-Eighth of a
Sphere*
black granit, height, 19¾″,
(50 cm)

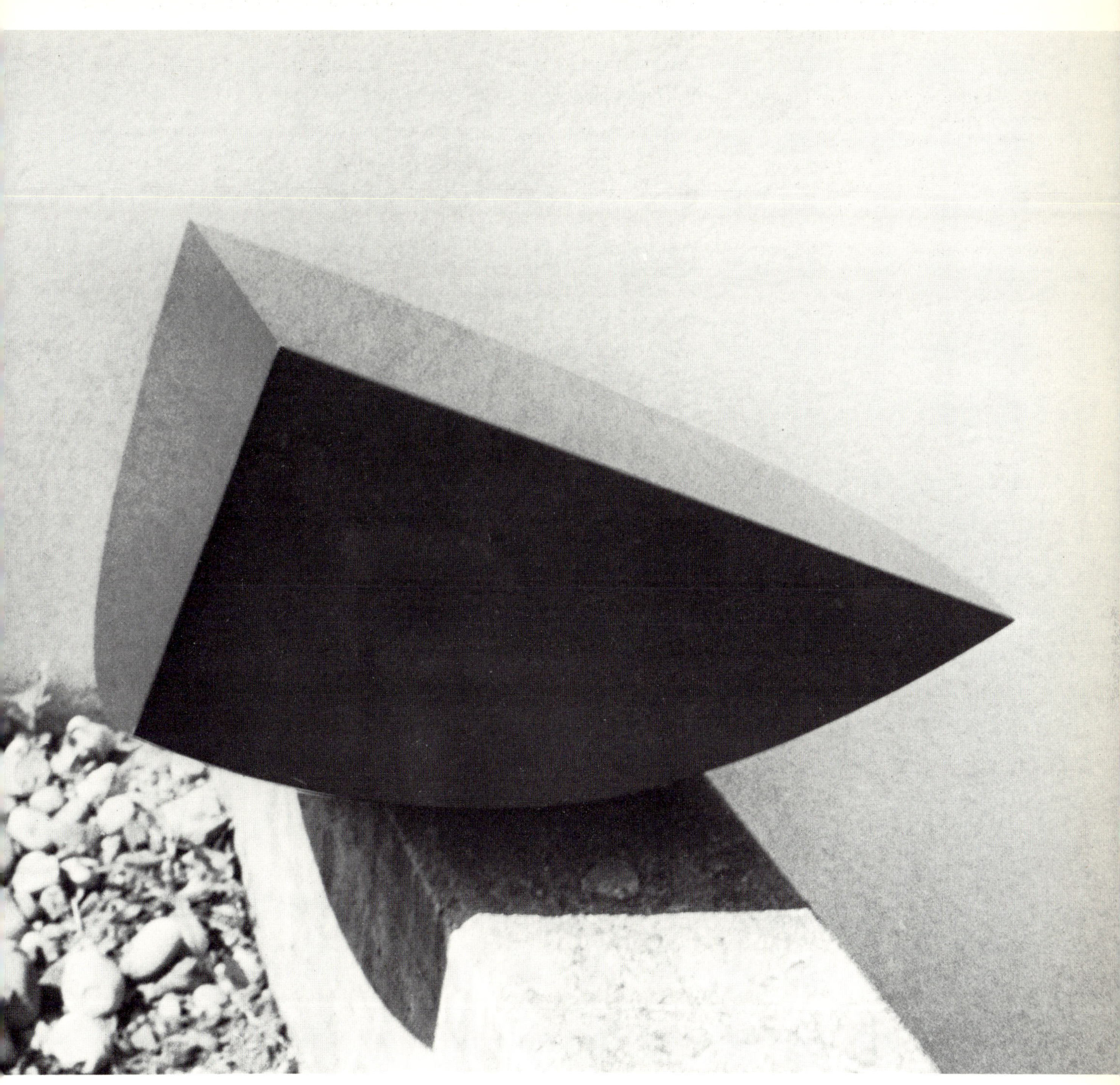

1965
*Irregular Pyramid over Surface of a
Sphere*
black granite, 28⅜″ × 19¾″ × 9⅞″,
(72 × 50 × 25 cm)

Max Bill perceives a connection of cause between structure and concrete art. It is in this spirit that in 1960 he conceived the retrospective exhibition *Konkrete Kunst – 50 Jahre Entwicklung (Concrete Art – 50 Years of Development)* organized by him in Zurich. The text which we are publishing here, first appeared in the volume, *Vision + Values* (1965), edited by Gyorgy Kepes. (It was published also in the French and German editions of this book under Editions de la Connaissance, Brussels, 1965.)

Structure as Art? Art as Structure?

One can consider art to be essentially identifiable as invention. The invention of means of expression; the first thrust into realms which contain as yet unknown aesthetic and formal possibilities.

That is the sense in which art presupposes something novel. The newness of the idea, newness of the themes, newness of the form. This kind of newness can be achieved in two ways: (a) in an individual way – which has its origin in the intellectual and psychological make-up of the artist; (b) in a more general way – which bases itself on experimenting with objective possibilities of form. In an extreme case (a) will lead to «art informel» or to a neo-dadaistic combination of materials; (b) leads to structure. On the one hand: materials in their «natural» condition, individually interpreted. On the other: tectonic laws which ultimately are schematically applied in a uniform distribution.

Even though amorphous material can be considered to posses an inner configuration – a structure of its own – in its natural condition, we can eliminate this kind of structure from our consideration, for as an inherent structure it is not accessible to aesthetic or visual arguments, either in painting or in sculpture.

Tectonic laws are altogether different. They are accessible to aesthetic arguments for they are principally laws of order, and in the end art = order. In other words, art is neither a surrogate for nature, nor for individuality, nor for spontaneity. And where it appears as such, it is art only insofar as it informs the surrogate with order and form. Because order is so charactertistic of art, art begins to rely for order on the tectonic laws.

Now the question arises as to what a tectonic law, a law of order, as we know it in science, means with respect to art. That is, where does structure end and art begin?

Let us start with the extreme case: a plane is covered with a uniform distribution in the sense in which this is understood in statistics; or a uniform network extends into space. This is an order which could be uniformly extended without end. Such an order we here call a structure. In a work of art, however, this structure has its limits, either in space or on the plane. Here we have the basis for an aesthetic argument in the sense that a choice has to be made: the possible, aesthetically feasible extension of the structure. Actually it is only through this choice to limit the arbitrarily extensible structure on the basis of verifiable arguments that a discernible principle of order becomes comprehensible.

But is a choice, or the setting of limits, sufficient for the creation of a work of art? This question arises mainly because, since the radical attempt to dispense with all individualistic stylistic expression beginning with Mondrian, no reduction can be extreme enough. This also arises because the aesthetic information offered by the means of expression is dwindling sharply: *neither locatable nor measurable, neither expressing nor indicating an order:* producing a neuter with aesthetic pretensions. The aesthetic quality is beginning to withdraw into the most extreme reductions, into the most extreme objectivity, culminating ultimately in the negation of newness and of invention.

But invention always presupposes the discovery of new problems. The discovery of these new problems is individually determined. Art is unthinkable without the effort of the individual. Order on the other hand is impossible without an objectifying structure.

This means that art can originate only when and because individual expression and personal invention subsume themselves under the principle of order of the structure and derive from it a new lawfulness and new formal possibilities.

Such lawfulness and such inventions manifest themselves as rhythm in an individual case. Rhythm transforms the structure into form; i.e. the special form of a work of art grows out of the general structure by means of a rhythmic order.

[1965]

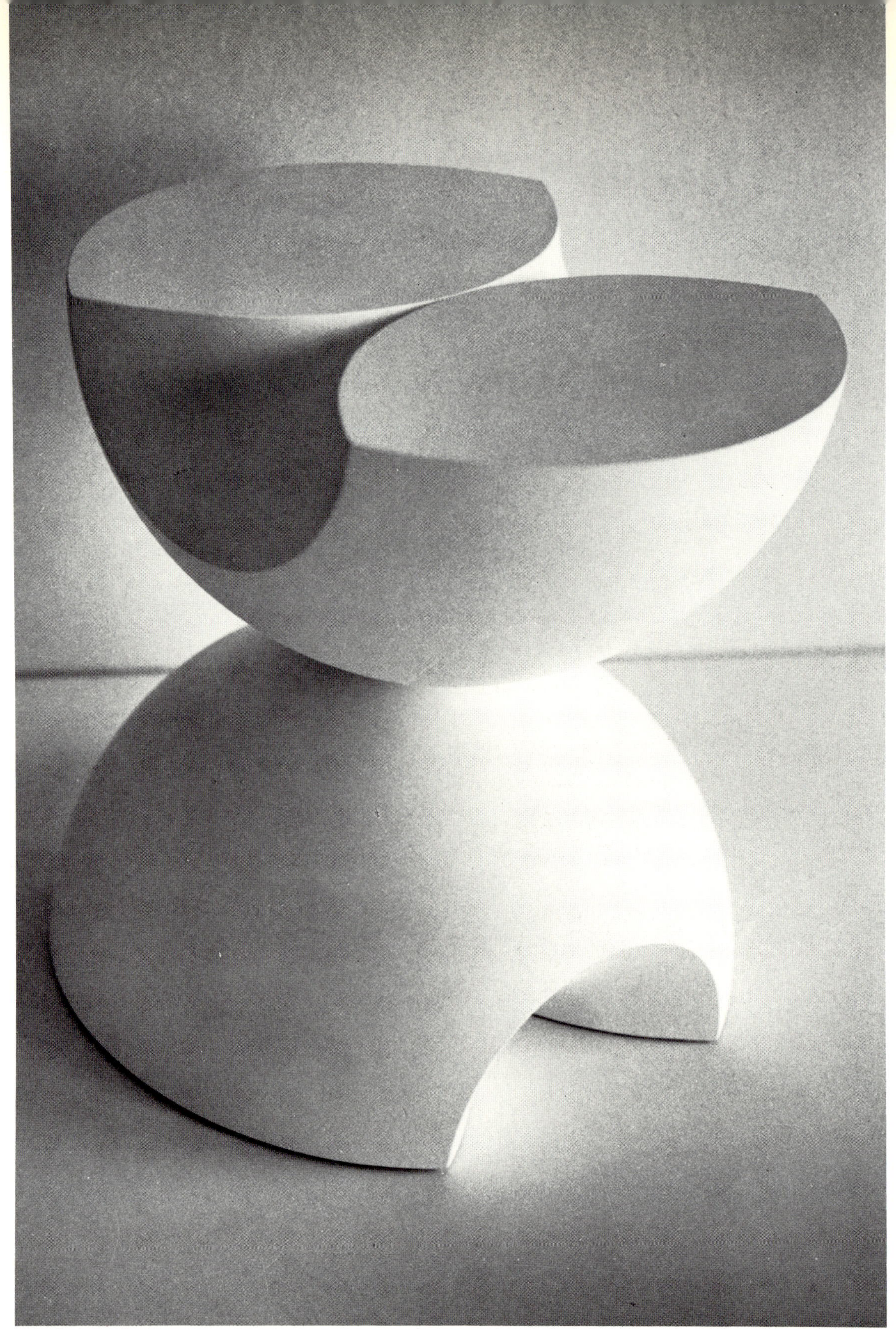

1965-66
Construction from a Spherical Ring
white silicon, 10½″ × 10½″
(26,5 × 26,5 cm)
The Carborundum Company, Niagara
Falls

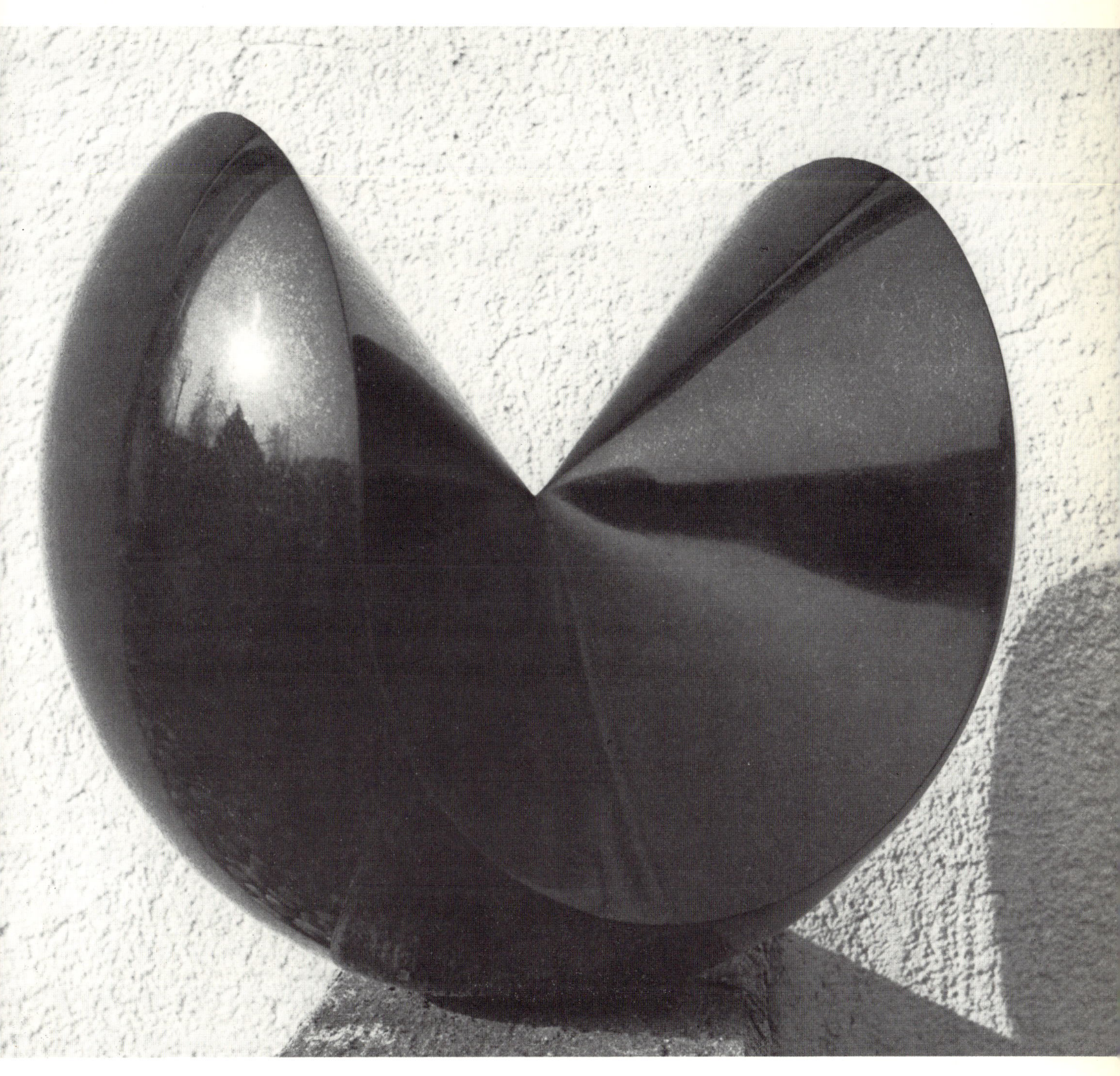

1965–66
Half Sphere Around One Axis
black granite, diameter, 39⅜″,
(100 cm)

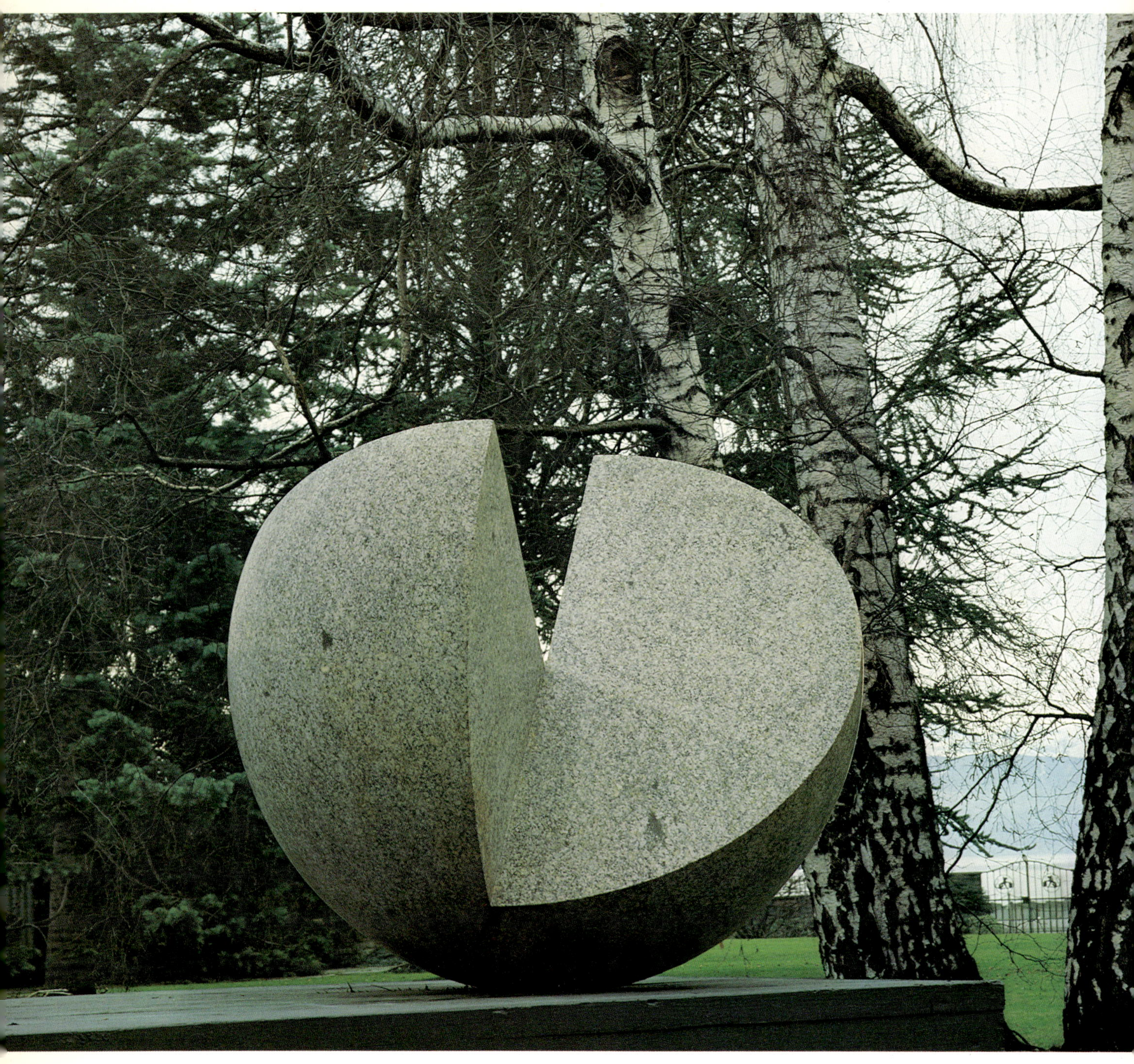

1965–66
Half Sphere Around Two Axes
grey granite, diameter, 47½″,
(120 cm)

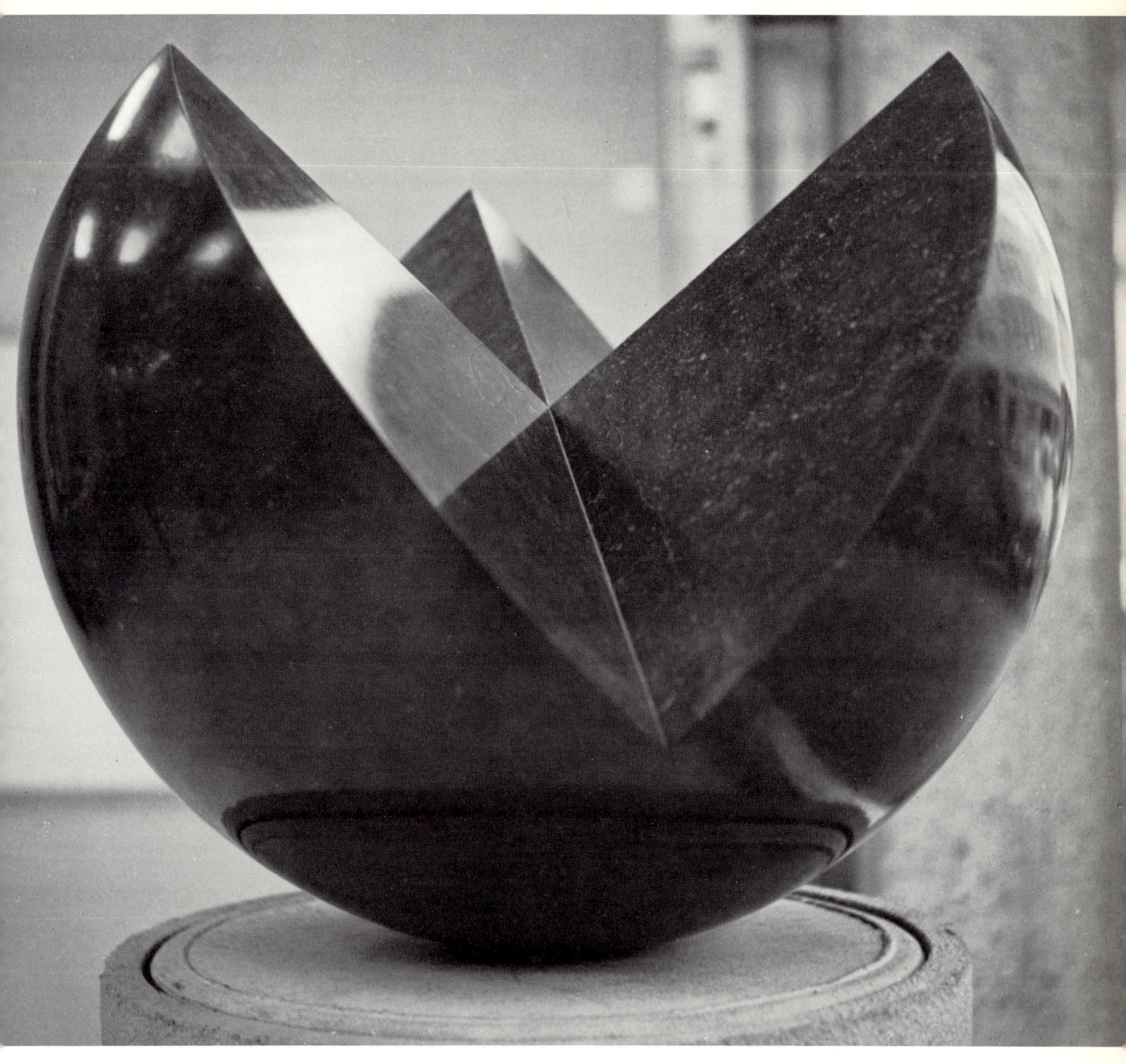

1965–66
Half Sphere Around Three Axes
black granite, diameter, 18″, (46 cm)

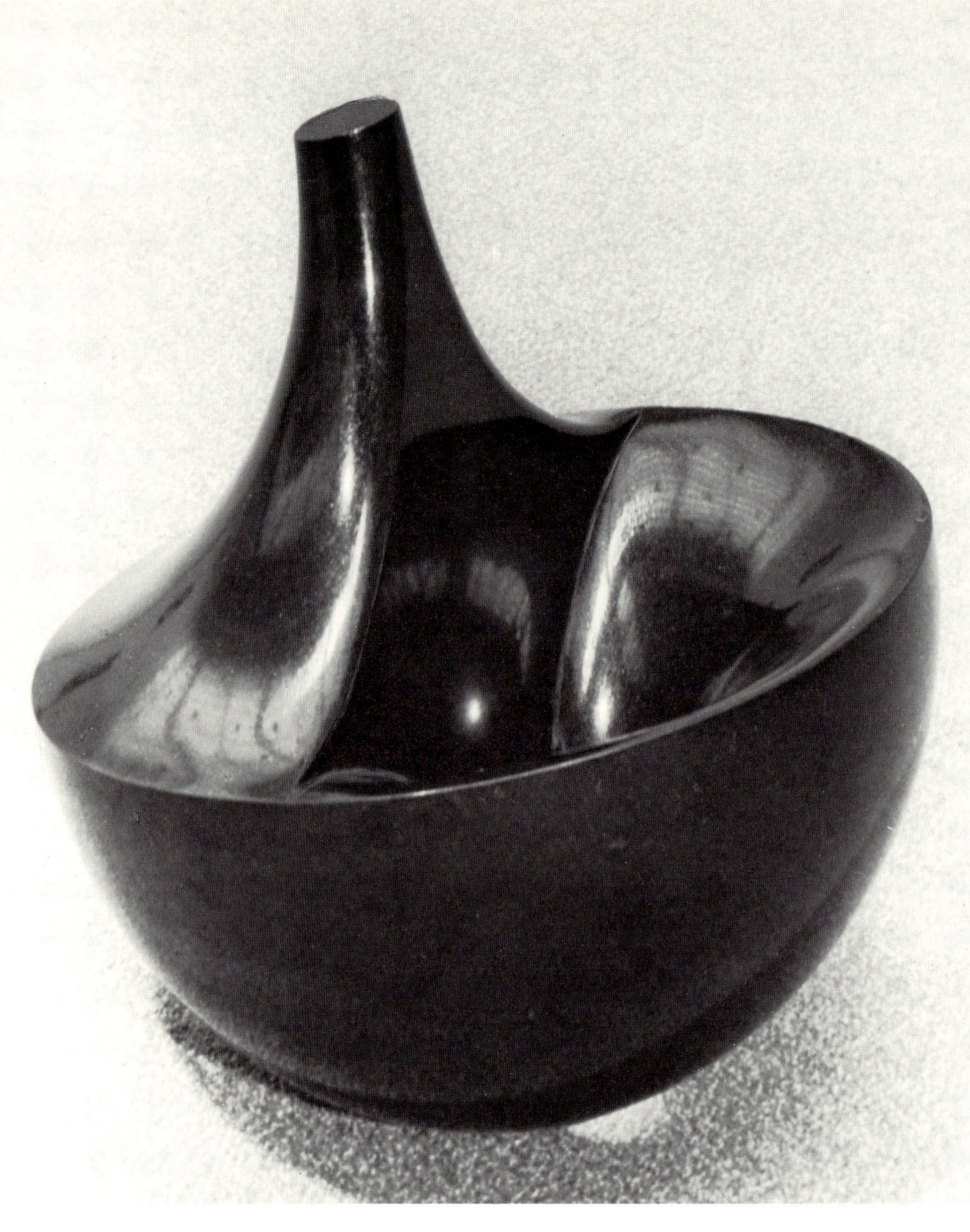

1965-66
Half Sphere no. 5
black granite, diameter, 15¾",
(40 cm),
Coll. Janice Ury, Belvedere, California

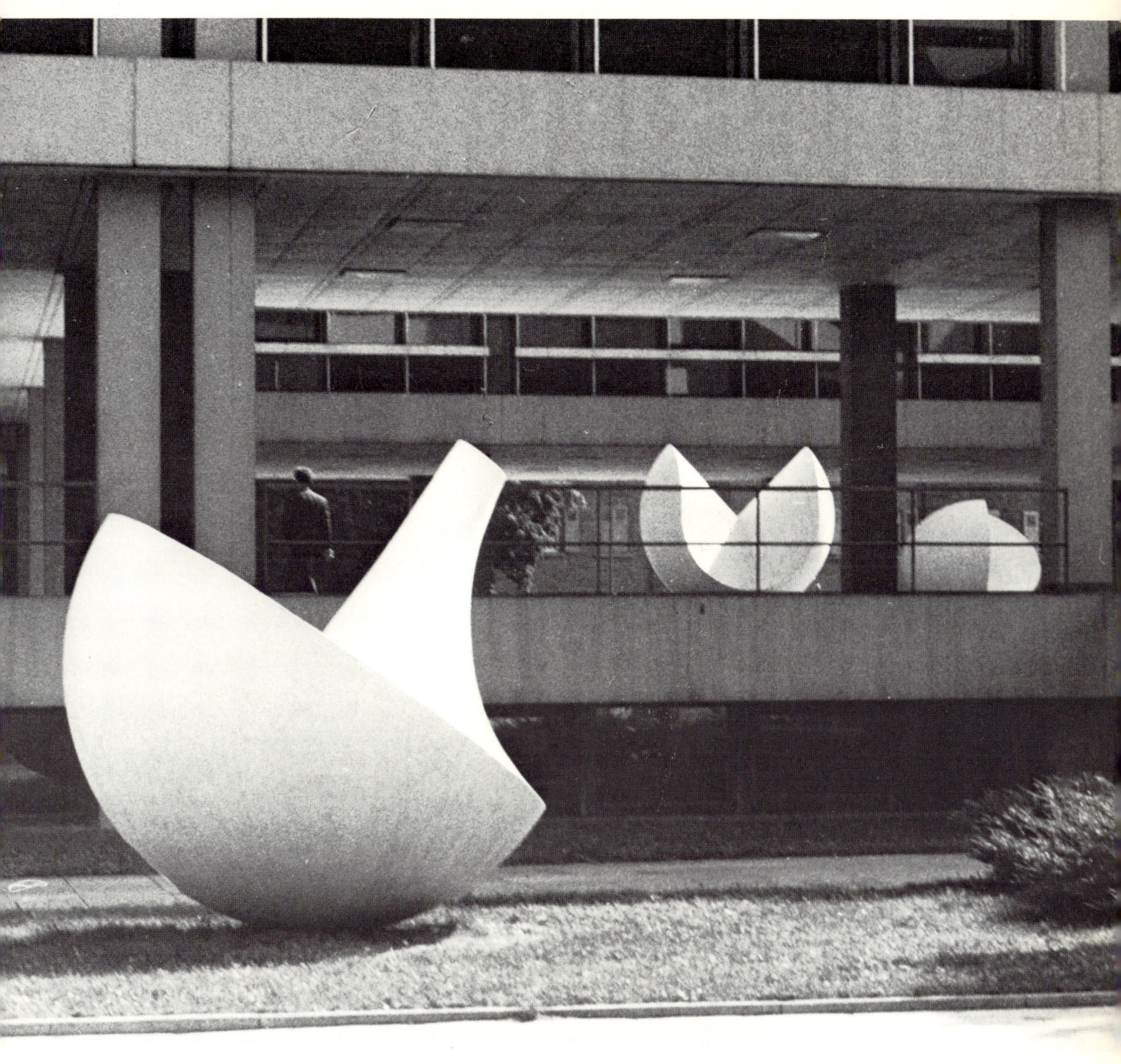

1965–66
Family of Five Half Spheres
artificial Stone, diameter 94–½″,
(240 cm),
University of Karlsruhe, Mathematical Institute

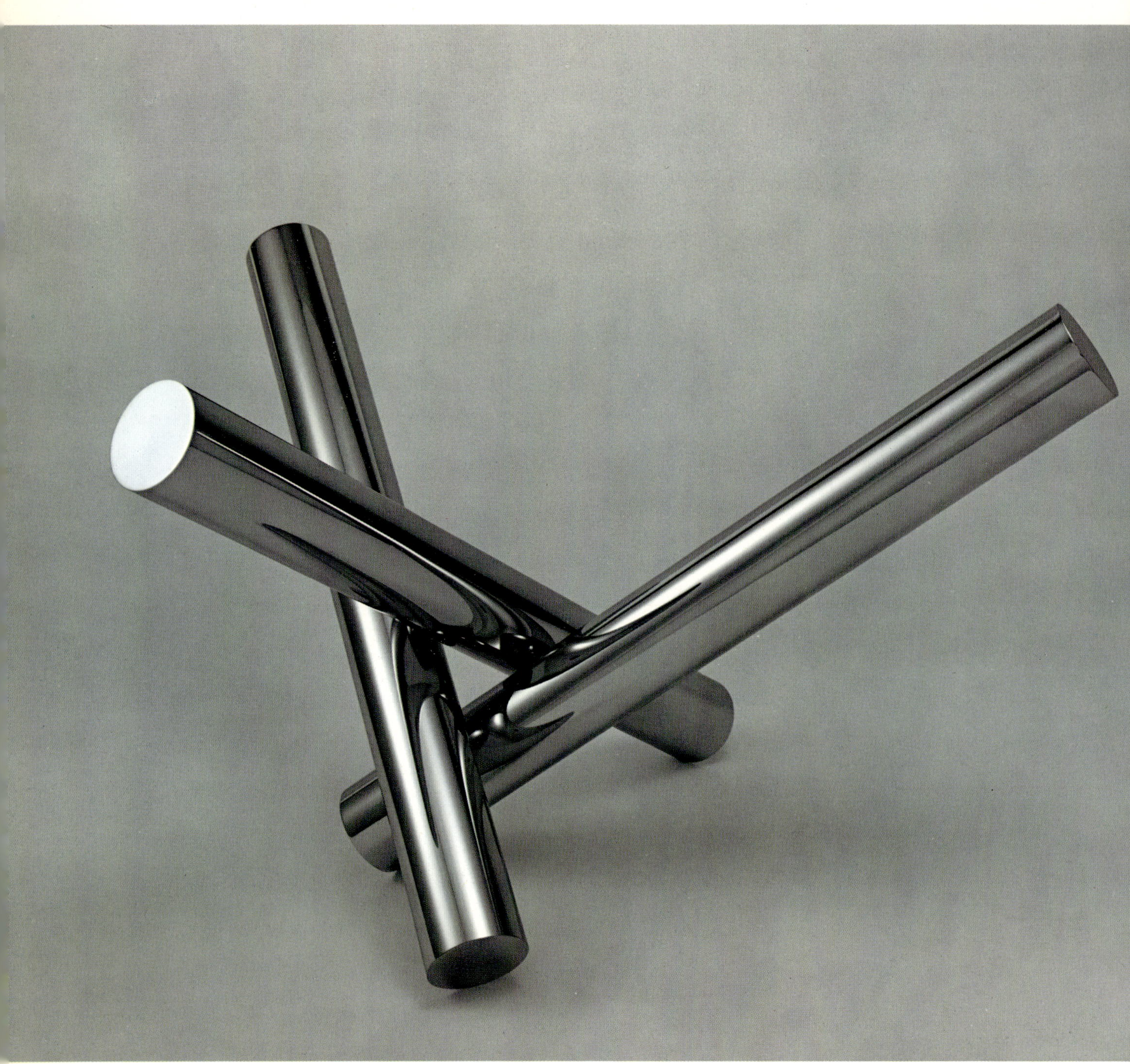

1966
Unity of Three Equal Cylinders
gilt brass, 26″ × 14″ × 19″,
(66 × 36 × 48 cm)
(illustrated: version in chromed brass)

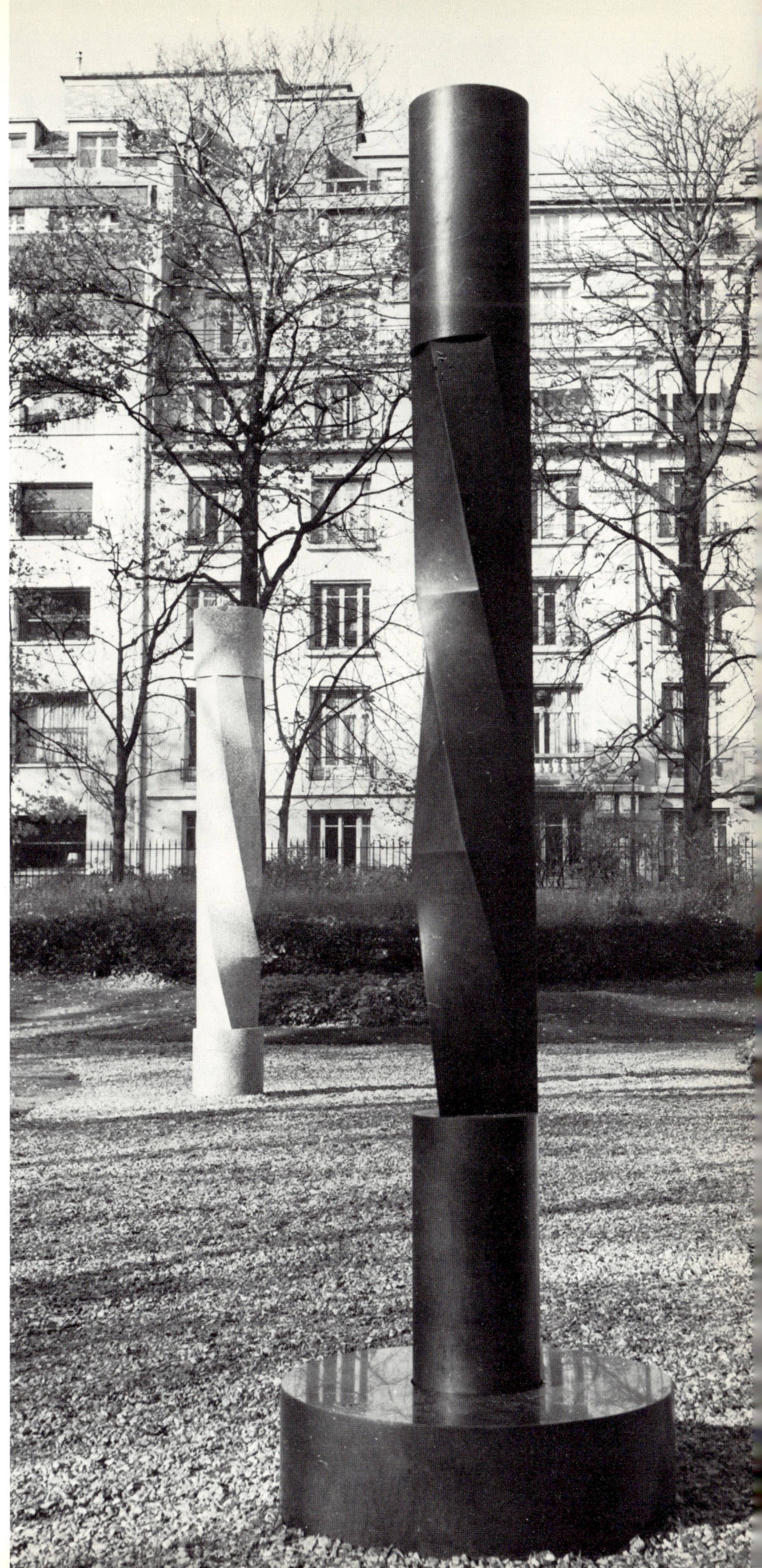

1966
Column with Triangular and Hexagonal Sections
black granite, 11⁷/₈″ × 128⁷/₈″,
(30 × 328 cm),
Marlborough Gallery, Inc., New York

145

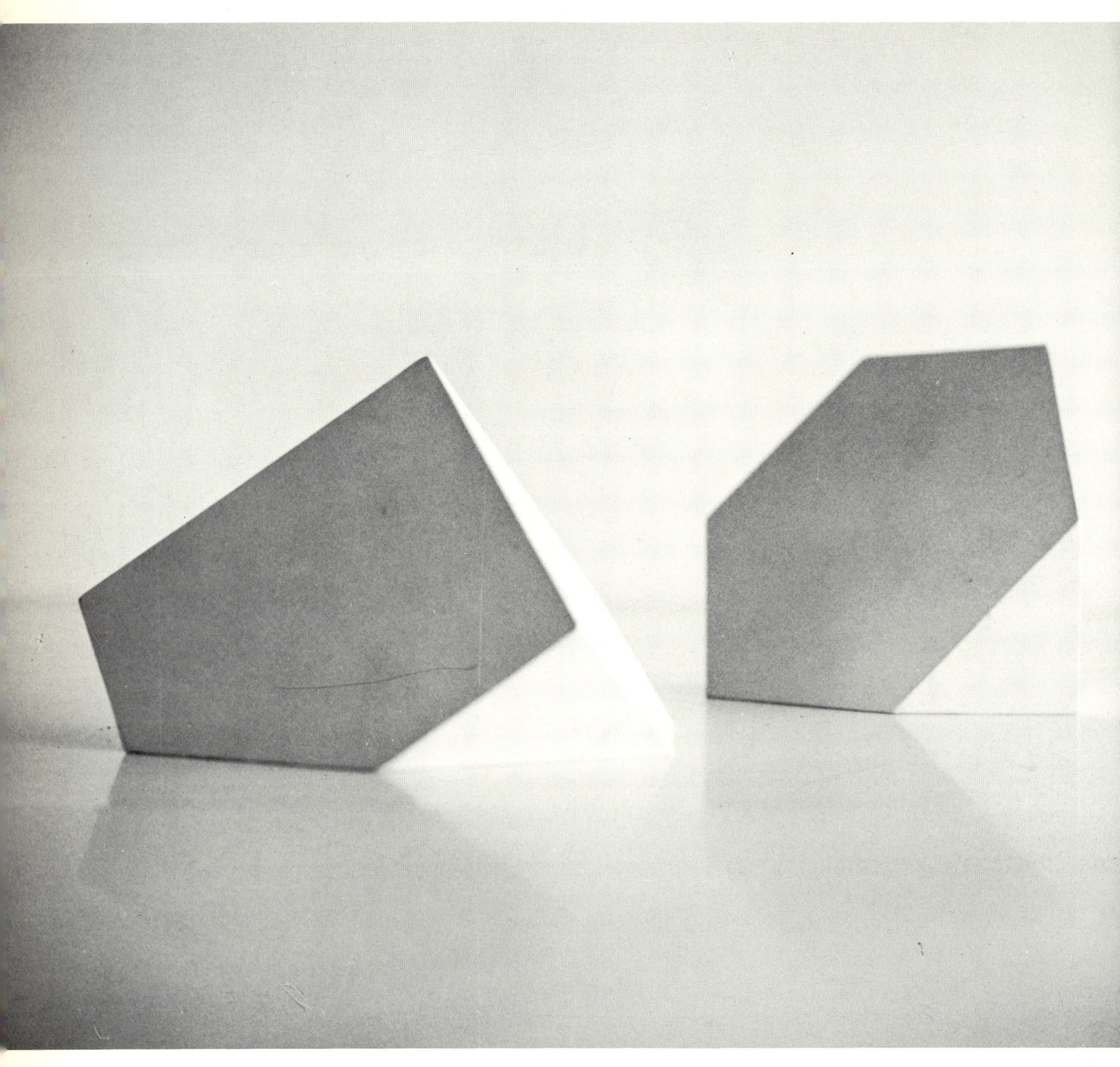

1966
Two Demi Cubes
black marble, 11″ × 11″ × 11″,
(28 × 28 × 28 cm),
The Tel Aviv Museum, Tel Aviv
(reproducted: the plaster models)

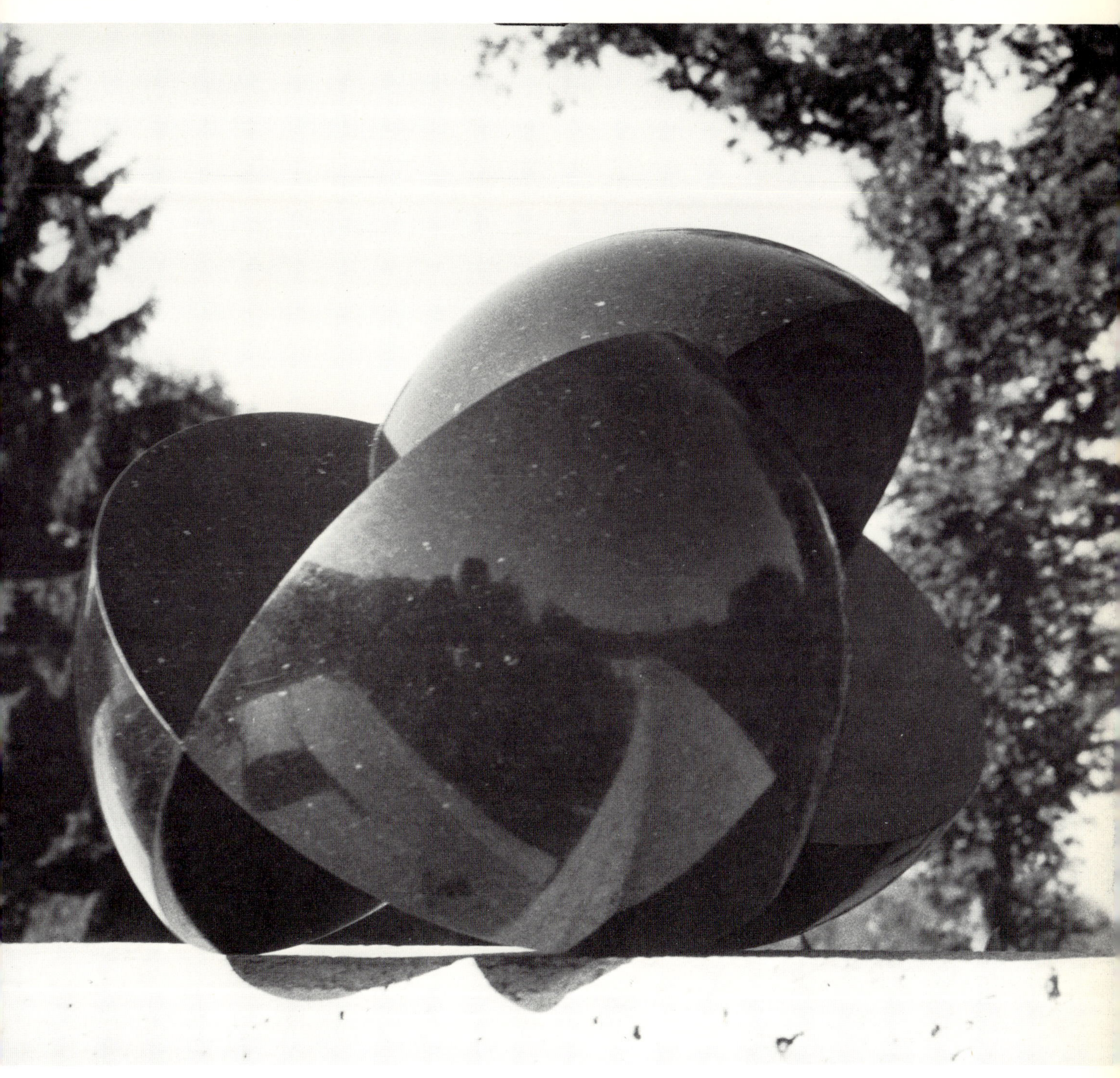

1966–67
Striving Forces of a Sphere
granite, 35½″ × 23½″ × 23½″,
(90 × 60 × 60 cm)

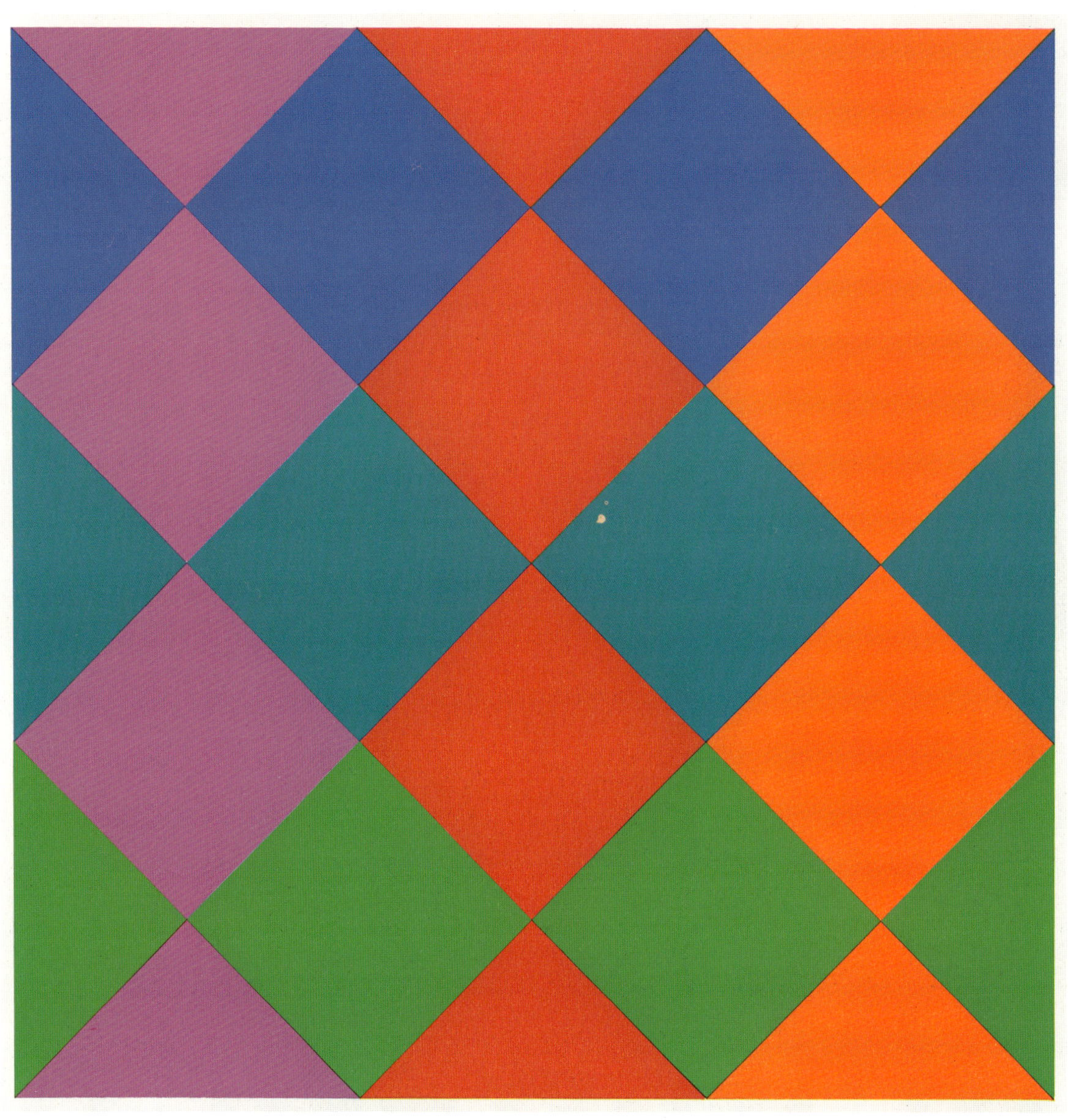

1966
Field of Six Penetrating Colors
oil on canvas, 52″ × 52″,
(132 × 132 cm)

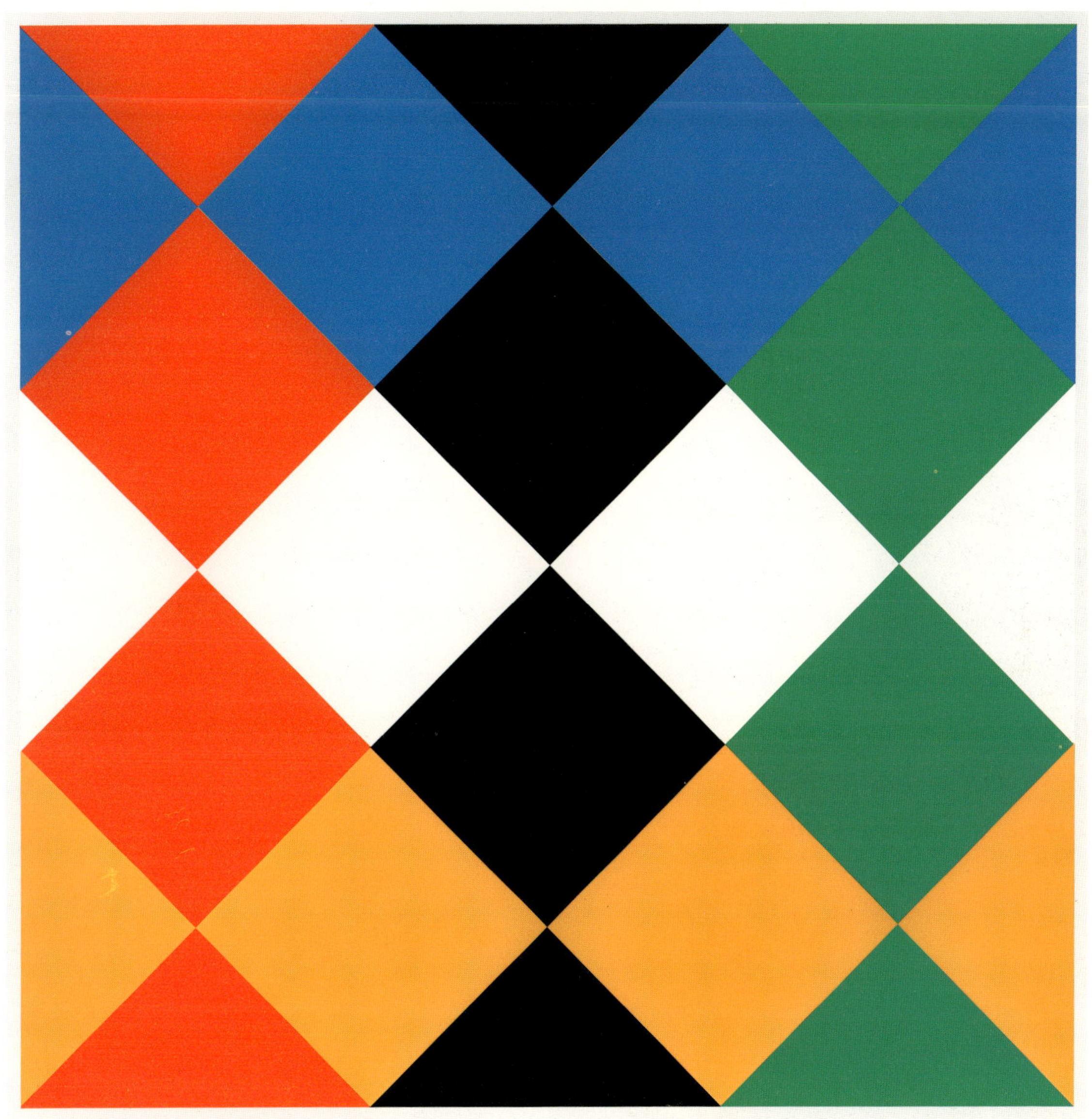

1966–67
Six Penetrating Colors
oil on canvas, 59″ × 59″,
(150 × 150 cm)

149

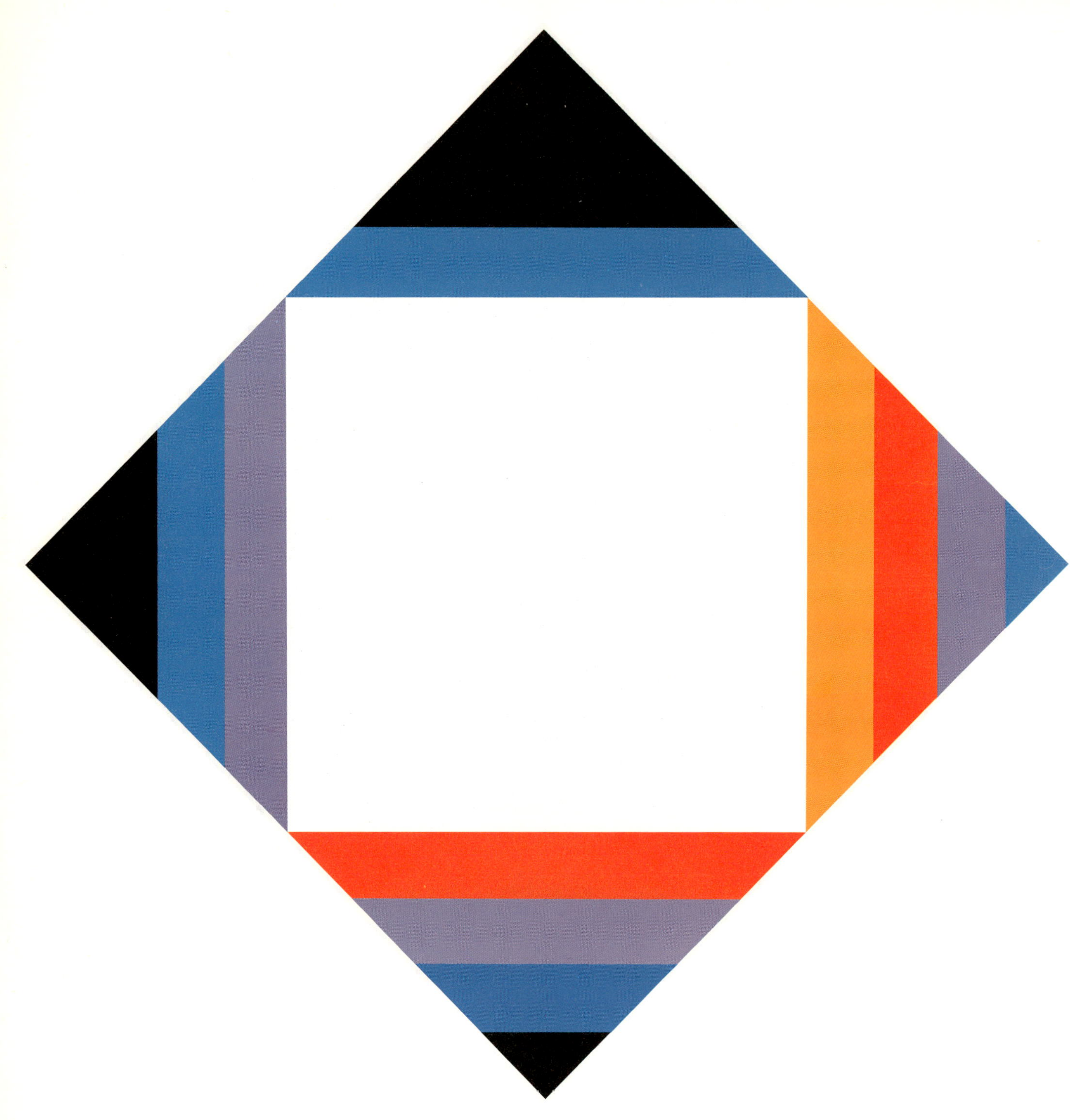

1967
Construction on a Theme from 1946
oil on canvas, diagonal, 64″, (162 cm),
Marlborough-Godard, Ltd., Toronto

Art as Non-Changeable Fact

Max Bill published *Art as Non-changeable Fact* in *Data – Directions in Art, Theory and Aesthetics,* published under the direction of Anthony Hill, Faber and Faber, London, 1968. The contents of this essay are indistinguishable from the notion of structure which Max Bill understands as fundamental to art.

It has always been said by avantgardists – the constructivists, the dadaists, the kinetic artists and the pop and op-artists – everything changes, everything is life, everything is in motion. Using such arguments a new state of being has been proclaimed for the fine arts. More exactly, new states of being – the changeable work. In a similar way to introducing time into the domain of physics, time has been introduced into the fine arts. So far this has been limited to literature and music, but one now hopes to realize the element of time in painting and sculpture, too. A wave has thus been started which is still sweeping on. I want to find out what in this context is mere fashion, what an error, and what might be right.

The understanding that everything moves is nothing new. The only new fact has been the proof that matter and energy are the same and different only in regard to their density and their order. The understanding that something produced artificially, and moving, generates a typical form, is nothing new either. Consider clocks, carriages, airplanes. The understanding that it is possible to make new machines out of old useless ones, which have no other purpose but to move and to present familiar things to a new audience, is equally not so new.

The understanding that fireworks, water displays, light and shadow projections can be created and purposefully planned, reaches back to antiquity and has not yet been replaced by something better and more impressive.

All this has been known for a long time. Why had it to be proclaimed again?

We can ask that every means which is appropriate to originate a work of art be actually used. But that does not dispense with a thorough investigation of where the meaning and the possibilities of art lie.

If we start from the principle that art is aesthetic information, we have to ask: information for whom? by whom? by means of what? Information on what: on an aesthetic fact? But what is an aesthetic fact? an elementary truth? a comprehensible order? an understandable law?

Presuming that art could be described in this way one should also know what purpose this aesthetic information serves. I say: it serves as an unchangeable message from today to today and into the future.

I say that it is the scope of art to create a kind of non-changeable, elementary truth. A kind of truth which can be inter-

preted differently but which remains nevertheless the
same.

Though the environment and the onlooker are subject to
change, this does not go for the aesthetic object.

This shows why essentially the subordination of plastic art to
the laws of change contradicts the meaning of plastic art. The
purpose of art is to give an aesthetic measure. If one knows
how difficult it is to give an absolute measure, as against physical nature, then one recognizes that this problem in the spiritual field can only be solved by art. How difficult it is to
measure exactly: time, distance, weight! And how important
it is for the whole of our society that this measuring functions
correctly so that our environment may be well and durably
established.

However, to measure in the field of aesthetics we are quite
insufficiently equipped. The spiritual life limps behind the
technical development of our artificial limbs, moving toward a
culminating point which at present conflicts with the
unsolved problems of humanity: an adequate social order in
general and an adequate spiritual order for the single human
being. Elements of such a spiritual order we find in the field of
basic aesthetic truth. And this can do without kinetics, without modernism, without the so-called up-to-date material. Its
basis is the durability of its newness as aesthetic information.

In the end: what is the use of all those aspirations of kinetics?
Art should remain the serene play it has always been! The kinetic artists belong to the domain of jugglers, conjurers, the cir-
cus and the fairground. We find pleasure in their friendly and
funny ways, their mischief and their tricks. But one should not
see more than there really is: entertainment. This, however,
has never been the idea of art and (fortunately) will never be.

[1967]

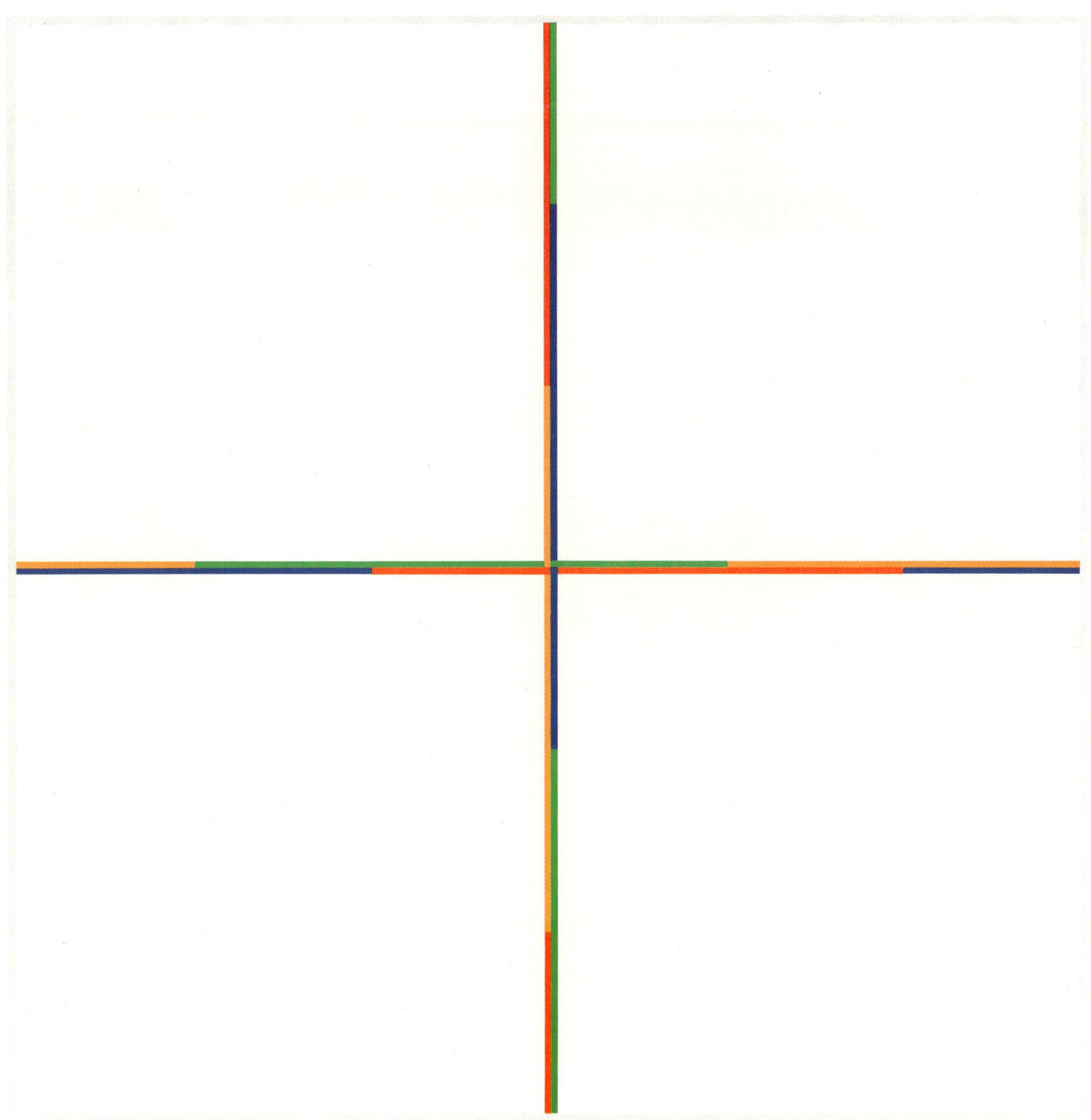

1967–68
Rythm of Four Colors in the White
oil on canvas, 78¾″ × 78¾″,
(200 × 200 cm)

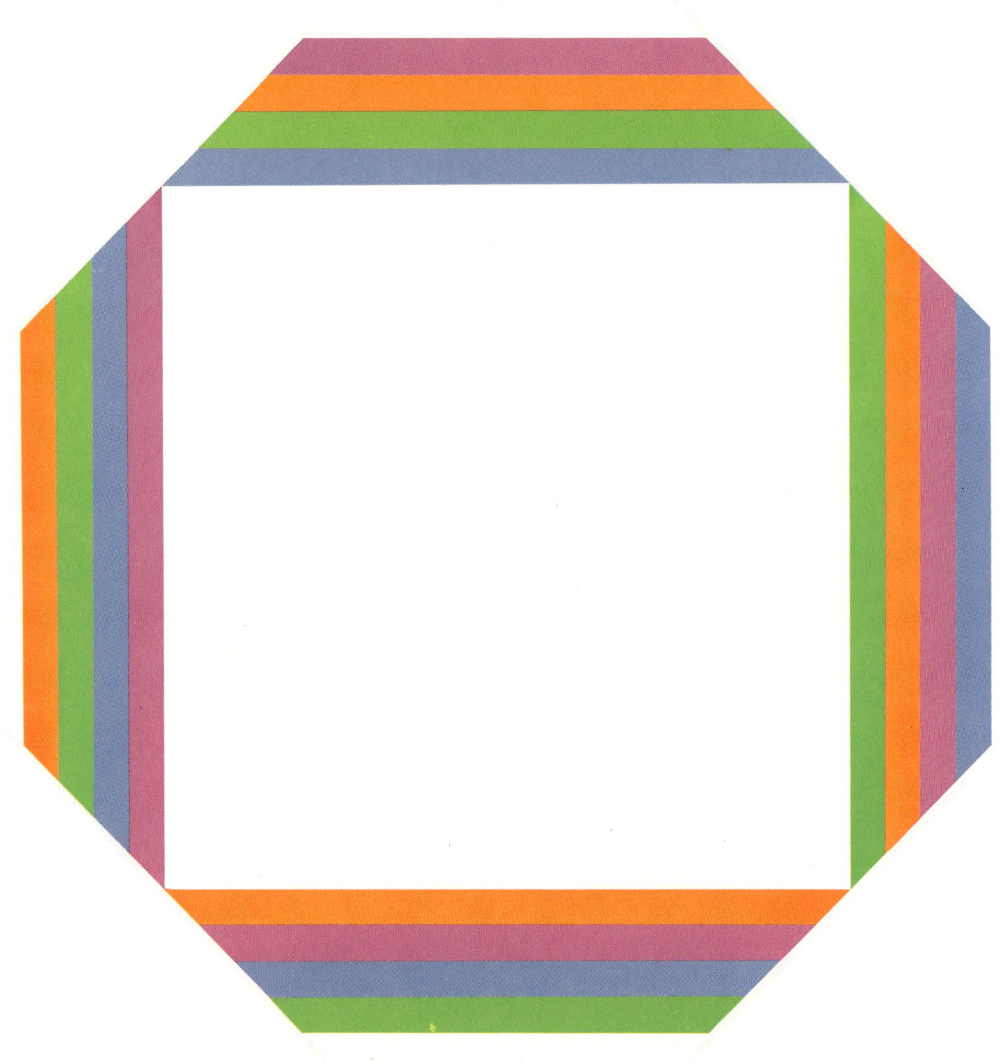

1969
Enclosed Nucleus
oil on canvas, diagonal, 67³/₄″,
(172 cm)

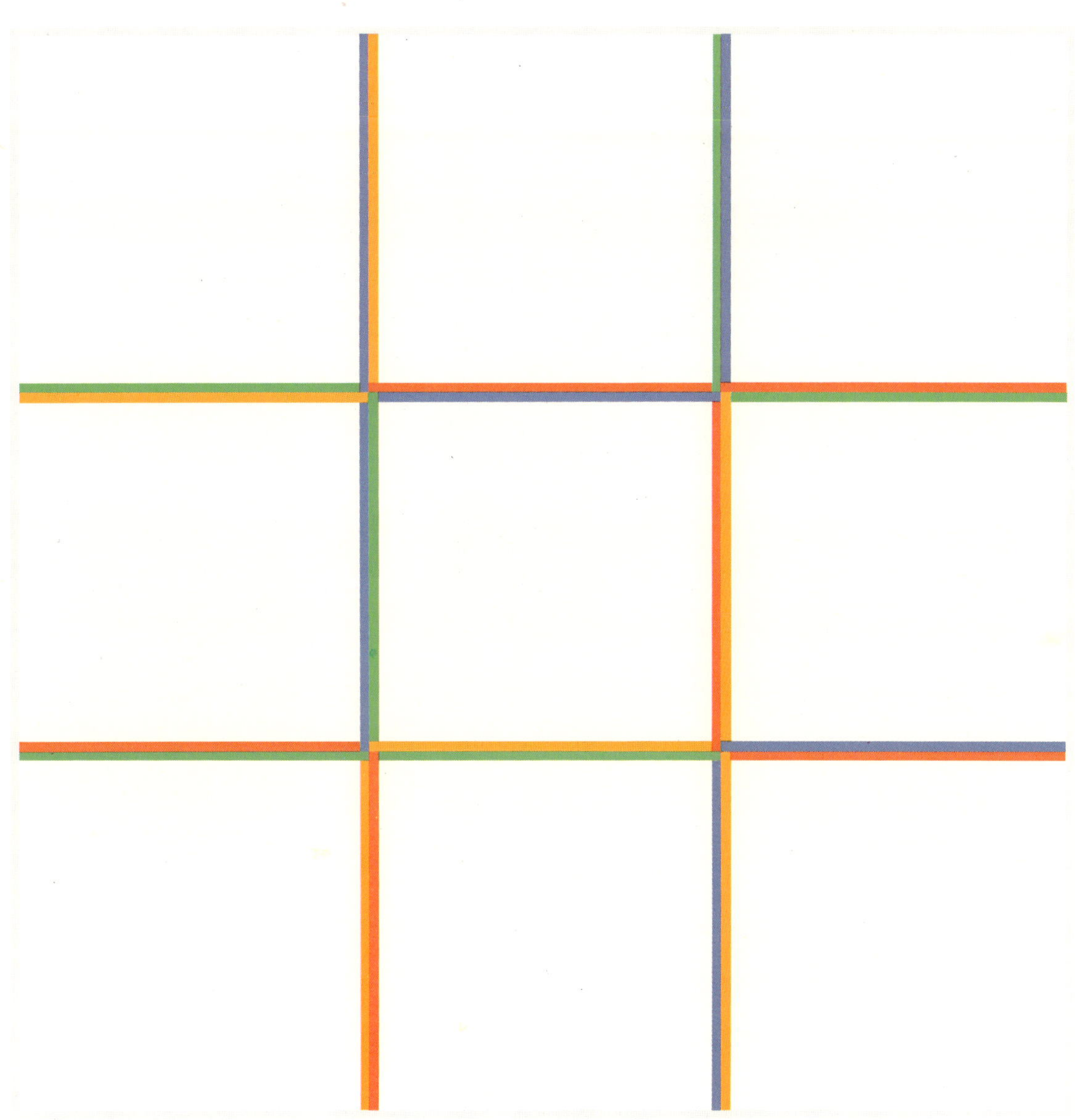

1968
*Nine Fields Divided by Means of Two
Colors*
oil on canvas, 47″ × 47″,
(120 × 120 cm),
Albright-Knox Art Gallery, Buffalo,
Gift of Seymour H. Knox

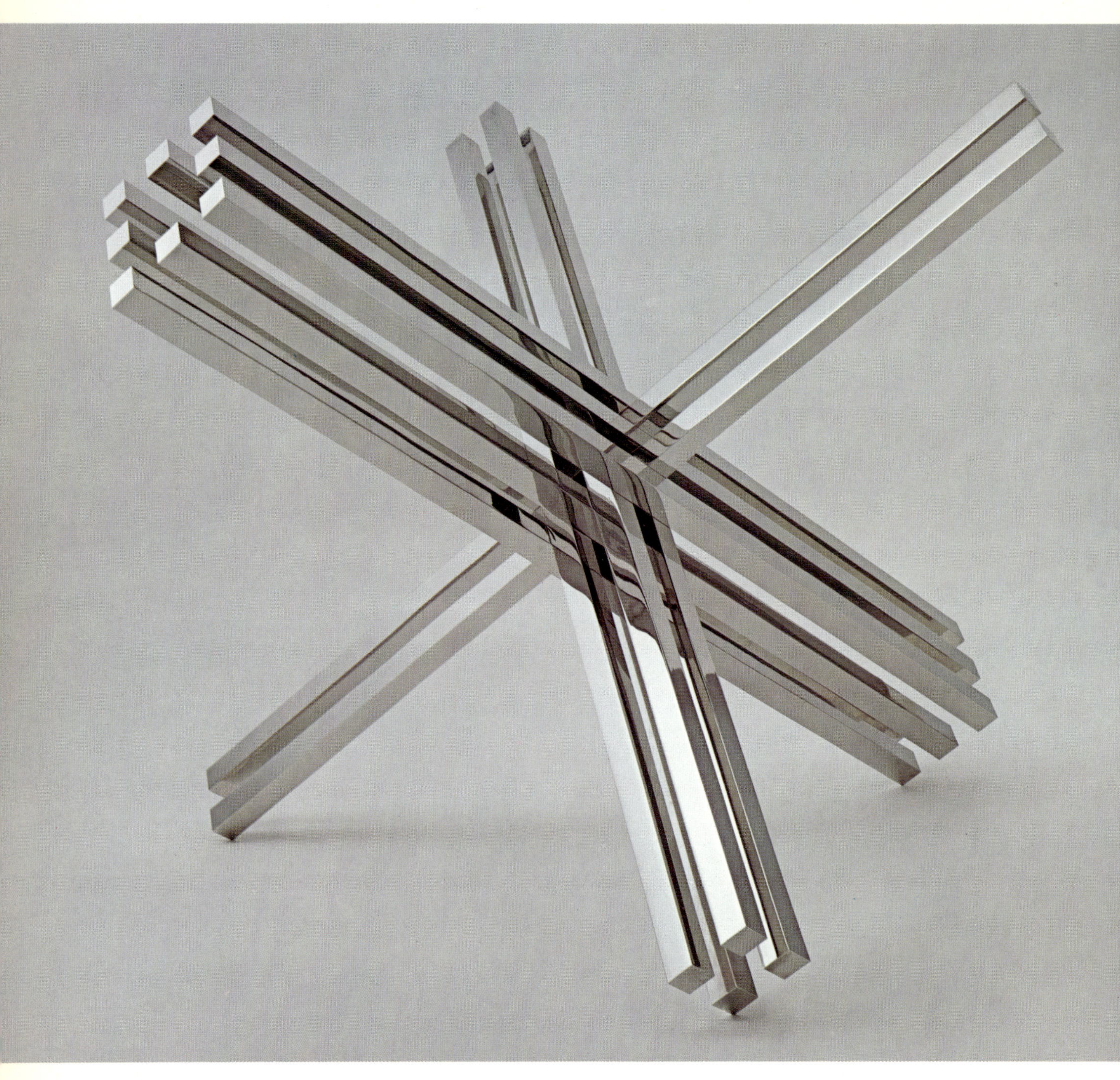

1968–69
Nucleus by Doubling II
nickel-plated aluminum,
44″ × 39⅜″ × 31½″,
(112 × 100 × 80 cm)

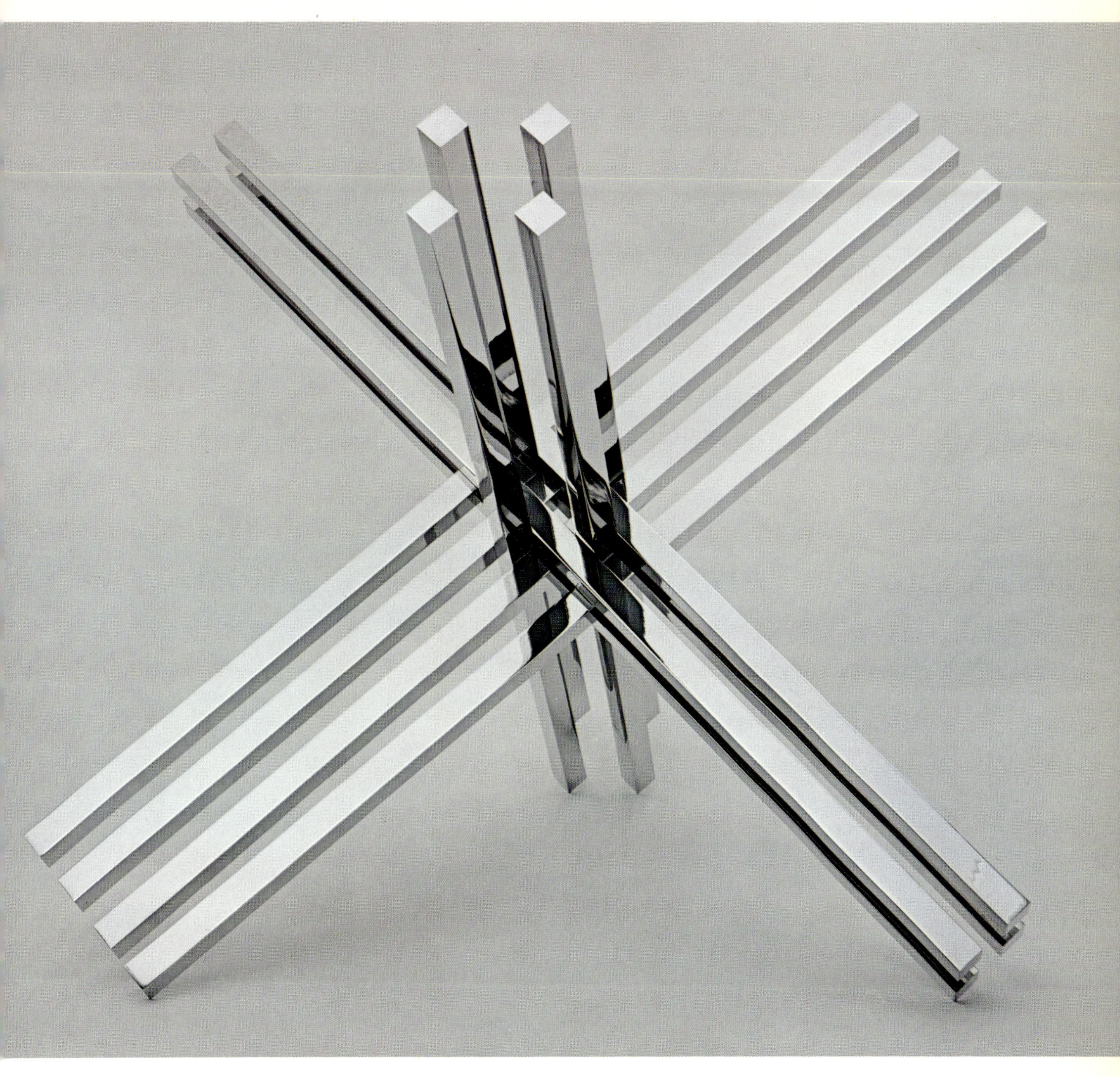

1969
Nucleus From Groups of Four Elements
Each
nickel-plated aluminum,
41⅜″ × 39⅜″ × 32″,
(115 × 100 × 81 cm)

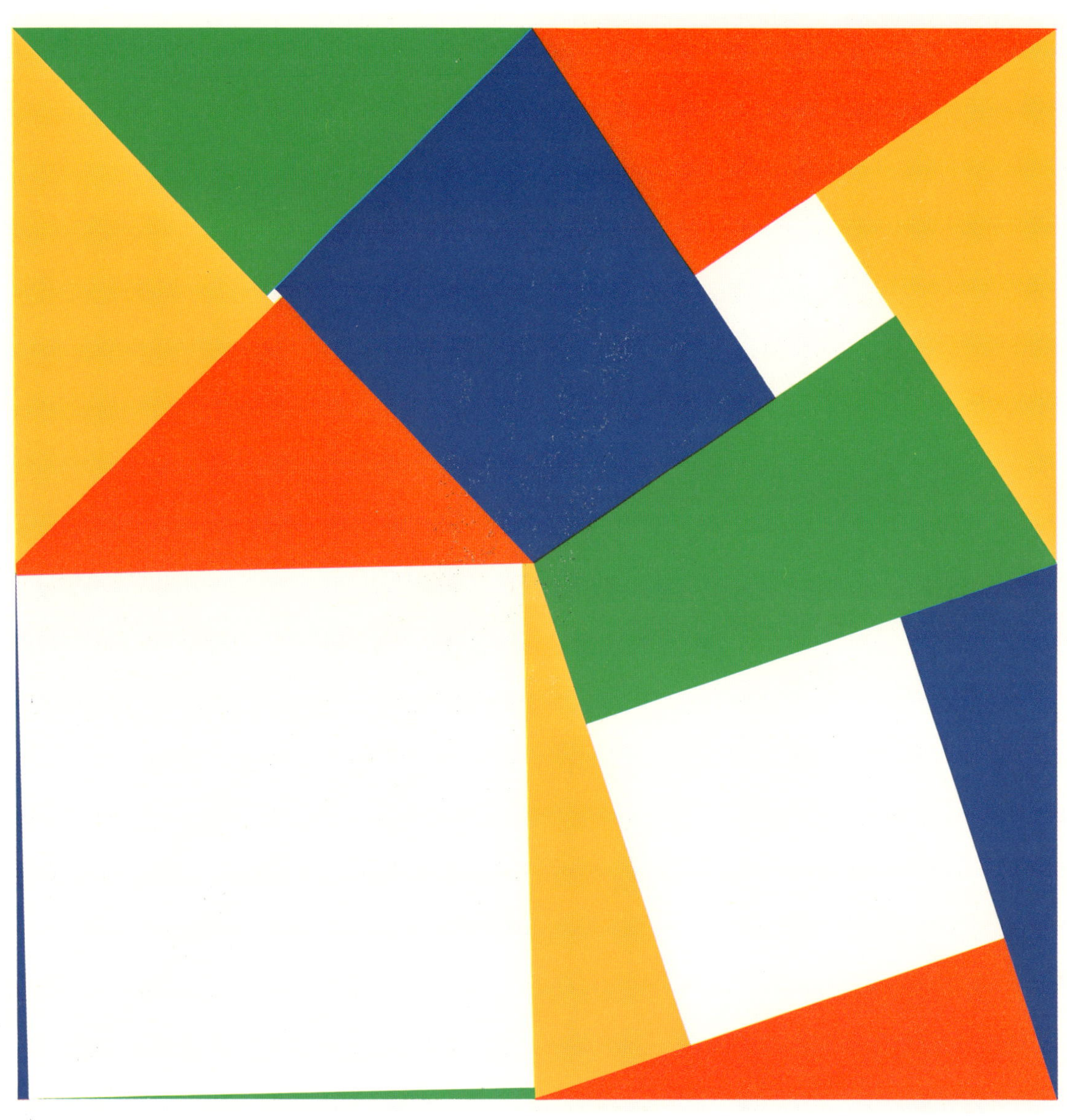

1969
Rotation of Equal Color Quantites around
White Centers
oil on canvas, 78³/₄″ × 78³/₄″,
(198 × 198 cm)

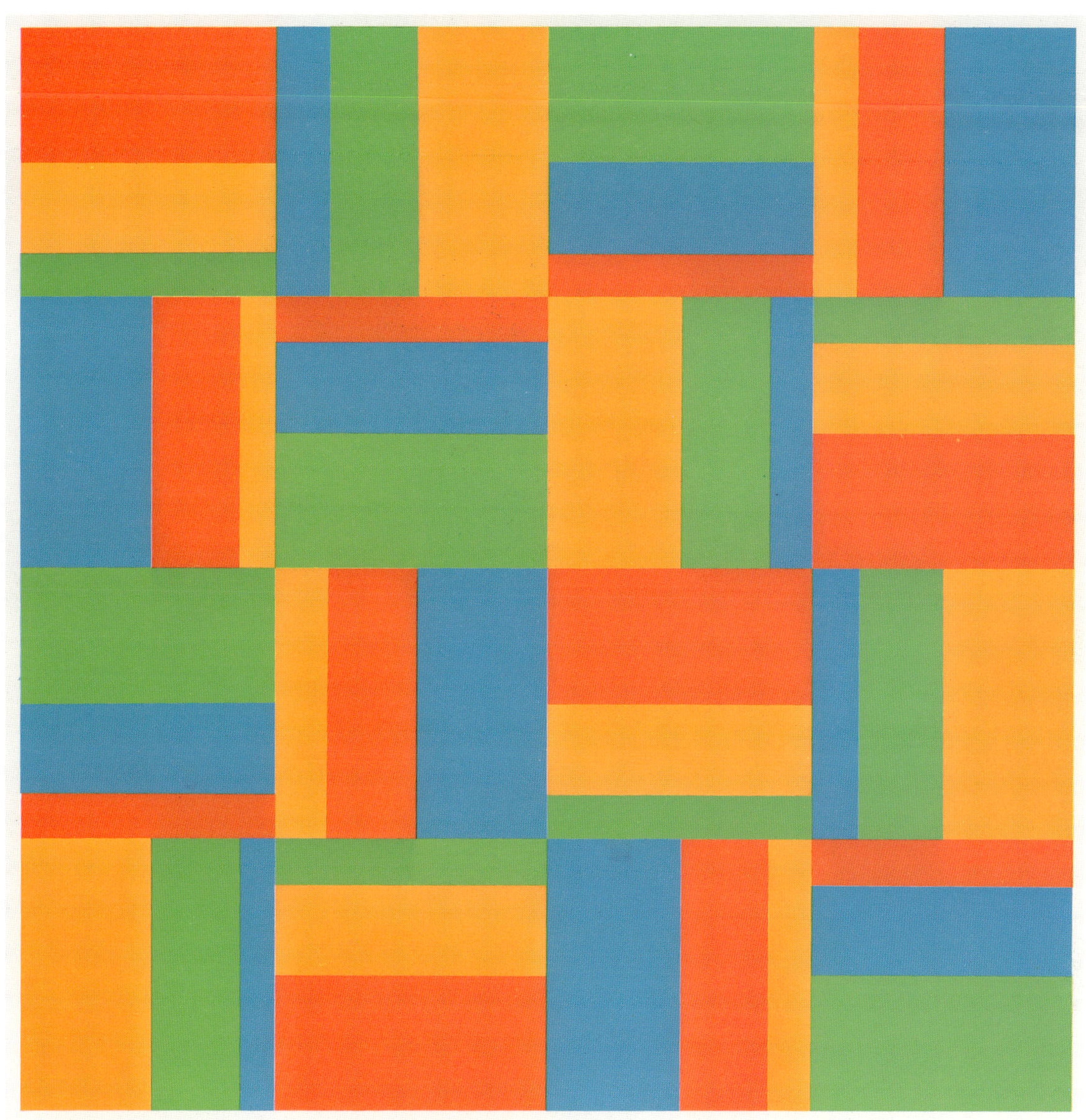

1970
System with Five Four-colored Centers
oil on canvas, 47″ × 47″,
(120 × 120 cm),
Migros-Genossenschaft, St. Gallen

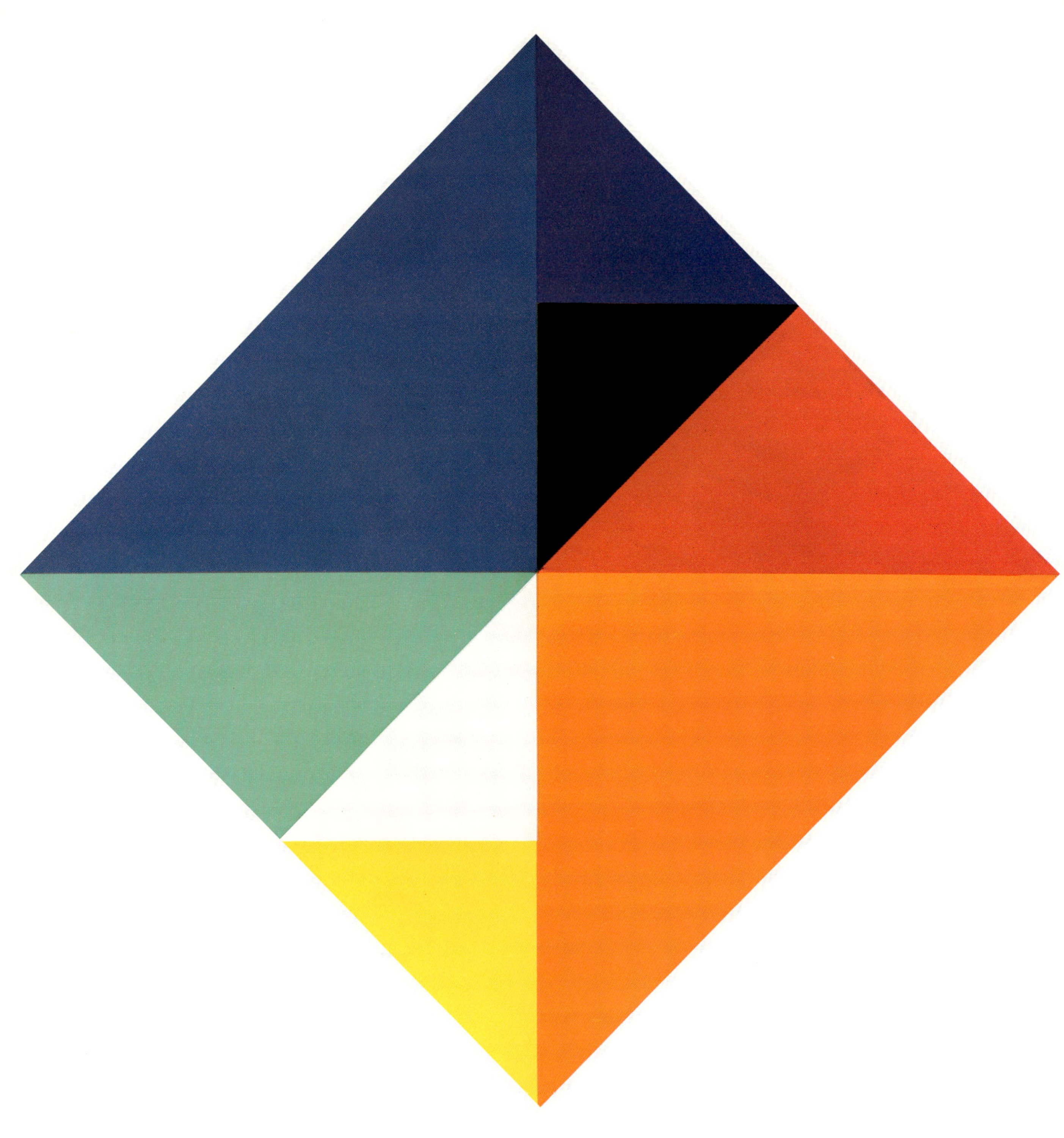

1970
Complementary Rotation
oil on canvas, diagonal, 111½″,
(283 cm)

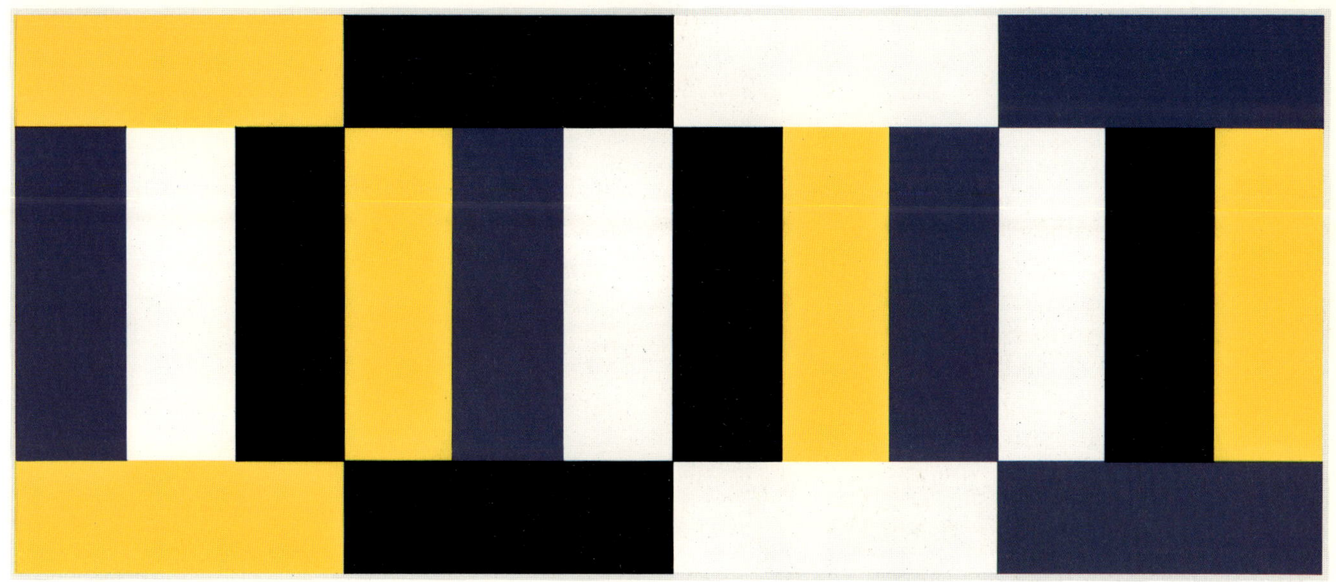

1970
System in Four Colors
oil on canvas, 94½″ × 39⅜″,
(240 × 100 cm)

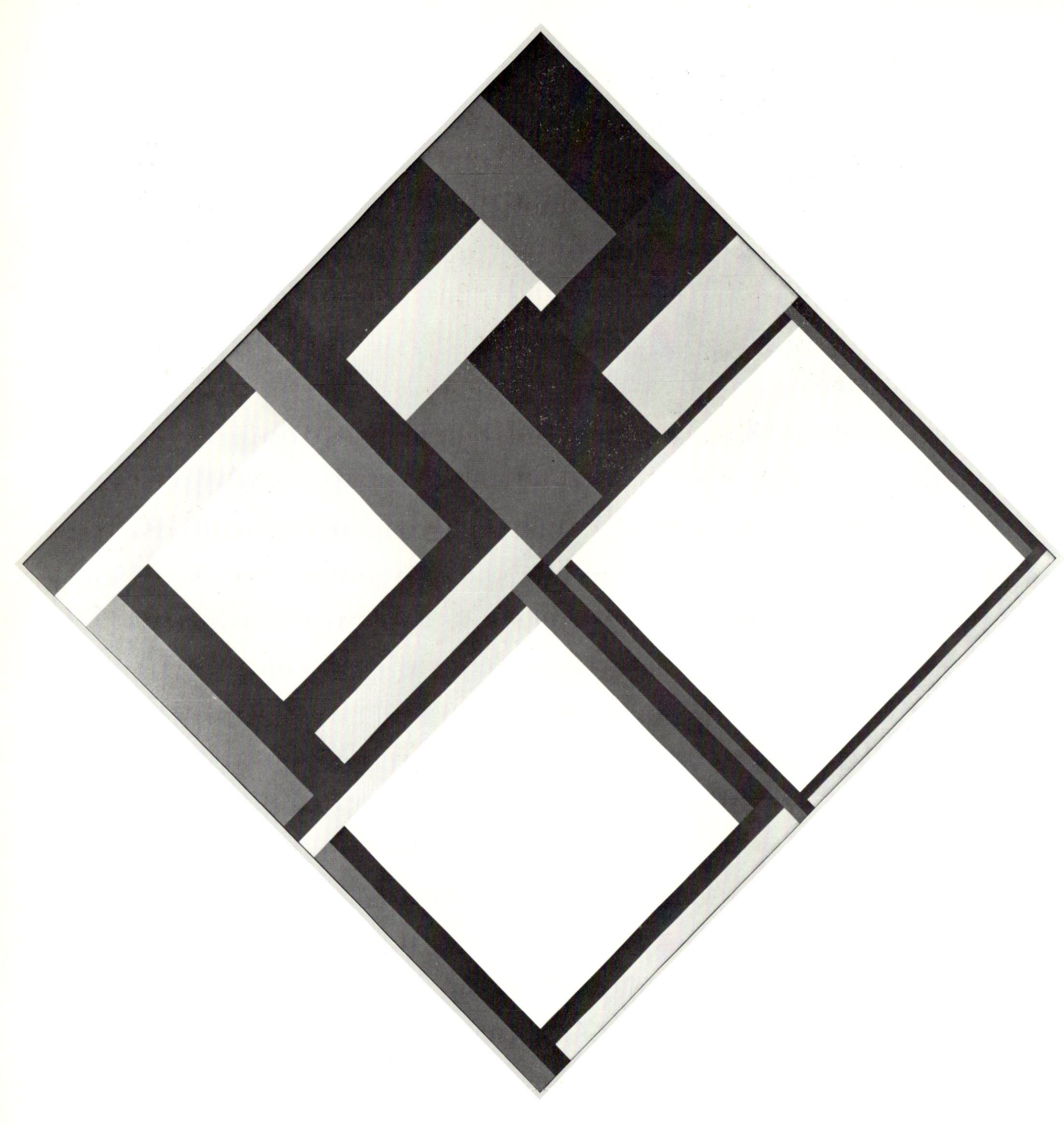

1970–71
Double Colors in Four Directions
oil on canvas, diagonal, 83½″,
(212 cm)

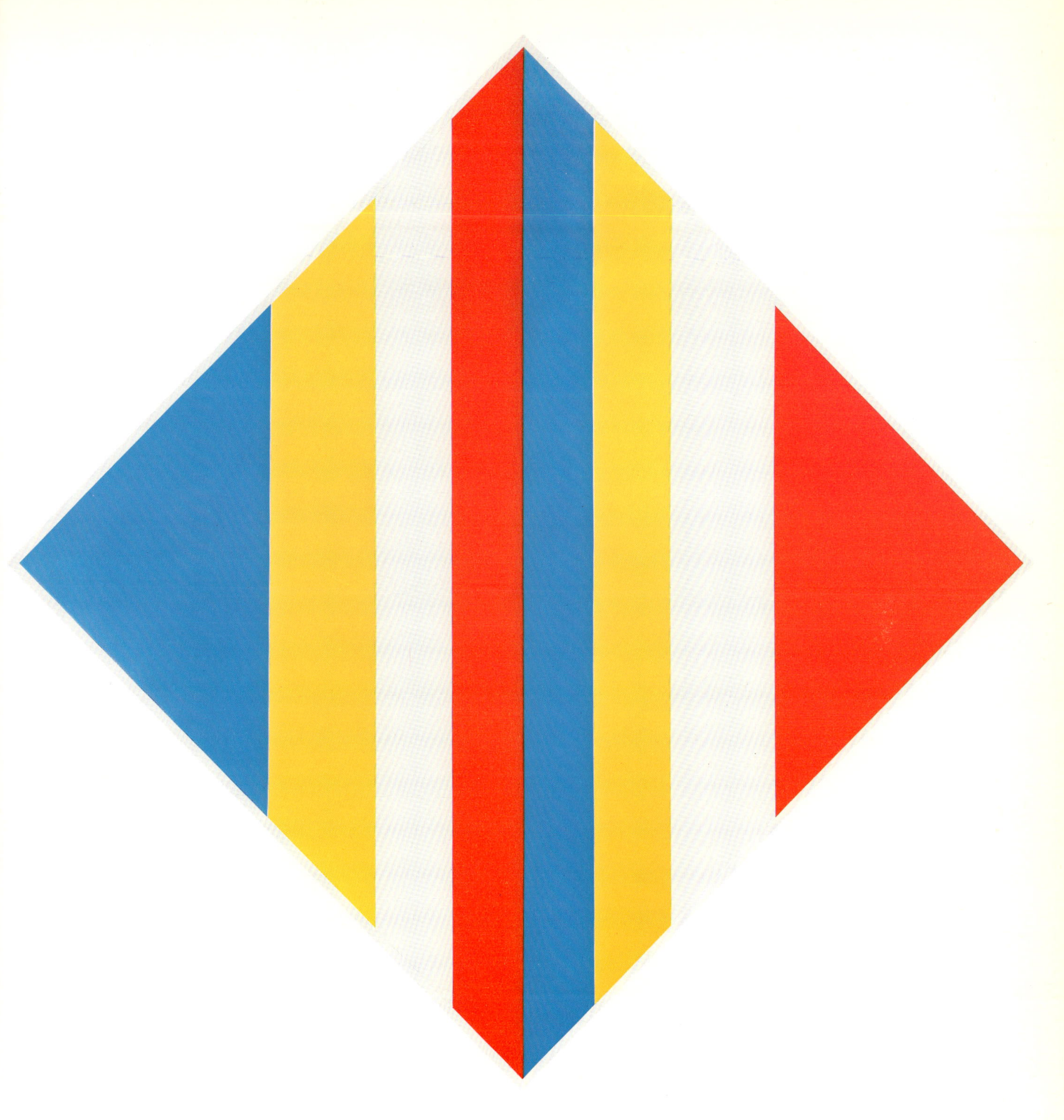

1970–71
Eight Fields of Equal Surface
oil on canvas, diagonal, 67″, (170 cm),
Marlborough Gallery, Inc., New York

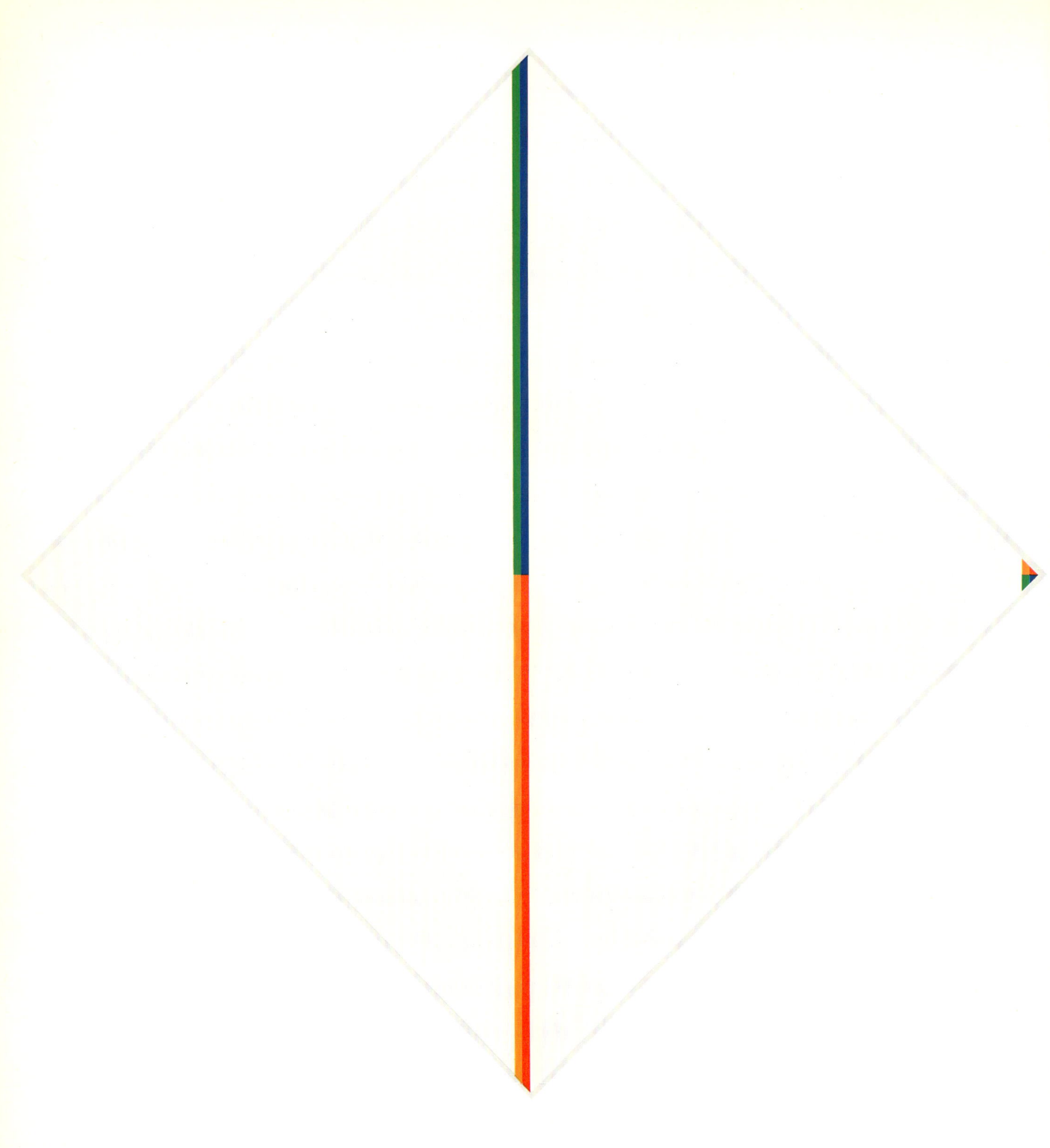

1970–73
Parallels of Double Colors in Space
oil on canvas, diagonal, 83½″,
(212 cm)

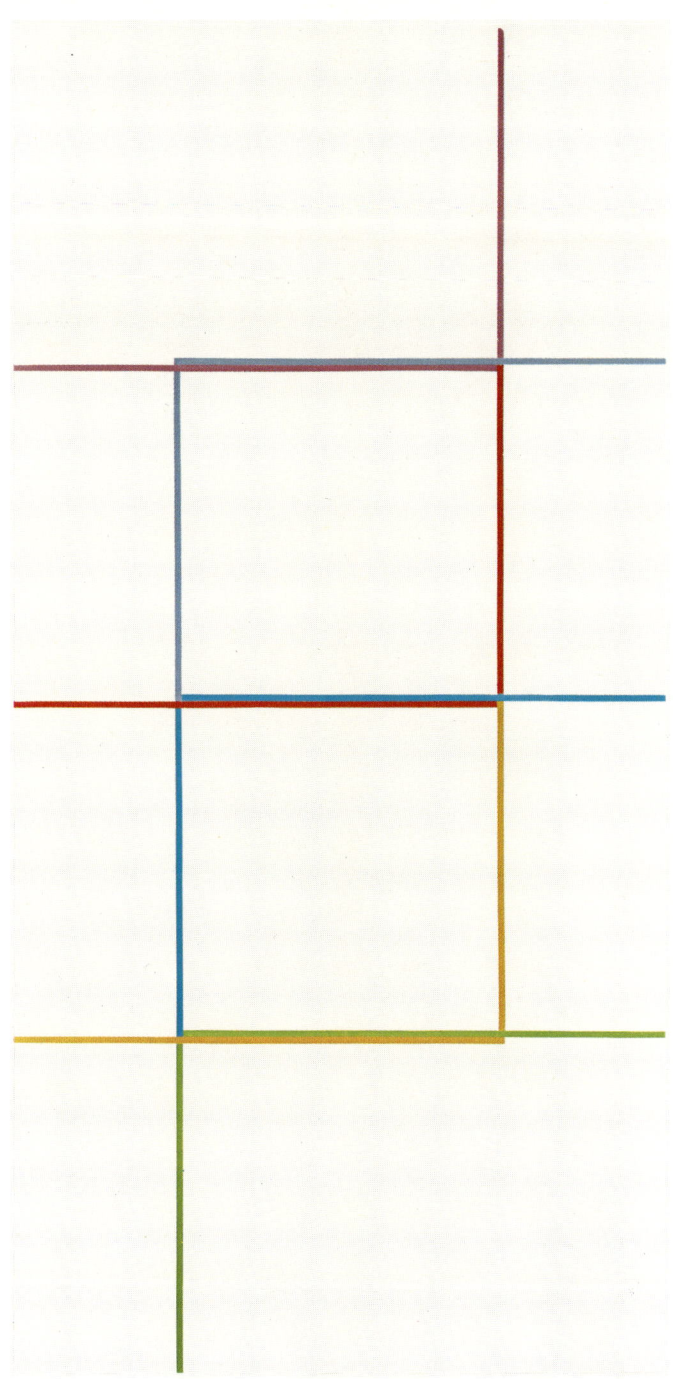

1971
Two Surrounded Squares
oil on canvas, 39⅜″ × 78¾″,
(100 × 200 cm)

165

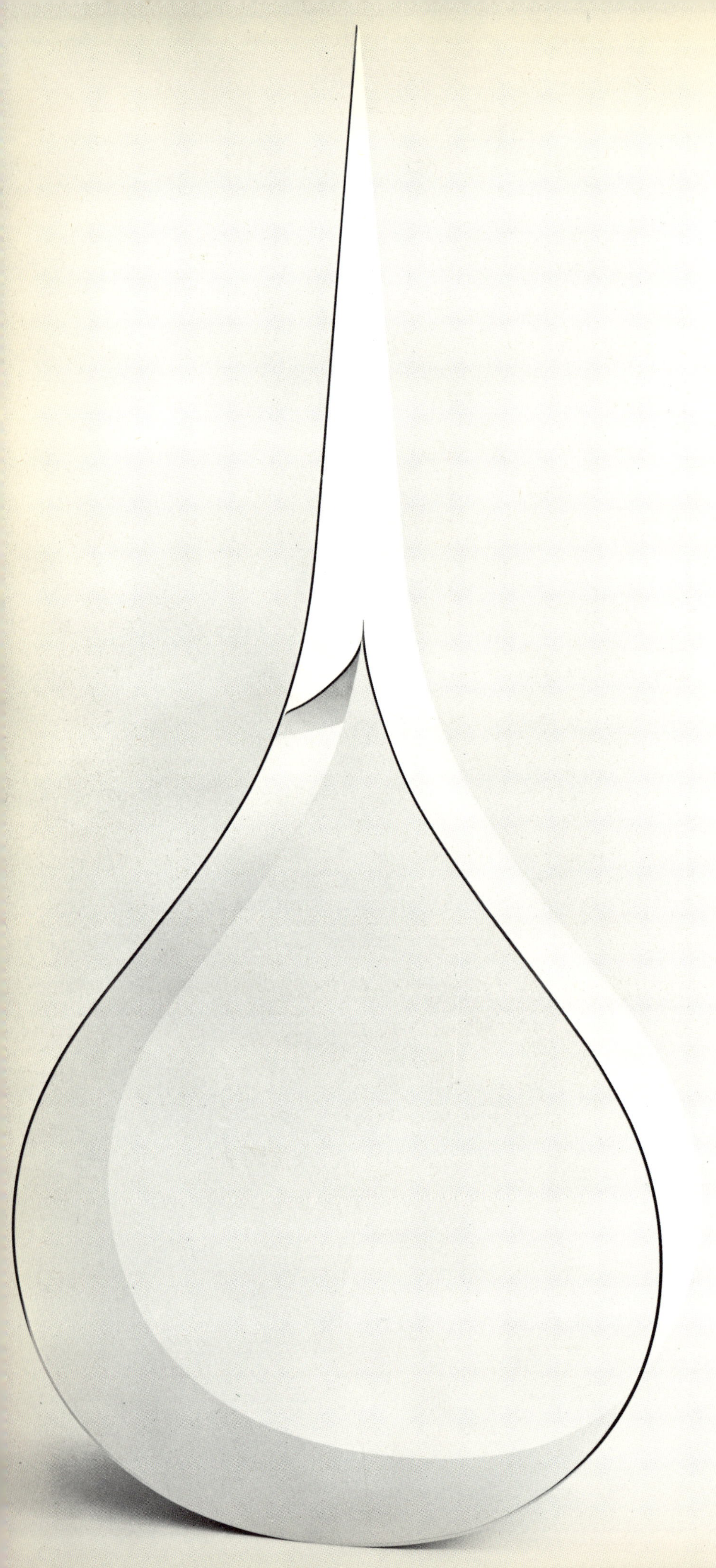

1971
Surface in Space with Two Corners
gilt brass,
$7^{7}/_{16}'' \times 17^{5}/_{8}'' \times 39^{13}/_{16}''$,
(19 × 45 × 101 cm)

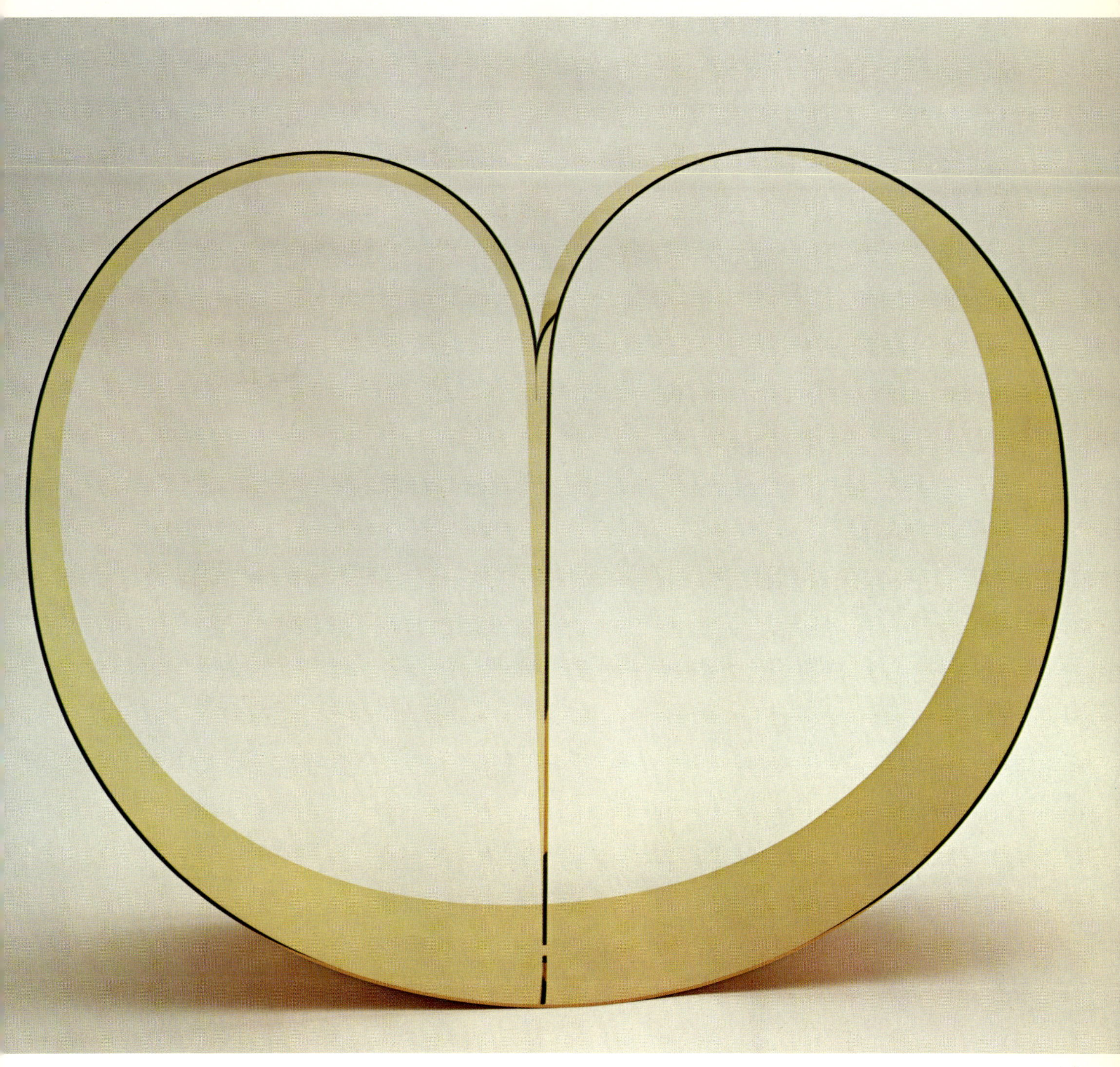

1971
Inverse Surface in Space with Two Corners
gilt brass, 7½″ × 18⅛″ × 17½″,
(19 × 46 × 44.5 cm)
Marlborough Fine Art (London) Ltd.,
London

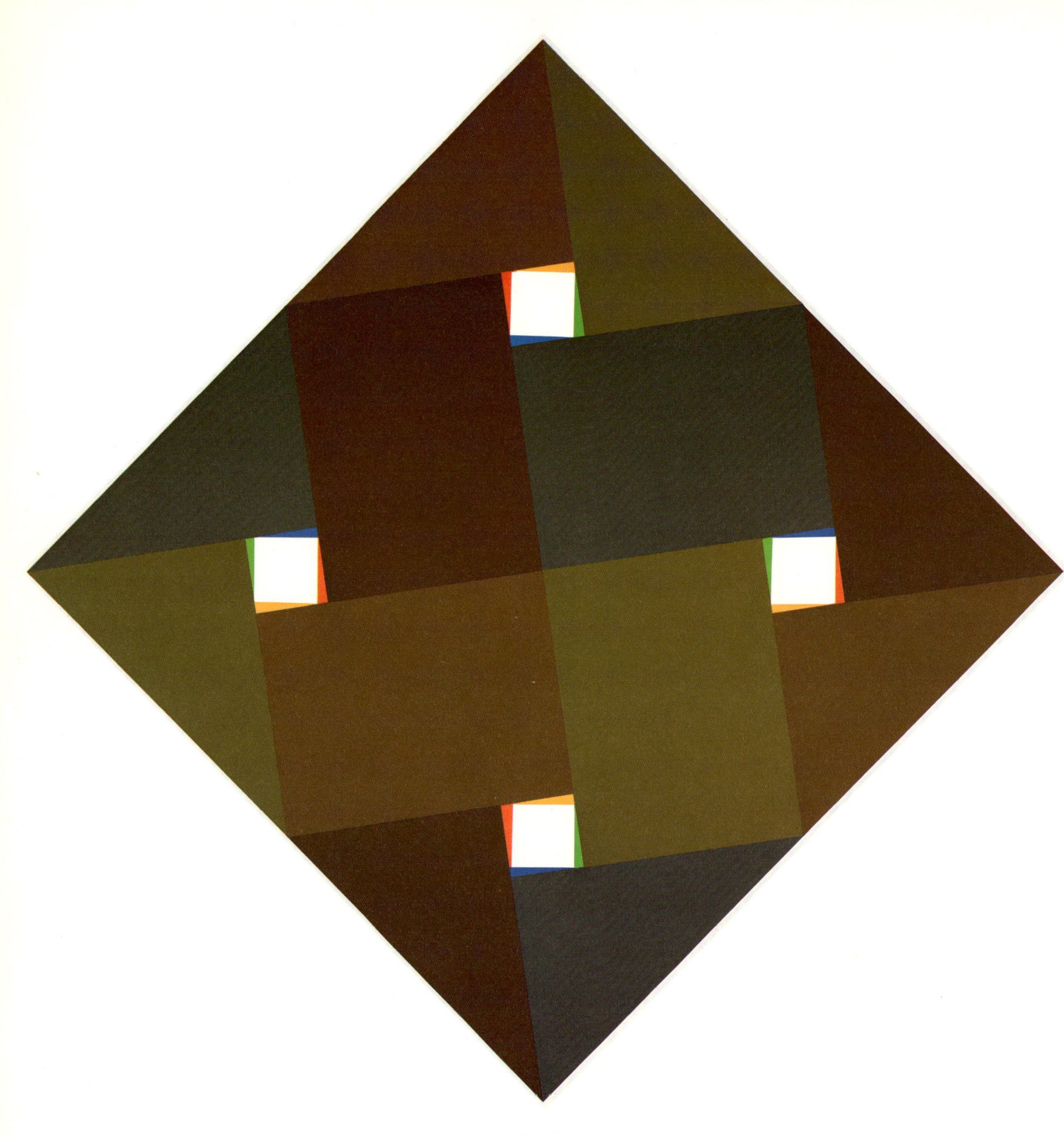

1971–72
Rotation around White Nuclei
oil on canvas, diagonal, 83½″,
(212 cm)

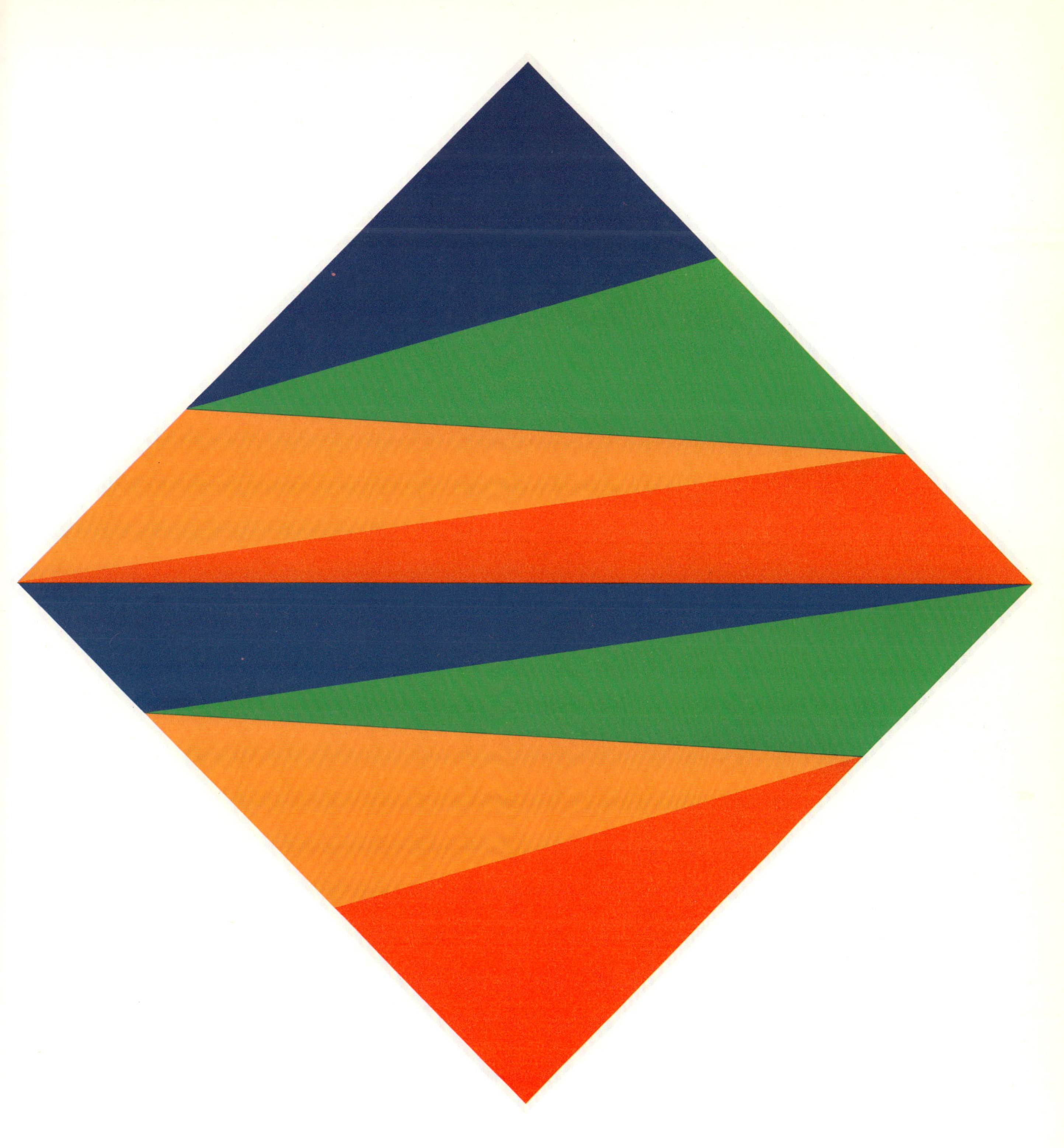

1972
Unity from Equal Colour Quantities
oil on canvas, diagonal, 67″,
(170 cm)

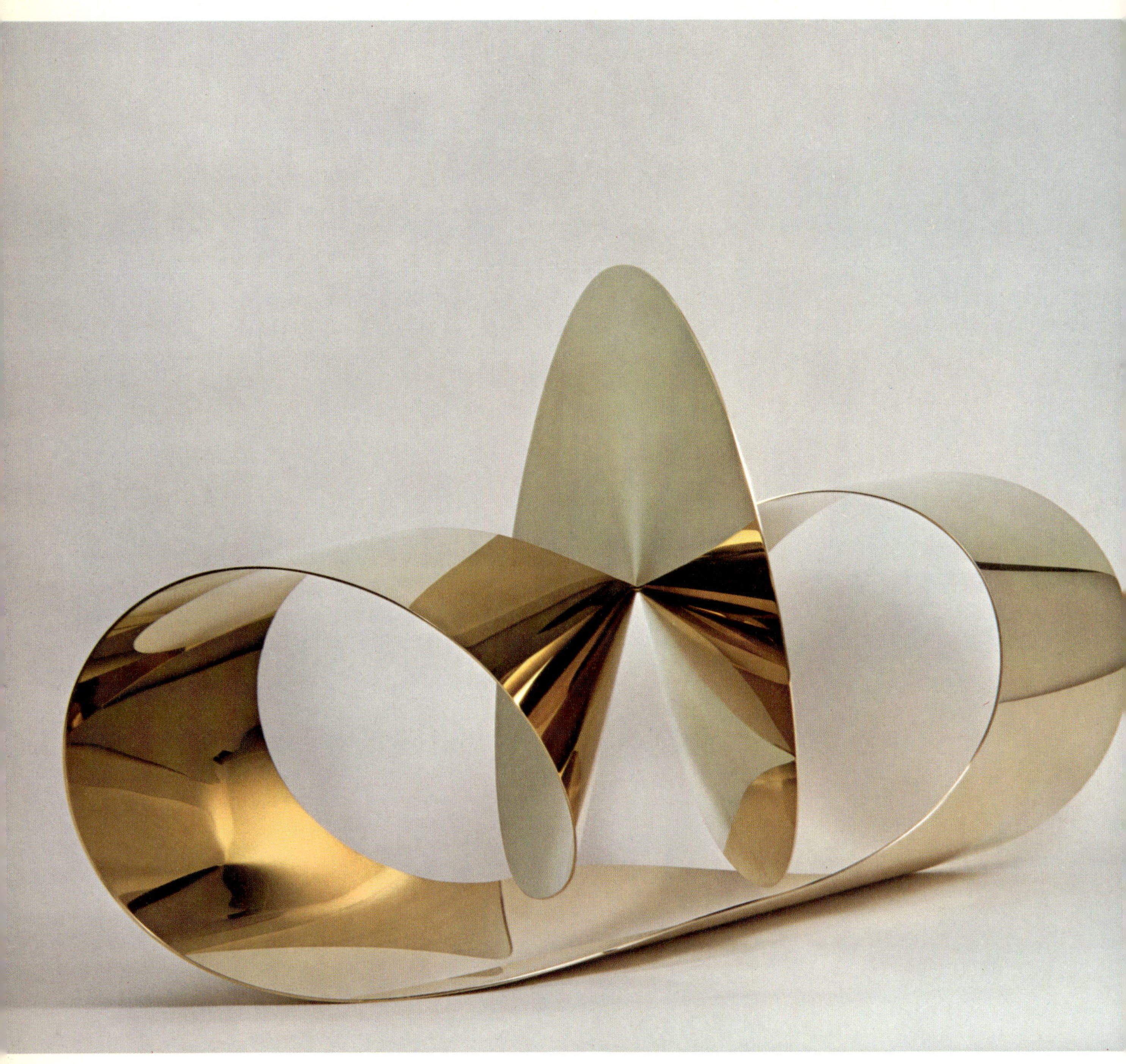

1972
Contour Passes Through the Center
gilt brass, 33½″ × 16½″ × 15″,
(85 × 42 × 38 cm)

1972
The Solid Half of a Sphere
black granite, diameter, 31½″,
(80 cm)

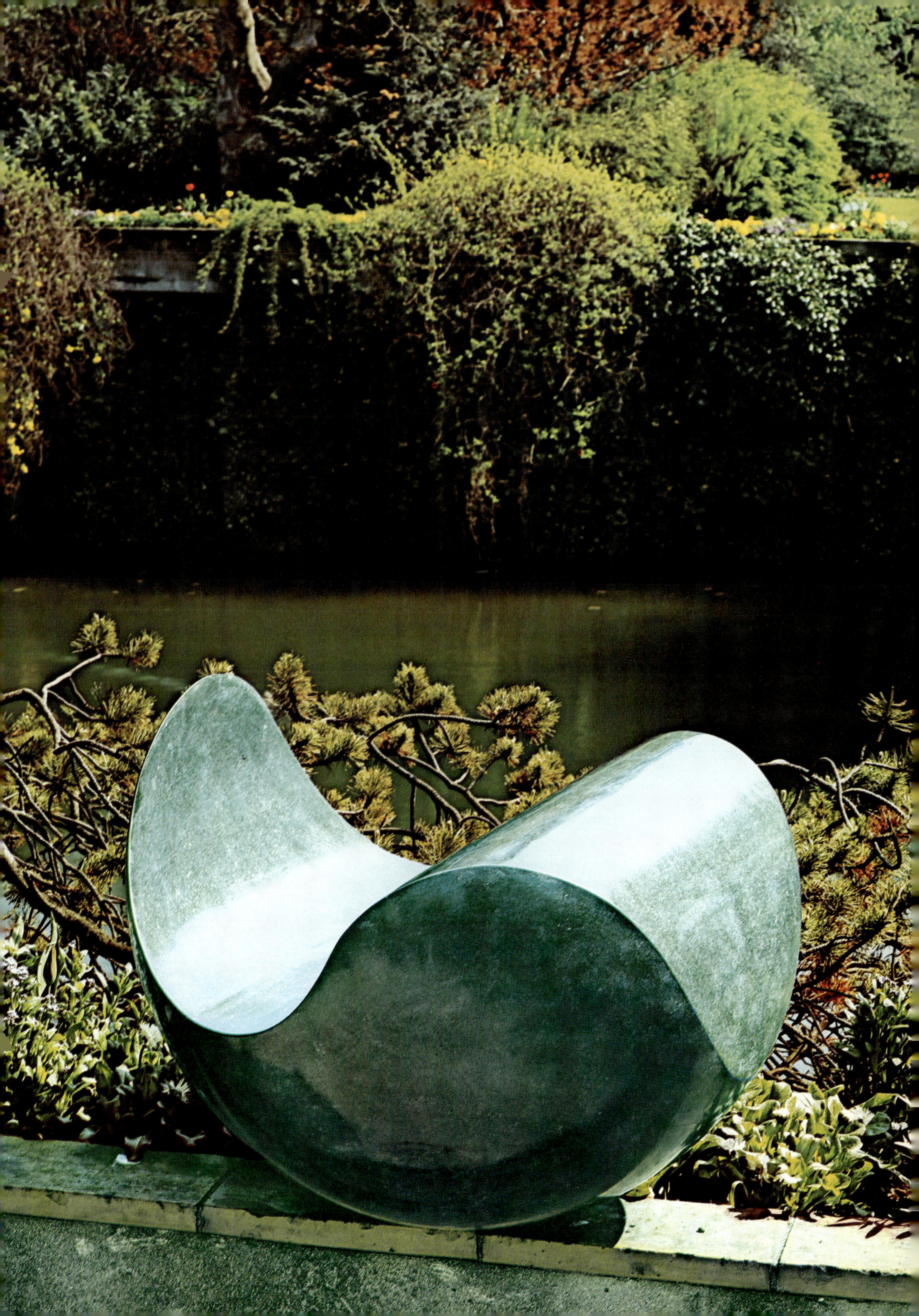

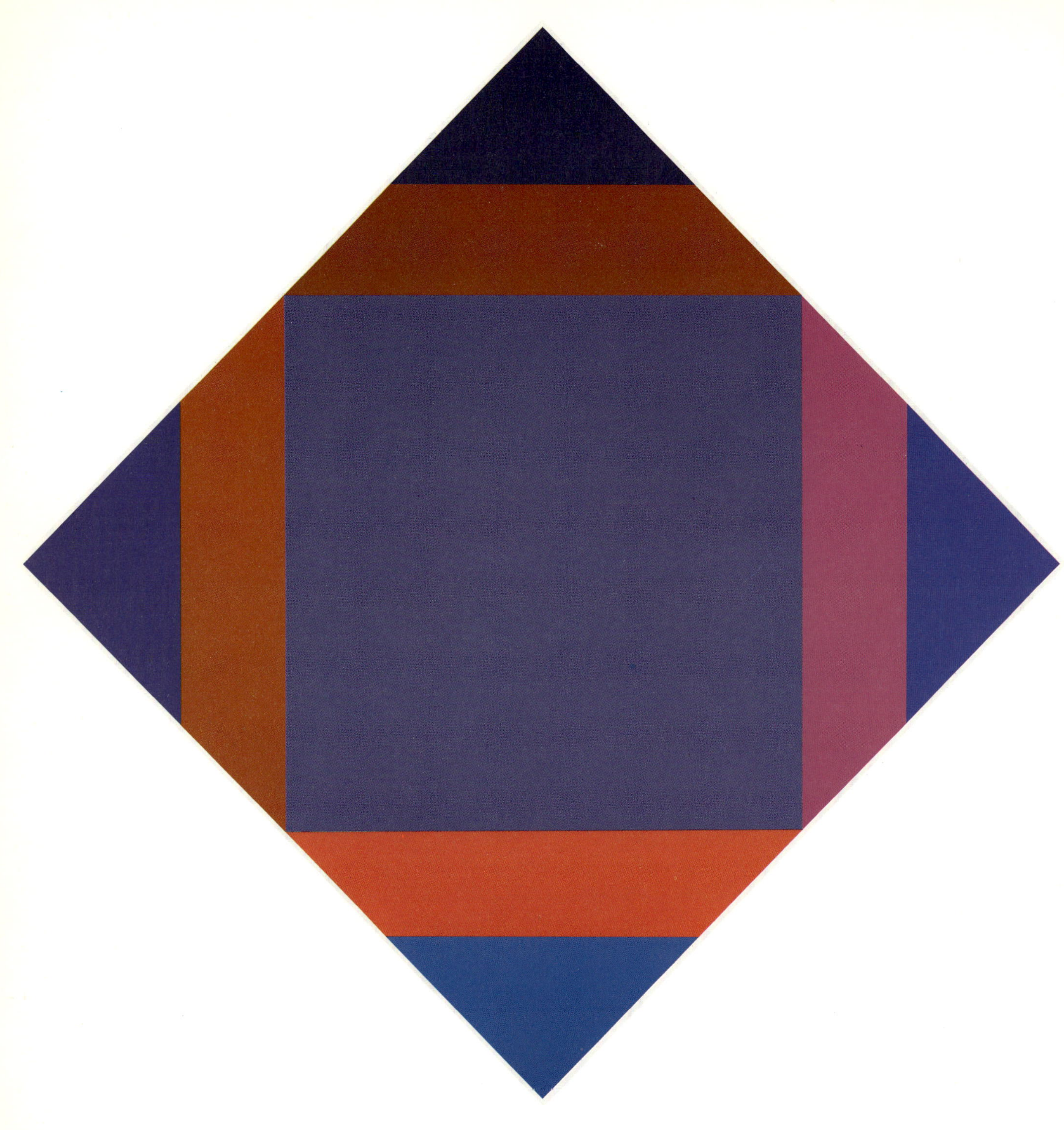

1972
Radiation from Violet
oil on canvas, diagonal, 67″,
(170 cm)

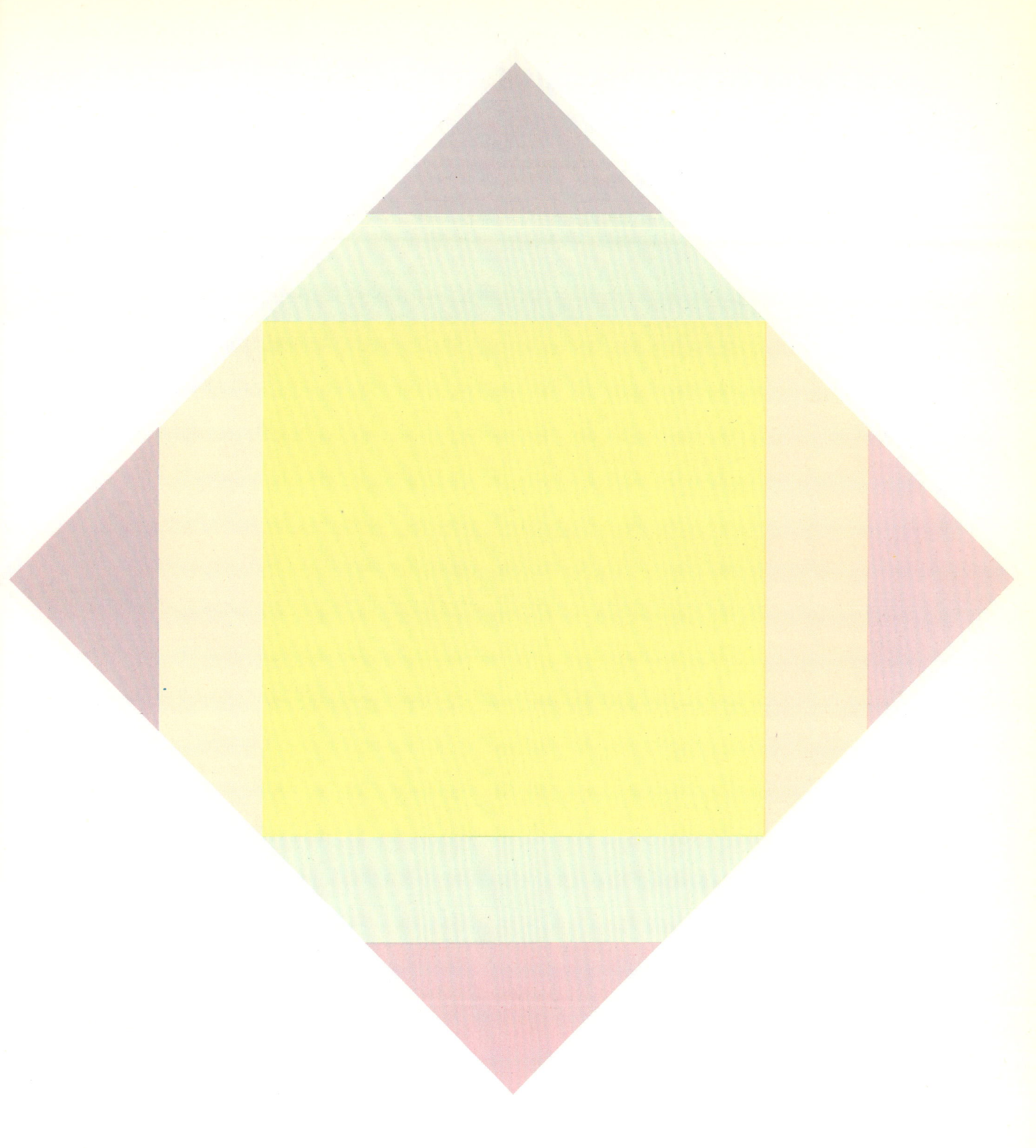

1972
Transcoloration from Yellow I
oil on canvas, diagonal, 34⅝",
(88 cm)

173

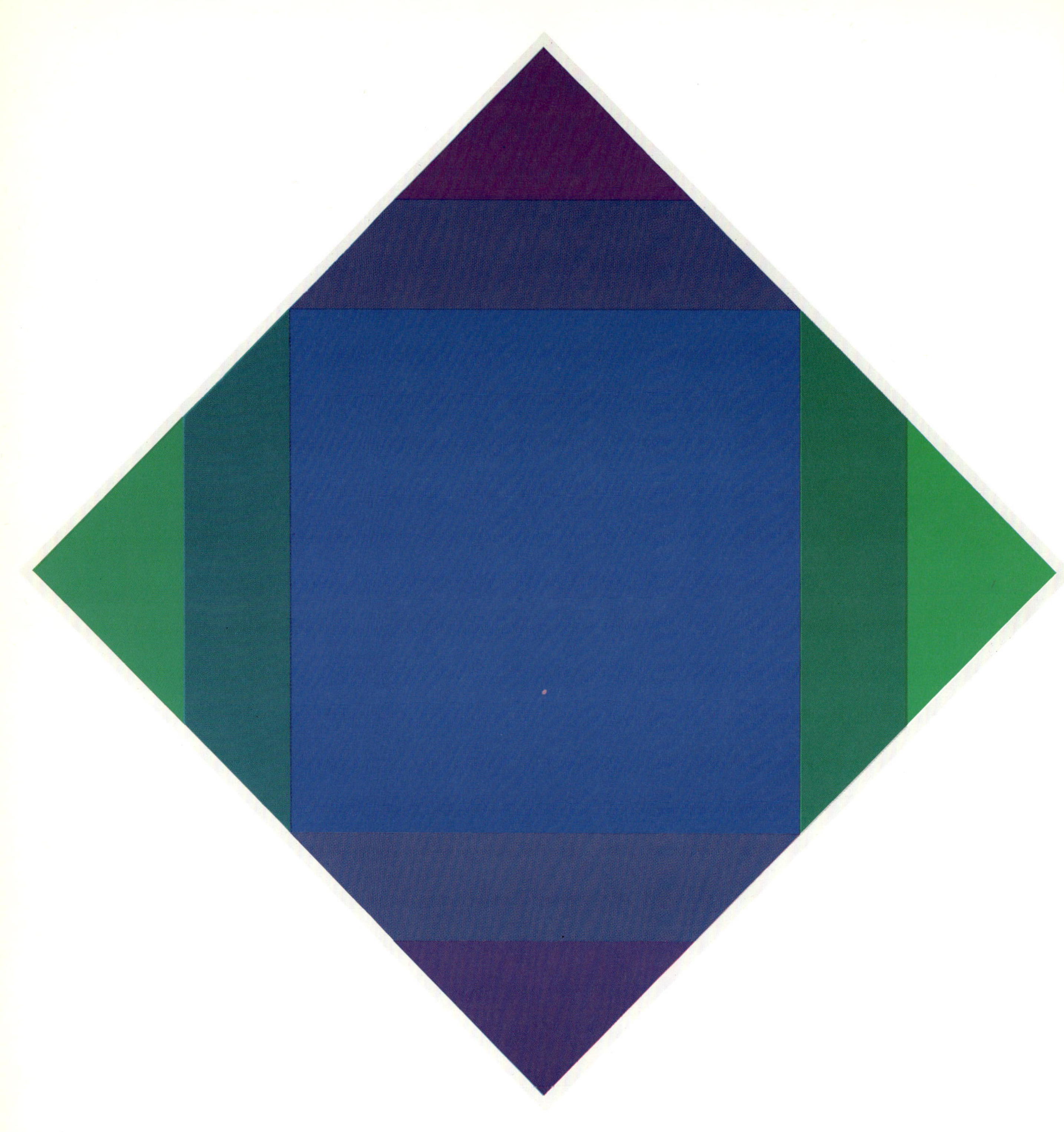

1972–73
Radiation from Blue
oil on canvas, diagonal, 34⅝″,
(88 cm)

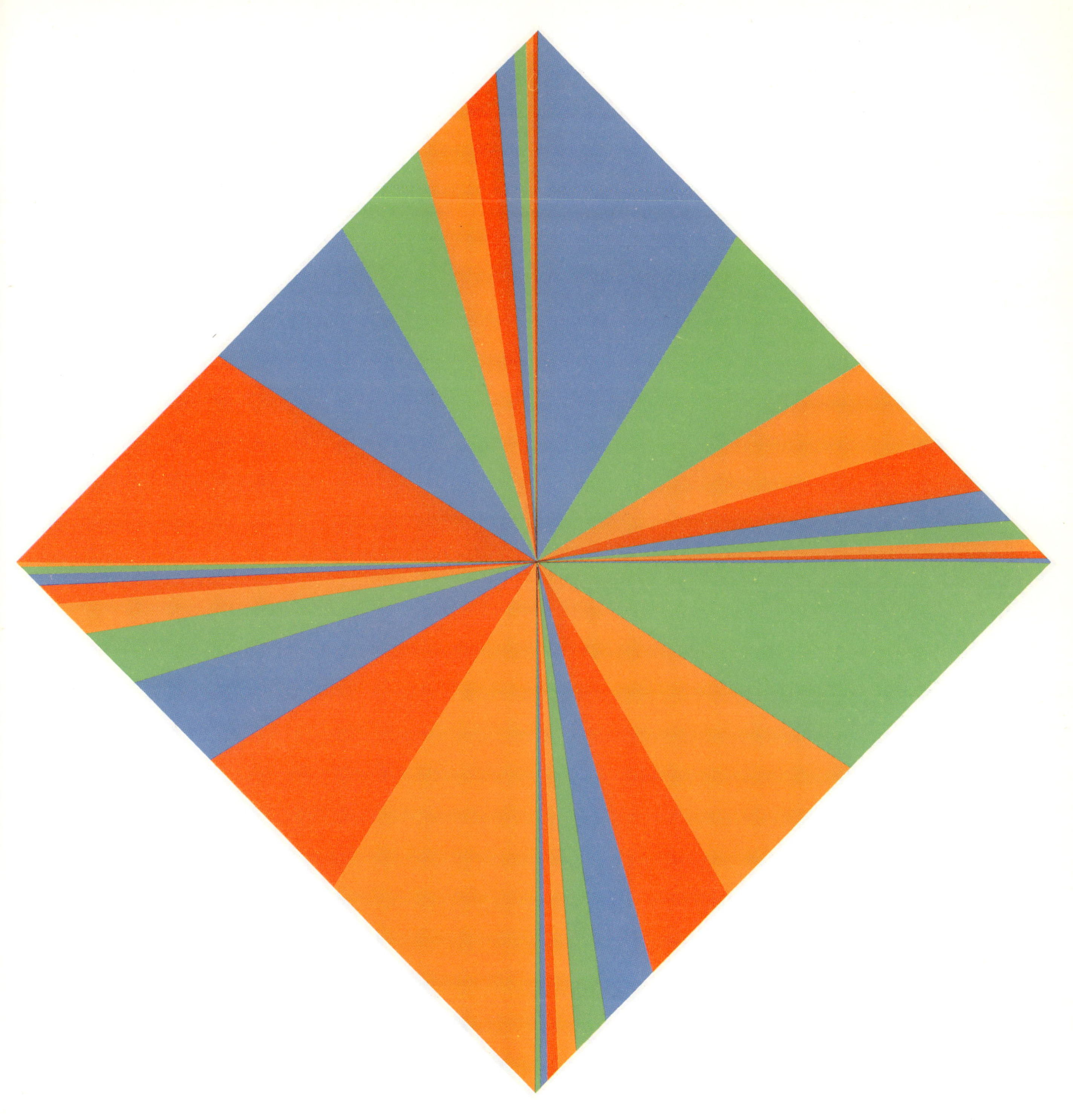

1972–73
*Radiation Through Four Equal Color
Quantities*
oil on canvas, diagonal, 111½″,
(283 cm)

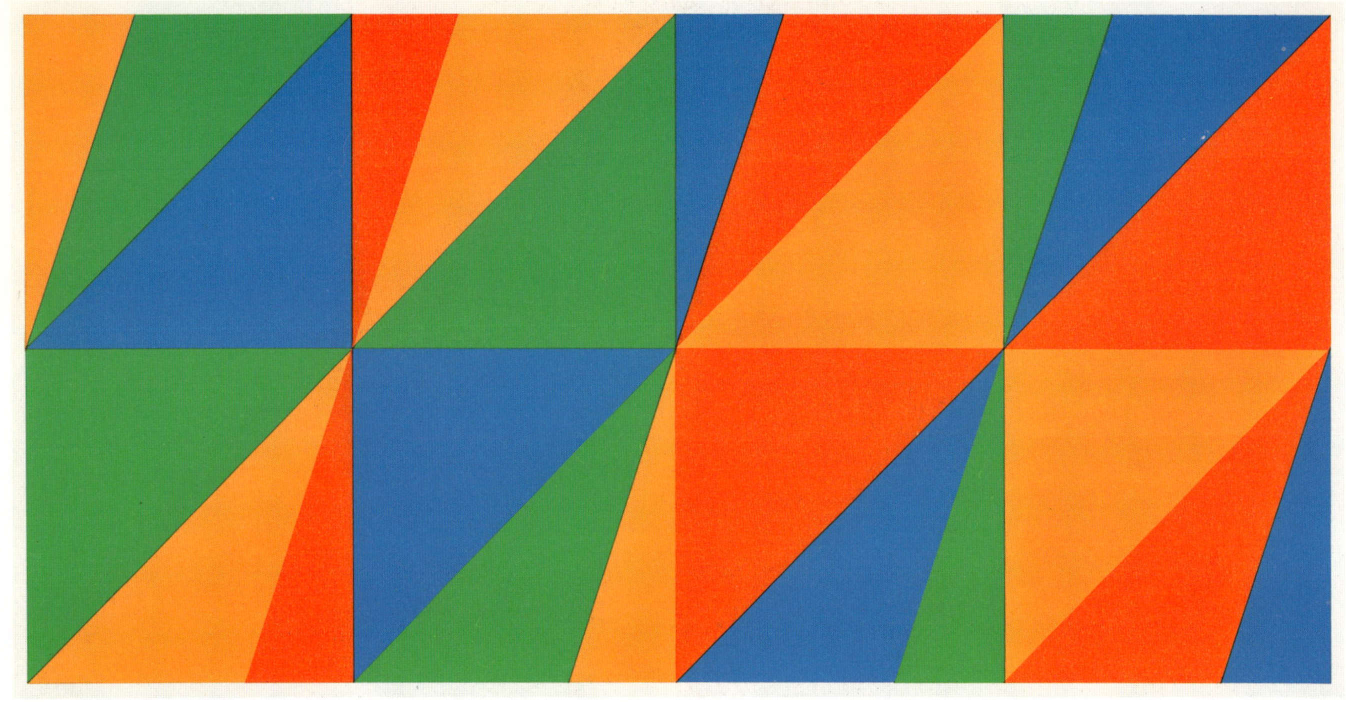

1973
Four Colors of Equal Quantities in Eight
Equal Fields
oil on canvas, 70⅞″ × 35½″,
(180 × 90 cm)

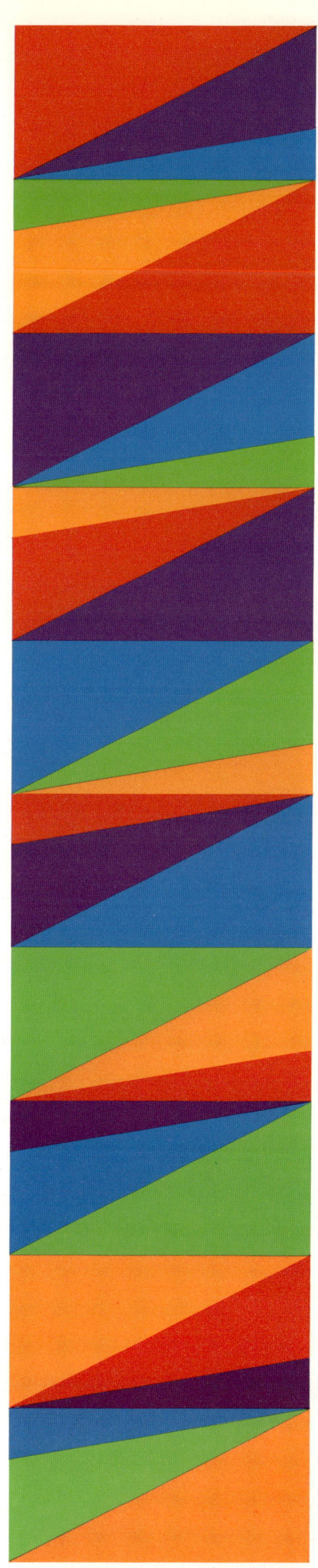

1973
*Transcoloration of Five Equal Color
Quantities*
oil on canvas, 23⅝″ × 118⅛″,
(60 × 300 cm)

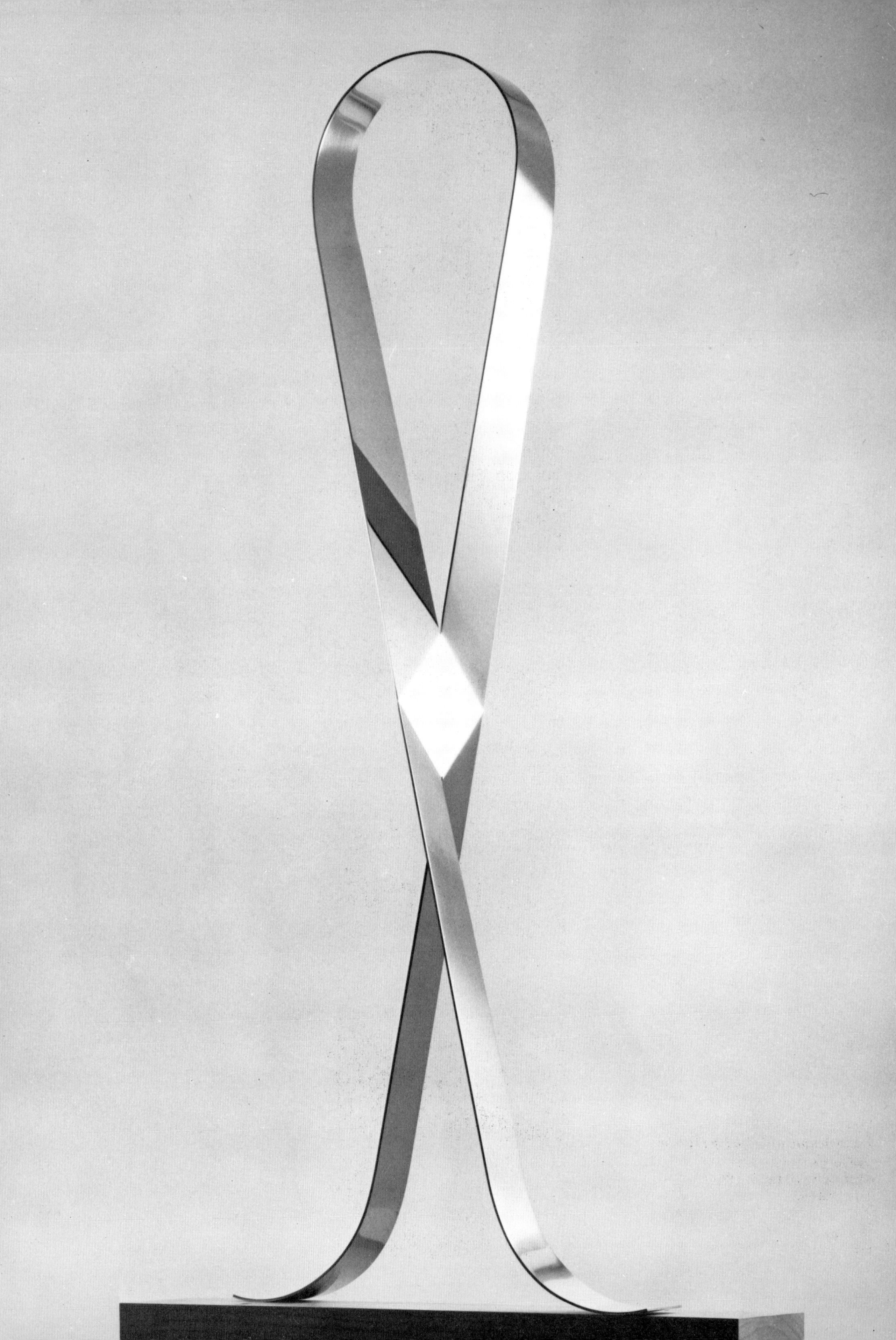

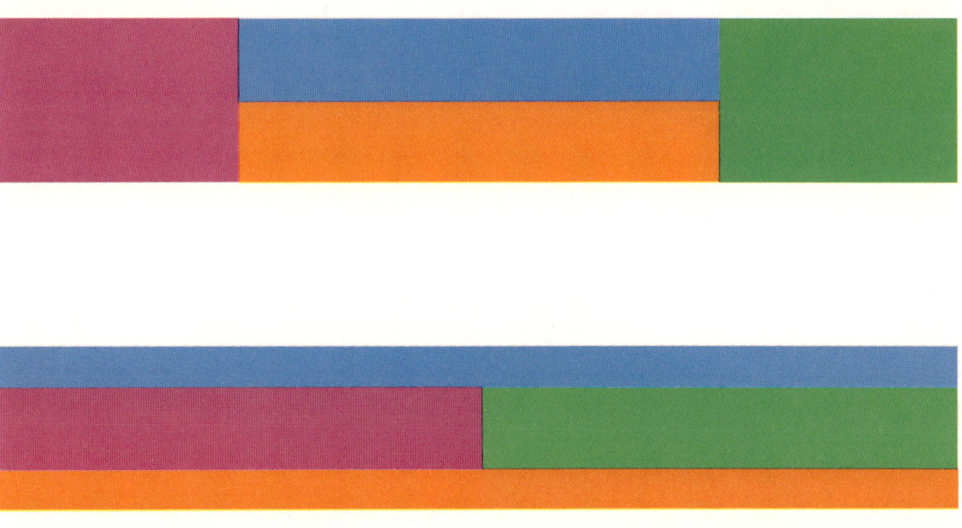

1973
Hexagonal Surface Around Two Squares
gilt brass, heigh 53½ ″
(136 cm)

1974
8 = (2 · 4/4) = 8
8 silkscreens, 27½″ × 27½″,
(70 × 70 cm)
intruduction plate

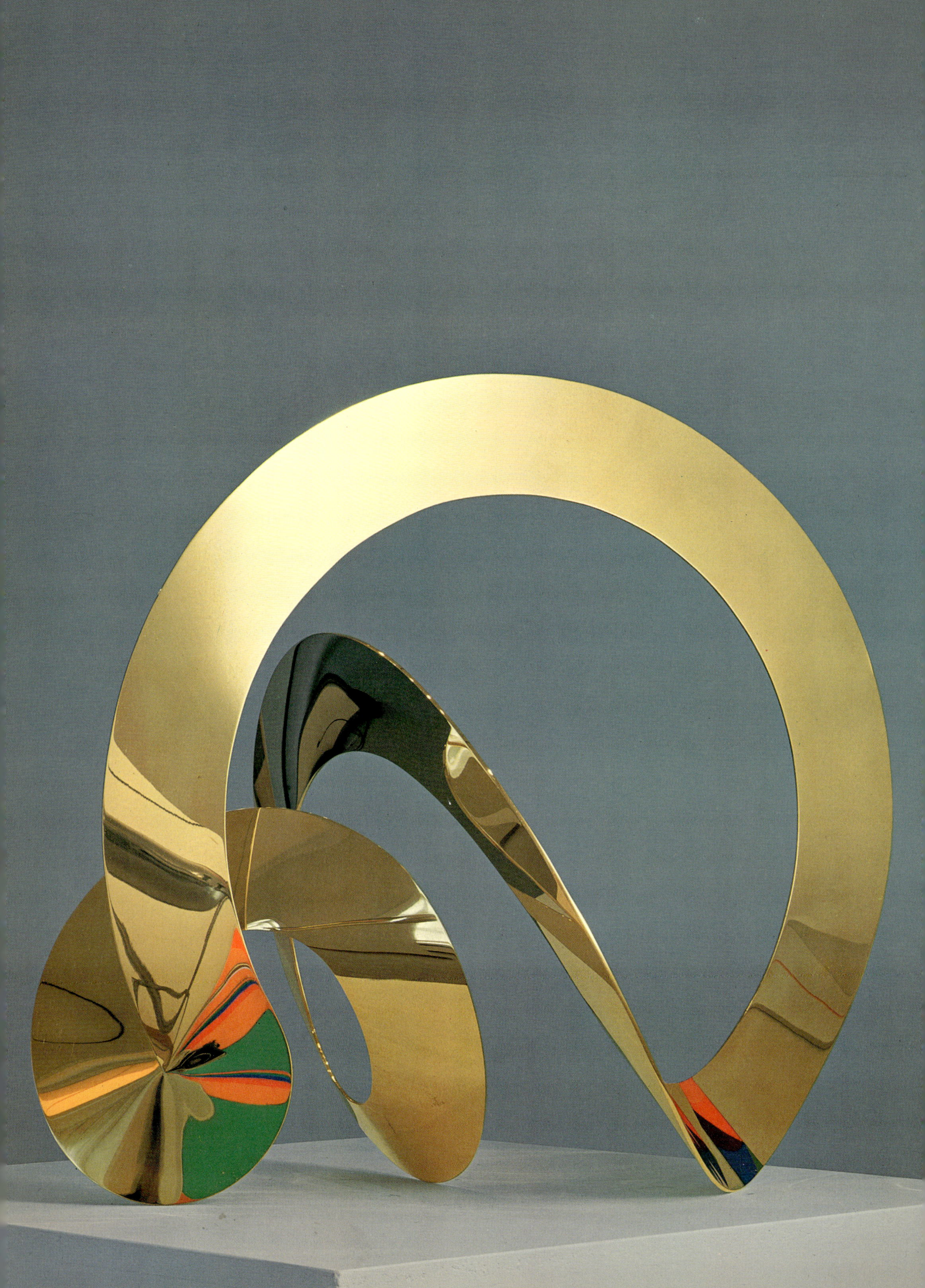

the suite of sixteen constellations is a
closed series that deals with the theme of
three circular lines of the same length.

the system on which this theme is based
was first carried out in a painting of 1944
that was made up of three circular curves.
this was the beginning of my research into
problems related to the vibration that
takes place on the edges of colour. in 1945
i transformed the theme and did a lithograph in 1946 entitled «four accents of the
same length». in a painting of the same
year i interpreted each line by a different
colour. this also belongs to my research
into the vibration of colours. in the last
version (lithograph as well as painting) the
fourth line was a straight line.

in 1960 i took up this theme again and
modified it into its present form.

my friend gualtieri di san lazzaro, who in
1938 published the portofolio «fifteen
variations on a single theme» (paris, édi-
tions des chroniques du jour) expressed
his desire to publish a second one.

a few weeks after the printing of the
sixteen constellations, gualtieri di san lazzaro
died, the seventh of september 1974.

max bill

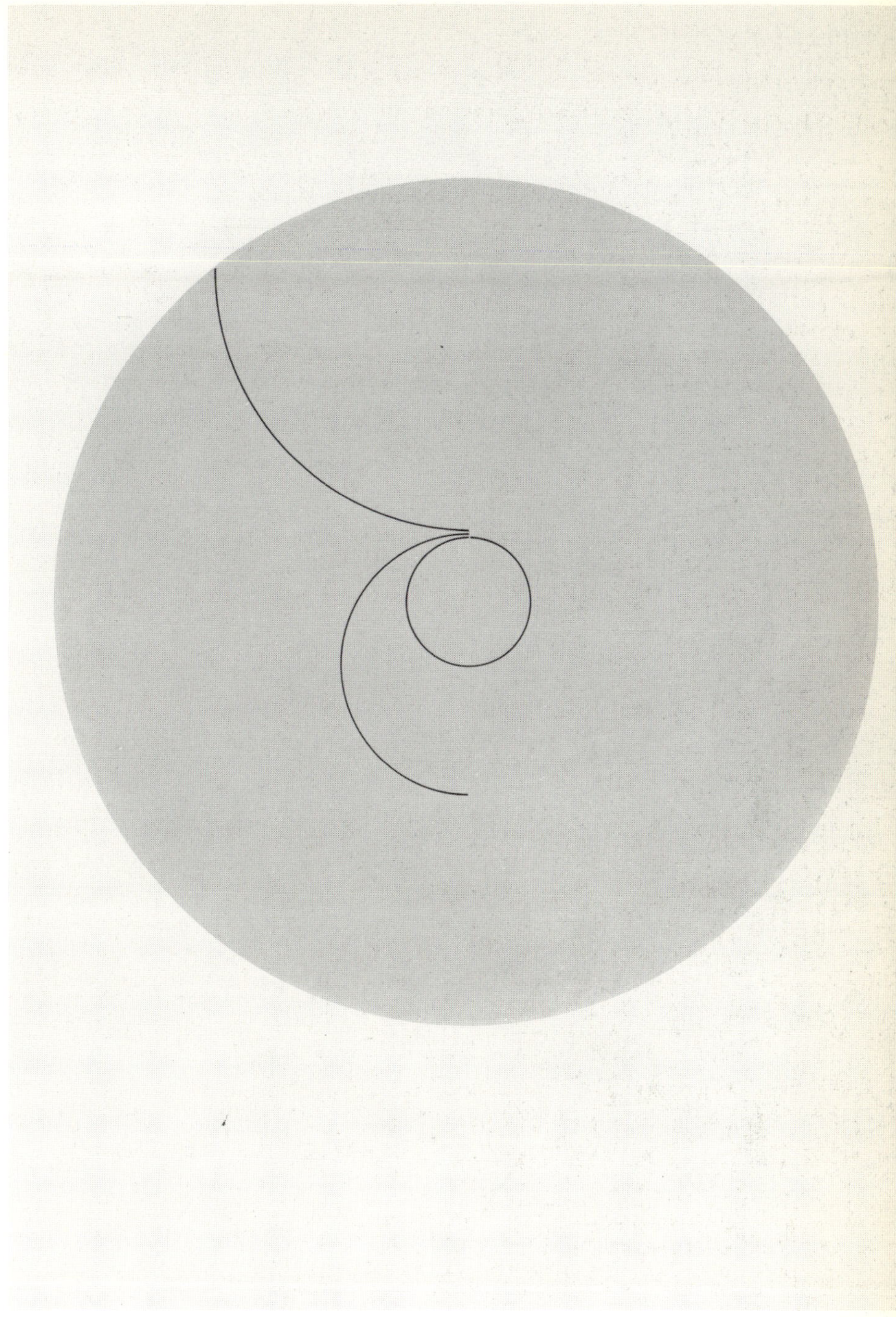

1974
Surface from an Entire Spiral
gilt brass, 30²/₄″ × 19³/₄″ × 24½″
(77 × 50 × 62 cm)

1974
Nr. 1, of *«16 Constellations»*
16 lithographs, 14¼″ × 20″,
(36 × 50.5 cm)

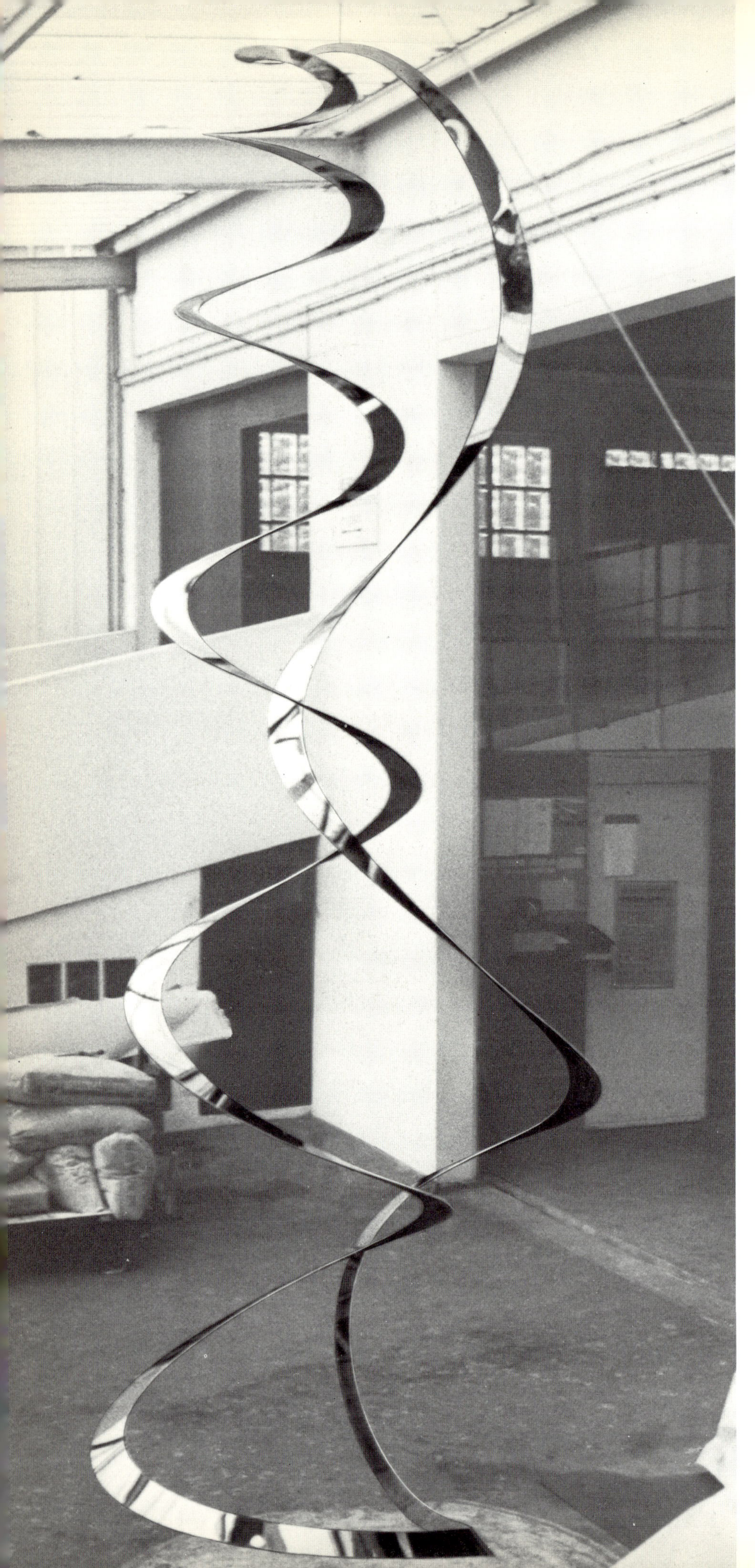

1973–74
Endless Spiral-Surface
stainless steel, diameter 5″ × 14″ height,
(150 × 420 cm)
Rapid-American Corp., New York

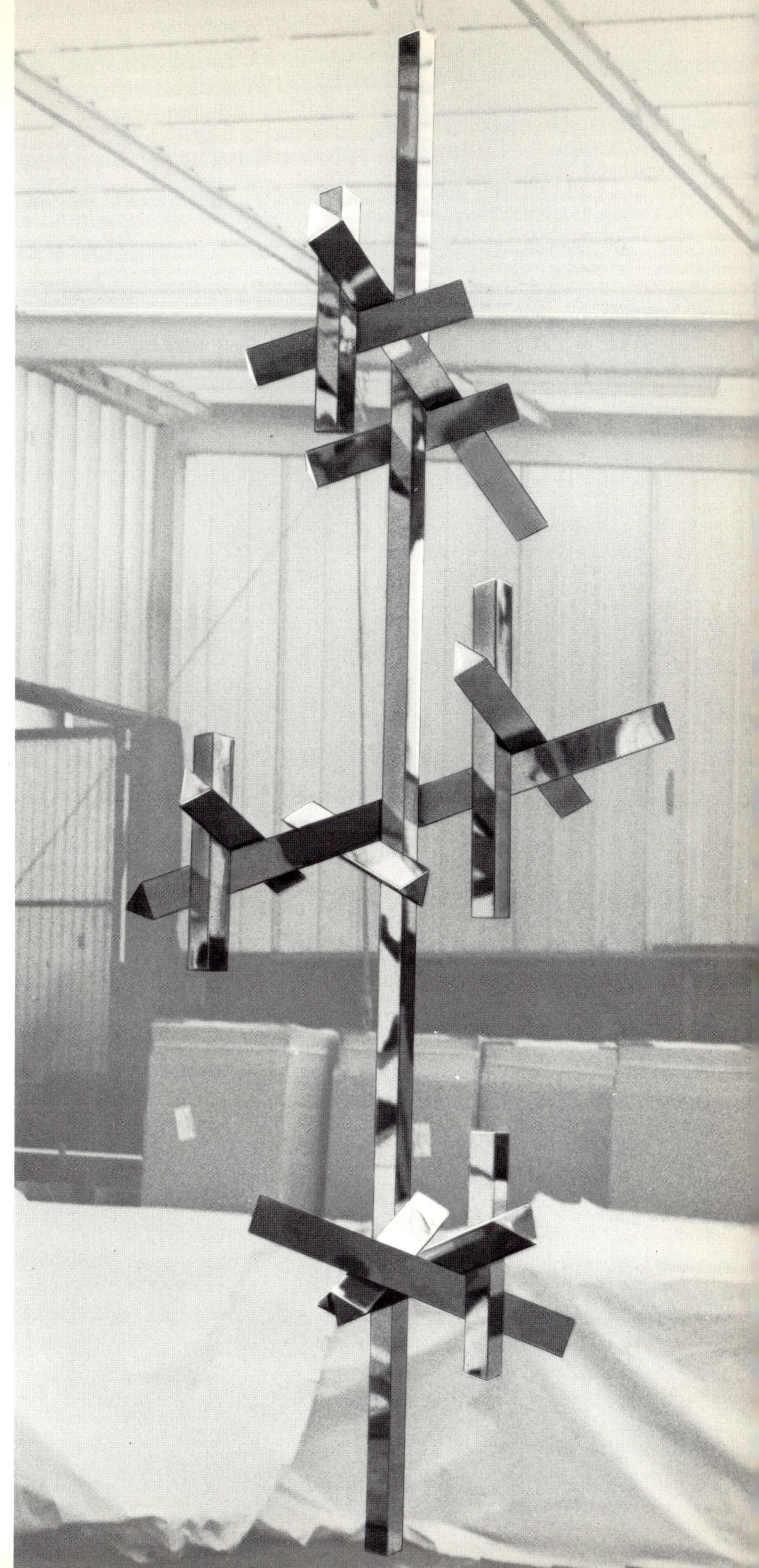

1973–74
Construction from Four Equal Prisms
stainless steel, diameter 5″ × 14″ height,
(150 × 420 cm)
Rapid-American Corp., New York

Lenders to the Exhibition: Mrs. Binia Bill, Zumikon/Zürich, Switzerland
Mrs. James Gray Ury, Belvedere, California
Mr. Richard Zeisler, New York

Albright-Knox Art Gallery, Buffalo, New York
The Art Institute of Chicago, Chicago, Illinois
Detroit Institute of Arts, Detroit, Michigan
Kunsthaus, Zürich, Switzerland
Kunstmuseum, Basel, Switzerland
Kunstmuseum, Bern, Switzerland
Kunstverein, Winterthur, Switzerland
Musée National d'Art Moderne, Paris

The Carborundum Company, Niagara Falls, New York
Migros-Genossenschaft, St. Gallen, Switzerland
Rapid-American Corporation, New York

Galerie Beyeler, Basel, Switzerland
Marlborough Fine Art (London) Ltd., London
Marlborough Galerie AG, Zürich, Switzerland
Marlborough Gallery, Inc., New York
Marlborough-Godard Ltd., Toronto, Canada

Works by Max Bill   **in the following Public Collections**

Amsterdam	Peter Stuyvesant Collection
Antwerpen	Middelheimpark/Open-Air Museum for Sculpture
Basle	Kunstmuseum
Belfast	The Ulster Museum
Berne	Kunstmuseum
Bochum	Städtische Kunstgalerie

Brugg	City of Brugg/City Administration Building
Brussels	Musées Royaux des Beaux-Arts de Belgique
Buffalo	Albright-Knox Art Gallery
Cambridge, USA	Busch-Reisinger Museum/Harvard University
Chicago	Art Institute of Chicago
Detroit	Institute of Arts
Duisburg	Wilhelm-Lehmbruck-Museum
Geneva	City of Geneva
Geneva	Musée d'Art et d'Histoire
Grenchen	City of Grenchen/Park Theatre
Grenoble	Musée de Peinture et de Sculpture
Hamburg	City of Hamburg/Kennedy Bridge
Hannover	Niedersächsisches Landesmuseum
Humlebaek/Danmark	Louisiana Museum
Kaiserslautern	Pfalzgalerie
Karlsruhe	University of Karlsruhe/Building of the Mathematical Institute
Locarno	Museo d'Arte Contemporanea/Castello Visconti
Los Angeles	County Museum of Art
Marl	Town Hall
Montreal	Museum of Fine Arts
Montreal	Museum of Contemporary Art
Mountainville N.Y.	Storm King Art Center
Nagaoka	Nagaoka Museum of Contemporary Art
New York City	Ciba-Geigy Collection
New York City	McCrory Corporation
New York City	New York University Art Collection
Paris	Musée National d'Art Moderne
Paris	Centre National d'Art Contemporain
Rio de Janeiro	Museu de Arte Moderna
Rome	Galleria Nazionale d'Arte Moderna
São Paulo	Museu de Arte Moderna
Stuttgart	Staatsgalerie
Tel Aviv	Modern Art Museum
Tokyo	Hakone Open-Air Museum
Toronto	Art Gallery of Ontario
Uster	City of Uster, Town Hall
Vienna	Museum des 20. Jahrhunderts
Washington D.C.	The Hirshhorn Museum and Sculpture Garden
Winterthur	Kunstmuseum
Winterthur	City of Winterthur
Zurich	City of Zurich, extended loan to the Kunsthaus
Zurich	Kunsthaus

statement 1974

one often speaks of the mathematics, the structure, the systems in art. i also did it. looking for a non-individualistic approach to so-called art problems, i did different kinds of research and i wrote a few statements which were worldwide publicized and interpreted.

as life – and so ideas and art as one of the human activities – is in constant motion, and as we hope in permanent development, my ideas also have developed and became clearer. this because of more experience and an accumulation of knowledge.

when i wrote a quarter of a century ago about «the mathematical approach in the contemporary art» this was a new way to see art which until then had been considered mostly as the more or less uncontrolled experience of an individual.

today i know better that mathematics are only a part of the methods to be adapted for the regulation of so-called works of art. i know that a concept has to conform to its inner organization and its visual existence. this means that a concept and the finally executed work have to be a unity. this unity is the result of the logical approach to the solution of the problem and its realization.

i prefer today to describe this process as the logical approach to the problems of art. this means that every part of the creative process follows step by step consciously a logical analysis and feedback. this is the way i hope to realize my vision best.

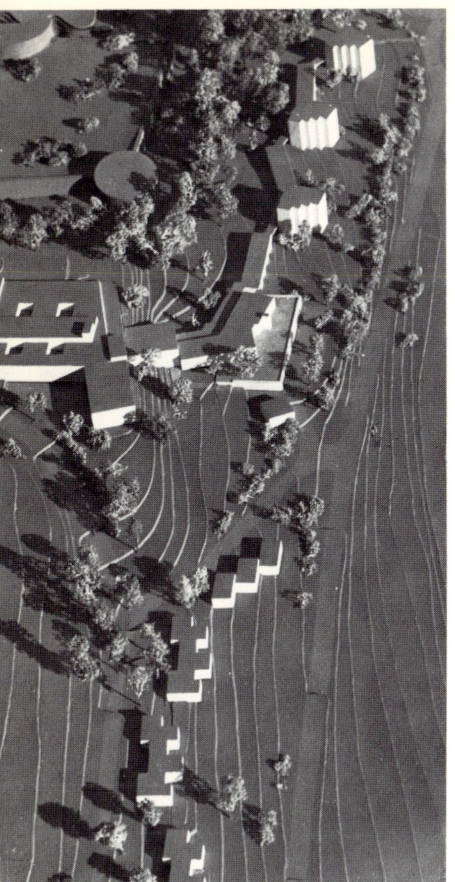

1953–55. «Hochschule für Gestaltung» Ulm (Institute of Design). Model of the project 1951–53.

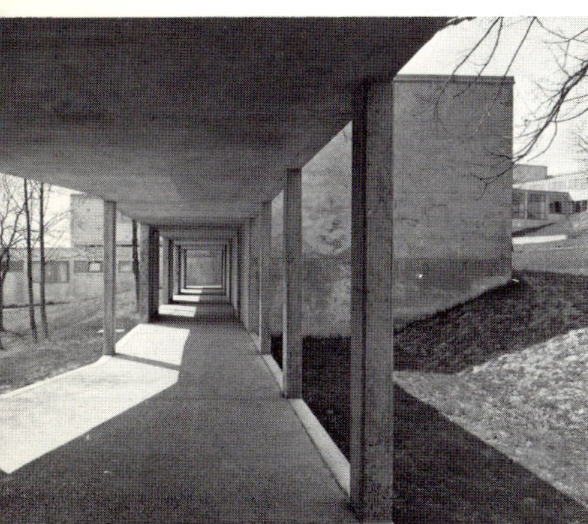

1955. Corridor between mainbuilding and the student dormitories underneath the student studios.

Biography

1908
Born on December 22 in Winterthur, Switzerland, of a family originating from Moosseedorf (Canton of Berne)

1924–27
Studies at the Kunstgewerbeschule (School of Applied Arts), Zürich, training as a silversmith

1927–29
Studies at the Bauhaus, Dessau (Germany)

1929
Settles in Zürich, where he works as an architect, painter and graphic artist, as a sculptor (from 1932), a publicist (from 1936), and a product designer (from 1944). In all these fields he is also active as a theorist, teacher and lecturer both in Switzerland and abroad.

1951–56
Co-founder and rector of the Hochschule für Gestaltung, Ulm, where he was in charge of the Departments of Architecture and of Product Design («Produktform»), and of designing the buildings.

1961–64
Chief Architect of the «Educating and Creating» Section of the Swiss National Exhibition, Lausanne, 1964

1961–68
Member of the Swiss Federal Art Commission
Member of the City Council, Zürich

1967–71
Member of the Swiss Parliament

1967–74
Professor of Environmental Design at the State Institute of Fine Arts (Staatliche Hochschule für Bildende Künste), Hamburg

1930–62
Member of SWB (Schweizerischer Werkbund, Swiss Arts and Crafts Society)

1932–36
Member of the «Abstraction-Création» Group, Paris

1937
Joins «Allianz» (Association of Modern Swiss Artists)

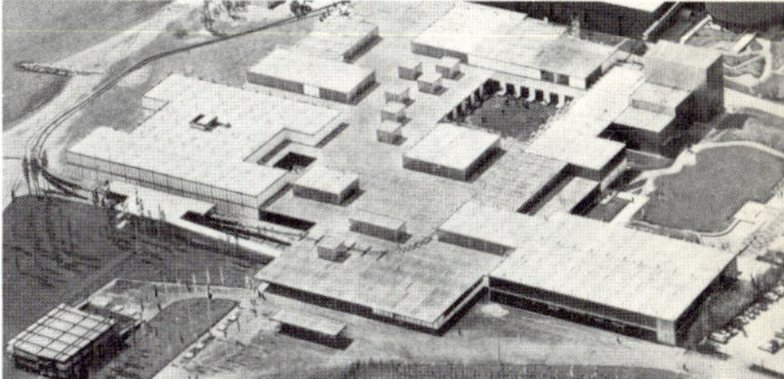

1964. «Swiss National Exhibition» East entrance and «Educating and Creating» Section.

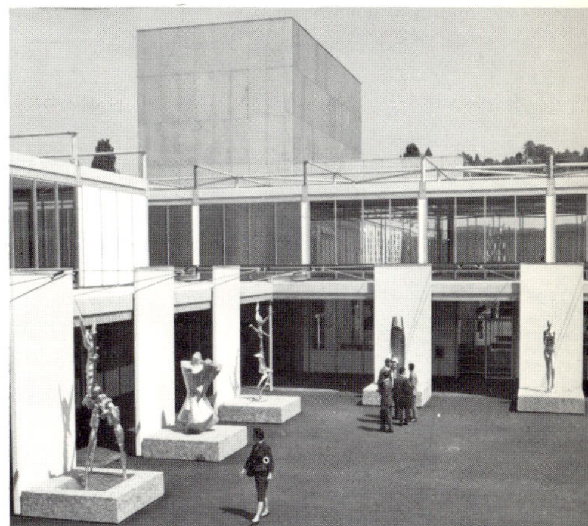

1964. The «Court of the Arts» in the Section «Educating and Creating» at the «Swiss National Exhibition» Lausanne.

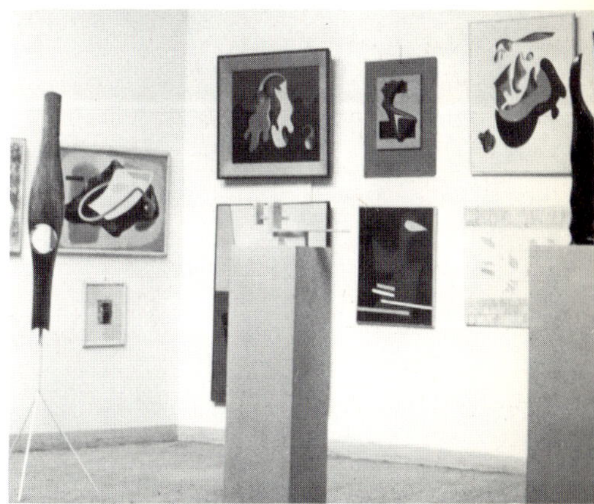

1933. Exhibition «Abstraction-Création» Paris. Sculptures by Bill, Vantongerloo, Béothy.

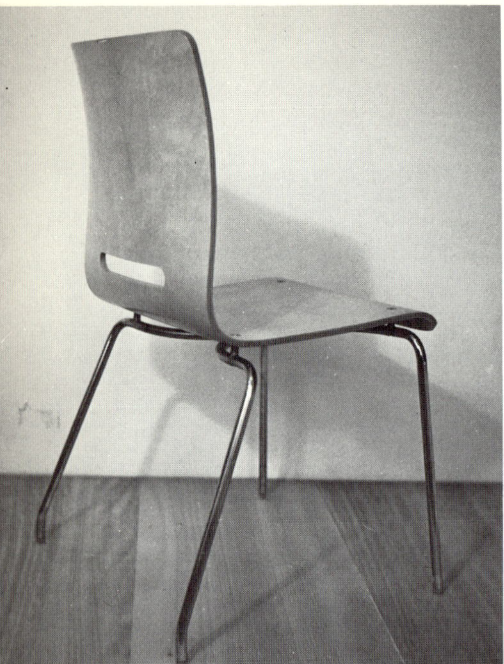

1951. Stacking chair of plywood and steel.

1938
Member of CIAM (Congrès International d'Architecture Moderne)

1949
Member of UAM (Union des Artistes Modernes), Paris

1953
Member of the Institut d'Esthétique Industrielle, Paris

1956
Member of DWB (Deutscher Werkbund, German Arts and Crafts Society)

1959
Member of BSA (Bund Schweizer Architekten, Society of Swiss Architects)

1964
Honorary Fellow of the American Institute of Architects, Hon. FAIA

1965
Honorary Member of «Oeuvre» (Swiss Association of Artists, Craftsmen and Industrialists)

1968
Member of GSMBA (Society of Swiss Painters, Sculptors and Architects)

1972
Extraordinary Member of the Academy of the Arts, Berlin

1973
Nonresident Member of the Royal Flamisch Academy of Science, Literature and the Arts

1973
Honorary Consultant, International Association of Fine Arts (UNESCO)

1936
Swiss section at the Milan Triennale gets Grand prize for his presentation

1949
Kandinsky Prize, Paris

1951
First International prize for sculpture at the São Paulo Bienal
Grand prize at the Milan Triennale for his presentation of the Swiss section

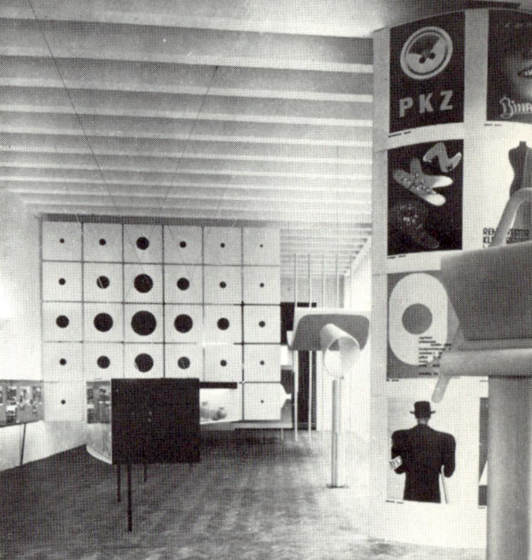

1951. Swiss Section at the Milan Triennale.

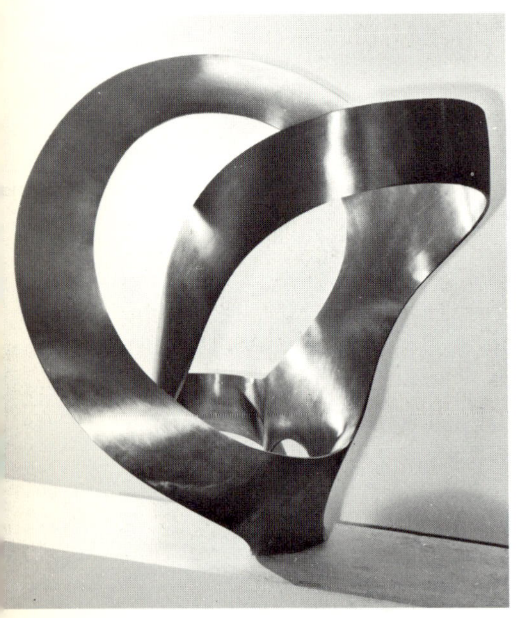

1947–48. «Tripartite Unity», stainless steel. First International Sculpture Price at the «São Paulo Biennal 1951». Collection Museu de Arte Moderna, São Paulo.

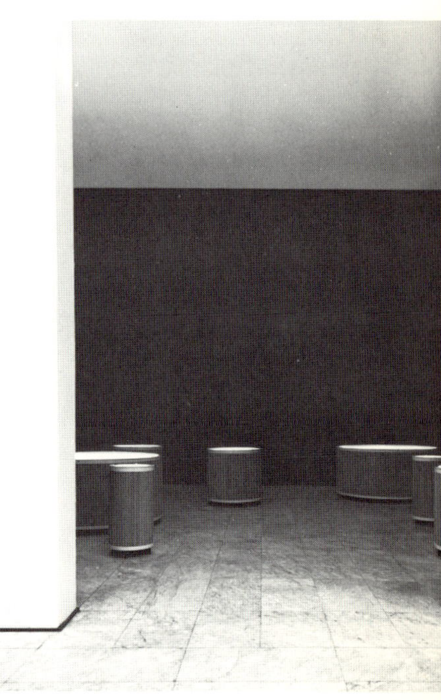

1936. Swiss Section at the Milan Triennale.

1953
Honorable mention (3rd prize) in the
International Competition for the monu-
ment to «The Unknown Political Priso-
ner», Institute of Contemporary Arts,
London

1966
Gold Medal of the Italian Chamber of
Deputies on the occasion of the Interna-
tional Congress of Artists and Critics at
Vérucchio

1968
Awarded the art prize of the City of
Zürich

1971
One of the ten equal prizes at the 1st
International Biennale of Small Sculpture,
Budapest

One-Man Exhibitions

1928
Bauhaus, Dessau (with Albert Braun)

1929
Atelier des Künstlers, Zürich

1930
Kunsthalle, Bern (with Probst, Steck, Val-
lotton, von May)

1939
Kunstmuseum, Basel (Fifteen variations
on a single theme)

1943
Kunststuben im Rösslyn, Zürich (with
Wiemken and Leuppi)

1946
Galerie des Eaux-Vives, Zürich

1948
Galerie Herrmann, Stuttgart (with Albers
and Arp)

1949
Galerie d'Art Moderne, Basel
Galerie Gerd Rosen, Berlin (with Albers)
Kunsthaus, Zürich (with Pevsner and Van-
tongerloo)

1950
Museu de Arte Moderna de São Paulo,
São Paulo

1951
Kunstverein, Freiburg i. Br. (with Bissier
and Vantongerloo)

1956–57
Travelling Exhibition:
Ulmer Museum, Ulm
Die Neue Sammlung, Staatliches Museum
für angewandte Kunst, München
Städtisches Kunstmuseum, Duisburg (now
Wilhelm-Lehmbruck-Museum der Stadt
Duisburg)
Städtisches Karl-Ernst-Osthaus-Museum,
Hagen

1957
Helmhaus, Zürich

1958
Biennale di Venezia, Pavillon suisse,
Venezia
Galerie Suzanne Bollag, Zürich (with Har-
tung and Poliakoff)

1958–59
Galerie Suzanne Bollag, Zürich

1959
Kunsthalle, Basel (with Aeschbacher,
Linck and Müller)
Galerie Gelbes Haus, St. Gallen
Städtisches Museum Leverkusen, Schloss
Morsbroich, Leverkusen studio f, Ulm

1960
Staatsgalerie, Stuttgart
Kunstmuseum, Winterthur
Galerie Suzanne Bollag, Zürich
Galerie im Ronca-Haus, Luzern

1961
Galerie du Perron, Genève
Galerie Anna Roepke, Wiesbaden

1962
Galerie Hilt, Basel

1963
Galerie Suzanne Bollag, Zürich
Galerie Gimpel & Hanover, Zürich
Staempfli Gallery, New York
Pace Gallery, Boston
studio f, Ulm

1964
Galleria Cadario, Milano
Galerie Suzanne Bollag, Zürich
Galleria del Deposito, Genova-Bocca-
dasse
Galleria dell'Accademia, Roma

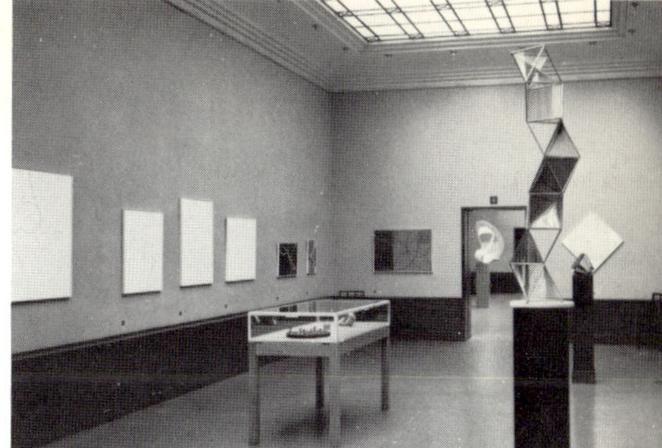

1949. Max Bill's rooms at the Exhibition
«Pevsner, Vantongerloo, Bill», Kunsthaus
Zürich.

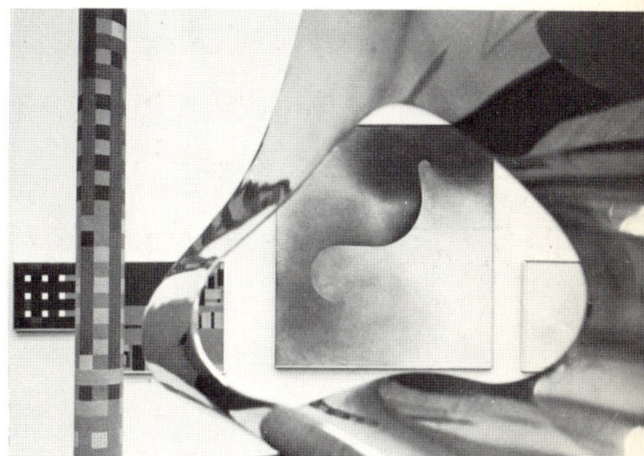

1950. Part of the Exhibition at the Museu
de Arte, São Paulo.

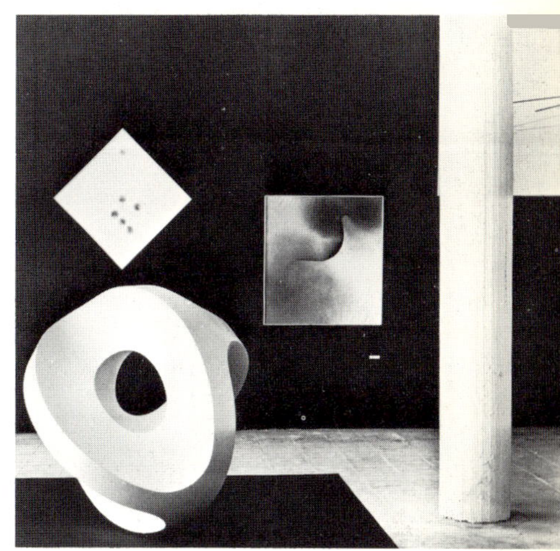

1955. Max Bill at the first
«Documenta» Kassel.

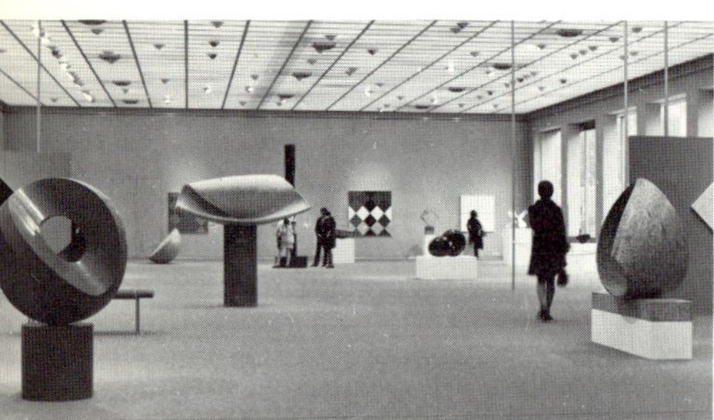

1968–69. Exhibition at Kunsthaus Zürich.

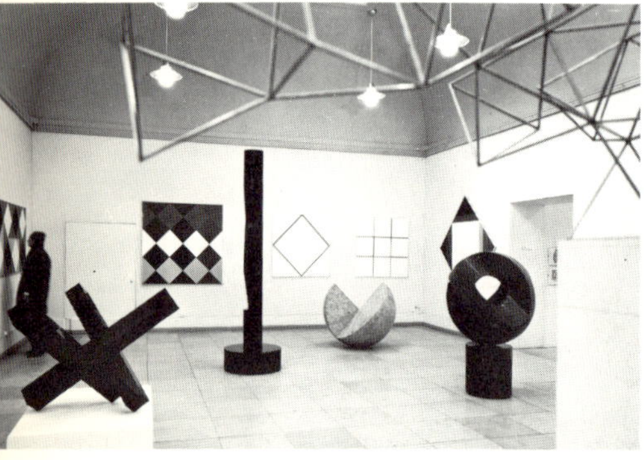

1969. Max Bill Exhibition at the Biennale Nürnberg.

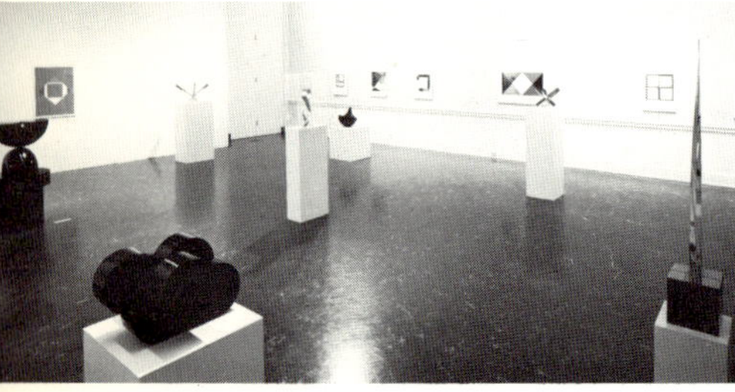

1970. Max Bill Exhibition at the San Francisco Museum of Art.

1965
Galerie Aktuell, Bern
(Op)-Art Galerie, Esslingen
Galleria Flaviana, Locarno
Galerie Suzanne Bollag, Zürich
Galerie 58, Rapperswil
Gemeindehaus, Uster

1966
Staempfli Gallery, New York
Galerie Suzanne Bollag, Zürich
Galerie Hilt, Basel
Hanover Gallery, London

1967
Galerie Im Erker, St. Gallen

1968
Kunsthalle, Bern
Kestner-Gesellschaft, Hannover
Kunstverein für die Rheinlande und West-
falen, Düsseldorf
Haags Gemeentemuseum, Den Haag
Musée des Beaux-Arts, La Chaux-de-
Fonds
Albrecht-Dürer-Gesellschaft, Kunsthalle,
Nürnberg
Galerie Aurora, Genève (with Le Corbu-
sier)

1968–69
Kunsthaus, Zürich
Galerie Suzanne Bollag, Zürich

1969
Arts Club of Chicago, Chicago
Galleria La Bertesca, Genova
Galleria La Polena, Genova
Galleria Vismara, Milano
Galerie Godard Lefort, Montreal
Staempfli Gallery, New York
Biennale 1969 Nürnberg, Kunsthalle,
Nürnberg
Galerie Denise René, Paris
Galleria Martano/Due, Torino
Galerie Bischofberger, Zürich
Centre National d'Art Contemporain,
Paris

1969–70
Musée de Peinture et de Sculpture, Grenoble

1970
Biennale di Venezia, (Linea di Ricerca),
Venezia
Edition Bischofberger, Zürich
Galerie Loeb, Bern
Neue Galerie, Baden-Baden
Galerie im Weissen Haus, Winterthur
San Francisco Museum of Art, San Fran-
cisco
Galerie Appel und Fertsch, Frankfurt

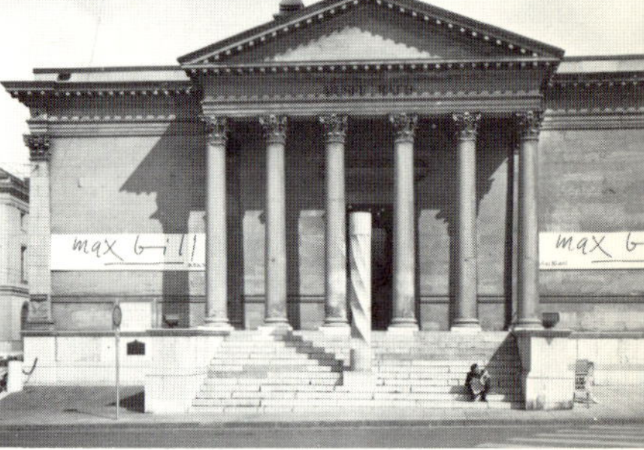

1972. Musée Rath, Geneva.

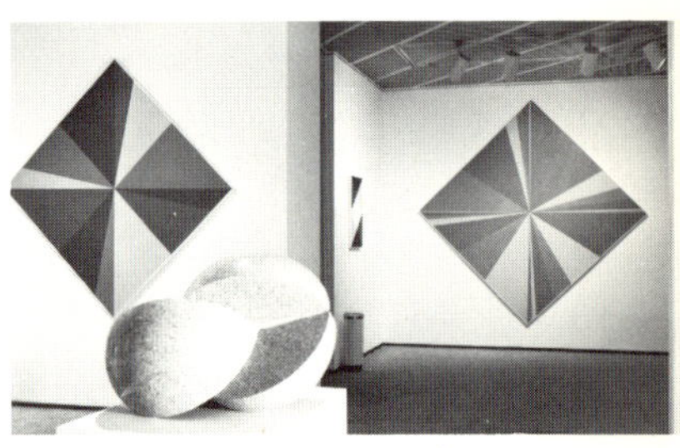

1974. Exhibition at Marlborough Fine Art,
London.

Galleria del Cavallino, Venezia
White Gallery, Lutry
Galleria Arte Studio, Macerata
Galerie design 1, Hamburg
Galerie Fürneisen, Hamburg
Galleria d'arte «Peccolo», Livorno
Galleria del Cortile, Roma
Galerie Klubschule, Zürich
Staempfli Gallery, New York

1971
Galerie Reckermann, Köln
Galerie Denise René, Paris
Galerie Suzanne Bollag, Zürich
Galerie im Erker, St. Gallen
Galerie Denise René/Hans Mayer,
Kunstmarkt, Köln

1972
Musée Rath, Geneva
Galleria Lorenzelli, Milano
Marlborough Galerie, Zürich
Kunstmuseum, Aarhuis
Galerie Hauswedell, Baden-Baden
Marlborough-Godard, Ltd., Toronto
Marlbourogh-Godard, Ltd., Montreal

1973
Galerie 58, Rapperswil

1973–74
Galerie Ziegler, Genève

1974
Marlborough Fine Art, London
Galleria Lorenzelli, Bergamo
Galerie Media, Neuchâtel
Galleria Medea, Milano
Marlborough Galerie, Zürich
Galerie Watari, Tokyo

1974–75
Travelling Exhibition:
Albright-Knox Art Gallery, Buffalo, New
York
Los Angeles County Museum of Art, Los
Angeles
San Francisco Museum of Art, San Fran-
cisco

Bibliography

Writings about Max Bill

Monographs and selected articles

Georg Schmidt. «Variations on a Single
Theme in the Fine Arts», XXe Siècle
(Paris), no. 4, 1938.

Georg Schmidt. «Max Bill's ‹Kontinuität›
Werk (Winterthur) vol. 35, no. 3, 1948

Rogers, Ernesto N. «Max Bill». *Magazine
of Art* (New York), vol. 46, no. 5, 1953.

Hill, Anthony. «Max Bill, the search of the
unity of the plastic arts in contemporary
life.» *Typographica* (London), no. 7, 1953.

Maldonado, Tomás. *Max Bill.* Buenos
Aires: Editorial Nueva Vision, 1955.

Gomringer, Eugen, ed. *Max Bill, Festsch-
rift zum 50. Geburtstag.*
Teufen: Arthur Niggli, 1958.
Texts by Max Bense, Eugen Gomringer,
Will Grohmann, R. P. Lohse, Kurt Marti,
Anni Müller-Widmann, Carlos Flexo
Ribeiro, Ernesto N. Rogers, Ernst Schei-
degger.

Plüss, Eduard. «Max Bill.» In *Künstlerle-
xikon der Schweiz, XX. Jahrhundert.*
Frauenfeld: Huber & Co., 1958.

Gomringer, Eugen. «Max Bill, variety and
unity of the shaped environment.» *Architects' Year Book* (London), no. 10, 1962.

Staber, Margit. «Max Bill und die
Umweltgestaltung – Über die Wechsel-
wirkung von Theorie und Praxis.» *Zodiac*
(Milan), no. 9, 1962.

Bense, Max. «Max Bill 1963.» *Art International* (Lugano), vol. VII, no. 3, 1963.

Staber, Margit. *Max Bill.* London: Methuen & Co., 1964. Contains bibliography.

Staber, Margit. «Max Bill» *Art International* (Lugano), vol. X, no. 5, 1966

Farner, Konrad. «Max Bill oder die
Gerade in der Spirale.» *Tendenzen*
(München), no. 39, 1966.

Staber, Margit. «Max Bill, Umweltgestaltung nach morphologischen Methoden.»
Kunst Nachrichten (Lucerne), vol. 4., no. 3,
1967.

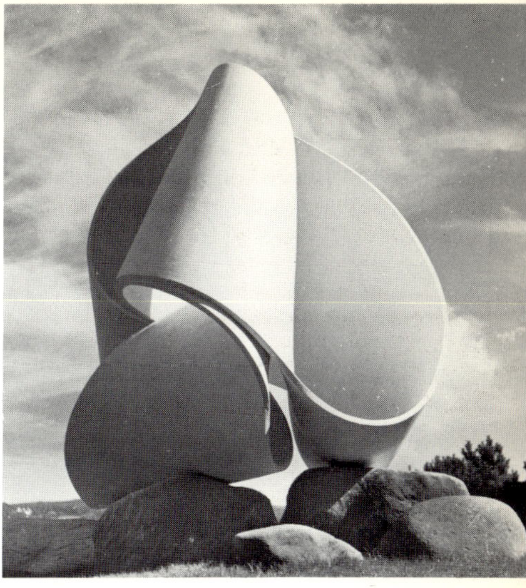

1946–47. «Continuity»,
destroid Zürich 1948.

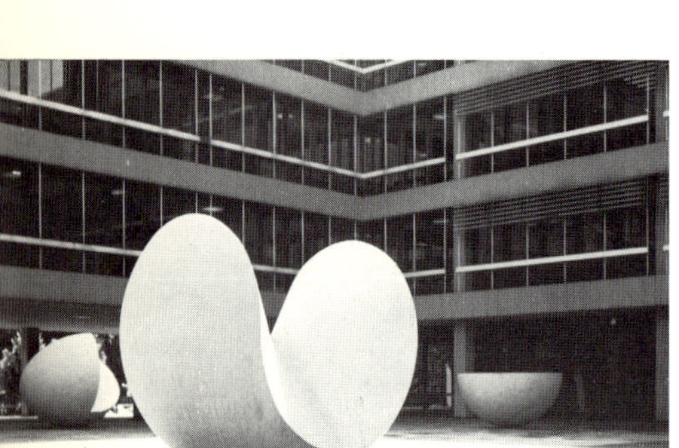

1965–66. Three of the «Family of Five Half Spheres» University of Karlsruhe.

Clay, Jean. «Max Bill». *Réalités* (Paris) no. 274, nov. 1968.

Grohmann, Will. «Thèmes et variations dans l'œuvre de Max Bill.» XXe Siècle (Paris), no. 32, 1969.

Staber, Margit. *Max Bill.* St. Gallen: Erker-Verlag, 1971.
Contains extensive bibliography.
Bense, Max. «Le principe et le cas dans l'œuvre de Max Bill.» *XXe Siècle* (Paris), no. 40, 1973.

Staber, Margit. «Quando Pitagora dipinge.» *Bolaffiarte* (Torino), no. 27, 1973.

Nueva Forma (Madrid), September 1973. Special number on Max Bill.

Reichardt, Jasia, «Max Bill: About Two of his Themes» *Art International* (Lugano) vol. XVIII, no 7, 1974.

Exhibition catalogues of one-man shows (some with text by Max Bill)

Ulm. Ulmer Museum, 1956.
Text by Max Bill, Will Grohmann, Ernesto N. Rogers.

Zürich. Helmhaus, 1957.
Text by R. Wehrli, Max Bill.

Venice. 29 Biennale di Venezia, Swiss Pavilion, 1958.
Text by Franz Meyer.

Leverkusen. Museum Schloss Morsbroich, 1959.
Text by Udo Kultermann, Eugen Gomringer, Max Bill.

Stuttgart. Staatsgalerie, 1960.
Text by Adolf Max Vogt.

Winterthur. Kunstmuseum, 1960.
Text by Eduard Plüss.

Geneva. Galerie du Perron, 1961.
Text by Ernesto N. Rogers, Will Grohmann (same text as for catalogue of exhibition at Ulmer Museum, Ulm, 1956).

Milan. Galleria Cadario, 1964.
Text by Umbro Apollonio.

Genoa-Boccadasse. Galleria del Deposito,
1964.
Text by Margit Staber.

Locarno. Galleria Flaviana, 1965.
Text by R. Bianda, Max Bill. (Also text by
Margit Staber from the catalogue of the
exhibition at Galleria del Deposito,
Genova, 1964).

Basel. Galerie Hilt, 1966.
Text includes interview with Max Bill by
Rudolf Pollozek.

New York. Staempfli Gallery, 1966.
Text by Margit Staber.

London. Hanover Gallery, 1966.
Text by Max Bense.

St. Gallen. Galerie Im Erker, 1967.
Text by Will Grohmann, Max Bense, Max
Bill.

Bern. Kunsthalle, 1968.
Text by Adolf Max Vogt, Max Bill.

Hannover. Kestner-Gesellschaft, 1968.

Text by Wieland Schmied. (Also text by
Will Grohmann, Max Bense, Max Bill
from the catalogue of the exhibition at
Galerie Im Erker, St. Gallen, 1967.)

Dusseldorf. Kunstverein für die Rhein-
lande und Westfalen, 1968.
Text by Karl-Heinz Hering. (Also text by
Will Grohmann, Max Bense, Max Bill
from the catalogue of the exhibition at
Galerie Im Erker, St. Gallen, 1967.)

The Hague. Haags Gemeentemuseum,
1968.
Text by L. J. F. Wijsenbeek. (Also text by
Will Grohmann and Max Bill from cata-
logue of the exhibition at Galerie Im
Erker, St. Gallen, 1967.)

Zürich. Kunsthaus, 1968.
Text by René Wehrli, Georg Schmidt.
(Also text by Will Grohmann from the
catalogue of the exhibition at Galerie Im
Erker, St. Gallen, 1967.)

Nuremberg. Albrecht-Dürer-Gesellschaft,
Kunsthalle Nürnberg, 1968.
*Max Bill – Das Druckgrafische Werk bis
1968.*
Text by Zdenek Felix, Max Bill. (Also
excerpts from the text by Adolf Max Vogt
for the catalogue of the exhibition at
Kunsthalle, Berne, 1968).

Genoa. Galleria La Polena, 1969.
Text by Orlandini.

Nuremberg. Biennale 1969 Nürnberg,
Kunsthalle Nürnberg, 1969.
*Konstruktive Kunst: Elemente und Prin-
zipien.*
Text by Margit Staber to the special con-
tribution by Max Bill.

Turin. Galleria Martano/Due, 1969.
Text by Max Bill.

Paris. Centre National d'Art Contempo-
rain, 1969.
Also at Musée de Peinture et de Sculpture,
Grenoble, 1970.
Text by Maurice Besset, Max Bill, Harald
Szeemann.

Venice. Galleria del Cavallino, 1970.
Text by Ernesto Luciano Francalanci.

Livorno. Galleria d'arte «Peccolo», 1970.
Text by Luigi Lambertini.

Paris. Galerie Denise René, 1971.
Text and drawings by Max Bill.

Geneva. Musée Rath, 1972.
Text by Valentina Anker, and Max Bill.

Zurich. Marlborough Galerie, 1972.
Recent Works.
Max Bill answers questions by Margit
Staber.

Toronto. Marlborough-Godard, Ltd., 1972.
Surfaces. Also at Marlborough-Godard,
Ltd., Montreal, 1972 Containing two
essays: «The principle and the individual
case; theoretical notes on Max Bill», by
Max Bense and «How I started making
single-sided surfaces», by Max Bill.

London. Marlborough Fine Art, 1974.
Also at Marlborough Galerie, Zürich,
1974. Text consists of selected critical
quotations from 1936–1973 compiled by
Margit Staber.

Buffalo. Albright-Knox Art Gallery, 1974.
Also at Los Angeles County Museum of
Art, Los Angeles, 1974 and San Francisco
Museum of Art, San Francisco, 1975. Text
by Lawrence Alloway, James Wood, Max
Bill.

das thema:
  4 gleiche quadrat-gruppen
jede aus 4 gleichen elementen
  4 + 4 + 4 + 4 = 16 quadrate

in diesem portofolio besteht jede komposition aus einer anderen farbgruppe, das heisst, wenn man sämtliche verwendeten farben zusammen auf alle elf kompositionen anwenden würde, könnten innerhalb des gegebenen themas und seiner struktur 1034 verschiedene kompositionen entstehen.
wenn man aber alle diese farben, ohne die einschränkung durch die elf gegebenen gruppen verwenden würde, dann wäre es möglich, viele tausende solcher kombinationen zu produzieren.

der schritt von einer gruppe zur folgenden erfolgt durch veränderung des platzes eines einzigen elementes der gruppe.

es gibt elf mögliche kompositionen von denen jede aus vier identischen gruppen besteht. weggelassen sind fünf varianten, die lediglich spiegelungen sind der gruppen II, III, IV, V und XI

es gibt innerhalb dieser elf kompositionen 66 möglichkeiten von kombinationen wenn man sich auf nur vier farben beschränkt. wenn man die spiegelungen mit berücksichtigt, dann sind 94 kombinationen möglich.

the theme:
  4 equal groups of squares
of 4 equal elements each
  4 + 4 + 4 + 4 = 16 squares

in this portofolio each composition is done with a different colour group. that means, that when taking all this colour it would be possible to combine in the given theme and structure, 1034 different compositions.
by using all colours of the eleven given compositions, without the restriction of equal groups and limited colorcombinations, there would be many thousends more possibilities of combinations.

the step from one group to the next by changing the place of only one element.

here are eleven possible compositions, each of four identical groups.
excluded are five variants by the reversion of the groups II, III, IV, V and XI.

there are 66 possibilities within this eleven compositions by using only four identical colours.
The reversions included, there would be 94 possible combinations

I · II · III · IV · V · VI · VII · VIII · IX · X · XI

identisch mit I → ← identical to I

1970
11 × 4:4
11 silkscreens, 21⅝″ × 25⅝″,
(55 × 65 cm)
Introduction plate

Selected Writings by Max Bill

Books and edited works since 1938

Quinze Variations sur un même Thème. Paris: Editions des Chroniques du Jour, 1938.
Sixteen Lithographs with text in English, French, German. Edition of 250.

Le Corbusier & P. Jeanneret: The Complete Works. vol. 3, 1934–1938. Zurich: Dr. Hans Girsberger, 1938.
Edited by Max Bill.

Leo Leuppi: 10 Compositionen. Zurich: Allianz-Verlag, 1943. Ten original woodcuts with introduction by Max Bill.

Hans Arp: 11 Configurations. Zurich: Allianz-Verlag, 1945. Edited by Max Bill with texts by Hans Arp, Max Bill, Gabrielle Buffet-Picabia.

Wiederaufbau. Erlenbach-Zürich: Verlag für Architektur, 1945.

Vantongerloo, Georges. *Georges Vantongerloo: Paintings, Sculptures, Reflections.* Problems of Contemporary Art Series, no. 5. New York: Wittenborn, Schultz, Inc., 1948.
Preface by Max Bill.

Wassily Kandinsky, 10 Farbige Reproduktionen. Basel: Holbein-Verlag, 1949.
Selected and introduced by Max Bill. English version by John Richardson, Holbein Publishing Co., Basel, 1949.

Moderne Schweizer Architektur 1925–1945. Basel: Karl Werner, 1950.

Wassily Kandinsky. Paris: Editions Maeght, 1951.
Also at Institute of Contemporary Art, Boston, 1951. Edited by Max Bill. Text by Jean Arp, Max Bill, Charles Estienne, C. Giedion-Welcker, Will Grohmann, Ludwig Grote, Nina Kandinsky, Alberto Magnelli. English, German and Spanish translation of French text in Institute of Contemporary Art edition.

Form – A Balance Sheet of Mid-Twentieth Century Trends in Design. Basel: Karl Werner, 1952.
Text in English, French and German.

Kandinsky, Wassily. *Über das Geistige in der Kunst.* Bern: Benteli-Verlag, 1952. Edited and introduced by Max Bill.

Mies Van der Rohe. Milan: Edizione Il Balcone, 1955.

Kandinsky, Wassily. *Essays über Kunst und Künstler.* Stuttgart: Gerd Hatje, 1955. Edited and introduced by Max Bill. 2nd enlarged edition: Bern: Benteli-Verlag, 1963

Die Gute Form. Winterthur: Buchdruckerei Winterthur AG, 1957.

Kandinsky, Wassily. *Punkt und Linie zu Fläche.* 4th ed. Bern: Benteli-Verlag, 1959. Edited and introduced by Max Bill.

Enzo Mari. Milan: Muggiani, 1959.
Text by Max Bill and Bruno Munari.

Robert Maillart, Bridges and Construction. Text in English, French and German. First published in Zurich in 1949. New York: Praeger, 1969.

11 × 4:4. Zurich: Edition Bischofberger, 1970.
Portfolio of 11 serigraphs with text by Max Bill in English and German. Edition of 100.

System mit Fünf Vierfarbigen Zentren. St. Gallen: Erker-Verlag, 1972.

Transcoloration in fünf Quadraten. Norderstedt: Meissner Edition. 1974
Portofolio of 5 serigraphs with text by Max Bill in German.

8 = (2 ¼) = 8. Neuchâtel: Edition Media. 1974.
Portofolio of 8 serigraphs with text by Max Bill in French

16 Constellations. Paris: Société internationale d'art XXe siècle 1974
Portofolio of 16 lithographs with text by Max Bill in French, English, German.

Articles and exhibition catalogues since 1936

Konkrete Gestaltung. (exhibition catalogue). Zurich: Kunsthaus, 1936.
For the exhibition *Zeitprobleme in der Schweizer Malerei und Plastik.* Revised as *Konkrete Kunst* for the exhibition *Zürcher Konkrete Kunst* in Galerie Otto Stangl, Munich, 1949.

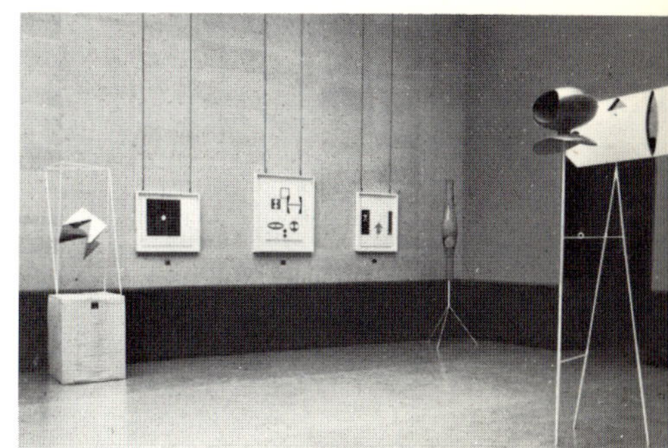

1936. Max Bill in the exhibition. «Zeitprobleme in der Schweizer Malerei und Plastik», Kunsthaus Zürich.

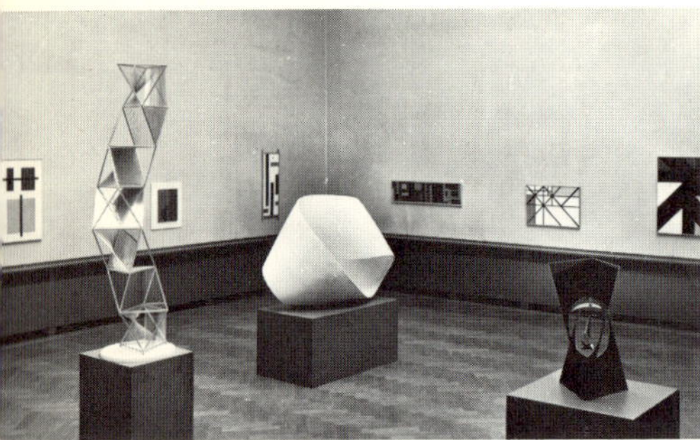

1944. Max Bill's room at the Exhibition «Konkrete Kunst», Kunsthalle Basel.

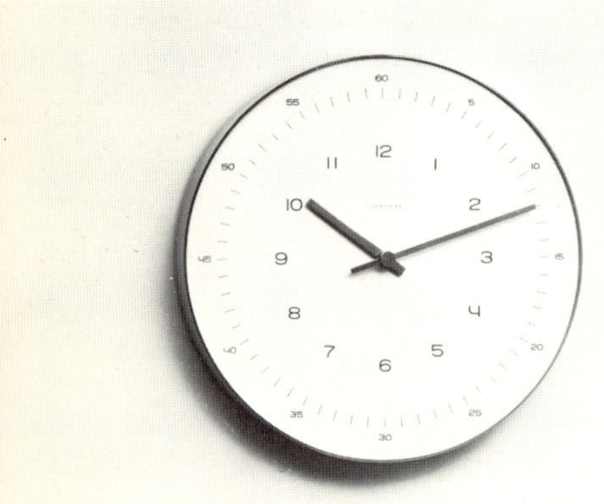

1957. Wall clock.

«Über konkrete Kunst.» *Werk* (Winterthur), no. 8, 1938.

«The mastery of space.» *XXe Siècle* (Paris), vol. 2, no. 1, 1939.

«Sophie Taeuber-Arp.» *Werk* (Winterthur), no. 6, 1943.

«Von der abstrakten zur konkreten Malerei im XX. Jahrhundert» *Pro Arte* (Geneva) vol. 2, no. 15/16, 1943. Revised for exhibition catalogue *arte astratta e concreta* Milan, 1947.

Konkrete Kunst. (exhibition catalogue). Basel: Kunsthalle, 1944. Exhibition organized by Max Bill with text by Hans Arp, Max Bill. et al.

«Über Typografie.» *Schweizer Grafische Mitteilungen* (St. Gallen), no. 4, 1946.

Worte rund um Malerei und Plastik. (exhibition catalogue). Zurich: Kunsthaus, 1947.
For the exhibition *Allianz.* Also used for the exhibition *Konkrete Kunst: 50 Jahre Entwicklung,* in Helmhaus, Zurich, 1960.

«Ausstellungen – Ein Beitrag zur Abklärung von Fragen der *Ausstellungsgestaltung.*» *Werk* (Winterthur), no. 3, 1948.

«Graphic art in the world of the atom.» Graphis (Zurich), vol. 4, 1948.

Die Gute Form. (exhibition catalogue). Zurich: Kunstgewerbemuseum der Stadt Zürich, 1949.
For the exhibition of the Schweizerischen Werkbundes.

«Schönheit aus Funktion und als Funktion.» *Werk* (Winterthur), no. 8, 1949.

«De la surface à l'espace.» *XXe Siècle* (Paris), no. 2, 1951.

«Typography today.» *Typographica* (London), no. 5, 1953.

«The Bauhaus idea: From Weimar to Ulm.» *Architects' Year Book* (London), no. 5, 1953.

«The mathematical approach in Contemporary Art.» *Arts and Architecture* (Los Angeles), no. 8, 1954.
Originally published in *Werk* (Winterthur), no. 3, 1949.

«Base et but de l'Esthètique au Temps du Machinisme.» *Esthètique Industrielle* (Paris), no. 10, 1954.

Piet Mondrian. (exhibition catalogue). Zurich: Kunsthaus, 1955. For the exhibition of the same name.

«The beginning of a new epoch in architecture.» *Architectural Design* (London), no. 11, 1955.

«Die Komposition I/1925 von Piet Mondrian.» *Jahresbericht 1956 der Zürcher Kunstgesellschaft* (Zurich), 1956. Also included in the catalogue for the Piet Mondrian centennial exhibition at the Solomon R. Guggenheim Museum, New York, 1971.

Josef Albers, Fritz Glarner, Friedrich Vordemberge-Gildewart. (exhibition catalogue). Zurich: Kunsthaus, 1956.
For the exhibition of the same name.

«Ein Denkmal.» *Werk* (Winterthur), no. 7, 1957.

«Aktuelle Probleme der Gestaltung.» *VIR* (Cologne), no. 3, 1957.

«Josef Albers.» *Werk* (Winterthur), no. 4, 1958.

«Der Modellfall Ulm – zur Problematik einer Hochschule für Gestaltung.» *Form* (Cologne), no. 6, 1959.

Konkrete Kunst: 50 Jahre Entwicklung. (exhibition catalogue). Zurich: Kunsthaus, 1969.
For the exhibition of the same name.

Zu Marcel Duchamp. (exhibition catalogue). Zurich: Kunstgewerbemuseum der Stadt Zürich, 1960.
For the exhibition *Dokumentation über Marcel Duchamp.*

«Une lettre à Zodiac: le Bauhaus de demian.» *Zodiac* (Milan), no. 5, 1960. With English translation.

Georges Vantongerloo. (exhibition catalogue). London: Marlborough Fine Art, Ltd., 1962.
For the exhibition of the same name.

«Einige Erfahrungen mit der Vorfabrikation und einige Schlüsse daraus.» *Form* (Cologne), no. 24, 1963.

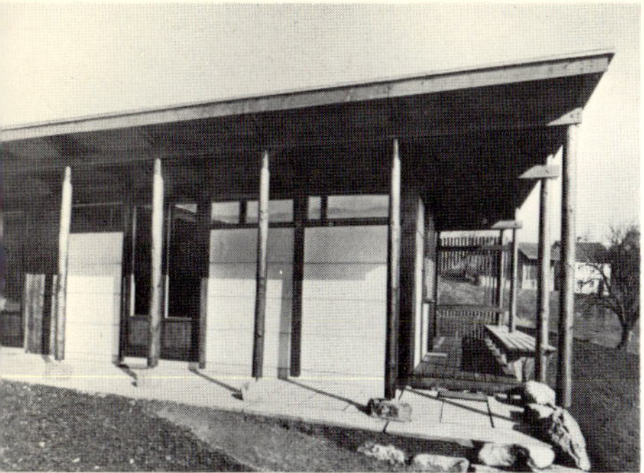

1945. House constructed with prefabricated elements under war restrictions.

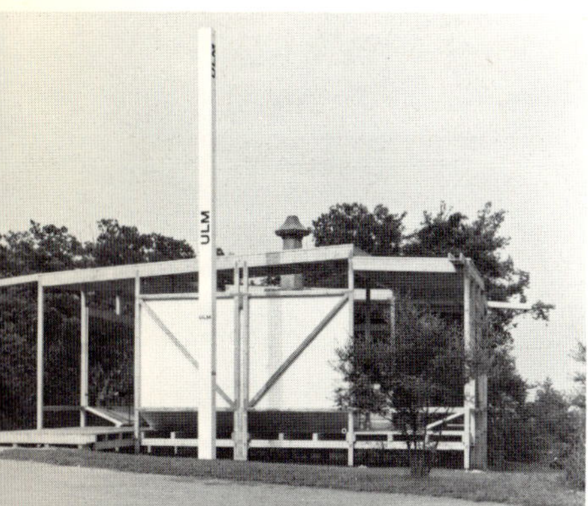

1955. Pavillon for the city of Ulm at the «County Exhibition Baden-Württemberg», Stuttgart.

«Structure as art? Art as structure?» In *Structure in Art and in Science,* edited by Gyorgy Kepes. New York: Braziller, 1965.

«Le Corbusier.» *Neue Zürcher Zeitung* (Zurich), no. 3867, 1965.

«Das Individuelle und das Allgemeine in der Architektur.» In *Diskussionsforum Schöner Wohnen.* Stuttgart: Teppichgemeinschaft e. V., 1966.

«Vantongerloo.» *XXe Siècle* (Paris), no. 28 (sup. 31), 1966.

«Responsibility in design and information.» *American Scholar* (Washington, D.C.), vol. 35, Spring 1966.

«La formation de l'architecte.» *UIA, Revue de l'Union Internationale des Architectes* (Paris), no. 44, 1967.

«Laudatio für Max von Moos» *Neue Zürcher Zeitung* (Zürich) no 932, 1967, reprinted in «Max von Moos» Zürich: Scheidegger, 1974.

«Josef Albers.» In *Josef Albers – Graphic Tectonic,* edited by Margit Staber. Cologne: Galerie der Spiegel, 1968.

«Lieber Will.» In *Lieber Freund – Künstler Schreiben an Will Grohmann,* edited by Karl Gutbrod. Cologne: DuMont Schauberg, 1968.

«Art as non-changeable fact.» In *DATA, Directions in Art, Theory and Aesthetics,* edited by Anthony Hill. London: Faber & Faber, 1968.

Fritz Glarner. (exhibition catalogue). Venice: Swiss Pavilion, Biennale di Venezia, 1968.
For the exhibition *Fritz Glarner/Hans Aeschbacher.*

«ars multiplicata.» *Kunst* (Mainz), no. 29, 1968. Interview with Max Bill. Later used as text for the exhibition at Centre National d'Art Contemporain, Paris, 1969.

«Das Behagen im Kleinstaat – Eine Rede von Max Bill.» *Neue Zürcher Zeitung* (Zurich), no. 795, December 1968.

«Zur kulturellen Situation in Zürich.» In *Zürcher Almanach.* Zurich: Benzinger Verlag, 1968.

Zürcher Künstler: Abstrakte und Nichtfigürliche Richtungen (exhibition catalogue) Zurich: Helmhaus 1968. Introduction by Max Bill.

«Walter Gropius zum Gedenken.» *Neue Zürcher Zeitung* (Zurich), no. 428, 1969.

«Walter Gropius – Architekt und Erzieher in unserer Zeit.» *Universitas* (Stuttgart), no. 11, 1969.

«Ludwig Mies van der Rohe, 1886–1969.» *Neue Zürcher Zeitung* (Zurich), August 1969.

«Ludwig Mies van der Rohe – Baumeister unserer Zeit.» *Universitas* (Stuttgart), no. 9, 1969.

«Einige Feststellungen über Kunst.» *Neutralität* (Bern), October 1969.

Zürcher Künstler: Konkrete und Phantastische Richtungen. (exhibition catalogue). Zurich: Helmhaus, 1969. Introduction by Max Bill.

«Wassily Kandinsky.» In *Die Grossen der Weltgeschichte,* edited by Kurt Fassmann with the assistance of Max Bill, Hoimar von Ditfurth, Hanno Helbling, Walter Jens, Robert Jungk, Eugen Kogon. Zurich: Kindler Verlag, 1970.

«Piet Mondrian.» In *Die Grossen der Weltgeschichte,* edited by Kurt Fassmann with the assistance of Max Bill, Hoimar von Ditfurth, Hanno Helbling, Walter Jens, Robert Jungk, Eugen Kogon. Zurich: Kindler Verlag, 1970.

Design? Umwelt wird in Frage gestellt. Berlin: Internationales Design-Zentrum, 1970. Includes contribution by Max Bill.

«22 questions to Max Bill: an independent production of H. P. Walker and Czadina-wor Film.» In «Architecture, the film and society», by E. Mühlestein. *Werk* (Winterthur), vol. 57, August 1970.

Zürcher Künstler: Figurative Malerei und Plastik (exhibition catalogue). Zurich Helmhaus 1970 Introduction by Max Bill.

«Funzione dell'arte e dell'artista nella società.» *La Biennale di Venezia* (Venice), vol. XXI, no. 67–68, 1971.

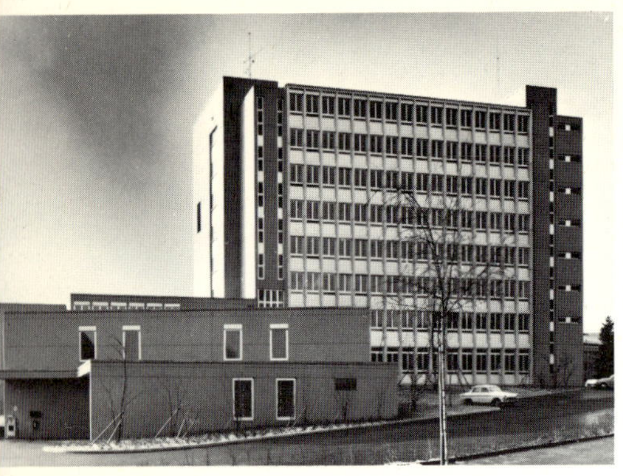
1964–74. Radio-Studio Zürich.

Fritz Glarner, (exhibition catalogue) Bern:
Kunsthalle 1972.
For the exhibition of the same name

Georges Vantongerloo. (exhibition cata-
logue) Zürich: Galerie Scheidegger und
Maurer *«Splitter»,* no. 6, 1972.
For the exhibition of the same name.

«Radio-Studio Zürich.» *Werk* (Winterthur), vol. 60, October 1973.

Credits:
5000 copies of this catalogue, compiled and edited by Max
Bill and James N. Wood, have been printed in Switzerland by
Genossenschaftsdruckerei Zürich, with photolithographs by
Cliché & Litho AG, Zürich, and binding by Hch. Weber AG,
Winterthur, for the Albright-Knox Art Gallery, the Los
Angeles County Museum of Art and the San Francisco
Museum of Art on the occasion of the exhibition, *Max Bill.*